ORGANIZATIONS AND THE PSYCHOLOGICAL CONTRACT

Managing People at Work

ORGANIZATIONS AND THE PSYCHOLOGICAL CONTRACT:

Managing People at Work

Peter J. Makin

Cary L. Cooper

Charles J. Cox

Manchester School of Management
University of Manchester
Institute of Science and Technology

BPS Blackwell

© Peter J. Makin, Cary L. Cooper, and Charles J. Cox 1996

Editorial Offices:
108 Cowley Road, Oxford OX4 1JF, UK
    Tel: +44 (0)1865 791100
350 Main Street, Malden, MA 02148-5018, USA
    Tel: +1 781 388 8250

English language edition, except in the United States and Canada, published by BPS Books (The British Psychological Society).

First published 1996 by The British Psychological Society
As a BPS Blackwell book
Reprinted 2002

ISBN 1-85433-168-X pb

A catalogue record for this title is available from the British Library.

Set by Fakenham Photosetting Ltd, Fakenham, Norfolk
Printed and bound by Athenaeum Press, Ltd., Gateshead, Tyne & Wear.

For further information on
Blackwell Publishers, visit our website:
www.blackwellpublishers.co.uk

A hardcover edition of *Organizations and the Psychological Contract*
is available from Quorum Books, an imprint of Greenwood Publishing
Group, Inc.

The Library of Congress has catalogued the hardcover edition as follows:

Makin, Peter J.
    Organizations and the psychological contract: managing people at work / Peter J.
    Makin, Cary L. Cooper, and Charles J. Cox
        p.   cm.
    Includes bibliographical references and index.
    ISBN 1-56720-091-5
    1.   Psychology, Industrial.   2. Industrial management.
    3. Communication in personnel management.   I. Cooper, Cary L.
    II. Cox, Charles.   III. Title.
    HF5548.8.M3   1996
    658.3 – dc20
                                                            96–7011

CONTENTS

LIST OF FIGURES

ACKNOWLEDGEMENTS

Figure 2.2 from H.J. Eysenck *The Equality of Man* © 1975, published by Fontana/HarperCollins Publishers Ltd; *Figure 4.2* from J.R. Hackman/G.R. Oldham, *Work Redesign* © 1980 by Addison-Wesley Publishing Co., Inc. Reprinted by permission of Addison-Wesley Publishing Company, Inc. *Figure 5.1* from *Behaviour Modification in Applied Settings* by A.E. Kazdin. Copyright © 1994, 1989, 1984, 1980, 1975 Brooks/Cole Publishing Company, Pacific Grove, CA 93950, a division of International Thomson Publishing Inc. By permission of the publisher. *Figure 5.3* from H.C. Berthold, Jnr. 'Transitional contingency contracting and the Premack principle in business' in R. O'Brien, A. Dickinson and M. Rosow (Eds) *Industrial Behaviour Modification: A management handbook* © 1982 Pergamon Press/Elsevier Science Inc.; *Figure 6.2* from A. Bryman *Leadership in Organisations* © 1986 Routledge Limited; *Figure 6.5* from G.A. Randell, P. Packard and J. Slater *Staff Appraisal, 3rd edn* (now out of print) © 1984 Institute of Personnel and Development; *Figure 6.6* from P.L. Wright and D.S.

Taylor *Improving Leadership Performance* © 1994 Prentice Hall Paramount Publishing; *Figure 7.2* from *Comparative Studies in Administration*, James D. Thompson *et al.*, (Eds) © 1959 by University of Pittsburgh Press. Reprinted by permission of the University of Pittsburgh Press. *Figures 8.1–8.3* from G. Hofstede *Cultures and Organizations: Software of the mind* © 1991 Geert Hofstede, reproduced by permission of the author; *Figure 8.4* from R. Likert *New Patterns of Management* © 1961 McGraw-Hill Inc.; *Figures 8.5 and 8.6* from K.K. Tse Marks and Spencer: *An anatomy of Britain's most efficiently managed company* © 1985 Pergamon Press/Elsevier Science Inc; *Figure 8.8* from S. Baddely and K. James 'Owl, fox, donkey and sheep: Political skills for managers' in *Management Education and Development, 18,* 3–19, © 1987 AMED; *Figure 9.2* from Robert F. Bales, *Interaction Process Analysis* © 1950 by Addison-Wesley Publishing Company, Inc. Reprinted by permission; *Figure 9.3* Reprinted with the permission of The Free Press, a division of Simon & Schuster from *Communication of Innovations* by Everett M. Rogers with F. Floyd Shoemaker. Copyright © 1962, 1971 by The Free Press; *Figure 9.4* from R.N. Ottaway 'Defining the Change Agent' in B. Evans, J. Powell and R. Talbot (Eds) *Changing Design,* © 1982, reprinted by permission of David Fulton Publishers; *Figure 9.5* from C.A. O'Connor *The Handbook of Organizational Change* © 1993, McGraw-Hill Book Company Europe.

PREFACE

This book is a revised and much expanded version of *Managing People at Work*. However, the revised chapters of the original book constitute slightly less than half of the present text, and in addition, we have taken the opportunity to look at many of the topics covered in terms of the relatively new concept of the 'psychological contract'. For these reasons we decided to give the book its new title.

OBJECTIVES AND STYLE

As with our previous book our objective is to describe how psychological theories and practice can be effectively and usefully applied to the behaviour of people within organizations, in particular to the process of managing and being managed. In doing so we have tried to present the theories in a way that can be understood by someone with little or no knowledge of psychology. As one reviewer of the previous book commented in *Personnel Psychology*, 'I enjoyed reading this book – others will too'. We hope we have achieved the same with this book.

All the authors, as well as being members of the academic staff of one of the top university management departments in the UK (The Manchester School of Management at UMIST), have acted as consultants to a wide range of organizations, both commercial and industrial, public and private. Accordingly we draw on our experiences as consultants to provide real-life examples to illustrate the practical applications of the theories. In addition, many of the chapters contain practical exercises, often drawn from consultancy work, to help the reader apply the techniques to their own circumstances.

READERSHIP

The book is aimed at a wide range of potential readers. The case studies and exercises mean that the individual manager can use the book to analyse, understand and, we hope, improve their managerial effectiveness. The book's main audience, however, is those undertaking management courses that include organizational psychology or organizational behaviour, whether at diploma, undergraduate, or post-graduate level.

CONTENT

The content of the book is indicated, not surprisingly, by the chapter titles which, we trust, are self-explanatory. However, it may be worth pointing out how the current text differs from *Managing People at Work*.

As we have mentioned before, one of the features of the book is that it uses the concept of the 'psychological contract' to understand some of the topics. The concept is explained and explored in the introduction, as is its relation to the other chapters in the book. As we mention in that chapter, however, the book is structured so that it can be used, if the reader so wishes, without applying the concept of the psychological contract. Each chapter concludes with a section that links back to the psychological contract and how it relates to the particular chapter. This can, if you wish, be ignored.

Totally new chapters have been added on *Selection, Placement, and Careers, Understanding and Coping with Change*, and *Empowerment and Self-Management*. The chapter on *Personality and Individual Differences* has been expanded into two new chapters. This has also been done with the chapter on *Motivation*. Additional material has been added to produce a chapter which concentrates on the rapidly expanding behavioural approach to *Motivation*. The chapters on *Leadership and Management Style, Identifying Organizational Problems*, and *Organizational Change* have been expanded and only the chapters on *Group Dynamics at Work*, and *Managing your Boss* remain largely unchanged.

We hope that our additions and amendments add to the value of this book and that it will encourage more people to consider the psychological aspects of work.

Peter J. Makin
Cary L. Cooper
Charles J. Cox

mitment. Unlike personality, which is generally perceived as very stable, attitudes are more responsive to the organizational environment that the individual experiences. We consider these two attitudes and discuss what impact they have on an individual's performance and other work-related behaviours. As Robinson and Rousseau (1994) have shown, violations of the psychological contract can have a negative effect on job satisfaction and commitment to remain with the organization.

CHAPTER 3: INTER-PERSONAL PERCEPTION AND INTERACTION

Laymen, like psychologists, use personality traits to describe other people; how accurate are these perceptions? In this chapter the way people perceive others is considered, and its accuracy assessed. We consider how people form impressions of others and, in particular, how they use categories such as stereotypes. We also consider how people decide whether an event is caused by the personality of the person involved, or whether they were the victim (or beneficiary) of circumstance. Finally, we consider a particular approach (Transactional Analysis) to understanding, analysing, and improving interactions between people at work.

The psychological contract often involves relationships with others, and how we expect to be treated by them. This chapter shows how these relationships might be improved, and how changes in the contract should be negotiated.

CHAPTER 4: MOTIVATION

The major 'classical' theories of work motivation are discussed, largely in historical order, moving from Taylor's 'scientific management' to Herzberg's 'two factor' theory, and McClelland's 'managerial needs' theory. Current approaches, such as 'work design' are then explored. These theories have implications for the psychological contract, especially in understanding the 'needs' that individuals expect their jobs to fulfil.

Perhaps the most important theory, from the view of the psychological contract, is 'equity theory'. Equity theory is concerned with the underlying principles by which rewards are distributed, and how these are perceived as fair or otherwise. As well as considering what is distributed, equity theory also considers perceptions of the fairness of the process by which such decisions are taken. The theory is based upon concepts of fairness and reciprocity. The effects of breaches of the norms of fairness are demonstrated using evidence from studies in organizations. The links between equity theory and the psychological contract are clearly drawn.

CHAPTER 5: BEHAVIOURAL APPROACHES TO MOTIVATION

The behavioural approach combines the theories of 'goal setting' and 'organizational behaviour modification'. The emphasis of these theories is very much on the precise specification of behaviour and the rewards that will be gained for performing the behaviour. This is in line with our contention that organizations would benefit from making the psychological contract more explicit. Issues such as performance-related pay are discussed and analysed. An example from the authors' own work is used to demonstrate the potential of the approach.

Whilst the explicit emphasis of the chapter is on the economic contract, the example used demonstrates how change in one area can have important implications for the psychological contract.

CHAPTER 6: LEADERSHIP AND MANAGEMENT STYLE

The major theories of leadership are discussed, including the Ohio and Michigan studies, Fiedler's Contingency Theory, and Hersey and Blanchard's theory of situational leadership. The recent renewed interest in charismatic and transformational leadership is discussed. The chapter ends with a section on the theory and techniques of staff appraisal – leadership in action.

Expectations about the type and nature of leadership are likely to figure large in the psychological contract. In addition, it is in situations such as the appraisal interview that the negotiation and continuing renegotiation of the psychological contract is perhaps best achieved.

CHAPTER 7: GROUP DYNAMICS AT WORK

The functions of groups, decision-making in groups, and team roles are discussed in this chapter. In addition, the nature, causes, and cures of inter-group conflict are discussed.

People's expectations of, for example, the extent to which they participate in group decision-making may have important effects. The psychological contract will probably contain such expectations, and their breach may damage the group's effectiveness.

CHAPTER 8: IDENTIFYING ORGANIZATIONAL PROBLEMS

Following consideration of first the individual, then the group, this chapter considers the organization. Different types of organization are considered, together with the metaphors by which we try to understand them. Organizational culture and its significance are discussed, as are methods by which the culture may be changed. Associated with this is the process that organizations go through as they attempt to deal with growth and change. Different types of organizational structure and climate are described, which often correspond to different stages of organizational development. Methods of producing such change are described and discussed.

The effect of organizational culture is all-pervasive for the psychological contract. It will define, at the macro-level, how people are dealt with in organizations, and what the possibilities are for change. Changing the culture will have, therefore, an enormous impact on the psychological contract, and hence on the organization's effectiveness.

CHAPTER 9: ORGANIZATIONAL CHANGE

Having discussed in the previous chapter various organizational problems, this chapter considers how the organization can change and adapt. This adaptation will involve individuals, teams, and top management. Topics such as resistance to change and how it may be minimized are discussed. If change is to be effective it will need to take into account the psychological contract of those whom the change affects. The nature of these contracts and the process of negotiating their change is considered in some detail, as is the development of a contract to cover the process of change itself.

The three final chapters of the book build, to a considerable extent, on the material presented earlier. Where appropriate, new material is introduced, but the major emphasis is upon the application of the theories to practical situations. In **Chapter 10: Managing your Boss**, the focus is upon understanding and influencing the individual whose actions are likely to have most impact on the extent to which your psychological contract is fulfilled. **Chapter 11: Understanding and Coping with Change** moves the focus back to the individual. It examines the stages that people go through when faced with change, and analyses them in terms of three psychological approaches. Advice on how the individual can cope with change is drawn from each of these theories. Finally, **Chapter 12: Empowerment and Self-Management** considers a particular form of change that is receiving considerable attention within organizations. Many organizations are devolving power and decision-making downwards. This has considerable implications, both positive and negative, for the psychological contract. Advice on how individuals and organizations can achieve this without disruption is offered.

1

Selection, Placement, and Careers

The process of selecting people for jobs, especially in large organizations, is now often the task of specialists. These specialists are also often involved in placement, or internal selection for promotion. This chapter will not attempt to make the reader a specialist, but will instead concentrate on those areas of most use to non-personnel managers. In our view this means that a manager should be able to talk to selection specialists in their own language, improve their own involvement in the selection process, and have an insight into the types of selection procedures to which they may themselves be subjected during the course of their managerial careers.

Accordingly, the chapter will concentrate on:

- providing an appreciation of the background to personnel selection, so as to enable a manager to talk effectively to personnel specialists

- giving some insight into how that most widely used selection technique, the interview, can be improved

- developing an understanding of the theory and practice of 'assessment centres' in selection and placement.

All of these concentrate on how the organization can improve its effectiveness by selecting the right candidate for the job. It is often assumed that this candidate, once selected, will accept the job. What is also often disregarded is the impact on those candidates who are not selected. In the latter part of the chapter we will turn our attention to the views and choices of the candidates; why people choose the careers they do, and the effect on them of being unsuccessful candidates.

PERSONNEL SELECTION

The process of systematic personnel selection is based upon four main assumptions.

1. Any particular job has relatively stable characteristics.

2. Individuals have relatively stable characteristics.

3. The characteristics of both job and individuals can be matched.

4. Accurate matching will result in better job performance, or other organizational outcomes such as reductions in lateness, staff turnover, etc.

These assumptions carry other implications which will need to be addressed. For example, job characteristics, especially those of managerial jobs, may change over time. Individual characteristics may also change. In addition, the process of matching requires that characteristics of both job and people are capable of accurate measurement. We will consider these as we progress through the chapter.

It will be logical to structure the chapter roughly on the various stages of the personnel selection process.

The first step of personnel selection is *job analysis,* which can be used to produce a *job description,* which can then be used to produce a *personnel specification*.

The second step is to produce *selection techniques* that can be used to differentiate between individuals.

Finally, the two are matched to indicate who should be offered the job.

The way in which we have just stated the process assumes that the job comes first and that the purpose is to identify an individual best suited to the particular job. This, of course, is what organizations are normally trying to do. However, it should not be overlooked that matching is a two-way process.

Rather than starting with the job, it is equally possible to start with the individual. What characteristics does the person have, and to which job, or type of job, would they be most suited? When stated this way, the process becomes one of career guidance rather than that of personnel selection. The processes are very similar; they differ in their starting points – the job or the individual. Neither one can be considered without the other. Organizations may offer jobs, but individuals have the choice as to whether or not to accept them.

JOB ANALYSIS, JOB DESCRIPTION, AND PERSONNEL SPECIFICATION

Methods of job analysis range from the very simple to the very sophisticated. The latter are the province of selection specialists, and we will not concern ourselves with those. However, no matter how simple or sophisticated the method, they all depend on three techniques:

- Asking
- Observing
- Doing

These are often used in combination.

Asking involves seeking information about the job from those who are doing the job, or who know it well. Perhaps the simplest technique involves asking the job incumbents, either individually or in groups, about the characteristics of the job. Other possible sources are the supervisor and trainer (both of whom may well have done the job in the past). The source of this information need not only be oral. Written material such as training manuals, previous job descriptions and operation and service manuals may also provide useful information. More sophisticated techniques tend to be more structured and precise. For example, rather than asking incumbents about the job, they are asked to fill in a questionnaire, which can then be scored along certain pre-determined dimensions.

A particular method involving asking is the 'critical incidents technique' (Flanagan, 1954). As its name suggests, this technique asks job incumbents, or others with detailed job knowledge, to identify critical incidents in their jobs. This identifies not only aspects of the job but their relative importance. It is also useful for identifying those important aspects of a job which may occur fairly infrequently and hence may be overlooked by more routine methods of analysis.

Observing often provides information that may be missed by merely asking. People may not be aware of, or take for granted, certain aspects of their jobs that others might consider important. Observations should be carried out at different stages of the job, often at different times of the day. Once again, observation can be simple or sophisticated. Video cameras may be used to record activities which may then be broken down into more and more precise observations. The degree of specificity will depend upon the use to which the analysis is being put. Such observation techniques can even be used on oneself. Diary-keeping is often a useful technique. This not only gives an indication of what is done, but how often different tasks require doing.

Doing involves just that: gaining information from actually doing the job. There are, of course, limitations to this. Some jobs require much experience and if performed by a novice may involve unacceptable danger. It often, however, provides an insight into skill requirements that may not have been obvious to the observer.

Having analysed the job, the manager must turn the results into a job description and then into a personnel specification. The examples we will use to illustrate job description and personnel specification are fairly straightforward. However, as with job analysis, there are other, more sophisticated techniques. But again, these are the province of specialists and we will not consider them here.

There are many formats for writing a job description, but perhaps the most effective way is to group the information about the job into a number of categories. Smith and Robertson (1993) suggest a six-stage method, based on six categories: job identification, main purpose of the job, responsibilities, relationships with people, physical working conditions, and pay and promotion. For example, the category 'job identification' would include the job title, the physical location of the job, and the title of the person to whom the job-holder reports. Within the category of 'responsibilities' would be a list of the main results the job-holder would be expected to achieve and their responsibilities for people, material, and money, for example. Job descriptions, it should be noted, are written in terms of outcomes or of activities, not in terms of the personal characteristics required to achieve them. This is the function of the personnel specification.

As with job descriptions, it is helpful to use categories to help organize the information required in a personnel specification. One such system is Rodger's 'seven point plan'. (This is often, but incorrectly, referred to as an interview plan.) The seven categories suggested by Rodger are:

- physical make-up
- attainments
- general intelligence
- special aptitudes
- interests
- disposition
- home circumstances

Smith and Robertson (1993) suggest that aspects of each of these categories may be classified as either 'essential' or 'desirable'. The following example, for the job of upholsterer, is adapted from their book.

Physical characteristics	Essential	• Able to work in standing condition
	Desirable	• Neat and clean appearance
Attainments	Essential	• Time-served apprentice
Intelligence	Desirable	• Not in bottom third of population
Special Aptitudes	Desirable	• Manual dexterity
Disposition	Desirable	• Willingness to work alone
Home circumstances	Essential	• Ability to work shifts

Having assessed the characteristics of the job, and turned these into a specification of the personal characteristics required, we will turn our attention to how these characteristics can be assessed. Before this, however, we will need to consider some technical issues, namely those of reliability and validity.

RELIABILITY AND VALIDITY

We mentioned earlier that one of the requirements for developing an effective selection procedure is that job characteristics and individual characteristics were capable of being measured. Before moving on to look at specific selection techniques, we need to be aware of the issues surrounding measurement and, in particular, those concerned with measuring individual characteristics.

Individual characteristics such as height and weight can be physically measured. Characteristics such as personality, intelligence, and career interests are not susceptible to such direct, physical, measurement. We have to devise measuring instruments specifically to measure such attributes. These measuring instruments need to be both *reliable* and *valid*.

Reliability. The concept of reliability can perhaps best be understood by analogy with the measurement of physical characteristics, such as height. Height, like any other distance, is normally measured by some form of standard length, such as a ruler or tape measure. We take it for granted that, in measuring a distance, our measurements are, within certain limits, reliable. We would be very surprised, for example, if on measuring the height of an individual on two occasions, we obtained measurements of 1.72 metres and 1.93 metres. There could be a number of possible reasons for such a difference occurring. One would be human error in taking the measurement. But if we rule this out, there are others. For example, the person may have grown between our first and second measurements. Assuming that the time between the two measurements is days rather than years, we can rule this out also. Having eliminated these possibilities, we would be likely to turn our attention to the measuring instrument itself. We could, for example, repeat the measurement using another tape measure. If we now find that we get consistent measures we might rightly conclude that there is something wrong with the original tape measure (for example, it was constructed of material that stretched) and discard it.

The same applies to psychological measures. They, like tape measures, need to give consistent results. This consistency is referred to as reliability. But how is this reliability to be assessed, and how much consistency is required?

Returning to the analogy of the tape measure, one way to assess its reliability would be to carry out the measurement process twice and compare the results. This is known as 'test/re-test' reliability. For some types of psychological measure, however, it is inappropriate. For example, if the same intelligence test was given within a short period to the same people it is probable that they would remember some of the answers. This would be likely to increase their scores on the second occasion, and hence give an inaccurate estimate of the test's reliability. Another option is to develop two versions of the same test, using slightly different questions. The scores of people on both of the tests could then be compared. This is referred to as 'parallel form' reliability. This can also be done using just one version of the test. Most psychological tests, for example intelligence tests, consist of a large number of questions, all trying to measure the same thing in slightly different ways. If there is a large enough number of questions two 'artificial' forms can be created. For example, the total produced by summing the scores on evenly numbered questions can be compared with the total for the odd numbered questions. This is referred to as 'split half' reliability.

Finally, perhaps the most common method of estimating a test's reliability is the 'internal' reliability, sometimes known as Cronbach's alpha (after Lee Cronbach, who devised the method). This technique compares the scores on each question in the test with those of every other question. By entering the level of agreement between all the questions into an equation, a figure is produced that represents the test's internal consistency, or reliability.

Thus far we have not considered how the degree of reliability can be measured or expressed, so it is to this that we must now turn.

The degree of reliability and, as we shall see, validity is usually expressed as a *correlation coefficient*.

There are a number of different types of correlation coefficient, depending upon the type of data being used. Most of these need not concern us here. Perhaps the two most common were developed by two British psychologists, Spearman and Pearson. Of these, Spearman's 'product moment' correlation coefficient is the most common. (Pearson's 'rank order' coefficient is used for what is called rank order data, that is, data arranged in increasing order of size.) All correlation coefficients express, in numerical form, the degree of association between two variables (e.g. height and weight, or the scores on two tests). The correlation coefficient is calculated by combining data from a large number of cases (e.g. the heights and corresponding weights of all the children in a school). The calculation produces a figure that varies between -1 at one extreme, through zero, to $+1$ at the other extreme. For the moment we will only concern ourselves with correlations in the range from zero to $+1$.

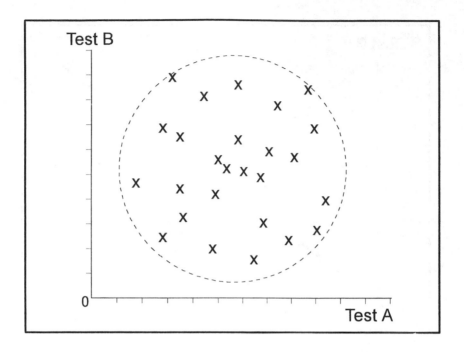

Figure 1.1. Correlation between test scores of zero

Perhaps the easiest way to understand the meaning of a correlation coefficient is to depict coefficients of 0 and +1 graphically.

Figure 1.1 represents a coefficient of 0. Each point on the graph represents an individual's score on two tests, A and B. As can be seen, there is no relationship between the scores on the two tests. The fact that an individual scored high (or low) on test A does not mean they will score high (or low) on test B. Compare this with the solid line in Figure 1.2. Here there is a perfect correlation (+1) between the scores of individuals on the two tests. If an individual scored high (or low) on test A, they scored similarly on test B. In fact, their score on either one of the tests allows us to predict, with almost complete accuracy, their score on the other test. Unfortunately this rarely happens in practice. In real life most correlation coefficients lie somewhere between 0 and +1. The dotted ellipse in Figure 1.2 represents an approximate correlation of +0.3.

As we have said, so far we have concerned ourselves only with positive coefficients, in the range 0 to +1, but what of negative coefficients? Negative coefficients represent exactly the same degree of association as positive ones, but the nature of the association is reversed, so that as the value of one of the variables increases, the

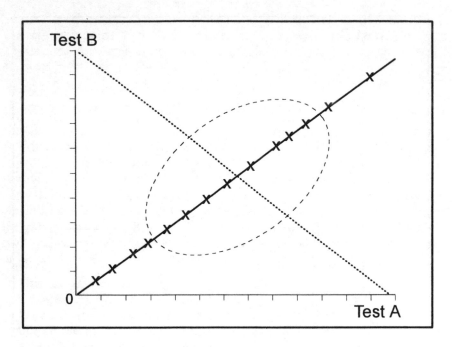

Figure 1.2. Correlation between test scores of + 1,–1, and approximately + 0.3

other decreases. The line for a coefficient of −1 would, therefore, be exactly as that for +1, but sloping the other way, as shown in the dotted line in Figure 1.2.

Now we have a measure of the degree of association, this can be used to assess reliability. But what constitutes an acceptable level, that would allow us to use a test with confidence?

There is no hard and fast rule on this, but generally reliabilities of 0.9 are considered excellent, 0.8 good, 0.7 acceptable, and 0.6/0.5 poor. Below this is considered abysmal. Without reliability it is nonsense to talk about a measure's validity. Reliability is a *sine qua non* for validity.

Validity. The concept of validity, like reliability, can also be compared with measures of physical characteristics, such as length. Whilst reliability is concerned with the consistency of measurement, validity is concerned with whether the measure is measuring what it is supposed to be measuring. For example, a tape measure that had been incorrectly calibrated would produce consistent measures, but it would not produce measures that were *valid*.

As with reliability, there are a number of methods of assessing validity. Perhaps the most important, for our purposes, are

- content validity
- criterion-related validity
- construct validity
- face validity.

Content validity is concerned with the extent to which the measuring instrument accurately samples the supposed content. All tests are, to a greater or lesser extent, samples of the behaviour they are intended to measure. Like opinion polls, the assumption is that the sample chosen will be representative of the whole. In general the larger the sample, the higher will be the content validity. Consider, for example, a test that most of us will take at some time in our lives – a driving test. A driving test is intended to assess our ability to drive safely. Part of the driving test in the UK consists of a practical test of driving, usually lasting about half an hour. This takes place on roads and streets around the driving test centre. Because of its practical nature, the test involves many of the skills involved in everyday driving. These are assessed by the examiner, who decides whether the candidate passes or not. It could be argued, however, that there are many important aspects of driving that are not included in the test. For example, motorway driving, which accounts for most mileage and which, many would argue, requires skills not required in driving on ordinary roads. These considerations all concern the content validity of the test. The greater the degree of correspondence between the test and the behaviour it is trying to sample, the higher the validity.

For our purposes *criterion-related* validity is perhaps the most important. Returning to the example of the driving test, criterion-related validity concerns the degree to which performance on the driving test predicts later driving behaviour. In order to determine whether this is, or is not, the case we would need to compare performance on the driving test with some measure of driving behaviour.

The first step in this process would be to get driving examiners to produce a 'score' for the performance of each candidate taking the test. (At the moment this is not possible as the UK driving test is not scored, other than 'pass' or 'fail'.) The next step would be to develop a *criterion* of driving behaviour with which the score on the driving test could be compared. The driving test is supposed to assess whether a person is a safe driver. This would suggest that some measure of safe driving behaviour could be obtained for each driver. One possibility would be to look at the number of accidents per thousand miles driven. Finally, the scores of the examiner would be correlated with the accidents per thousand miles. (As you will recall, the correlation coefficient is a measure of the degree of association between the two measures.)

DEVELOPMENT OF CRITERIA

The development of criteria is never as easy as most people first imagine. For selection purposes the criteria required are usually some measure of 'performance'.

We will shortly look at the problems associated with developing measures of job performance but, as an introduction, let us return to the example of driving performance.

We have suggested that a useful measure of safe driving would be the number of accidents per thousand miles. This would appear to be a good indicator of safe behaviour that can be measured. But let us consider this in a little more detail and think about some of the problems associated with this, apparently objective, measure.

- Are all accidents counted, or only those for which the driver was held liable?

- Given that our main reason for driving safely is to protect people, rather than property, do we count only those accidents involving injury?

- If we count accidents both to people and property, how do we weight them? Is a person who is involved in one fatal accident a worse driver than a person involved in ten non-fatal accidents?

- Some roads, for example motorways, are safer than others. Should this be taken into account?

- Some cars, for example those with anti-lock braking, may be better able to avoid accidents. Should the car a person drives be taken into account?

- What about those people who may not have any accidents but who, by their inconsiderate or dangerous driving, cause others around them to have accidents?

These are only a few of the problems associated with developing a meaningful criterion of safe driving behaviour. As we will now see, similar sorts of problems bedevil the creation of performance criteria.

Performance criteria

Exercise

Before reading this section try to generate, for your own job, an objective measure of performance. It should be such that you think it provides a fair method of judging your performance relative to those in a similar job. In other words, you would be happy if it was used as the basis for determining your pay.

Anyone who has tried to measure work performance soon becomes aware of the enormous problems associated with this apparently simple task. Even for simple repetitive jobs the creation of an objective and meaningful measure of performance is extremely difficult. Why should this be so?

In order to produce a measure of performance that allows individuals to be compared accurately with each other, the following are required: individuals with exactly the same training, and exactly the same experience, must be doing exactly the same job, under exactly the same conditions, using exactly the same equipment and resources, and with exactly the same type of supervision. Quite a list of exactlys! If you have tried the exercise we suggested at the beginning of this section you may have already come across some of these restrictions.

The main problem is the amount of variety in each job. To this can be added factors over which the individual has little or no control. For example, managers often have little or no control of the choice of staff for whom they are responsible. In addition, in complex organizations different parts of the organization are dependent upon each other. The failure of materials to arrive is rarely under the control of the person whose performance is being measured. Without such control it would be unfair to apportion responsibility to them. Without such responsibility it would again be unfair to use this as a measure of performance. As a result of the considerable difficulty in devising an accurate measure of performance, many organizations fall back on a subjective assessment of a person's performance, usually by their immediate boss. This, of course, is also open to criticism, especially that of bias. However, it could be argued that this is what the organization often uses to make decisions such as who to promote, and hence may be a useful criterion to be able to predict.

For all of these reasons, therefore, performance criteria are usually derived from rating scales completed by supervisors. (These are often used in formal performance appraisal exercises.)

Criteria other than performance may also be useful. The costs associated with high levels of absenteeism and staff turnover are well known. It may well be therefore that these should be among the criteria to be included in any validity study.

VALIDATING THE SELECTION METHOD

The final step in developing a selection procedure is to correlate the test scores with the performance scores to select the best predictor. Ideally this should be done as follows. The test (or tests) should be administered to all applicants for a job. The selection process should then take place *ignoring the results of the test*. Some time later, after the job incumbents have had time for training and gaining job experience, their performance should be measured. This measurement should then be correlated with the original test scores. This procedure is a specific form of criterion-related validity known as *predictive validity*. It is unusual, however, for this to be done. For obvious reasons, organizations are reluctant to ignore the results of selection tests, even though they do not know precisely how accurate they are at predicting future performance. (There are good reasons for this, as we shall see shortly.) What is more likely to happen is that the validation process will be carried out using current staff. This is known as *concurrent validity* which, like predictive validity, is a type of criterion-related validity.

In assessing concurrent validity the selection tests are administered to people presently doing the job. Assessments of their current levels of performance are then compared with their scores on the tests. This allows the validity of the tests to be determined relatively quickly. Unfortunately, there are some drawbacks with this technique. The most important of these are rather technical, but motivational influences may also be important. Those applying for jobs are highly motivated to perform well on tests. Those already doing the job may not be so well motivated, thus depressing their test scores.

Construct validity is not as clearly demonstrated by analogy with the driving test as content- and criterion-related validity. Essentially construct validity concerns the degree to which the test measures a particular construct. This construct is usually abstract and often psychological. A good example would be 'intelligence'.

Intelligence is an abstract psychological construct, so how do you know if your test of intelligence measures it? The normal way of solving this problem is to reach agreement on what abilities constitute what we refer to as intelligence, for example verbal ability, memory etc., and then devise a standard test to assess it. Such standard tests are usually administered on a one-to-one basis and may take up to an hour to complete. (Examples are the Stanford-Binet Intelligence Test and the Weschler Intelligence Scale for Adults; WAIS.) If you wish to devise a shorter, 'paper-and-pencil', intelligence test that can be administered to large numbers at once, you will need to show that it has construct validity. This is achieved by correlating the scores of individuals on the new test with their scores on one of the standard tests.

Finally, we turn to *face validity*. Face validity addresses the question 'Does the test *look* as if it is measuring what the job requires?' This may be important, especially for applicant reactions. It is desirable that all applicants, perhaps especially the unsuccessful ones, are left with a positive image of the organization. This is more likely to occur if the applicants feel that the selection procedure is fair. Selection techniques that are clearly related to the job demands are likely to be perceived as being fair. It should not be thought, however, that a test that has face validity necessarily has criterion-related validity. This has to be demonstrated empirically.

For selection purposes, perhaps the most important of the above is criterion-related validity. This is usually expressed, as we have seen, as a correlation coefficient. But what levels of validity are acceptable? Generally speaking, validity levels in excess of 0.5 are considered excellent, those in the range 0.40–0.49 good, those in the range 0.30–0.39 reasonable, and below 0.3 poor.

SELECTION METHODS

Having considered the requirements for both reliability and validity, we can now move on to consider various selection methods.

All selection methods are meant to collect information about individuals that, ideally, will predict aspects of job-related behaviours. But what sort of information is required, and how should it be collected?

Some information, such as specific educational or training data, may be easy to collect. What we are concerned with, however, is information that would allow the organization to identify which of the suitably qualified candidates is likely to be best at the job. For example, who would be the 'better' lawyer or motor mechanic?

One obvious method to determine who would be the best employee would be to give the job to every suitable applicant on a probationary basis. In other words, let them all do the job, then retain only the best. The problems associated with this are, however, obvious. In addition, the cost is likely to be prohibitive.

If the applicants have already been doing a similar job, perhaps in another organization, then their performance in that job might provide such information. It is often difficult, however, to determine what their performance was like. The only source of such information is the individual person or their current boss. There is an obvious potential for distortion in self-report and even their present boss may have reasons for either over-stating or under-stating the person's performance.

Given the problems with letting a person do the job to see how they perform, virtually all selection procedures have to make do with *samples* of relevant behaviour. In fact, the samples can be either of *behaviour* related to the job, or of *constructs* which are assumed to underlie behaviour. Let us take an example to demonstrate the difference between behaviours and constructs.

Imagine that you are seeking to select a trainee motor mechanic to work with a small group of mechanics. One way of sampling the applicants' mechanical ability would be to give them a practical test. Such tests are available, but the cost of administering them to a large number of applicants would be high. Another possibility, therefore, is to measure the applicants' 'mechanical aptitude'. This is a psychological construct that is assumed to underlie practical mechanical skills. The advantage of using this approach is that it can be assessed by 'pencil-and-paper' tests. These can be administered fairly cheaply to large numbers of applicants.

Exercise

In the descriptions of specific selection methods that follow, consider whether they are trying to assess behaviours or constructs, or a mixture of the two.

META-ANALYSIS

As we have seen, we need to assess the criterion-related validity of various selection methods to know which is most effective. But in making our initial choice we are likely to want to know how valid each of the methods has been shown to be in other organizations, and for other jobs. In this way we can concentrate on developing those methods that have a proven track record.

Many studies have been published over the years which have reported the criterion-related validity of various selection methods used for a wide variety of jobs. The range of reported validities for any one selection method is, however, often large. One way of assessing the overall validity of any particular method would be to average all the reported validities. This, indeed, was what happened for many years, and the estimated validities for virtually all methods rarely exceeded 0.3. More recently a new statistical technique has been developed that allows a more accurate assessment of 'true' validity. This technique is known as *meta-analysis* (Schmidt and Hunter, 1977). In the descriptions that follow the validity levels reported for each selection method will be that generally accepted by most experts as a result of meta-analysis.

TRADITIONAL METHODS

Application forms. The application form, it could be argued, does not really form part of the selection process proper. Rather it is part of the pre-selection process. However, it fulfils a number of functions. From the manager's viewpoint these are:

- The information given allows the generation of a short-list of suitable candidates (pre-selection).

- The information given on the form also provides the basis for an interview, where areas may be explored in more depth.

It should not be forgotten that the application form also performs a public relations function. The form is likely to be seen by a large number of people, and their impression of it is likely to influence their impression of the organization.

The form should be designed with care. Organizations often have a number of forms, depending on the type of job or the type of recruit, for example school leavers, managerial positions etc. The information requested on the form should take into account the personnel specification. (See Smith and Robertson, 1993, for examples.)

Interviews. Interviews are perhaps the most widely used method of selection (Shakleton and Newell, 1991). This is the case irrespective of the size of the organization (Robertson and Makin, 1986). Unfortunately, the validity of interviews has consistently been found to be poor. The best current estimate, provided by meta-analysis, suggests a validity of 0.2 (Robertson, 1994) for the 'traditional' interview.

One of the reasons for this poor validity lies in the lack of reliability of the interview. There are two main methods by which reliability can be assessed. One method is to use two interviewers in the same interview and then compare their views of the interviewee. This is known as '*inter*-rater' reliability. The other method is to get the same interviewer to interview the same interviewee on two separate occasions. This is referred to as '*intra*-rater' reliability. Inter-rater reliability is consistently poor, that of intra-rater reliability 'reasonably good'. This figure, however, is likely to be artificially high because it is probable that the interviewer will retain some memory of the first interview.

The usefulness of the interview, therefore, is somewhat suspect. Indeed, on the evidence available, the advice from experts would almost certainly be that the traditional interview should be abandoned. Yet, despite this evidence, organizations are reluctant to offer jobs to people without interviewing them. Let us, therefore, examine the uses of the interview and see how it may perhaps be improved.

Interviews have three main functions. One function is the collection of information about the personality and, perhaps, the inter-personal and social skills of the candidate. The second, and most obvious, function is the collection of job-related information about the candidate, often probing in more detail the information given on the application form. Finally, the interview has a public relations function. It should never be forgotten that selection is a two-way process. Organizations select individuals, but individuals also select organizations. We will return to this later in this chapter.

The assessment of personality by means of a job interview is difficult. The interview, like almost every other selection method, assesses a sample of behaviour. But, like the driving test, there can be questions concerning its content validity. In other words, is the behaviour observed in the interview a representative sample of the person's behaviour in other situations? It may well not be so. Interviews are very 'role-constrained' situations (we will discuss this in some detail in the next chapter). Put simply, an interview is a situation where people are following behaviour patterns that are determined, to a large extent, by social conventions. For example, the interviewer is largely in control and will ask most of the questions. The interviewee is expected to be polite, if not deferential, and answer the questions asked. Towards the end of the interview the interviewee will be expected to ask some intelligent questions about the job and/or the organization. Assessing personality from such controlled behaviour is difficult. In addition, some people may 'interview' better than others. As with examinations, some people may not give their best because of the stress of the situation. Also like examinations, the more you take the better your technique becomes. Interview behaviour, like exam technique, is likely to improve with practice. Those who have had most interviews may perform better in the interview, but not necessarily in the job.

Collecting job-related information in the interview is not subject to the same problems as those associated with trying to assess personality. It has, however, problems of its own. Perhaps the main reason for the lack of reliability of interviews is that they vary so much. Different interviewers rarely ask the same questions. Indeed, the same interviewer rarely asks the same questions from one interview to the next. Compare this with psychological tests. As we will see shortly, psychological tests have very high reliabilities. They achieve this because they ask *exactly* the same questions of every candidate.

Given that organizations are wedded to the use of interviews, what can be done to improve their reliability and validity?

The first step is to improve the reliability of the interview. As we have already suggested, one way to achieve this is to *standardize* the interview, so that the same questions are asked of each candidate. The second step is to improve the content validity of the interview. Improving the content validity by sampling more relevant job-related behaviours should lead to an increase in the criterion-related validity, that is how well it predicts how a person will perform. Both of these steps are included in the development of a situational interview.

The situational interview. Situational interviews (Latham *et al.*, 1980) attempt to sample job-related behaviours reliably. They do so as follows:

- Questions which sample job-related behaviours are developed from a systematic job analysis.
- The questions developed from the job analysis are asked of every candidate.
- 'Objective' scoring techniques are applied to the candidates' answers.

A description of the use of the technique will perhaps help to illustrate the process. The following description is based upon the original article by Latham *et al.* (1980) which outlines the procedure for developing a situational interview for, amongst others, hourly-paid workers in a sawmill.

The job analysis was carried out using the critical incidents technique referred to in the section on job analysis. These critical incidents reflected such job-related behaviours as attendance, safety, interaction with peers, work habits etc. These were then examined by a small number of superintendents who had experience in both supervising workers and interviewing applicants. Each superintendent picked an incident that he believed 'exemplified the criterion under consideration'. He then turned this into a question which was read aloud to the other superintendents. The group then discussed the questions and chose no more than two for each criterion. (This restriction was required so as to ensure that the interview lasted no more than one hour.)

The example given by Latham concerns attendance. A supervisor described a worker who used whatever excuse he could to stay off work, often not even phoning in. This was turned into the following question:

'Your spouse and two teenage children are sick in bed with a cold. There are no relatives or friends available to look in on them. Your shift starts in three hours. What do you do in this situation?'

Having developed the job-related questions, the next stage requires the creation of a method of scoring possible answers.

Each supervisor was asked to provide an example of answers that they had heard (or might have heard) from an interviewee who had proved to be either an outstanding, mediocre, or poor attender. The answers were then read to the other superintendents and, again after group discussion, an example of each was chosen. For example, for the question above, a poor response was 'I'd stay at home – my wife and family come first', a mediocre response was 'I'd phone my supervisor and explain the situation', and an outstanding response was 'Since they only have colds, I'd come to work'. It might be thought that candidates would realize what was required and give the response that they thought was expected. This proved not to be the case.

The technique raised inter-rater reliability levels to approximately 0.8, and produced concurrent validities of between 0.28 and 0.51 with various criteria. Robertson and Downs (1989) used a similar technique for administrative jobs in a bank. In their study they used the interview to assess five major constructs such as 'adaptability', 'commitment to a career', and 'positive outlook'. The construct of adaptability, for example was assessed with a question concerning their response to a customer presenting a new product. Examples of high, medium, and low scale point responses were: 'Ask them if they have a prototype', 'Tell them to recruit a business person', 'Tell them not to go ahead', 'Too risky, no market'. Robertson *et al.* report that the average score on the situational interview correlated 0.28 with a supervisor's rating of job performance, and 0.33 with their rating of future potential. These figures are similar to those derived from meta-analysis. These may certainly be considered to be 'acceptable' to 'good' and this means that a well developed situational interview has to be classed among the best of modern selection methods. The reasons for this, as we have described, are related to its increased reliability and content validity. Another reason for the improvement in validity may be its high face validity. Candidates can see the obvious relevance of the questions to the job and hence are likely to be motivated to perform well.

In these examples the situational interview has been used on interviewees with job experience. However, it has also been successfully used on inexperienced interviewees. Hunter and Hirsch (1987) suggest that the interview may be measuring different things in each case. For experienced interviewees they suggest the interview is acting as a job sample test. For inexperienced interviewees hypothetical examples are often used which may be acting as a test of intelligence in assessing the desirability of a particular response. We will return to both job sample and mental ability tests shortly.

References. Like interviews, references continue to be widely used, yet their reliability and validity leave much to be desired. Unlike interviews, however, there is very little research into references.

The process of producing and assessing a reference involves two stages. First the referee has to assess the individual concerned. The reference has then to be assessed by the person undertaking the selection process. According to Reilly and Chao (1982) the problems arise at the stage where the reference is being generated. When the same people are assessed by more than one referee, reliabilities rarely exceed 0.40. The reliability of assessment of the same reference by two assessors is, according to Reilly and Chao, usually acceptable.

Given that most applicants choose their own referees, it is likely that references will tend to give a positive, yet unreliable, picture of the candidate. This assumes, of course, that you are able to obtain the reference. Studies have shown that response rates are often low (see Smith and Robertson, 1993). Even when responses are obtained the generally accepted level of validity is considered by Reilly and Chao to be poor.

Little distinction is made, in the limited amount of research into references, between the two purposes for which they are used. References may be used to verify past history, or to obtain information about present and possible future performance. It is likely that the former use will probably be more reliable and valid. References should, therefore, be used to check on factual data and also, perhaps, to weed out the few candidates who are likely to be unsuitable.

MODERN METHODS

There are a number of modern methods of personnel selection. Many (but not all) have one characteristic in common. They all try to achieve what has been called 'point-to-point correspondence' (Asher and Sciarrino, 1974). Put simply, this requires a direct link between the various aspects of the selection procedure and those of the job. The situational interview we have just been discussing is an example of such point-to-point correspondence. The job-related questions are designed to correspond directly to job-related behaviours. Indeed the situational interview could easily have been included in this section rather than as a traditional method.

Accomplishment records. The construction of an accomplishment record is similar in many ways to that of a situational interview. The critical incidents technique is used to analyse the job and produce dimensions of job performance. However, rather than questions being developed to assess each dimension, the applicants are asked to provide descriptions of their own major accomplishments. These are intended to be illustrative of their performance on each of the dimensions. These are then scored by experts in the field. The technique has been used by Hough and her colleagues (Hough *et al.*, 1983; Hough, 1984) with lawyers. Each lawyer was asked to provide a general description of what they had achieved, a precise description of what was actually done, any formal recognition received, plus the name and address of a person who could verify the facts. Expert lawyers then used these descriptions as a basis for scoring.

Initial analysis showed a strong relationship between the score on the accomplishment record and the length of time in practice. When this was statistically controlled for, there was a relationship between the scores and various performance ratings, ranging from 0.16 to 0.27. Interestingly, there was no relationship between the scores and Bar examination results. The accomplishment record appears, therefore, to tap something other than professional expertise.

Accomplishment records have high face validity and may be particularly suited to the selection of professionals. Professionals often object to methods of selection such as psychological tests. Their argument is often that they should be judged on their track record. The accomplishment record provides a systematic way of assessing this. (See Makin, 1989 for a fuller discussion of some of the problems associated with the selection of professional personnel.)

Work sample tests. Work sample tests have the highest point-to-point correspondence of any method, other than a probationary period. Whereas structured interviews and accomplishment records assess verbal and written *reports* of behaviour, work sample tests assess the behaviour *directly*. However, like the other two techniques, work sample tests are based upon a thorough analysis of the job concerned.

There are a number of different types of work sample tests. They are usually classified with regard to the main skills that they are sampling. The following classification, for example, is adapted from Robertson and Kandola (1982).

- Tests of *psycho-motor* skills.
- Tests of *individual* decision-making.
- Tests of *group* decision-making.

Earlier in this chapter we used the example of the driving test when discussing various types of validity. The driving test is probably the most widely used psycho-motor work sample test. This is *not* the reason for the inclusion of the word 'motor' in the description of this type of test! These tests are referred to as motor tests because they test the effectiveness of the motor component of the nervous system. This is the part of the central nervous system that controls the movement of our bodies, in particular our limbs. The driving test mainly examines our ability to control the car through the use of our hands and feet. (It could also be argued that it assesses some aspects of decision-making associated with these motor activities. Hence the inclusion of the prefix 'psycho'.)

As mentioned earlier, the foundation for a valid work sample test is a thorough job analysis. The process is almost identical to that for a situational interview; the job is analysed, behaviours identified, and a scoring system developed. The difference is that the behaviours identified are developed into a practical test that each applicant is required to undertake.

Work sample tests have been developed for many manual skills, including operating a sewing machine and repairing a gearbox (see Asher and Sciarrino, 1974). Their validity is generally good.

Whilst psycho-motor tests tend to be associated with manual work, tests of individual decision-making tend to be used for selecting managers. There are, however, exceptions. Pilots, for example, are tested on psycho-motor flight simulators, which also assess aspects of individual decision-making.

There is a subtle yet important difference between psycho-motor tests and those for decision-making. This concerns the distinction made earlier between selection methods that assess behaviour, and those that assess constructs underlying the behaviour. Psycho-motor tests assess behaviour directly, while tests of decision-making tend to assess the underlying constructs. (These constructs may also be referred to as 'dimensions' or 'competencies'.)

A widely used individual decision-making test for managers is the 'in-tray' or 'in-basket' test. This test, again based on job analysis, presents the candidate with a full 'in-tray' for the job they have just taken over. (The explanation for the in-tray being full is that the previous incumbent died suddenly, or was sacked.) The candidate has to sort through the contents of the in-tray, which includes memos from others in the organization, telephone messages, etc., and respond as they think appropriate. This may involve making notes on action to be taken, sending memos in reply, and so on. The way in which the applicant responds is then scored on various dimensions (underlying constructs) of decision-making such as 'ability to set priorities', 'delegation and control' etc.

Like individual decision-making tests, group decision-making tests tend to be used for the selection of managers. The most common examples of such tests are Committee exercises and Leaderless Group Discussions (LGDs). In both of these applicants take part in group discussions to solve a set problem. In the Committee exercise each applicant, in turn, chairs the committee discussion. In the LGD no formal chair or leader is appointed, hence its title. In both cases the discussions are observed by a number of people who may include managers trained in observation techniques, personnel specialists, and psychologists. The performance of each candidate is observed and recorded. The dimensions on which such observations are made include 'inter-personal skills', 'leadership potential' etc. Tests of individual and group decision-making often form part of assessment centres and for this reason we will defer consideration of their reliability and validity until the next section.

The main drawback with most work sample tests is that they are costly to develop and administer. They tend to be very job-specific (especially psycho-motor tests) and usually only one applicant can be tested at once. However, in situations where the number of suitable applicants is low and the cost of selecting the wrong person is likely to be high, they may be very effective.

Robinson (1981) reports the use of work sample tests, plus a situational interview, in selecting a construction superintendent for a small construction business. (Selection for small businesses is often overlooked as the majority of selection specialists are employed, either directly or indirectly, by large organizations.) The business arranged the building of family homes. They bought the land, designed the houses, and then used subcontractors for the building work. This work was overseen by the construction superintendent. Following a job analysis, four work sample tests were developed: a blueprint reading test, a construction error recognition test, a scheduling test, and a 'scrambled subcontractor' test. The latter involved scheduling subcontractors according to a critical path so that each task was completed in the right order. The situational interview covered various aspects of the relationship between the construction superintendent and the building inspectors, physical security of building materials, and some other job aspects. Sixteen applicants took the tests and one applicant stood out clearly as best suited to the job. This candidate was offered the job and accepted. The candidate was doing the job satisfactorily more than a year later.

The tests described so far have been for experienced applicants. It is also possible to use a modified version to assess *trainability*. A trainability test differs from a work sample test in one respect. The trainability test includes a period of standard training, identical for each applicant, prior to the work sample test being taken. Such tests have been developed for trainee bricklayers and welders, amongst others (see Robertson and Downs, 1989). Their validity is generally good.

Assessment centres. Assessment centres have a long history. It could be argued that they developed from the British Army's officer selection methods of the Second World War. These were known as War Office Selection Boards (WOSBs) which were developed by the Civil Service into the Civil Service Selection Boards (CSSBs). In America a similar process for officer selection was introduced in 1942, a year after the introduction of the WOSBs (Dulewicz and Fletcher, 1982). It was American companies, however, and in particular AT&T, that developed the method for commercial and industrial use. Their use has increased in recent years. In 1986 Robertson and Makin found that only 20 per cent of UK companies used assessment centres in their selection process. By 1991 Shackelton and Newell reported use by 60 per cent.

Assessment centres use various methods to assess a variety of dimensions or competencies. The particular methods vary between organizations, and also within organizations, depending on the type of job for which candidates are being selected. The development of the battery of exercises is, however, similar. As with previous methods a systematic job analysis is performed to identify the important dimensions to be assessed. The number may vary from seven to almost 30. Examples of such dimensions are 'initiative', 'career ambition', 'oral skills', and 'delegation of authority'. Exercises are then chosen which, it is hoped, will give some indication of the candidate's strength on each dimension. Examples of such exercises include the 'in-tray' and decision-making exercise described earlier. In addition, candidates may undergo an 'in-depth' interview and/or be required to give a presentation. The candidates' performances are observed, often by senior managers, personnel staff, and psychologists, who score the performance on the relevant dimensions. In addition, psychological tests, of either cognitive skills or personality may be used (see next section).

The reported validity of assessment centres is generally good, but there is a wide variation in reported validities. The main reason for low validities appears to be, as might be expected, the degree of care associated with their construction and use. Organizations that implement them without due care, often because they are the latest 'fad', are unlikely to find that they are particularly valid. As with work sample tests, assessment centres are costly to develop and run. Centres usually take between one and five days to conduct, involving from six to eight candidates, plus the observers. These observers have to be well trained in observing, recording, and drawing inferences from the candidates' performances. There is considerable evidence to suggest that a well constructed and well run assessment centre can have high criterion-related (predictive) validity. There is some argument, however, as to how this is attained. The arguments are rather technical but we will attempt a simplified description.

When individuals take part in an assessment centre exercise their performance should be scored along certain underlying dimensions, *not* on their global performance on the exercise. For example, an individual's performance on an in-tray exercise is scored on such dimensions as 'ability to set priorities', 'delegation and control', etc. They should not be scored on a dimension of 'ability to do in-tray exercises'. Unfortunately, when the observers' scores are statistically analysed, the evidence suggests that this is just what the observers *are* doing. (See Robertson *et al.*, 1987, for evidence and a fuller discussion.) Despite this lack of construct validity, however, their criterion-related validity remains high. It is not clear why this is so.

Biodata. Many methods of selection seek data about a person's past history, particularly as it relates to their skills and/or work experience. Application forms and interviews are often used to collect such information. Biodata uses more structured and detailed methods of collecting information about a person's personal biographical history. These data are then correlated with performance criteria to identify those factors of individuals' life history that predict job-related behaviours.

Application forms usually collect basic biodata such as age, education, work history, etc. Biodata forms, on the other hand, ask very specific questions. For example there may be as many as 30 specific questions about the individual's school history. These may include not only questions about the number of examinations taken and the results, but also how much homework was set and how long it took to complete. Even questions concerning parents' reactions to exam success or failure may be included. Not only are the questions very specific, but the format is similar to a multiple choice test. The answers are often required in a 'tick box' format which may be computer scored. These scores are then correlated with criteria to see which aspects of past history, if any, are related to work performance.

The choice of information to be collected is, of course, important. Many selection methods have a clear view about the kind of information required, usually derived from systematic job analyses. Biodata, on the other hand, often does not have such a clear view. Large amounts of personal history data are collected, in the hope that one or two will prove to be predictive. For example, one of the authors was told by a selection consultant of a rather interesting finding. The analysis of biodata for a particular job revealed that the best predictor of work performance was whether the individual had been on holiday in North Africa the previous year! This is one of the criticisms of biodata. There is no obvious link between the biodata items and work-related behaviours. It could be argued that this does not matter. If a particular item helps in selection, does it matter why it works? Yes, it does.

One problem is that of face validity. If applicants feel that the application procedure is unfair it may influence their perception of the organization. More importantly, however, the fact that there is no *logical* reason for the relationship means that it could be unstable. For example, if you carried out the same analysis on a similar group there would be few grounds for confidence that the results would be the same. This is the major problem with the crude usage of biodata. However, it would appear reasonable to assume that *some* aspects of personal history should be related to certain aspects of work-related performance. To overcome these reservations, more sophisticated biodata forms target specific areas of personal biography. For example, some ask a series of questions grouped into specific areas.

These might include 'academic ability', 'leisure activities', 'career choice', etc. Some also include self-description items such as 'risk-taking behaviour'.

The validity of biodata is considered to be reasonable. However, as well as the theoretical problems mentioned above, there is a major practical problem. The relationship between the items and performance is revealed by calculating correlation coefficients between the two. Unfortunately, some apparently high correlations can occur by chance. In order to rule out such chance correlations, it is necessary to have data on a large number of individuals, all doing the same job. This means that the use of biodata tends to be limited to organizations with large numbers of employees.

PSYCHOLOGICAL TESTS

The main characteristic of psychological tests is that they are highly standardized. The same questions are asked in exactly the same way of each candidate, under exactly the same conditions. The questions are very carefully chosen and for this reason the psychological tests produced by reputable publishers have very high levels of reliability.

Psychological tests can be classified according to several criteria. We will use two of the major methods of classification. These tend to be based upon *what* is being tested, and *how* it is tested. Let us deal first with what is being tested.

Tests may be classified as to whether they assess *attainment* or *aptitude*. Tests of attainment measure what the individual can do now. The driving test is an example. Aptitude tests, on the other hand, measure an underlying potential which will indicate later performance. It might, for example, be possible to develop a series of tests to assess driving aptitude. Such a test battery may, for example, include tests of reaction time or hand/foot co-ordination. Such tests of aptitude are often used to select trainees, whilst attainment tests are used to select experienced workers.

The main method of classification of test content, however, is according to the type of psychological characteristic being assessed. One generally accepted method of classifying this is according to whether the test measures 'mental ability', 'mechanical ability', 'job and/or career interests', or 'personality'. We will briefly discuss each of these, with the exception of personality tests which form a large part of the next chapter.

Mental ability. Perhaps the best known test of mental ability is the 'intelligence test'. For psychologists, intelligence consists of a number of different factors. At the most general level is 'general intelligence', often referred to as 'g'. This comprises two secondary factors; 'verbal intelligence' and 'performance intelligence'. The former is assessed by questions involving verbal understanding and reasoning. The latter is assessed in many different ways, but often by tests of spatial perception and reasoning. Underlying these two factors are specific mental abilities, often assessed by tests specifically designed to measure those abilities. The list of such abilities is long, but examples include numerical ability, space relations, and abstract reasoning. Such tests are often referred to as 'cognitive tests', as they measure aspects of cognition and reasoning, rather than, for example, personality. The validity of such cognitive tests has consistently been found to be good.

Mechanical ability. The abilities required for mechanical jobs can be divided into physical manipulation and mental manipulation. Tests in the former category are designed to measure physical abilities, often requiring fine manipulation or speed of assembly. Examples of such tests include the Purdue Pegboard Test, in which the candidate is required to assemble simple items involving pins and washers and insert them into holes on the pegboard. Such abilities are required in fine assembly work. The mental abilities involved vary according to the particular job, but may include speed and accuracy in detecting faulty items. This may be important in such jobs as quality control.

Many tests of mechanical ability tend to assess the sort of knowledge taught in school physics courses. Some, however, do attempt to assess mechanical aptitude. The Bennett Mechanical Comprehension Test, for example, presents candidates with problems involving pulleys and gear trains. The candidates have to decide what the effects will be of moving a gearwheel or lever which is part of a larger system.

Invariably included in any battery of tests for mechanical ability are tests of spatial ability. These may involve the comparison of a remembered figure with others in different spatial orientations. This involves mentally rotating the figure in either two or three dimensions, an ability which may be important for draughtsmen or design engineers. As might be expected, tests of mechanical ability are used for selection of trainee mechanics etc. Their validity is acceptable.

Interests. Tests of occupational interest are not generally used in personnel selection. Such tests often ask the individual to choose between a number of different occupations and/or interests. The various options are offered in different combinations, producing a test with a moderate number of questions. The test is scored to produce a ranking of the individual's interest in a number of different occupational areas. It is very clear what these tests are designed to assess, and hence cheating is very easy. They are normally used in career guidance where the individual is motivated to tell the truth, rather than 'fake good'.

Occupational-specific tests. As well as the tests already mentioned there are tests that are designed for specific jobs, or categories of jobs. For example, there are tests for assessing clerical ability, typing ability, and word processing ability.

There are also tests that measure managerial abilities. Often these assess such factors as the ability to think abstractly or critically. However, as we have said, the trend in assessing managerial abilities has been away from psychological tests and towards those involving greater point-to-point correspondence.

As well as being classified according to their content, psychological tests may also be classified according to the method of assessment they use. The basic distinction is between *individual* and *group* tests. Individual tests are administered on a one-to-one basis. They are thus expensive to use. Group tests, on the other hand, allow a number of people to be tested at once. These tests are usually of the paper-and-pencil variety. Because several can be tested at once, they are cheaper to use. However, whilst group tests are more economical, their results lack the depth that is achieved by an individual test administered by a skilled psychologist.

'NON-STANDARD' METHODS

There are a number of non-standard methods of selection that are used by some organizations. Perhaps the most interesting are graphology and astrology.

Graphology is an analysis of individuals based upon samples of their handwriting. Although it is widely used in continental Europe, particularly France (Shakleton and Newell, 1991), evidence for its validity is weak. The claims made for graphology are based on two premises. The first, that individuals have unique styles of handwriting, is uncontentious. Handwriting does appear to be stable over time, although there is some evidence that it can be faked. The second premise, however, is open to dispute. It is that specific differences in handwriting reflect underlying differences in personal characteristics. There is no evidence from psychological research to support this contention. Research into the use of graphology in selection is confounded by the fact that the analysis of the writing in, for example, a job application, may be influenced by the content.

Astrology, on the other hand, has some interesting links with occupations. There is research which has consistently demonstrated a link between planetary positions and career choices. The most famous of this work is by Gauquelin (1978) who looked at the planetary positions at the time of birth of 500 eminent French medical practitioners. He found a relationship beyond that which might have been expected by chance. He found similar relationships when he looked at successful scientists and artists. The reasons for these relationships are not entirely clear, but Eysenck and Nias (1982) suggest that the association is the result of personality factors. They produce evidence to suggest that planetary position at time of birth is associated with different personality factors, notably extraversion/introversion. This then is associated with occupational success. It should be pointed out that the relationship between planetary position and occupation is statistically very small. In any case, planetary positions are related not to the signs of the zodiac, which are determined by the earth's annual progress around the sun. Rather, they are determined by the earth's daily rotation on its axis. Therefore, in order to know the planetary positions at the time of a person's birth, it is necessary to know the exact time of their birth. This is recorded in France, but not in the UK.

The link between personality and astrology is not without its critics. For example, it appears that personality and star sign are only related for those who believe in astrology (see Nias, 1982). The possibility of a self-fulfilling prophecy presents itself. The person behaves in the way they do because they believe that this is the way they should behave, according to their star sign. Despite these links, however, the validity of astrology for personnel selection purposes is low. More evidence that it is related to job-related behaviours would be needed before its use could be recommended.

USING SELECTION METHODS

There are a number of factors that need to be taken into account when using selection methods. Firstly, they should not discriminate between applicants *except* on the basis of their likely ability to do the job. Any method that is used should be well validated. A systematic validation is likely to provide a good defence against claims of discrimination. (See Smith and Robertson, 1993, for a fuller discussion of this important topic.)

Discrimination need not only be direct, for example on the grounds of race, creed, colour, or gender. It may also be indirect. Smith and Robertson report an interesting example. In an American police force there was a minimum height requirement. This discriminates indirectly against women, who tend, on average, to be shorter than men. A job analysis was carried out which revealed that a police officer had to be at least tall enough to fire a revolver over the top of a police car. As a result the minimum height requirement was lowered. This still discriminated against women, but it could now be shown that the requirement was directly related to job requirements. One of the authors came across a maximum height requirement, which would discriminate against men. This was for the job of air steward/stewardess on a small regional airline in the UK. The cabin height was such that those above 5'2" (1.57m) would have difficulty working without continually bending.

Whatever methods are used, there comes a point when decisions have to be made on the basis of the results of the selection process. There are two ways in which the decision can be made, either *clinically*, or *actuarially*. The clinical approach involves making a subjective judgement based on the experience of the person making the decision. Such a decision may involve the results of various aspects of the selection process, but the decision rests on the judgement of the selector. The actuarial method, on the other hand, uses sophisticated statistical techniques (e.g. multiple regression) to weight the scores mathematically from the various selection methods. This produces an overall score for each candidate which becomes the basis for the decision. According to Smith and Robertson (1993) the evidence suggests that the actuarial method is superior, but rarely by more than 10 per cent. In the absence of specialists, therefore, selectors will have to use their best judgement in deciding how to weigh all the evidence and produce a decision.

EVALUATION

We have examined the validities of a number of selection methods and it is clear that the validity of even the best method rarely exceeds 0.5. Another way of indicating the usefulness of any method is to express it as the percentage of variation in the criterion that is explained by the particular method. The calculation to arrive at this figure is simple. The correlation coefficient is squared and multiplied by 100. So, for example, the variance explained by a selection method with a validity of 0.3 is 0.3^2 (0.09) multiplied by 100, which gives a figure of 9 per cent. (A correlation coefficient of 1.0 would, therefore, explain 100 per cent of the variation.)

Given that the best of methods rarely explain more than 25 per cent of the variance ($0.5^2 \times 100$), this leaves three-quarters of the variance unexplained. Even the most valid selection methods, therefore, will produce errors. It might appear that, despite the resources devoted to developing valid methods, the benefits are likely to be small. Fortunately, this is not the whole story.

The effectiveness of any selection procedure is referred to as its *utility*. A number of factors will influence the utility of a selection procedure, only one of which (albeit an important one) is its validity.

Let us consider the selection process diagrammatically. Figure 1.3

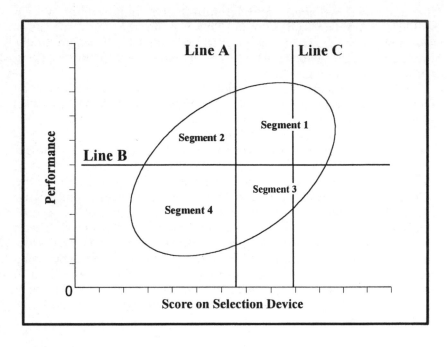

Figure 1.3. *Effect on errors in selection of different 'cut-off' points*

represents a correlation coefficient of approximately 0.3 between the performance criterion (the vertical axis) and scores on the particular selection method being used (the horizontal axis).

Let us now decide that we will only employ those with a score on the selection test higher than line A on the horizontal axis. In other words, only those with scores to the right of line A will be employed. This will mean that some of those who are likely to be poor performers will be rejected.

Let us also decide that we have a minimum level of performance that we require from our employees. This is represented by line B. We have now divided the ellipse into four segments. Segment 1 consists of those individuals who scored above the cut-off point on the test, and whose job performance will be above the minimum required. Segment 4 consists of those who scored below the cut-off point on the test and who would not have performed to the minimum standards required. So far, so good; this is precisely what a good selection method is meant to do.

The other two sectors are somewhat different. Those in segment 2 scored below the cut-off point on the test, but would have performed above the minimum required. They would have been wrongly rejected. This is an unfair outcome as far as an individual in this position is concerned, but from the organization's point of view this does not matter. Segment 3, however, is a different matter. These are individuals who have scored above the cut-off point on the test and hence have been employed. Their performance, however, turns out to be below the minimum required. They have been wrongly accepted. They can, of course, be sacked, but the costs of their training plus the costs of replacing them may be considerable. What else can be done?

One option would be to increase the cut-off point on the test. For example, by raising it to line C. One effect of this is to reduce considerably the size of segment 3, that is the number of wrongly accepted applicants. From the organization's point of view this is the desired effect. The utility of the selection procedure has been increased. However, whether or not the cut-off point can be raised depends, crucially, on the number of applicants. Assuming that the applicants are spread evenly throughout the ellipse, moving the cut-off point to the right will mean there will be fewer applicants who meet that requirement. Where you are able to set the cut-off will be determined by matching the number of vacancies that have to be filled with the number above the cut-off point. The ratio of the number of applicants for each job vacancy is known as the *selection ratio*. For a valid selection process, the higher the selection ratio, the higher will be its utility.

Another factor that affects the utility concerns levels of job performance. Consider two different scenarios, in both of which there is no systematic selection process. Applicants are accepted at random. In the first case the levels of job performance vary widely. The difference between the best and worst performer is large. In the second case there is virtually no difference in performance between different employees. In this latter case there would be no need to implement a systematic selection procedure. Everyone who is given a job performs at the same level. A systematic selection system would produce no benefit for its cost. In the first case, however, it will be highly desirable to produce a selection system that identifies the good and the poor performers. This then is the general point. The larger the spread (in statistical terms the 'standard deviation') of performance, the greater the utility of any valid selection process.

Other factors also influence utility, including the validity of the previous selection process, and the length of time those accepted remain with the organization. However, the main message is clear. The greatest benefits are to be obtained from valid selection procedures, applied to jobs where the spread of performance is largest, and the number of applicants per vacancy is highest. Under such circumstances the potential savings can be considerable. For example, Hunter and Schmidt (1982) estimated the utility of the Programmer Aptitude Test for selecting computer programmers for the US Government. The number of such programmers selected for employment was large, approximately 600 per year. This produced estimated savings of $5.6 million!

THE IMPACT ON CANDIDATES

It is often forgotten by those who design and operate selection systems, that selection is a two-way process. Not only do organizations select potential employees, but applicants select the organizations for which they will work. The impact of the selection procedure on the candidates is, therefore, important. Unfortunately, it is only recently that the issue has been seriously addressed.

Any selection procedure involves two stages. Candidates are first assessed, and then decisions are taken on the basis of that assessment. Each of these stages can have an impact on candidates. Assessment involves the provision of information about a person of which they may or may not have been aware. This information may be fed back to the candidate formally. However, even if the results of tests are not fed back, candidates often have a reasonable idea of how they performed. Sometimes the effects of this information may be beneficial. For example, Downs *et al.* (1978) used a work sample test for sewing machinists. Each applicant took the test and was rated on a scale from A (highest) to E (lowest). None of the applicants were informed of their score. Unusually, all the applicants, irrespective of their score on the test, were offered jobs. Of those assessed A, over 90% took up the offer and started work. Of those assessed D, slightly over 50% started, whilst of those assessed E, only 23% started. (This may also have been influenced by the relative availability of alternative work. In times of job shortages the pattern may be different.)

Potential skill at operating a sewing machine, however, is rarely central to a person's self-image or self-worth. This may not be the case for other factors, such as intelligence, personality, or managerial potential. The effects of receiving evidence that contradicts an important aspect of a person's self-image may be psychologically damaging.

The effects of the decision that is made on the basis of the assessment may also be significant, especially to those who are rejected. We have mentioned the importance of face validity and its role in leaving the unsuccessful candidates with a positive view of the organization. However, rejection, especially from a job or career that was important for the individual's self-image, is also likely to have detrimental effects. Fortunately, as we will see later in the book, most people bounce back fairly quickly from such disappointments.

The negative effects we have described may be unfortunate in the context of selection. When they take place in the context of internal selection, or placement, the consequences for the organization may be much more serious. For example, Fletcher (1991), examined the effects on successful and unsuccessful candidates of an assessment centre. Six months after the feedback of the results, the unsuccessful candidates were showing a drop in self-esteem. In addition, there were indications that they were less motivated to work hard. Fletcher states that his findings 'give cause for concern about the unsuccessful candidates' psychological well-being'.

This negative impact on the unsuccessful is all the more worrying when the effects of setting high cut-off points is recalled. The effect of selecting only a few successful candidates, for example for 'fast track' promotion, means that many candidates will be rejected who would have performed the job well. Robertson *et al.* (1991) have shown that the effects of not being selected have an impact on the candidates' attitudes to the organization, and on their intentions to leave. The cost of selecting a few 'high flyers' may be the loss of a larger number of solidly performing individuals, the backbone of any organization.

How can these negative effects be mitigated? First, the limitations of the assessment process need to be understood and explained. Second, reliable and valid methods should be used, bearing in mind the need for good face value. Third, feedback on the candidates' performance should be given in a constructive manner. In particular, the value the organization attaches to its solid performers should be stressed. In addition, the feedback should be developmental rather than judgemental in nature. Rather than 'this is what you are like', the emphasis should be on 'this is how you can improve'.

CAREER CHOICE AND DEVELOPMENT

The process of selection described in this chapter is strongly influenced by a set of assumptions about the nature of work and the notion of career and career progression. These assumptions developed during the twentieth century. Both the nature of work and the concept of career is, however, rapidly changing, and it may be that in the near future these assumptions will no longer be valid. We will start by looking at the current beliefs concerning the notion of career and return to these changes later.

The notion of someone having a career is a comparatively recent idea. *The Oxford English Dictionary* defines 'career' as

'a person's course or progress through life (or a distinct portion of life): (now esp.) a profession according opportunities for advancement'

and gives the date for the first recorded usage in this form as 1803, when reference was made to a 'diplomatic career'. It is significant that this usage developed at the time of the industrial revolution when the nature of work was also undergoing dramatic change. Over a relatively short period individuals moved from agricultural employment, or work as individual craftsmen, to being employed by large organizations. As a result of this change there developed a range of factory work and a cadre of 'managers'. Thus it became possible, for the first time, for there to be a choice of occupation, development within an occupation, and even movement between occupations. Prior to this, the occupation that a person entered was largely determined by their parent's occupation, and the individual remained in this for life.

In more recent times the term 'career' has been used in a number of ways. Three major types of definition can be distinguished. The first emphasizes notable achievement in any occupation, the second any pattern of occupational change, and the third a succession of related occupations that are hierarchically arranged, and through which the individual rises in an ordered sequence. A more comprehensive classification has been suggested by Hall (1976) who categorizes a number of uses of the concept of career as follows:

Career as advancement. This is perhaps one of the most widely used popular definitions of a career, which is seen as a sequence of moves or promotions, each succeeding position being, in some global assessment, 'better' than the one preceding. Although this sequence may be within the same occupation there is no requirement that this is so. There is a tradition, for example, of those in government, be they politicians or 'mandarins', moving between public office and professional or business positions.

Implicit within this definition, however, is a value judgement concerning the general direction of movement. Whilst an individual may make moves which appear to be 'sideways' or even 'down a rung' in order to improve their future prospects, such moves cannot be made often for, in general, advancement implies 'upwards'.

Career as profession. Certain occupations are referred to as careers whilst others are not. Whilst some of the former are obviously related to the career-as-advancement theme, the emphasis may perhaps be on the relatively long period and high level of training required for these occupations. Although formal promotion may also be involved, the crucial aspects may be the 'regularized status passages' through which the incumbents pass during training, together with the emphasis, at least in theory, upon client-centred service based on general rules of competency and confidentiality. Thus a lawyer is considered to have a career whether he has a small one-man practice or is a Lord of Appeal in Ordinary. Cotgrove (1967) has suggested that the difference between a career and a job is equivalent to that between tenancy and leasehold. Thus 'a career offers reasonably secure expectation of continued employment', compared with the more transient nature of a 'job'.

These are the two major definitions in widespread popular use, the first concentrating upon the 'opportunities for advancement' mentioned in the *OED*, the second upon the professional element. These popular definitions, however, limit the usage of the term to a minority of the working population, and to 'objective' assessments of success. Behavioural scientists have tended to adopt broader definitions.

Career as a lifelong sequence of jobs. This definition removes the rather value-laden emphasis of both the previous usages and considers the series of jobs held and organizations worked for, irrespective of the particular occupation or hierarchical level. In this way anyone who works may be considered to have a career. Although this increases the number of individuals to whom the concept can be applied, the emphasis on the jobs rather than the individuals holding those jobs means that their experiences within the job are not considered. Whilst the objective classification of such careers is often most useful, for example, in looking at patterns of social mobility, it will be argued that a better understanding will only be obtained by looking at individuals and their experiences.

Career as a sequence of role-related experiences. This, the broadest of the definitions to be discussed, is the furthest from the job-related, advancement-orientated usage which we considered first. It has its origins in the desire of sociologists to draw attention to the developing aspects of roles which might, on the surface, be thought to be unchanging. Thus, as Goffman (1961) has said:

'Traditionally the term career has been reserved for those who expect to enjoy the rises laid out within a respectable profession. The term is coming to be used, however, in a broadened sense to refer to any social strand of a person's course through life.... Such a career is not a thing that can be brilliant or disappointing; it can be no more a success than a failure.'

This emphasis upon individual roles encompasses both objective and subjective assessments. As Goffman goes on to claim:

'One value of [this definition] is its two-sidedness. One side is linked to internal matters held dearly and closely, such as image and felt identity; the other side concerns official position, jural relationships and style of life, and is part of a publicly accessible institutional complex.'

This sociological definition does not limit itself to roles that are work-related. For example, Becker (1963) has examined the 'career' of the marijuana user, and Goffman (1961) that of the mental patient. In relation to the theories discussed below we are, however, using the term career in its common meaning, as defined in the first two categories above. That is, career as advancement and/or as a profession.

As organizations got larger and increasingly complex, following the industrial revolution, there was a need to attract, develop, and retain appropriately skilled employees (both shop-floor and managerial). As Schein (1977) noted, the wider and deeper the range of skills required to operate successfully in an increasingly complex environment, the more vulnerable will the organization be to critical shortages of the required human resources. The need for human resource planning thus developed, leading to yet another 'career opportunity' in human resource management, as this particular specialism has now come to be known. In parallel with this development it became necessary for the individual to plot a course through the increasingly complex set of employment opportunities being offered, both in industry and the professions. Thus developed the notion that individuals should consider and develop a career plan. The twin specialisms of vocational selection and vocational guidance arose from these developments. It is significant that both these related specialisms are firmly rooted in a belief in differentiated organizations (see Chapter 8).

THEORIES OF CAREER DEVELOPMENT

Theories of career development tend to have their origins in the work of developmental psychologists, who have conceptualized personality and intellectual development as proceeding through a number of stages, e.g. Freud (1974) and Piaget (1952). Others, notably Eriksen (1973) have extended these stages to explain methods of adjustment beyond adolescence. Eriksen defines four stages:

- Adolescence. At this stage the individual is concerned with developing a sense of identity. If issues are not resolved the individual remains unclear concerning their self-concept; too hasty a resolution can lead to a rigid and inflexible view of self. Eriksen suggests that this stage typically takes place between the ages of 15 and 24.

- Young adulthood. Here the individual is concerned with issues of intimacy and involvement. This can be in relation to other people, or organizations or causes. There is a need for balance between isolation and being taken over by others. These concerns are typical of ages 25 to 34.

- Adulthood. The concern at this stage is essentially coping with mortality. It is about developing something of lasting value; something that will be remembered after the individual has gone. The worry is that nothing of lasting value will be achieved. This is the concern of ages 35 to 64.

- Maturity. This is seen as the final stage of life where, if the previous stages have been satisfactorily resolved, the individual can relax in the satisfaction of past achievements. If earlier stages were not satisfactorily worked through, then this will be a period of dissatisfaction and regret. This covers the period from age 65 on.

Obviously, the ages quoted indicate the typical range. There will be considerable individual variation. They are also based on a traditional male western working life, leaving school in late adolescence and retiring at 65.

One of the most influential career development theories is that suggested by Donald Super (1957). This is based on a stage development theory, similar to that of Eriksen, originally put forward by Charlotte Buehler (1933, quoted in Osipow, 1973). Super suggests that there are five 'vocational life stages':

- Growth stage (from birth to age 14). In this stage the self-concept develops through identification with key figures in the family and school. There are three substages which include an early fantasy role-play stage; followed by a phase where the individual's likes and interests begin to determine aspirations and activities; and finally abilities are given more weight as real life job requirements are considered.

- Exploration stage (age 15–24). Self-examination and occupational exploration take place in school, leisure activities, and part-time work. Substages consist of a *tentative* stage, where interests, capacities and opportunities are considered and tried out in fantasy; a *transition* stage where reality is given more weight as the individual enters work or professional training; and a *trial* stage where an appropriate occupational field having been located, a starting job is tried out as a potential for a life work.

- Establishment stage (age 25–44). Having found an appropriate occupational field, effort is put into making a permanent place in it. There may also be some continuing trial and subsequent shifting. Thus the two substages are; *trial*, where there may be some more exploration and shifting, before moving to *stabilization* where as the career pattern becomes clear, effort is put into stabilizing it and making a secure place in the world of work.

- Maintenance stage (age 45–64). Having made a place in the world, the concern now is to hold on to it. There is little new development; the individual continues with the established pattern.

- Decline stage (age 65 on). As physical and mental powers decline, work activity changes and eventually ceases. The individual moves from being a participant to being an observer. There are two sub-stages; *deceleration* as the pace of work slackens; followed by *retirement*, when work ceases, although there may be a continuing and gradually decreasing part-time occupation.

Early Adulthood

Early-Adult Transition, 17–22

- Start thinking about place in the world separate from parents and educational institutions.
- Test initial preferences for living.

Entering Adult World, 22–28

- Develop sense of personal identity in work and non-work.

Thirties Transition, 29–33

- Evaluate accomplishments of twenties and make adjustments.

Settling Down, 34–39

- Strive towards achieving personal goals.
- Make commitments to family and work.

Middle Adulthood

Mid-life Transition, 40–45
- Review life structure adopted in thirties.
- Recognize mortality limits on achievement.

Entering Middle Adulthood, 46–50
- Developing a greater stability as questions raised in mid-life transition are answered.

Fifties Transition, 51–55
- Raise questions about life structure previously adopted.

Culmination of Middle Adulthood, 56–60
- Answer questions raised and adjust life choices.

Late adulthood (over 60)

Figure 1.4. Career stages according to Levinson et al.

It is doubtful, of course, whether anyone's actual career follows such neatly defined stages, and a great deal of research has been done to try to determine what really does happen to the individual, in career terms, during their working life. Perhaps one of the most thorough of these researches was that by Levinson *et al.* (1978). This was based on in-depth interviews with 40 American men, and showed that there tended to be alternating periods of stability and change. Levinson suggested that careers could be seen as developing through three stages related to age – Early Adulthood (ages 17–39), Middle Adulthood (40–60) and Late Adulthood (over 60). As can be seen from the summary in Figure 1.4, each stage is characterized by periods of development followed by re-appraisal and more development. Perhaps the major contribution of Levinson and his co-workers is the concept of *mid-life transition*, where a major review and, possibly, re-adjustment of career and life plans may take place.

CAREER TYPES

Rather than looking at the process of how careers develop, other researchers have investigated 'types' of career that different individuals follow. Driver (1982), for example, has suggested four types of career path:

- Steady state. The individual selects an occupation and stays within it for their whole working life, showing a high level of commitment to this one area. Many professional occupations would show this pattern, e.g. solicitors or accountants.

- Linear. The individual makes a steady progression through a particular occupation, for example, the manager who steadily climbs the corporate ladder.

- Spiral. The individual switches from one occupation to another, spending only a few years in each. But each stage utilizes and builds on the skills and experience of the earlier jobs, for example, the person who spends a few years in management, moves to lecture in a business school and then becomes a management consultant.

- Transitory. The individual changes jobs frequently with little, or no, connection between the jobs taken, variety being the defining characteristic. For example, the person who on leaving school takes a semi-skilled job in a local factory, after a year or two joins the merchant navy, on returning home gets a job as a warehouseman and then, perhaps, decides to train for some more skilled occupation.

In a slightly different approach Schein (1978) has suggested, based on his research into careers, that individuals can be classified into five types:

- Managers, who set out to climb the corporate ladder see themselves as generalists who are able to manage others.

- Technicians, who tend to be specialists concentrating on the details of their profession.

- Security-orientated, who are concerned with a safe work environment, and who find promotion rewarding because it shows that the organization values them and wants to keep them.

- High autonomy needs, who value freedom and will find ways to carve out their own niche in an organization.

- Entrepreneurs, who tend to start up their own ventures to fulfil their own creative needs.

Schein (1982) later identified other basic career orientations, which he termed 'career anchors'. A career anchor is defined as a basic value or motive which plays a significant role in influencing the direction of a career. Examples include:

- dedication to an ideology, a cause, or a group
- pure challenge – thriving on competition, adventure, or risk
- maintaining a balance between professional and private life.

Career anchors will influence the direction or type of career that an individual takes.

DEVELOPING CAREERS

The question arises as to what use are these theories (apart from giving academics something to talk about at conferences). The answer is that they should help individuals to make sense of what is happening in their careers, and thus enable them to plan better. They should also provide a framework for careers advisers to understand their clients better. Against this background there are, in fact, a number of things that both individuals and organizations can do to improve career development.

Self-assessment and planning: the individual can take steps to assess his or her own abilities, skills and interests, as a basis for deciding possible occupations, and then develop a career plan.

Vocational guidance and counselling: it is obviously very difficult for individuals with limited knowledge of the job market, or little understanding of their own needs and abilities, to plan careers on their own. This is particularly the case for young people, who are still in the growth or exploration stage. Good assessment and careers counselling is essential at this time. Very often this is provided by schools and local authorities. The Confederation of British Industry have also recently proposed an extension of these services with a system they call 'Careership', which would involve the public education system in providing such things as 'good quality independent careers advice' and 'personal learning profiles, and action planning, focusing attention on the development of the individual'. This would be part of the standard curriculum, the purpose being 'to ensure that individuals can manage their own learning and careers – and take responsibility for their choices, which will prepare them for their adult working lives, and begin to make them think about their own career development' (Davies, 1994).

Organizational support for career planning: it is in the interest of any organization that its employees are experiencing career satisfaction. There are a number of things which can be done to help this happen. Employees can be given feedback from the selection procedure, assessment centres can be orientated towards development as well as selection, developmental programmes can be offered. All of these should be accompanied by the availability of careers counselling. Part of the task of the manpower planning function of the organization should be to consider individual career progression in relation to the organization's manpower needs; the objective being to match, as far as possible, the individual's career needs with the needs of the organization. It may well be that as part of this process some individuals will realize that they cannot fulfil their career aspirations within the organization. It is in the interests of the organization, as well as individual, for the organization to provide help with finding better occupational prospects outside the organization.

CAREERS IN THE TWENTY-FIRST CENTURY

We suggested earlier that the current notion that an individual could look forward to a 'career', and indeed should do some planning for it, originated with the way that work changed with the industrial revolution. Now at the end of the twentieth century the way work is organized is again changing dramatically. Many organizations are drastically reducing the numbers of employees, and reducing the numbers of levels of management (downsizing and delayering, in current jargon). New organizational forms are developing, such as complex international networks of interrelated but independent companies, sometimes referred to as 'embedded' organizations (Berry, 1994).

Anthony Sampson, writing in *The Sunday Times* on 4 June 1995 gives a typical example of such changes. Referring to British Petroleum (BP), which once had a reputation for overmanning, he says:

'*Today BP's extravagant City skyscraper stands empty: a ghostly monument to earlier security. The company is now run from an Edwardian mansion. The new head of BP, David Simon, sees the skyscraper as the symbol of an outdated command system, passing down orders from the top. "We have to escape from that attitude", he told me. "Young recruits don't now expect to progress up the tower. The jobs for life syndrome is over."*'

There are many other examples of such change; Shell's head office staff is now only a fraction of its former size, ICI has split into two smaller companies (with the formation of Zeneca, based on the original pharmaceuticals division) and has shed large numbers of staff.

Charles Handy (1994a) suggests that in the future most organizations will have only a relatively small core of full-time, permanent employees, working from a conventional office. They will 'buy in' most of the skills they need on a contract basis, either from individuals working at home and linked by computers and modems to the company headquarters or regional offices (teleworking), or by hiring people on short-term contracts to do specific jobs or carry out specific projects. In this way companies will be able to maintain the flexibility that they need to cope with a rapidly changing world.

Much of this change is already happening. For example a recent survey found that 1 in 8 (13 per cent) of UK companies already allow some employees to work from home, and British Telecom claims that there are already more than 2.5 million people working from home on a full- or part-time basis in the UK, and that this figure is expected to rise to 4 million in 1996.

How will all this affect individual careers? Obviously far fewer (if any) people will have careers for life. Steady state and linear careers will virtually disappear. Spiral, and probably to a greater extent, transitory, careers may still exist. So to think in terms of career stages will, probably, also be meaningless. In fact, Handy (1994b) suggests that we shall have to change the whole way we think about work and having a job. He gives the following illustration:

'*There were two people in my house the other morning. My friend was saying: "It's terrible, there are no jobs any more for people like me, it's disgusting, civilisation is crumbling." And then the plumber who was there to fix the pipes said: "Oh God, it is terrible, I've got so many jobs on this week I can't cope." Interesting use of the word job. I said to my kids when they left college: "Don't get a job." "Horror!" they said, "Dad wants us to go on the dole." "No", I said, "Don't get a job, get a customer. Because if you can do something or make something which people are prepared to pay money for, you will be confident for the rest of your life."*'

In other words, we may be moving back to a view of work nearer to that which existed before the industrial revolution, where the individual thinks of himself or herself as a tradesperson or craft worker with a skill to sell. Apart from the traditional trades and crafts, these skills will include the older professions (such as law and accounting), as well as new ones, such as computer programming and information technology skills. What is also certain is that in a rapidly changing world, it will be necessary to update these skills continually and to acquire new ones.

SELECTION, CAREERS, AND THE PSYCHOLOGICAL CONTRACT

The selection process is where the individual and the organization have their initial contact. Both sides will approach the process with their own ideas of what is expected. What happens and, indeed, *how* it happens can have an influence on the psychological contract. The individual will approach this process with expectations. They may well expect to be subjected to a variety of selection devices. As we have seen, the face validity of these may well influence their performance. In addition, it may well influence their perception of the efficiency and 'fairness' of the organization. Professionals, in particular, may have expectations about the type of selection technique they consider appropriate.

The selection process is, of course, a vehicle for giving individuals information about the organization and the job to which they are being recruited. It is important that the organization, in its desire to attract good candidates, does not 'over-sell' the jobs available, hence setting up unrealistic expectations. The effects of such unrealistic expectations may be to lead to lower morale and higher turnover. As Robinson and Rousseau (1994) have shown, the violation of psychological contracts appears to be the norm rather than the exception.

One way of avoiding such unrealistic expectations is by the use of 'realistic job previews' (see Makin and Robertson, 1983). As we have seen, trainee sewing machinists are capable of assessing their own likely job performance, and of using this information when taking decisions as to whether or not to accept a job. It is possible to develop methods of giving applicants realistic job information. Such information may be in the form of written material, videos, or even allowing applicants to talk to current job incumbents. Indeed, it could be argued that giving job information in this way is a better method than using the valuable time of the selection interview. It is also important to give information not only about the job, but also about the expected career.

The concept of career is important because the beliefs we have about our likely career, or indeed whether we see ourselves as having a career or not, will determine many of the expectations we have about our world of work. Whether an employer sees himself or herself as offering a career, or simply a job, is also important. These expectations become part of the psychological contract both from the employee's and employer's point of view. Tsui *et al.* (1993) proposed that the psychological contract can be seen as either job-orientated or organization-orientated. The former is relatively short term and not career-orientated; the latter is more long term and could encompass the notion of a career within the organization. It is important that all parties have a similar perception of the nature of the contract, if the relationship is to be one of mutual satisfaction.

If the individual has the perception of career as a profession, this can bring an additional complication. In this case the individual could see his or her career within one organization (as is often the case in professional practice, such as the law) or through many (as is very likely in a career in marketing or data processing). In the latter case assumptions about the psychological contract based on beliefs about the profession may not be the same from one organization to another. Another problem, now very common, is that if conditions of employment change due to a changing environment, people will often feel that their psychological contract has been broken. For example, scientists in a government research organization which was in the process of privatization found themselves in the situation of having to sell their expertise, as consultants, on the open market. Many of them complained that this was not 'the contract' when they joined the organization, and that they wanted to be scientists, not salesmen. Many teachers in the UK feel that they are no longer getting the professional contracts that they expected when they joined the profession, because of political changes in the education system. Such changes may be inevitable but it is essential that the changes that affect the psychological contract are dealt with openly and fairly. We will return to perceptions of fairness, and their impact on behaviour, in Chapter 4.

2

Personality and Individual Differences

As with other sections of the book, the main emphasis of this chapter will be on those aspects of theory that, in our opinion, have most relevance to managers. We will not, therefore, spend too much time considering how personalities are formed, nor with the construction of personality tests. The manager can do nothing about the former; the latter is more the concern of specialists.

Exercise

Before we examine the descriptions generated by psychologists, we would like you to try to describe your own personality briefly. A series of single words or phrases will suffice. If you are brave enough, you might also ask someone who knows you well to describe you.

PERSONALITY THEORY

Personality is perhaps the area of psychology that is best known to the layman. Many reading this text will have completed, at some time or another, a questionnaire that attempted to measure their personality. These range from the highly developed and sophisticated measures used by psychologists, to the 'rough and ready' ones found in various popular magazines and books. Both 'pop' personality tests and the tests used by psychologists tend to be pencil-and-paper tests – questionnaires asking for your self-reported behaviour in various situations. Here the similarity ends! Properly constructed personality tests are highly sophisticated measuring instruments. Their reliability is accurately assessed, as are such factors as people's propensity to show themselves in a good light; this is referred to as 'social desirability'. Many tests contain 'lie scales' to help check on this propensity.

Scores on each of the personality dimensions being measured by the test are given as a point on a scale (usually of nine or ten points). Many personality tests measure a number of such dimensions, as we shall see. For an individual, a score will be produced for each dimension. As each of these dimensions is independent of the others, the score on each dimension can vary across the nine or ten points of the scale. A large number of personality 'profiles' is therefore possible, even though there may be as few as five dimensions.

Why are we so interested in personality? The concept of personality 'traits' is so widely used and accepted that, for the layman, it would appear to be the fundamental unit of psychological currency. Behind its widespread use is the underlying assumption that an individual's behaviour (including our own) is largely caused by their personality. Knowledge of their personality, therefore, allows us to predict how they are likely to behave in various situations. Is this assumption correct? And if it is correct, to what extent does personality cause behaviour?

Personality theory is not concerned with such observable characteristics as age or race, but with internal, unobservable mental states. Since personality cannot be observed directly it must be inferred from patterns of observable behaviour, or self-report questionnaires. From these observations or self-reports of behaviour are derived the abstract categories we refer to as dimensions of personality. The number and nature of these dimensions vary from theory to theory, but perhaps the two most influential schools of personality theory are those that consider personality as being either *traits* or *types*.

TRAIT THEORIES OF PERSONALITY

When asked to describe a person to others we tend to start with physical characteristics, followed perhaps by such things as their occupation, etc. We would also be likely to use shorthand descriptions of the way they tend to behave. Thus, we may describe people as aggressive, happy-go-lucky, lonely, introverted, or many other adjectives that are intended to give an indication of their personality. Each of these adjectives describe what psychologists would call a 'trait'. The list of such traits is obviously very large. Indeed, researchers have recently estimated that there are over 18,000 such words.

The trait is the basis of many influential theories of personality. It is a generalization made from observing the way a person habitually behaves. It is perhaps best summed up as 'a predisposition to behave in certain ways'.

Trait theories attempt to reduce the large number of traits in common use down to a smaller number of more general traits. There are a number of ways of achieving this. It would be possible to take an individual, or panel of individuals, and ask them to group together those traits that they consider to be alike in some respect. There is obviously scope for error in using such a method. For this reason, modern trait theorists use highly sophisticated statistical techniques to identify the underlying traits. The responses of thousands of individuals are subjected to these statistical procedures, thus reducing the possible errors.

Until recently there was much debate among psychologists about the number and description of personality traits. Cattell's widely used 16PF test (Cattell *et al.*, 1970) measured, not surprisingly, sixteen personality factors. These could, however, be reduced to a smaller number of more general factors (called 'second order' factors by Cattell). In the past few years a partial consensus has appeared concerning the number and, to a lesser extent, the descriptions of traits (but see Schneider and Hough, 1995, and Cattell, 1995, for criticism). This consensus has condensed around what have come to be known as the 'Big Five' personality traits. These are: Neuroticism, Extraversion, Openness, Agreeableness, and Conscientiousness.

There are obvious problems when the wealth of information about individuals is reduced to just five major factors, but there are advantages. In any system of categorization, the reduction in the number of categories used increases the generality of those categories. This makes them easier to work with, but reduces their specificity. This trade-off is inevitable. The choice has to be, therefore, to choose the level of category that most suits the purposes for which it is intended.

The 'Big Five' are referred to as *multi-faceted* traits because they are composed of a number of more specific *single-facet* traits. This relationship is shown in Figure 2.1. As we shall see, there are certain patterns of behaviour that can be predicted from traits such as neuroticism. However, on occasion it is useful to concentrate a little more specifically on, for example, 'hostility' or 'depression'.

There is another way in which single-facet traits may be useful. This is by combining single-facet traits from different parts of the 'Big Five' into what are referred to as *emergent traits*.

An example of an emergent trait is shown in the right-hand column of Figure 2.1. As can be seen, emergent traits are more specific even than single-facet traits.

As will be seen from Figure 2.1, traits are usually labelled by psychologists in much the same way as by the layman. At the beginning of this chapter we suggested that you might obtain a description of your own personality. It is likely that some of the traits in your description will match some of those in Figure 2.1.

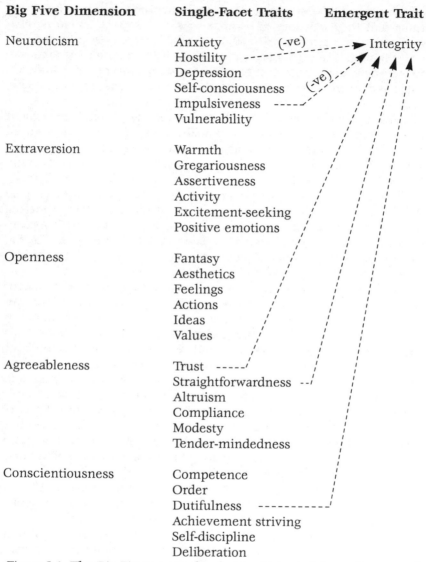

Figure 2.1. The 'Big Five' personality factors. (Adapted from: Deary and Mathews, 1993)

WHAT DO TRAITS PREDICT?

Space prevents us from considering all the relationships between traits and behaviour. We will limit our discussion, therefore, to the Big Five, and one emergent trait, integrity. This has been chosen because it has been used in organizational contexts.

Of the Big Five the two that have been shown to have the highest and most consistent relationship with behaviour are neuroticism and extraversion. For this reason many psychologists consider them to be the most important. (Conscientiousness is probably the next most important.) We will deal with these two first.

Neuroticism. As might be expected, neuroticism tends to be associated with a range of behaviours associated with mental health and stress. Those scoring higher tend to be more anxious and depressed (Eysenck and Eysenck, 1985). They also tend to have a poor image of their own body (Davis *et al.*, 1991), and to report having suffered more from minor medical symptoms (Deary *et al.*, 1991).

Neuroticism also appears to be related to stress-related syndromes (Wistow *et al.*, 1990) and also to methods of coping with stress. MacCrae and Costa (1986) suggest that high neuroticism is associated with 'emotion-focused' rather than 'problem-focused' coping strategies. The former tend to cope by withdrawing, or ignoring the source of stress. They may also tend to resort to self-blame. Such strategies are not likely to be effective in the long term.

As far as work-related behaviour is concerned, Tett *et al.* (1991) suggest that low neuroticism is related to overall job performance (r = −0.22).

Extraversion. The most obvious behaviour that might be expected to be predicted by extraversion would be that described by the single-facet traits. An extravert, by definition, is outgoing with other people, excitement-seeking, and assertive. It is true that extraverts will behave this way, *if they can* (we will return to this point later). However, extraversion is also linked with the way in which individuals cope with information. Extraverts appear to be better at handling rapid flows of information. Introverts, on the other hand, are better at processing infrequent information and reflective problem-solving (Deary and Matthews, 1993).

Barrick and Mount (1991; 1993) report relationships between extraversion and work-related behaviours. They found a correlation of 0.26 with 'training proficiency' and 0.14 with 'overall job performance'.

Extraversion and neuroticism, as well as being the most important, have another characteristic in which they are similar. They both appear to be based upon underlying *physiological* differences. Extraversion, for example, is thought to be influenced by the amount of activity in the brain. Extraverts have a low level of activity which has to be 'topped up' to an optimum level by stimuli from the environment. Hence the extravert is continually seeking stimuli. This underpinning by physiological mechanisms has led some to suggest that neuroticism and extraversion should be referred to as 'temperaments' rather than traits (MacCrae and Costa, 1991).

Despite their underlying physiological similarities, however, extraversion and neuroticism differ from one another in one important respect – the extent to which they determine behaviour. Extraversion has, on the whole, a weaker effect upon behaviour. For example, introverts can learn to behave in an extravert manner, when circumstances require. Thus the introvert manager knows the sort of gregarious behaviour that is expected at social events and can learn to behave accordingly. Their behaviour is, however, not as 'natural' as that of the extravert and this may show, especially during the early learning stages.

Neuroticism, on the other hand, appears to have a stronger influence on behaviour. Anxiety and depression appear to be related to the way that potentially threatening information is selectively attended to and/or recalled (see Mathews, 1993). Even so, it is possible to learn techniques that can help to minimize the deleterious effects of neuroticism (see Beck, 1976).

Other Big Five traits. The other traits are less well researched, but both Barrick and Mount (1991; 1993) and Tett *et al.* (1991) report correlations between various job-related behaviours and conscientiousness, agreeability, and openness. They found conscientiousness to be correlated with supervisor rating (0.35), job performance (0.18), and, on average, across a range of criteria (0.22).

The same authors report relationships of 0.25 and 0.27 between openness and 'training proficiency' and 'job performance' respectively. Finally, agreeability is reported by Tett *et al.* (1991) to be correlated 0.33 with 'job performance'.

Using the 16PF test, Bartram (1992) examined the personality characteristics of UK managers. He describes the average manager as

'an independent, stable extravert who is neither particularly tough-minded or tender-minded but who is somewhat more controlled and conventional than the average for the general population.'

As is often the case, however, the 'average' may hide a wide range of different personalities, all of whom may be successful in the right context.

Emergent traits. Emergent traits differ from multi-faceted and single-facet traits. The Big Five and the single-facet traits are considered to *cause* behaviour; emergent traits, on the other hand, are *caused by* the traits of which they are composed.

There are many emergent traits, but one which has attracted much attention recently has been that of integrity. Ones *et al.* (1993) report the results of a study in which 3,000 employers were asked to rate the importance of 86 employee characteristics. Of the top eight, seven 'were related to integrity, trustworthiness, conscientiousness, and related qualities'. (The other one in the top eight was 'general mental ability', which was rated fifth.)

Because of this perceived importance, many paper-and-pencil tests have been devised in order to try to measure integrity, and hence identify those who are likely to behave dishonestly. Collins and Schmidt (1993) used a number of different measures of integrity, and administered them to convicted white-collar criminals and to non-offenders of a similar occupational level. They found that they could discriminate between the two groups with a reasonable degree of accuracy.

Ones *et al.* (1993) combined the results from a large number of studies and concluded that the measures were effective across different situations and settings. Integrity measures predicted job performance and a range of organizationally disruptive behaviours such as theft, disciplinary problems and absenteeism. Correlations with the various behaviours were mainly in the range 0.29 to 0.40.

There is general agreement that the various tests of integrity are useful in predicting behaviour. There is less agreement, however, as to which traits cause integrity. Ones *et al.* (1993) suggest that it is the negative end of the conscientiousness trait, but Schneider and Hough (1995) review evidence from a number of studies and suggest that neuroticism may also be involved. It could also be argued that agreeableness may also be involved as Collins and Schmidt (1993), mention such single-facet traits as trust and straightforwardness. (For this reason, in Figure 2.1, the lines joining the emergent trait to other traits are dotted to show their tentative nature.)

TYPE THEORIES OF PERSONALITY

Type theorists start with traits, but then combine them to produce a small number of personality types. The number of traits commonly used is between two and four. This produces between two and sixteen distinct 'types'.

Perhaps the most influential type theorist has been Hans Eysenck, who is probably the best-known British psychologist. In his earlier work, Eysenck (1975) reduced the number traits to two, which have obvious overlaps with the trait theorists discussed earlier; extraversion/introversion and stable/unstable (sometimes called neuroticism). To these he has added a third: psychoticism. As might be expected, the stable/unstable dimension is concerned with emotional stability. Those with high stability tend to be calm and even-tempered, whilst those with low stability are anxious and moody. The trait of extraversion/introversion is part of everyday language and widely understood. It is composed of two closely related components, sociability and impulsiveness. People high on the psychoticism dimension tend to be uncaring about others, and opposed to accepted social norms.

The three traits, extraversion, neuroticism, and psychoticism, are independent of each other. In other words, knowing a person's score on one trait will tell you nothing about their scores on the others. For simplicity's sake, we will consider the two original traits. The third, psychoticism, is more appropriate to clinical uses.

Using these traits, a two-dimensional 'map' of personality emerges, as shown in Figure 2.2.

The names close to the centre of each sector, are those used by the ancient Greeks in their description of personality, and which Eysenck feels are equivalent to his own. The Greeks based their explanation of personality on the balance of the various bodily fluids in the individual. Thus, choleric is a preponderance of bile, sanguine of blood, and melancholic of black bile. Phlegmatic is, we trust, self-explanatory.

Another type theory widely used in organizations is that of Jung

INTROVERTED

STABLE INTROVERT	UNSTABLE INTROVERT
Passive	Quiet
Careful	Unsociable
Thoughtful	Reserved
Peaceful	Pessimistic
Controlled	Sober
Reliable	Rigid
Even-tempered	Anxious
Calm	Moody
(Phlegmatic)	(Melancholic)

STABLE —————————————————————— UNSTABLE

(Sanguine)	(Choleric)
STABLE EXTROVERT	UNSTABLE EXTROVERT
Leadership	Touchy
Carefree	Restless
Lively	Aggressive
Easygoing	Excitable
Responsive	Changeable
Talkative	Impulsive
Outgoing	Optimistic
Sociable	Active

EXTROVERTED

Figure 2.2. Eysenck's personality types. (Adapted from: Eysenck, 1975)

(1923), whose theory of personality is based upon four major differences in the way people prefer to

- relate to other people
- gather and generate information
- use information
- make decisions.

In addition, people also differ in the priority they give either to *gathering* information or *using* information. Let us look at these in a little more detail.

[In what follows, the letters in brackets refer to the labels used in the Myers–Briggs Type Indicator® (MBTI), the most widely used test for measuring these concepts (see Myers and McCaulley, 1985].

Relating to others: Extraversion (E) or Introversion (I). These terms were originated by Jung. We have already looked at this dimension, which has passed into psychological, and everyday, usage. Jung saw extraverts as orientated towards external conditions, whilst introverts were internally orientated.

Gathering information: Sensation (S) or Intuition (N). A 'sensing' person will prefer to deal with facts that can be objectively verified. Their approach is essentially practical. The 'intuitive' person, on the other hand, generates information through their own insight. Their emphasis will be on looking at things in new, and often theoretical, ways.

Using information: Thinking (T) and Feeling (F). The 'thinking' individual will emphasize logical analysis in the way they use information. The 'feeling' individual, on the other hand, makes decisions that are largely influenced by their own internal beliefs and values about what is right or wrong.

Gathering information or using it: Perceiving (P) or Judging (J). The 'gatherer' likes to collect (perceive) all the relevant information before reaching a decision. The 'user', however, will try to resolve an issue (judging) without waiting for a large amount of data to be generated. One of our colleagues suggests that this can be observed in PC users. There are those who must read all of the manual before touching the computer. Others prefer to 'leap in' and try operating the computer, only referring to the manual if they get hopelessly stuck.

    Combination of these four pairs of preferences gives sixteen different types. These are usually referred to by the letters of the types, e.g. ESFJ. (We should point out that, as with other type theories, there are no 'good' or 'bad' types, just different ways of operating. Each type has its advantages and disadvantages.)

Magerison and Lewis (1980), looked at the differences between British academics and managers. Only in the preferences for gathering information did they find any significant differences. A large majority (93 per cent) of the academics preferred the intuitive approach whilst over two thirds (68 per cent) of the managers preferred the sensing approach. Perhaps this could be seen as evidence for the belief amongst some that managers act without thinking whilst academics think without acting!

Studies using types to predict work-related behaviours are less common, and rather more difficult to interpret. In general it would be fair to say that their level of predictability is similar to that for trait measures.

THE USEFULNESS OF TRAITS AND TYPES

The usefulness of personality in predicting job performance, as measured by questionnaires, does not appear to be high. In the relationships reported above, the strength of those relationships is not great. As Blinkhorn and Johnson (1990) remark, 'we see precious little evidence that even the best personality tests predict job performance'. In statistical terms they can, at best, predict up to about 10 to 15 per cent of the variance in performance levels. This means that 85 to 90 per cent of work performance is due to non-personality factors. More recently, Robertson (1994) has reviewed the evidence and has suggested that carefully chosen personality tests can predict carefully chosen and specific aspects of work performance. Developing a point made in the previous chapter, he argues that higher validities are likely to be generated by trying to achieve greater point-to-point correspondence between particular traits and specific job requirements. Westoby (1994) has recently developed a questionnaire to measure job incumbents' perceptions about the personality factors required for their jobs. Initial results are encouraging.

Given this low level of predictability of work-related behaviour, you may well be harbouring some doubts as to the value of personality traits. Whilst they may only predict behaviour rather weakly they may, nevertheless, be extremely valuable to organizations. Their main value is in selection and, as will be recalled from the previous chapter, even a test with only a moderate ability to predict behaviour (say 0.3) may produce massive savings for an organization. Despite the possible savings in selection, however, the question still remains: why is the relationship between personality tests and work-related behaviour so weak?

Mischel (1968) threw doubt on the whole of personality theory. His argument was simple: if you ask people to describe the personality of an individual, yourself for example, you would expect a high degree of consistency. (This is one of the requirements of a trait.) However, the descriptions given by those who know you in different situations are often very different. The descriptions of your personality given by those who know you as boss, subordinate, workmate, spouse, parent, personal friend, golfing partner, etc. often differ so widely that it is difficult to know if they refer to the same person! The fundamental point made by Mischel is that our behaviour appears to be determined more by the *situation* in which we find ourselves than by our personality. It is the roles we play, and the norms within which we operate, that seem to have the greatest influence on our behaviour. Writing in an organizational context, Mitchell and Larsen (1987) concluded:

'It seems unlikely that personality will ever become the *predominant variable explaining all, or even most, behavior in organizations....... But if we start taking account of factors such as situational strength and self-monitoring tendencies, it is quite possible that new organizational circumstances can be discovered in which personality does play a vital role.'*

At first sight these suggestions are somewhat disconcerting, and yet they also appear to contain an element of truth. It is obvious that our behaviour does change as we adapt from one situation to another, and yet we also feel that there is an underlying stability that is essentially *us*. As we shall see, we need to consider the influence of both the individual's personality *and* the situation in which they are acting.

ROLES AND NORMS

At work, as in the rest of life, we interact with many different individuals, and the nature of these interactions differs. Our interactions with a bank clerk will differ from that with our boss, as it will with our family. Many of these interactions will take place between individuals who are taking on a particular *role*. Roles consist of patterns of behaviour that are largely standardized and pre-determined. The function of such roles is to differentiate between participants so that each knows what behaviour is expected, both of themselves and others.

The behaviour of those taking part in the interaction of roles is highly scripted. Like actors in a play, the behaviour of people in roles is highly constrained. In most of our interactions as a 'customer' we are playing a role, as is the assistant who is serving us. In acting out such roles there is little opportunity for our behaviour to be determined by our personality. True, we may act in a manner that differs in terms of its 'friendliness' or 'politeness', but in general our behaviour is dictated by the social demands of the role. An example of role-constrained behaviour is the job selection interview, which we referred to in the previous chapter. The roles of interviewer and interviewee are recognized by both parties, and the behaviour is structured accordingly.

Roles vary in the time-span over which they are appropriate. Our role as a customer is usually fairly short-lived, whilst that of the assistant, dealing with many customers, is rather more protracted. Some roles become so all-encompassing that they pervade the person's whole life. Examples of these roles include long-term prisoners and patients. In these circumstances the individuals may become 'institutionalized'. Their behaviour is so constrained that they often find it difficult to adapt when returned to environments that are not so constraining.

Like roles, *norms* are also socially determined. Their function is different, however. Roles are intended to *differentiate* between participants, so that the common expectations of each other's performance leads to a smooth and effective interaction. Norms, on the other hand, lead to a greater *integration* of the participants. For example, the roles of manager and subordinate are, in most organizations, fairly well-defined. In general, the manager gives instructions and the subordinate carries them out. These roles, however, are embedded within organizational norms. The manager may give instructions, but there may be norms about how this is done, or about how much consultation is expected before a decision is made.

Roles and norms, therefore, have a powerful influence over aspects of our behaviour. In general, the more constraining the role or norm the less influence a person's personality will have over the way they behave. Only if they behave 'out-of-role' is their personality likely to be determining their behaviour. Returning to the example of the job interview, the behaviour of the applicant is likely to be determined more by their role than by their personality, yet we often draw conclusions from the interview about their personality.

Situations, therefore, vary in the strength with which they constrain behaviour. The range of behaviour allowed at a football match is wider than that allowed in a place of worship, but there are constraints nevertheless. Organizations, in fact, are very 'strong' situations (Davis-Blake and Pfeffer, 1989). Behaviour within most organizations is highly institutionalized. They have their own culture; common understandings about the goals of the organization and 'how things are done around here'. As Zucker (1983) puts it, a large proportion of behaviour in organizations is determined by 'common understandings about what is appropriate and, fundamentally, meaningful behavior'. Often these constraints and limitations are implicit, rather than explicit. People often do not *feel* constrained or limited, rather they accept as 'natural' the common patterns of behaviour. They may only notice the norms when they move to another job where the norms are different.

To summarize, when behaviour is highly constrained by the roles the actors are required to play, and/or by the norms governing behaviour, personality traits are unlikely to be useful predictors of an individual's behaviour. It is, perhaps, to less constrained situations that we should turn to find personality traits having a strong influence on behaviour.

PERSONALITY OR SITUATION?

We have looked at behaviour as determined either by the individual's personality or by the situation in which they are acting. This dichotomy is, of course, an over-simplification. It is rare to find circumstances where either one or the other is totally controlling the behaviour. Most psychologists now adopt an *interactionist* approach. As one of the doyens of personality theory, Pervin (1989), puts it 'most personality psychologists now are interactionists'. The trait provides the predisposition, but the situation determines whether there are possibilities for the trait to manifest itself. For example, although an individual may score high on 'anxiety' this will not manifest itself in behaviour unless they are in a situation which they regard as anxiety-provoking. The interaction between the person and the situation is complicated even further. The individual is not a passive object upon whom the situation acts. The individual can, by their actions, influence the situation. For example, someone who finds heights anxiety-provoking can avoid them. People, therefore, actively interact with their environment. Sometimes this takes the form of choice, as in avoiding heights. On other occasions the individual may go further, actively shaping the environment to suit their purposes.

Recently, personality theory has begun to take into account the fact that people set themselves *goals* that they wish to achieve. As Pervin (1989) has commented, people's behaviour is now being viewed as determined as much by their motivation as by their personality. (It is often difficult for authors, including ourselves, to decide if certain topics belong in a chapter on 'personality' or in one on 'motivation', or 'leadership'. You will therefore find overlaps between these chapters.)

The problem for a personality theory which sees behaviour as goal-directed revolves around the concepts of 'equifinality' and 'equipotentiality'.

Equifinality suggests that there are many different ways of achieving the same outcome. In other words, the same goal may be achieved by different behaviours. My goal of influencing a fellow worker may be achieved by threats, pleading, ingratiation, or many other different behaviours.

Equipotentiality is, in some ways, a mirror image of equifinality. Whereas equifinality suggests that the same goal can be achieved by different behaviours, equipotentiality implies that the same behaviour may be satisfying different goals. For example, my reason for attending a conference may be to acquire information, make social contacts, or even to take the opportunity to visit friends or family nearby. The concept of goal-directed behaviour has undoubtedly added to our understanding of behaviour. It has, however, further weakened the trait/behaviour link. (We will return to goal-directed behaviour in Chapter 5.)

We have now looked at some of the reasons for the weakness in the links between personality and behaviour. Is there anything we can do, nevertheless, to improve the predictability of personality traits?

One way in which the predictability may be improved is by taking the strength of the situation into account. We have already seen that personality will tend to express itself more in those areas where there is freedom for it to be expressed, i.e. where there are high levels of job autonomy, and/or weak role requirements or norms. There may, however, be other moderating factors that influence the strength of the trait/behaviour relationship. It appears that individuals differ in the extent to which they respond to situational demands and constraints. It is suggested that the reason why people differ in this respect is that whilst some people are outer-directed, others are inner-directed. People differ, it is argued, in the extent to which they *self-monitor* (Synder, 1974).

Someone who is a high self-monitor will tend to be outer-directed. Their attention will be concentrated on the situation and, as a result, they will tend to adapt their behaviour to the demands of the situation. A low self-monitor, on the other hand, will tend to be inner-directed. Their behaviour will not be affected as much by situational demands, but will be more determined by their personality traits.

The predictive power of personality can be improved, therefore, by considering the situational demands, and the extent to which the individual responds to those demands. Even when these are taken into account, however, personality is less than perfect as a predictor of behaviour. Why, then, does it remain such an attractive concept? The reason probably lies in the unstated assumption that personality traits give us a concise description of individuals that allows us to predict their behaviour. This belief may be inaccurate, but it is comforting.

Given the weak links between performance and behaviour, are there any other differences between individuals, other than personality, that might help us understand and predict people's behaviour at work?

As well as differing in terms of their personalities, people also differ in the extent to which they can process information, and in the ways in which they prefer to process it. It is to these individual differences that we will now turn, as they may throw light upon some of the so-called 'personality clashes' that often occur in organizations.

INDIVIDUAL DIFFERENCES

The best known difference between individuals concerns their capacity to process information. The name most commonly given to this ability is intelligence. Most intelligence tests measure the ability to process certain kinds of information, which is usually verbal, mathematical, or abstract in nature. Some theorists suggest that there are many different types of intelligence, depending upon the nature of the material being processed, and the operations being carried out on it. As well as differing in our capacity to process information, we differ in the way in which we prefer to carry out the processing. It has not been shown that any particular method of processing information is superior to others. However, the way in which we prefer to work can cause problems if, for example, it differs substantially from those of our colleagues, or indeed from the organizational culture. One such difference, suggested by Kirton, is particularly relevant to behaviour in organizations.

ADAPTORS AND INNOVATORS

The distinction between the two styles of adaptor and innovator was made by Michael Kirton (1984), based on his study of the way in which management initiatives are taken, how they proceed through the organizational decision-making structure, and why they succeed or fail. As a result of his studies, Kirton suggests that many of his observations can be explained by the 'cognitive' (or thinking) styles of the individuals concerned, especially when dealing with problem solving.

The labels that Kirton gives to the two different approaches are that of 'adaptor' and 'innovator'. Strictly speaking, these are not two totally distinct styles. They are, in fact, seen as the opposite ends of a continuous scale. Thus, a particular individual does not necessarily have to be at one end or the other, but may be anywhere between the two extremes. For the purposes of description, however, it is easier to stick with the two 'pure' types which lie at the extreme ends of the scale.

A shorthand explanation of the difference between the two styles is that while the adaptor likes 'doing things better', the innovator prefers to 'do things differently'. This difference has considerable implications, especially when the two styles have to work together, as we shall see.

In order to do things differently it is often necessary to consider, and even implement, solutions that lie well outside the current way of doing things. Thus, a major difference between the two styles is the extent to which they stay within the current framework, both for solutions and implementations. Unlike the innovator, the adaptor will try to modify the existing system in order to make it better. Let us look, therefore, at how the two styles differ in the way they define problems, seek solutions, and implement these solutions.

In terms of defining the problem, it could almost be said that adaptors wait to be given the problem, whilst innovators seek out problems. However, it is in the type of solution that the main differences occur. The adaptor is concerned to solve problems by modifying the existing systems; this produces greater efficiency, while maintaining the organization's continuity and stability. It is likely that they will feel comfortable in an organization that adapts itself slowly and is not likely to undergo substantial and rapid change. For the innovator, on the other hand, the challenge consists in finding new, and possibly unexpected, solutions to problems.

Each of these types has its strengths and weaknesses. The adaptor can effectively adapt the present system, but is apparently 'blinkered' in not seeing solutions that lie outside that system. The innovator, on the other hand, is happier generating new solutions. Unfortunately, such individuals often find difficulty in having their ideas accepted by others within the organization, and become frustrated by what they see as 'irrational' inertia within the organization. Their ways of implementing decisions also differ. The adaptor prefers work characterized by precision, method, and discipline, and is capable of maintaining high levels of accuracy over long periods of time. The innovator, on the other hand, appears undisciplined, and incapable of maintaining work of a routine nature for very long. To the rest of the organization, the adaptor is seen as safe, dependable and conforming, while the innovator is seen as a 'maverick', with apparently endless self-confidence, who is constantly coming up with lists of ideas, some hopelessly impractical.

As well as individuals having preferences in the way they work, there is evidence to suggest that organizations can also be classified as predominantly adaptive or innovative. This is not to suggest, of course, that the whole organization is the same. There may be differences between departments within the overall structure. Given that each organization or department has its particular adaptive or innovative climate, this will influence those who work within it. Adaptors will find an innovative climate not to their liking, and vice versa. This will lead them to resolve the resulting discomfort in one of two ways. First, and apparently most commonly, by leaving. Second, by finding a 'niche' within which they can happily isolate themselves from the dominant climate. Indeed, the majority may actually help them 'generate' such a niche in order to insulate themselves from the individual. This often occurs when the chances of moving the individual are small.

As we have said, the two styles can obviously complement each other, but the perception of each by the other may be a problem. To the adaptor, the innovator is seen as an extravert, generating new ideas but almost totally insensitive, both to the demands of the system, and to the feelings of others. This abrasive personal style means that the adaptor feels uncomfortable when working with such an individual, who constantly questions perceived wisdom. To the innovator, the adaptor appears as a conservative, timid conformist, always ready to agree, both with the system and with his boss.

The innovator is not deliberately rude and inconsiderate to others, but expects everyone else to be filled with the enthusiasm that he feels. Similarly, the adaptor does not agree with his boss because of weakness, but rather because his boss is also likely to be an adaptor, and hence have a similar way of approaching problems.

Kirton found that the clash of these styles could often explain why innovative ideas failed to be implemented in organizations. This, of course, is likely to be the sort of clash that takes place whenever departments with different climates interact. Each will see the other in the same way as differing individuals would do. Kirton found that adaptors tend to predominate in the public sector and in organizations such as banking. Both of these types of organization are, however, under pressure to react to market forces, either by adapting or innovating. This pressure may result in the creation of new departments, some of which may be given the job of innovating. Such new, innovative departments within organizations may lead to inter-departmental conflict because of the difference in perspectives. Ways in which such inter-group conflict may be minimized will be addressed in Chapter 7.

If, as is suggested, these styles are relatively permanent, what can managers do to avert or minimize clashes between individuals? The solution must lie in understanding, together with an acceptance of the other person's position. This may sound like 'pie in the sky' but, as will be seen later, the recognition that another person has a preferred way of working can often be enough to defuse situations that may otherwise lead to disagreement. Knowing 'the other's style' enables prediction of what they will, or will not, like, and hence reduces uncertainty. If both parties are familiar with the concepts and the 'jargon', it may even become a source of amusement when working together.

TYPE As AND TYPE Bs

Exercise
Before reading this section, please turn to Appendix 1 and answer and score the Type A/Type B questionnaire.

The concept of Type A and Type B personality was developed by Friedman and Rosenman (1974) during a study of patients with coronary heart disease. They found that many of their patients behaved in similar ways; they tended to be extremely competitive, high-achieving, aggressive, hasty, impatient, and restless. They were also characterized by having explosive patterns of speech, tenseness of the facial muscles, and always appeared to be under time pressures. Type As have also been described as being so deeply involved and committed to their work that other aspects of their lives become neglected. The connection between the Type A personality and coronary heart disease has since been confirmed by other studies. It should not be thought, however, that Type A personalities are automatically susceptible to heart disease. The danger occurs when Type As are subjected to high levels of demand and stress. (We will look at ways of managing Type A behaviour later in this chapter.)

The best shorthand description for extreme Type As is that they suffer from 'hurry sickness'. Everything has to be done at once. In addition, they are usually doing a number of different things at the same time. Waiting in queues is likely to prove highly stressful for Type As. All this frantic activity might be quite all right if it were not for the fact that they are unable to relax – when not *doing* something they feel vaguely guilty. Surely there must be something that they ought to be doing? The frantic activity of 'getting somewhere' also means that they are not able to enjoy the journey.

Type Bs are the opposite of Type As. They work without agitation and relax without guilt. The same pressures of time urgency do not affect them.

The descriptions so far have been those of extremes of each type. In reality, most people lie somewhere between the two. For the sake of convenience four different types are normally identified. If your score on the questionnaire was between 104 and the maximum possible score of 143, then you are an extreme Type A1. About 10 per cent of the population falls into this category. If your score was between 91 and 103 you are Type A2, and between 65 and 90 Type B3. About 40 per cent of the population falls into each of these categories. Finally, if your score was between 10 and 64 you are a Type B4. In our experience, most managers fall into the Type A1 and Type A2 categories, but this is not always the case.

Since many managers are Type As, it would be unfair to leave them without some specific suggestions as to how to manage their behaviour. Since Type A/Type B is a personality characteristic, there is no point in trying to change it. What can be managed, however, is the behaviour that results from it. Type As need to take steps to manage their behaviour style so that they do not set themselves up for a stress-related illness. These steps often include such things as relaxation exercises, but often what is needed is to refrain from those behaviours that characterize Type As.

Friedman and Rosenman recommend a number of 'drills against hurry sickness', which they claim to work for their Type A patients.

- Stop trying to be the centre of attention by constantly talking. Force yourself to listen to others, and don't keep finishing their sentences for them.

- If you do continue talking unnecessarily, ask yourself: a) Do I really have anything important to say? b) Does anyone want to hear it? c) Is this the time to say it? If the answer to any of these questions is 'No', then keep quiet, even if you have to bite your lip.

- Put yourself in positions that force you to slow down, or penalize yourself for hurrying. Friedman and Rosenman suggest that you should frequent restaurants were you know there will be long periods of waiting. They also suggest that if you find yourself speeding up to get through the traffic lights on amber, you should penalize yourself. You should turn left (or right) at the next corner, go back on yourself, and go through the same lights again. (They do not report the effects of this sudden manoeuvre on the Type A driver in the car behind!)

- Put your Type A behaviour into perspective by asking yourself the following questions: a) Will this matter have importance five years from now? b) Must it be done right away, or do I have time to think about the best way to do it?

- Take up some outside activities that require not only attention but patience, such as reading, theatre, etc. Beware, however, that you do not turn these into surrogates. We are aware of one individual who deliberately took up golf to manage his Type A behaviour, but then became obsessional about winning.

- Try not to make unnecessary appointments or deadlines. Remember, the more deadlines you make for yourself, the worse your 'hurry sickness' will become.

- Learn to say 'No' and protect your time. If you don't protect it, no one else will!

- Take 'stress-free breathing spaces' during the course of the day. They need not be long, but should be frequent. Research has shown that as well as reducing stress they can also increase efficiency. Many managers work in stretches that mean their performance declines. We advise students who are revising for exams to study for 50 minutes and break for 10. Such breaks give our metal processes time to recover, and also allow the brain to 'sort out' the information it has absorbed.

- Try to create opportunities during the day or night when you can totally relax. Do not try to work and relax in the same situation; while you try to relax all the reminders of work will be there. Have a room, or even just a chair, that is for relaxation only.

It is also important for Type As to realize the effect they have on other people. One of the characteristics of Type As is that they are perceived by others as being overly hostile. Type As should continually remind themselves of this fact. One way of countering this is to try to reward people for their efforts – not taking them for granted. Time spent in relaxed social interchange is, for many Type As, so much wasted time. They should realize that time spent this way is, in fact, time well spent.

Type As are extra-punitive; they place the blame for their own disappointments and failures on others. 'Over and over again we have listened to Type As rationalize their hostility as stemming from disappointment over the lack of ideals in their friends.' The search for 'idealists' is a waste of time because Type As are only looking for excuses to be disappointed, and hence hostile towards others.

As with adaptors and innovators, both Type As and Type Bs can be effective. It could even be argued that both are needed. All that can be done is to reach understanding by appreciating the other person's way of operating and making allowances for it.

JOB-RELATED ATTITUDES

No doubt many who are reading this book will have been 'subjected to', or may even have initiated the distribution of, questionnaires designed to measure job-related attitudes. What are these attitudes, and why are people so interested in them?

Before we attempt a definition of 'attitude', there is a major classification in psychology, knowledge of which will assist in the following sections. Most psychological concepts and phenomena may be classified as to whether they are:

- *cognitive* (concerned with information)

- *affective* (concerned with feelings)

- *behavioural* (sometimes called 'conative', and concerned with behaviour).

As with many concepts, there is overlap between these three classifications. They do, however, help in understanding concepts such as attitudes. The concept of personality traits provides a good example of this overlap.

Traits are considered to be predominantly cognitive. They supply information about people. It could also be argued that they have an affective component, i.e. good/bad. Similarly, because they are used as a predictor of behaviour, they could also be said to have a behavioural component. Despite this overlap, however, their main component is cognitive. Traits are concepts whose content is predominantly informational. Attitudes, on the other hand, are predominantly affective.

Attitudes, like personality traits, are considered to be 'internal'. They are a part of the individual and, like personality traits, they are thought to have an influence on the way people behave. Attitudes are considered less stable than traits, and hence more capable of change. It is also implicitly assumed that attitudes, although internal, are largely generated by the situations that people experience. For example, police attitudes towards criminals are likely to differ from those of the general public.

The central feature of attitudes, however, is that they are *evaluative*. Any attitude contains an assessment of whether the object to which it refers, e.g. work, political parties, is liked or disliked. Evaluation may be considered to be both cognitive (an emotionally neutral judgement) and affective (a feeling towards the object of the attitude). Some researchers would also argue that there is a behavioural component (a tendency to behave in a particular way towards the object). This argument, as to whether attitudes have only an affective component, or whether there are also cognitive and behavioural components, is ongoing amongst psychologists (see Pratkanis *et al.*, 1989, for a discussion). It will crop up in the sections that follow.

O'Reilly (1991) adopts an 'affective' definition of work attitudes and notes that they 'are typically defined as positive or negative evaluations about aspects of one's work environment'. There are many work attitudes, so we will need to limit our discussion. The most sensible way of doing so is to consider those work attitudes that have generated the most interest and research. 'Job satisfaction' undoubtedly satisfies this criterion. As O'Reilly pointed out in 1991, it is the most frequently studied job attitude. Nothing has changed since. Research into 'organizational commitment' does not have the same long history of research, but since 1979 the amount of research into this attitude has grown considerably.

ORGANIZATIONAL COMMITMENT

The most influential approach to organizational commitment, at least in its early stages, has been that of Mowday *et al.* (1982). They define organizational commitment in terms of the individual's involvement and identification with the organization. This is reflected in the items that comprise their Organizational Commitment Questionnaire (OCQ). The items tap three areas: a strong belief and acceptance of the organization's goals, a willingness to exert effort on behalf of the organization, and a strong desire to maintain membership of the organization. Although they measure these three different elements, organizational commitment is considered to be a single dimension.

The research work of Mowday *et al.* and others has largely concentrated on work outcomes such as absenteeism and turnover. The justification for this is that both of these outcomes have costs for an organization. Absentees need to be covered, whilst staff turnover involves costs of retraining, induction, and socialization. Numerous studies have shown that the OCQ does, indeed, predict turnover (see O'Reilly, 1991). It is even better at predicting 'intention to quit'. This latter finding is important as there may be some individuals who intend to leave the organization but are not able to. We will discuss this further.

More recently the work on organizational commitment has developed in new directions. First, the one-dimensional nature of the OCQ, and of the original concept of organizational commitment, has been questioned. Secondly, the work has been extended to examine commitment to other areas beside organizations, for example occupation, profession, career, union, etc. Given the limitations of space, we will not concern ourselves with the extension into other areas (see Meyer *et al.*, 1993).

The elaboration of commitment into a multi-dimensional scale has been accompanied by an extension to outcomes other than those of absenteeism and staff turnover. The most comprehensive development of this multi-dimensional approach has been carried out by Meyer and his co-workers (see Meyer *et al.*, 1993). Meyer suggests that the approach to commitment of Becker (1960) can usefully be added to that of Mowday. Becker sees commitment in the context of what he refers to as 'side-bets'. Side-bets, like those in gambling, are peripheral to, and additional to, the main bet. Examples of side-bets in organizations are things like accrued pension rights, seniority etc.

These are acquired over time and their effect is to make leaving the organization ever more difficult. Meyer and his co-workers suggest that the combination of these two approaches gives two dimensions, to which they have more recently added a third. These they refer to as affective, continuance, and normative. Affective commitment is concerned with the extent to which the individual identifies with the organization. Continuance commitment on the other hand, is more calculative. It concerns the individual's need to continue working for the organization. Normative commitment is in some respects similar to affective commitment. It is commitment that is influenced by society's norms about the extent to which people ought to be committed to the organization. In simple terms, therefore, people stay with the organization because they *want* to (affective), because they *need* to (continuance), or because they feel they *ought* to (normative).

As with other attitudes, the strength of an individual's commitment is measured by questionnaire. Examples of the questions for each dimension are shown below.

- Affective commitment questionnaire item: 'I feel like "part of the family" at my organization'.
- Continuance commitment: 'I feel that I have too few options to consider leaving the organization'.
- Normative commitment: 'This organization deserves my loyalty'.

All of them, it is suggested, are related to the relationship between the individual and the organization, and also to their desire to stay with or leave the organization. The strength of each of them, however, is influenced by different factors.

Affective commitment to the organization is, Meyer suggests, influenced by the extent to which the individual's needs and expectations about the organization are matched by their actual experiences. This has clear links with the psychological contract.

Continuance commitment, on the other hand, is determined by the perceived costs of leaving the organization. In particular, side-bets and other 'investments' are important determinants. Some authors (e.g. McGee and Ford, 1987; Somers, 1993) have proposed that this dimension may be further sub-divided. They suggest that continuance may be composed of 'personal sacrifice' associated with leaving, and 'limited opportunities' for other employment.

Normative commitment is a perceived obligation to stay with the organization. It is based upon generally accepted rules about reciprocal obligations between organizations and their employees. This is based on 'social exchange theory', which we will deal with later in the book. The theory suggests that a person receiving a benefit is under a strong 'normative' (i.e. rule-governed) obligation to repay it in some way. Thus the receipt by the employee of something 'over and above' what they might normally expect from their employer, places them under a social obligation to repay it in some way. Examples might include additional training, granting of compassionate leave, etc.

If the causes of the different types of commitment are different, what about their consequences?

Meyer *et al.* (1989) found that there were different relationships between measures of performance, and affective and continuance commitment. Supervisors' ratings of an individual's job performance and promotability were related positively to their level of affective commitment, i.e. as one increased, so did the other. For continuance commitment, on the other hand, the relationship was negative. Higher continuance commitment was associated with lower ratings of performance and promotability. This finding, of course, has implications for the way in which organizations try to obtain commitment from their employees. Some organizations try to 'buy' commitment from their employees by making it difficult for them to leave. They may, for example, restrict their training to that which is specific to the organization. The evidence would suggest, however, that such strategies may not be very effective. Whilst it may prevent people from moving too easily, it will do nothing to increase the extent to which individuals feel a part of the organization. It is only this latter type of commitment that produces better performance. Increased continuance commitment is, in fact, associated with *lower* levels of performance.

As mentioned earlier, there is some similarity between the causes of affective and normative commitment. Both are concerned with exchanges. In affective commitment these are concerned with what Rousseau (1990) has called the 'relational obligations' of the psychological contract. The exchanges in normative commitment are slightly more calculative than relational. In fact normative commitment may be seen, in one respect, as lying between affective and continuance. It is concerned with what Rousseau refers to as 'transactional obligations', but the underlying psychological mechanism is not calculative but based upon societal norms of what is 'fair'. Individuals often feel an obligation to repay the investment the organization has put into their training, even if this is not contractually stated.

The close relationship between the causes of affective and normative commitment is reflected in the fact that they tend to be correlated with the same things. Both are related to better performance and more 'pro-social' and 'organizational citizenship' behaviour. (We will define these in the next section.) They are also correlated with each other. Given that they are closely related, and that both are associated with positive organizational outcomes, does it matter which is encouraged by the organization? Although there is, as yet, no direct evidence, Meyer *et al.* (1993) suggest that it may be important. They suggest that normative commitment may be only short-lived. Once the individual perceives the 'debt' as having being repaid, normative commitment levels may drop. It is important, therefore, for organizations to develop high levels of affective commitment.

The most important determinant of affective commitment is the extent to which the expectations that the individual has of the organization are met. Job challenge, organizational dependability and role clarity are also important (Mowday *et al.*, 1982). Studies have also shown that the individual's experiences during the first few months of employment are perhaps the most critical in developing affective commitment. The message for organizations is clear. Affective commitment of the employees will depend upon positive experiences within the organization, especially early in their career with the organization.

JOB SATISFACTION

Job satisfaction is, according to Locke (1976), 'a pleasurable or positive emotional state resulting from the appraisal of one's job or job experiences'. Like other concepts in organizational psychology, the phrase has passed into everyday usage. As with other psychological concepts, you may come across definitions that differ slightly.

Some measures of job satisfaction operate at a global level. Agho *et al.* (1992) for example, asked respondents to what extent they agreed or disagreed with items such as, 'I find real enjoyment in my job', and 'I am seldom bored with my job'.

Others use a multi-dimensional approach, as does the most widely used measure of job satisfaction – the Job Descriptive Index (JDI) (Smith *et al.*, 1969).

The JDI measures five aspects of job satisfaction; satisfaction with:

* pay
* the job itself
* opportunities for promotion
* the supervisor
* co-workers.

The scores on each of the scales are usually added to produce a global measure. As we shall see in later chapters, each of these dimensions can be important in their own right, influencing, for example, motivation. For our present purposes, however, we will deal with job satisfaction only as a global concept.

As we have said, it is assumed that job satisfaction results from the experiences that people have at work. Jobs with high levels of pay, good supervisors, and interesting work, are likely to produce higher levels of job satisfaction than jobs lacking such characteristics. In general, this is so. There are, however, some interesting differences that appear to be unrelated to the perception of work. For example, there is a consistent relationship between age and job satisfaction. For men it appears that job satisfaction rises until middle age, levels off, and then rises again from the mid 50s. Women, on the other hand, do not appear to have the levelling off in middle age. It is thought that this general increase in satisfaction is due to a number of factors, including age-related differences in rewards, values, etc. (see Arvey *et al.*, 1991). At first sight there also appears to be a positive relationship between level of education and job satisfaction. When other factors are taken into account, such as the better educated having better-paid jobs, this relationship largely disappears.

The most important question, of course, is 'Are high levels of job satisfaction reflected in higher performance?' Unfortunately, the answer is almost certainly, 'No!' (See Arvey *et al.*, 1991; O'Reilly, 1991.) Initial theorists suggested that satisfaction *causes* high performance. When these links were not found, this theory was abandoned. Theorists then suggested that the link might be the other way round; satisfaction is the *result* of high performance, not its cause. This also has been shown to be incorrect. On reflection, this should come as no surprise. It is not difficult to identify members of an organization who are satisfied, but who are not high performers, and vice versa. But if job satisfaction does not produce high performance, does it have any value?

In answering this question we can be a little more optimistic. When we consider specific aspects of job satisfaction (e.g. satisfaction with pay), we will find more positive results. For global job satisfaction, although the performance link is tenuous, there are links with other organizational variables. Most importantly, there are strong relations between job satisfaction and 'organizational citizenship behaviour' (Organ and Konovsky, 1989).

Organizational citizenship behaviour (OCB) is behaviour that goes beyond that which is formally required by the organization. It is behaviour that is intended to assist the smooth running of the organization (a similar, and related, concept is that of 'pro-social behaviour'). According to Katz and Kahn (1966), within any organization there

. . . are countless acts of cooperation without which the system would break down. We take these acts for granted, and few of them are included in the formal role prescriptions for any job.'

It is just such behaviour that is related to job satisfaction. In addition, an individual who is satisfied with their job is likely to be a better 'ambassador' for the organization. The effects upon an organization of a positive or negative image among the family and friends of its employees is often important, if unquantifiable. Job satisfaction has also been shown to be related to staff turnover, and commitment to the organization. It also has been shown to have a link with absenteeism, although this link is rather weak (see Agho *et al.*, 1992).

Given that job satisfaction is an evaluation, it has both cognitive and affective components. It is important to know which of these is the more important. Is citizenship behaviour influenced more by what we *think* about our job and the organization, or how we *feel* about it?

Organ and Konovsky (1989) suggest that the cognitive component is the more important of the two. In other words, it is the subjective assessments of job outcomes, rather than the emotional feelings surrounding those outcomes, that influence our citizenship behaviour. In particular, the perceived 'fairness' of the way a person is treated by the organization appears to be important. (We will return to this concept in Chapter 4.) This finding, as we shall see, is important for reasons which may not be immediately apparent.

So far, we have made the assumption that attitudes are largely the result of experiences. They should, therefore, be capable of change over a reasonably short time-scale. For example, satisfaction with pay should be quickly affected by a reasonable pay rise. Some researchers have suggested, however, that job satisfaction may be dispositional rather than situational. In other words, it is similar to a personality trait, i.e. stable over a long period of time and relatively difficult to change. Staw and Ross (1985) found considerable stability over long periods (i.e. decades) for job satisfaction. In their study the best predictor of current job satisfaction was not satisfaction with current pay or job status, but prior levels of satisfaction. Similar stability, although over shorter periods, has also been reported by other researchers (e.g. Spector and O'Connell, 1994). Despite the evidence of some stability over long time periods, it is difficult to think of job satisfaction as a personality trait, like extraversion. As we will see in Chapter 4, there is considerable evidence to link aspects of jobs, such as the amount of autonomy, with job satisfaction. From experience many of us would recognize job changes that have had an impact on our job satisfaction.

Given these criticisms, subsequent theorizing and research has concentrated on two new personality traits; negative and positive *affect*. These traits, it is suggested, have a strong influence over a person's job satisfaction. The stability in job satisfaction is, it is argued, the result of the stability of these traits.

Positive and negative affectivity. The work on positive and negative affectivity started with Bradburn's book *The Structure of Psychological*

Well-being (1969). Positive and negative affectivity 'index the strength of the individual's disposition to experience, respectively, pleasure and pain, reward and punishment, self-enhancement and self-imperilment, and to behave and think in ways that are conducive to these experiences' (Tellegen, 1982, quoted in Arvey *et al.*, 1991). If this is somewhat abstract, a consideration of some of the items used to assess each of the scales might be useful. Items used to measure positive affect include 'I live an interesting life', and 'Every day interesting things happen to me'. Negative affect is assessed using items such as 'I often find myself worrying about something'. (See Deiner and Emmons, 1985; Agho *et al.*, 1992, for full descriptions of scales.)

At first sight it might appear that positive and negative affect lie at opposite ends of a single scale. Positive affect is surely just the opposite of negative affect? It would appear not. Various studies, e.g. Deiner and Emmons (1985), Agho *et al.* (1992), have demonstrated that although they are related, they are also distinct. In other words, it is possible to be high on both, low on both, or any other combination. This may appear strange, but closer examination reveals that it is not as strange as at first thought. Initial affective (i.e. emotional) reactions do tend to be either good *or* bad, happy *or* sad. At the moment of the emotion it is the case that we are either one or the other, but not both at the same time. With the passage of time, however, we look back on events with 'mixed' emotions. We can see that there were elements of both sadness and happiness associated with the events. Momentarily, therefore, positive and negative affect may be at opposite ends of the same scale. Over time they become independent of each other (Deiner and Emmons, 1985).

Despite the evidence for the independence of positive and negative affect from each other, there is still discussion about the status of these traits. Whilst demonstrating the independence of the two scales, Agho *et al.* (1992) still report a correlation of −0.48 between positive and negative affect. Other researchers have also doubted the distinction between affect and other personality traits. Meyer and Shack (1989), for example, report significant overlaps between positive affect and extraversion, and negative affect and neuroticism.

The question concerning job satisfaction, therefore, is the same as that with behaviour. Is it caused by internal dispositions (affect), or by external factors such as characteristics of the job? As before, the answer is a bit of both, but perhaps weighted towards the characteristics of the job. Spector and O'Connell (1994) argue for the importance of several personality factors, including negative affect. Their results show that negative affect is linked with a number of job characteristics, such as role conflict and role ambiguity. However, they found negative affect only weakly related to job satisfaction (−0.18). Indeed, the strongest links with job satisfaction were with job autonomy

(0.56), role ambiguity (−0.40), and role conflict (−0.33). The conclusion of Arvey *et al.* (1991) is worth quoting. Whilst they admit that their conclusion is only 'a hunch', it is a well-informed one. They suggest that

'*person factors account for between 10 and 30% of the variance in job satisfaction, that 40-60% of the variance is associated with situational factors, and that interactive elements account for between 10 and 20%.'*

This is encouraging. If job satisfaction were mainly determined by personality then we could use only selection procedures to get a satisfied work-force. At least we now know that the way we treat individuals will have an effect on their levels of satisfaction. Perhaps the best way of summing up the evidence on job satisfaction is to say that it is not related directly to performance, but that it does have an impact on organizational citizenship behaviours. As far as the causes of job satisfaction are concerned, it appears that there is a dispositional element, i.e. a tendency to be either satisfied (or dissatisfied), no matter what. More important, however, is what organizations do to people. It is this that will largely determine the level of satisfaction.

PERSONALITY AND THE PSYCHOLOGICAL CONTRACT

What can we conclude from our discussion of personality and work-related attitudes, and what implications does it have for the psychological contract?

First, we can conclude that psychologists can indeed identify personality dimensions and that individuals differ in the extent to which they exhibit these dimensions. The contribution they make to performance and behaviour at work is, however, a little more debatable. The selection of people in terms of their personalities can, under certain circumstances, improve organizational effectiveness. In addition, an understanding of the other person's preferred way of operating, as either an adaptor or an innovator, or as a Type A or Type B, will help to smooth possible inter-personal conflict.

The second conclusion that can be drawn is that the situation appears to have far more influence over people's behaviour than does their personality. Similarly with attitudes; people's attitudes tend to be determined to a large extent by their experiences. This is a fairly positive conclusion from the organization's point of view. If behaviour is influenced, and attitudes formed, by experiences then they can be changed, for better or worse, by the organization's actions.

Of particular importance will be the roles that the organization requires people to fill, and the norms within which it operates. Indeed, as we have seen, the psychological contract is largely concerned with these normative factors – how people expect to be treated. In particular, important aspects of organizational commitment are influenced by the extent to which people's expectations are met, especially during the early stages of their time with the organization.

So far we have considered personality theory as the domain of the psychologist. But how does the lay person perceive other people, and what impact does this have on the way we interact with each other? It is to these issues that we will turn in the next chapter.

Inter-personal Perception and Interaction

In the previous chapter we considered personality and individual differences as they are defined by psychologists. But how do people perceive each other, and how does this influence the way they interact?

PERCEPTIONS OF OTHERS

There are few things that can be said with certainty in psychology. Most statements are probabilistic in nature. This can be a source of annoyance to those with a background in the natural and physical sciences who are used to statements whose certainty is somewhat greater. (The possible exception to this are those with a background in quantum, or particle physics, who are also used to dealing with probabilities.) However, there are according to Simon (1990) a number of 'invariants' of human behaviour. Of these, perhaps the most important is that human beings are 'limited capacity information processors'. As Simon points out, once the first move has been made in a game of chess the number of possible moves is beyond the capabilities of even super-computers. Yet we play chess. Likewise, despite their limited capacity for processing information, humans manage to cope fairly well with a complex world. In their inter-personal interactions people try to understand and make sense of each other. They need to do this in order to guide their own actions and interactions as they seek to achieve their goals. They do so by simplifying, or categorizing, the information they receive from their environment. This applies to information about both physical stimuli and social stimuli. Our concern here is with stimuli about other people. Put simply, the amount of information we receive concerning other people is enormous. We need a system of classifying and categorizing people in order to simplify and make all this information manageable.

We need to simplify in order to help us predict and, to some extent, control our social environment. To deal with the behaviour of every individual with whom we interact without some form of simplification and categorization would be impossible. As we have seen, behaviour is often a function of the personality of the individual and the demands of the situation. We should, therefore, take both into account. Let us first consider characteristics of the person.

PEOPLE CATEGORIZATION

As already mentioned, we have limited information-processing capacity. Our purpose is to try to predict the behaviour of other people. This being so, it would make sense to consider the characteristics of people, before considering those of the situation. Our attention is, therefore, directed towards the individual rather than towards the situation. But in what ways do we categorize other people?

There are two principal methods of categorization; personality traits, and stereotypes. There is a very strong tendency for people to categorize other people according to personality traits. Indeed, it would appear that a judgement based on inferred traits or goals happens faster than one based on the characteristics of the situation. But what are the traits that people use when developing these categories?

Impressions of personality. There is considerable evidence that we each have an 'implicit personality theory'. Much as the traits theorists discussed in the previous chapter seek to group traits together, to make a more manageable number of higher-order traits, so each of us has an implicit theory about which traits go with which, and their relative importance. People tend to rate others on those dimensions that they personally consider important. Concerning which traits go with which, there appears to be some agreement between people, although individual differences do occur.

Exercise

Consider the 'and/but generator' shown in Figure 3.1.

You have to describe an imaginary person using two of the adjectives in the lists. Your description will, therefore, have one of the following patterns.

a) X is _____ and _____ .

b) X is _____ but _____ .

First of all choose two words, both from column 1 of Figure 3.1. Then choose two words, both from column 2. Finally choose two words, one from each column. Now decide whether each of these pairs should be linked together either using 'and', as in a), or 'but', as in b).

Column 1	Column 2
generous	ungenerous
wise	shrewd
happy	unhappy
good natured	irritable
humorous	humorless
sociable	unsociable
popular	unpopular
reliable	unreliable
important	insignificant
humane	ruthless
good-looking	unattractive
persistent	unstable
serious	frivolous
restrained	talkative
altruistic	self-centred
imaginative	hard-headed
strong	weak
honest	dishonest

Figure 3.1. The and/but generator. (Adapted from: Asch, 1946)

If you have tried the exercise you will notice that there is no logical or grammatical reason why either 'and' or 'but' should be preferred. Despite this, most people use 'and' when the words both come from the same column, whether it be column 1 or column 2. On the other hand, most people use 'but' when the words come from different columns. You will probably have noticed that those adjectives in column 1 are 'desirable', whilst those in column 2 are less so.

The use of 'and' as a conjunction implies that the two adjectives go together naturally. Using 'but', however, carries the implication that they are rather strange bed-fellows. This highlights a common phenomenon when considering personalities. Put simply, 'good goes with good' and 'bad goes with bad'. There is evidence that this even applies to physical characteristics; 'beautiful is good'.

This is further evidenced by the way that people are surprised when they discover that people they considered to be 'good' turn out to have faults. Perhaps the case of the American football star O. J. Simpson serves as an example. Many of his fans, it appears, find it difficult to come to terms with the fact that their hero may have his faults. To repeat, there is no logical reason to assume that one particular characteristic must be associated with others. It appears that we have a preference to reach a unified and global judgement about those with whom we interact, often in a way that does not do justice to their 'real' personality.

Having discovered the tendency to rate things as either 'good' or 'bad', are there common dimensions upon which many would agree?

It would appear that there are. There appear to be two major dimensions upon which we judge individuals. These two dimensions are almost, but not entirely, independent of each other. The first is that of intellectual ability, the second that of sociability. (In psychologists' terms these are 'cognitive' skills and 'inter-personal' skills, respectively.) Any manager who has read, or indeed written, a reference for an individual will probably recognize the format. Referees first tend to comment on the person's intellectual or technical skills, then to add something about how they get on with people.

There are two other aspects of impression formation, both related to the amount of information that an individual receives about the other person. The first of these is that of primacy. When we first meet someone else, the first pieces of information we receive about them will obviously be perceived as important, because previously we had none. The evidence suggests that we do, in fact, place great weight on this information. First impressions do count! For example, Kalma (1991) found that people interacting in twos or threes made judgements of a person's dominance at the beginning of group interactions. Indeed, these judgements were made 'after a first glance, before even one word was spoken'. These rapid judgements predicted the amount of talking each person did, and the judgement did not change as a result of the verbal interaction. An example, perhaps, of a self-fulfilling prophecy.

The second aspect of impression formation is that some adjectives, or traits, seem to carry more information and are more influential than others. For this reason they are often referred to as central traits. Asch (1946), in a very early study, found that describing an individual as either 'warm' or 'cold' had a considerable impact on how they were perceived on other personality traits. Subjects were presented with a list of seven adjectives which described an individual. Two lists were used which differed in only one detail. In one list the adjective 'warm' was used, in the other it was replaced by 'cold'. The subjects were then asked to rate the individual on eighteen personality dimensions. Whilst there were no differences for some traits, e.g. 'persistent', for others there were considerable differences. Someone described as 'warm' for example, was also described as 'generous' by 91 per cent of subjects. Only 8 per cent of subjects described the 'cold' individual as generous. Warm individuals were also much more likely to be described as 'humorous', 'sociable', and 'popular'.

In general, our impression of someone's personality is influenced by the first important piece of information we receive about the two dimensions – intellectual and social. Evidence also suggests that once we have formed such an impression we are loath to modify it. We seek information that confirms, rather than conflicts with, our initial view.

We have seen that people are very quick to categorize others. It is also the case that this initial categorization is based upon personality traits. It is now clear how these traits exert such an influence over our perceptions. The first impression we make of others is important, and this will almost inevitably involve a judgement based on traits.

The stability of these first impressions may be explained, to some extent, by the way they influence our processing of future information about the person. Almost anything people do is open to a number of interpretations. Their behaviours are, to a greater or lesser extent, ambiguous. The importance of our first, trait-based, impressions is that they provide a framework to interpret such ambiguous information. We tend, therefore, to interpret the information so as to fit the impressions we have already formed. Whether we look for positive or negative information depends, however, on the length of the relationship. When we first meet someone we tend to look for negative information that may serve as a warning for us not to get involved with them. As we get to know them better, however, we tend to look for information that confirms our original positive impression.

In summary, people make judgements about other people's personalities based upon first impressions of two major factors. A global judgement, either positive or negative, is the normal outcome. This initial judgement is usually quick and unchanging. According to Fiske (1993) 'trait inference appears to be spontaneous (without intent or awareness), but controllable'. We will return to the controllability aspect after we have considered the other major type of categorization – stereotypes.

Stereotypes. Stereotypes differ from traits in two important ways. They tend to be much richer than traits, and contain a wealth of information which is supposed to relate to the person to whom they refer. Not only do they summarize inter-personal characteristics, but also characteristics concerning life style, voting behaviour, hobbies, etc. Stereotypes also differ from traits in that they are not usually 'triggered' by observed patterns of behaviour, but by characteristics that are immediately accessible, e.g. visual. The most important of these have been consistently found to be gender, age, and race (see Fiske, 1993). To these we may perhaps add, in a British context, accent.

Stereotyping involves classifying people into groups. Inferences about them are then made, based on the characteristics of the group into which they have been classified.

Stereotypes are interesting, both in their formation and their influence on our perceptions of others. Despite their generally 'bad press' they are also perhaps essential to our everyday personal interactions. The process of the formation of stereotypes is complex. There is, however, one aspect of the process about which it is useful to be aware. As we have noted, human beings are limited in their capacity to process information. As a result, we use certain 'short-cuts' in information processing. These usually work well, but they may also lead us to make certain types of errors. One of these is referred to as 'illusory correlation' (Tversky and Kahneman, 1974). Put simply, on occasions we tend to see relationships that do not actually exist between variables, or to over-estimate their strength if they do exist. This can be important in stereotype formation. Illusory correlation often occurs when two infrequent, or unusual, events happen to coincide. In general, undesirable behaviours are more infrequent than desirable ones. Thus the coincidence of an undesirable event with, for example, the presence of a member of a minority group, may lead to establishment of a negative stereotype about that group.

The establishment of a group category for other people has some interesting effects. In particular, the boundaries between that group and other groups are sharpened. Analogies of this phenomenon are known in other areas of psychology. For example, when a boundary is projected on to the retina of the eye, the cells detecting the brighter side of the boundary 'fire' more strongly. This is to be expected. What might not be expected, however, is that the firing of those on the darker side is actually suppressed. The boundary is therefore heightened in perception. So it is with stereotypes; the distinctiveness of the group is over-estimated. Similarly, an effect occurs that is known as 'out-group homogeneity'. The group is seen as more homogeneous than it really is. It is relatively easy to demonstrate this effect. Think of a group of which you are a member, e.g. sports club, family, etc. Now think of an identifiable group of which you are not a member. Within your own group (the in-group) you will be aware that there is a wide range of different individuals, with their distinctive personalities and attitudes. When considering the group of which you are not a member (the out-group), you will tend to view it as more homogeneous, i.e. the members are more similar to each other. People consistently underestimate the differences between members of a group of which they are not themselves members.

To summarize, stereotypes are useful in that, like traits, they allow us to simplify a large amount of information. Generally, our perceptions are accurate enough but there remain a number of potential errors that can influence that accuracy. Whether traits or stereotypes will be invoked to classify someone depends upon the purposes for which the classification is being made. Traits are obviously more specific than stereotypes. Stereotypes may, however, be sufficient for our purposes if our interaction with the other person is at a fairly superficial level.

Do some people categorize more than others? We have assumed so far that the tendency to categorize people according to traits is universal. This is not so; there are age and cultural differences. For example, personality traits do not seem to be used significantly below the age of seven or eight years. In adolescence, however, their usage is at its highest. This can be accounted for by the needs of the individual to predict the actions of others. Adolescence is a time when the establishment of inter-personal relations, and hence the need for predictability, is at its highest. The prevalence of personality traits also appears to be culture-dependent. It is far more prevalent in western societies, which tend to be more individualist. Traits are not as widely used in more collectivist cultures. Again, this is understandable in terms of predictability. In a collectivist society, behaviour is more likely to be influenced by the social roles and norms than by the personality of the particular individual.

Even within our own society, some individuals use personality traits more than others. Individuals differ in what is referred to as their 'need for structure'.

Because one function of categorization is to provide structure and control to social interactions, and because individuals differ in the extent to which they desire control and structure, individual differences in personal need for structure (PNS) should moderate the extent to which people categorize. Spontaneous trait inferences (STIs) have been used to assess the use of traits in categorization. Subjects with a high personal need for structure were more likely to form STIs and more likely to recall the names of actors in stimulus sentences (Moskowitz, 1993).

We have seen, both in this chapter and the last, that behaviour is best explained by an interaction between personality (or attitudes), and the demands of the situation. But how do we decide on the relative contribution that each makes? In other words, how do we *attribute causality?* What influences our perception of the relationship between personality, situation, and behaviour, and what effect does that have on our inter-personal interactions?

ATTRIBUTION THEORY

Attribution theory examines the way in which people attribute causality for events. The way that we do this has considerable implications for how we think, feel, and behave; it also has a considerable influence on how we interact with others. (Because of this we will encounter attribution theory again in later chapters.)

The 'founding father' of attribution theory, Heider (1958), suggested that our attributions, or explanations, for events involving people (including ourselves) fall into two possible categories. On the one hand we can see the cause of events as being due to the *internal dispositions* of the person concerned. On the other hand, we may see the cause as being the *external situation*. Did your subordinate fail because they were incompetent (internal), or because the job was too difficult for anyone to do (external)? Our choice will influence what action we take. Indeed, at a broader, societal level our attributions will influence the behaviour of, amongst others, juries and governments. Is crime caused by 'bad' people, or 'normal' people driven to crime by their poverty and unemployment? Did the defendant do what they did because they were negligent, or because they were placed in an impossible situation? Counsel for the prosecution will try to prove the former, counsel for the defence the latter. For example, in May 1995 a junior hospital doctor was charged with manslaughter after delivering a fatal dose of penicillin to a patient's brain, instead of to their bloodstream. The doctor was acquitted after the jury heard that the mistake had occurred at the end of a 14-hour work shift, and that the doctor had worked for 110 hours during the previous week.

Given the importance of attributions, how do we make them? The way in which attributions are made is somewhat complex (see Hewstone, 1989, for a fuller discussion). Central, however, to most explanations are three factors:

- consensus
- distinctiveness
- consistency.

To see how these influence attributions, let us take 'Harry's being late for work today' as an example. How would we assess the consensus, distinctiveness, and consistency of this behaviour?

Consensus – how do *other people* behave in the same situation? Was Harry the only person late for work or were others also late? If others were also late then consensus is high. If only Harry was late, it is low.

Distinctiveness – how does Harry behave in *similar situations*? Is he late for other appointments? If Harry is usually punctual for appointments, then his present behaviour stands out as being unusual – its distinctiveness is high. If it is not unusual, it is low.

Consistency – how consistent over *time* is Harry's behaviour in these particular circumstances? Is he regularly late for work, or is this a 'one-off'? If he is regularly late, then consistency is high.

If consensus is high (most people were late), distinctiveness is high (Harry is usually punctual for appointments), and consistency is low (this is a on-off) then the 'blame' lies with the situation. If, on the other hand consensus is low, distinctiveness is low, and consistency is high, then Harry is likely to be seen as being at fault.

Returning to the case of the junior hospital doctor acquitted of manslaughter, what is likely to have led the jury to its decision? Although we cannot know for certain, it is likely that the jury took the view that many other people in that situation could have made the same mistake (high consensus). It is also likely that character witnesses will have been called to show that this was a temporary lapse in an otherwise conscientious person (high distinctiveness, low consistency).

In real life, however, events are not often as simple as those we have considered. For complex events there may be many possible causes. Which of the possible causes is *the* cause? Imagine you are involved in a car accident. It is likely that for some considerable time after the event you will mull over its causes. Part of this will concern the actual events of the accident, but you will also be likely to find a 'cause' in the events that led up to the accident. In doing so you will probably find yourself thinking 'if only x hadn't happened'. This 'x' is likely to be perceived as the cause. The 'x' is likely to be something abnormal, e.g. 'if only I'd gone by my usual route'. In our mental 're-run' of the events we will alter the abnormal event. If altering it changes our mental 're-run' such that the accident does not occur, we will then concentrate on this as the cause. This is known as *counter-factual reasoning*. We look for the odd event in any sequence leading to a bad outcome and mentally change it to the opposite of what happened (counter-factual). If this produces a scenario where we can imagine the bad event being avoided we will concentrate on it as the likely cause. Although this is not, perhaps, important in inter-personal interactions, it is in other contexts. We will return to these in later chapters.

Having considered how attributions are made, what are the effects of attributions? In fact, the attributions that people make for the behaviour of others can exert a powerful influence over their interactions with them. For example, in a relationship, if one of the partners sees the other's negative reactions towards them as being due to relatively permanent internal factors, they will behave differently than if they see them as being due to temporary, external factors. The former pattern is likely to lead to a 'downward spiral' in the relationship. Evidence from 'distressed' and 'non-distressed' marriages supports this view (Bradbury and Fincham, 1990). Non-distressed spouses tend to see positive actions by their partner as being due to relatively permanent, internal factors. Negative events are seen as being due to temporary, external causes. In distressed spouses this pattern is reversed.

Individuals and organizations are often aware of the implications of internal and external attributions, even if they are unaware of the theory. Because of this they often try to influence the attributions that others will make for their behaviour. This is known as *impression management*. At the individual level it can be seen in behaviour such as tripping in a crowded street. Notice how often the person who trips glares back at the pavement. The implication of this glare is obvious. It is an attempt to influence onlookers to believe that the cause of the trip was the poor repair of the pavement (external), not their clumsiness (internal). Organizations also try to influence attributions (Bettman and Weitz, 1983). There is clear evidence that in annual reports organizations try to blame their poor performance on external factors, such as the economic climate, or disadvantageous exchange rates. Successes, on the other hand, are invariably due to the expertise of the management!

Presented in this way, the 'causal calculus' we use to attribute causality seems logical and error-free. But is this so? Are there any systematic biases in the way we attribute causality? It would appear that there are.

One with which we are all familiar, if we care to admit it, is the *self-serving bias*. When things go right, it's because of my personal qualities. When things go wrong, on the other hand, the fault lies elsewhere. As a former colleague of one of the authors used to say, 'If I break a plate whilst washing up, and my wife is upstairs cleaning, it can sometimes take me as long as 30 seconds to work out why it's her fault'. Most people see their successes as being due to internal, stable causes, while failure is often seen as due to unstable, external causes, e.g. luck. This is especially so in areas in which we claim some expertise, and helps to protect our self-esteem against potentially damaging failures. It is especially noticeable in driving behaviour. When someone 'carves you up' on the road, they are a ****. When you 'carve' someone else up it is because you 'were late for an important meeting'.

Another bias, which is certainly less obvious, is called the *fundamental attribution error*. Here, when we judge the behaviour of others, we underestimate the power of the situation in determining behaviour. Again, let us take an example. This may be found in what social psychologists have referred to as the 'bystander phenomenon', or 'bystander apathy'.

The bystander phenomenon describes a pattern of behaviour of which most of us will have had experience. It occurs when a large number of people are present and something untoward is happening. For example, a person is lying on the ground in a busy thoroughfare. Apparently totally insensitive people are walking around, or even over, the person without offering assistance. It is naturally assumed that the reason people do not help is because they are uncaring. (This is often cited as evidence for the alienating effects of large cities.) This explanation is, however, incorrect. If 'tendency to help', or any other name you might like to give it, is a personality trait, then the bigger the crowd that assembles, the more likely it is that there will be someone in the crowd whose level of this trait is high enough such that they will offer help. Not so! Experiments in real life situations show exactly the opposite. The more people who gather, the less likely anyone is to help. This must mean that the situation is exerting an important influence over people's behaviour. It is likely that the reason for the lack of help lies in 'pluralist ignorance'. Everyone assumes that somebody else has offered help and found it not to be required. For example, they may assume that the person is sleeping off the effects of drink. That this is not due to 'uncaring people' can be easily demonstrated. Once someone has made the initial move and offered help, others around are only too keen to offer their assistance – uncaring people would continue to ignore the person. Experiments across a range of situations support the suggestion that the fundamental attribution error does exist, and that we consistently underestimate the effects of the situation.

Finally, there is the *false consensus effect*. This is the mistaken impression that the majority of other people share our own characteristics. Many people make the incorrect assumption that their attitudes, interests etc. are shared by the majority of others. Many fans of 'soap operas', sports, etc. are surprised to find that not everyone shares their tastes. Managers, similarly, often assume that their level of performance is the 'norm', and that others are motivated by the same things that motivate them.

The message from attribution theory is clear. The attributions we make will strongly influence our interaction with others. When making such attributions we should remain alert to the fact that we have a strong tendency to underestimate the situational causes of behaviour, especially when things go wrong.

MAKING ALLOWANCES FOR THE SITUATION

Although our initial reaction is to classify people according to personality traits, we do, in appropriate circumstances, make allowances for the effects of the situation. Often, as we have seen, the effects of the situation may be stronger than dispositional effects. Taking situational effects into account will, therefore, improve the accuracy of our perception of others. Fiske (1993) points out that adjustments can be made for the situation. Whether they will or not depends upon a number of factors.

Crude classifications, based solely on traits, may be acceptable for certain situations; for example, if the interaction with the other person is only temporary, or unimportant. If, however, we are accountable for our judgements, e.g. personnel selection, then we are more likely to take the situation into account. We are also more likely to expend more effort if the judgements are likely to be important for us, as for example in an 'asymmetrical dependence relationship'. Such relationships are characterized by a dependence between people, but where one has more power than the other. The best example is that of boss and subordinate. The subordinate, with less formal power, has a greater interest in predicting their boss's behaviour than vice versa.

When the need arises, therefore, information processing capacity can be devoted to analysing the situational characteristics. However, this analysis is often not carried out. As we have seen, the dispositional, trait-based, analysis takes place first. This is then corrected by an analysis of the situation. This analysis, however, takes time and effort. If constraints are placed on these the situational analysis may be abandoned, or not even started. A similar effect occurs in inter-personal interactions. Just before individuals take their turn to speak they are busy processing their contribution. This often means that they have little spare information processing capacity available at this point to analyse what the other person is saying. This often results in a 'disjunction' in the conversation. The person's contribution does not follow logically from that of the previous speaker. This is known as the 'next-in-line' effect.

Judgements are often made on the basis of first approximations, which are then refined and adjusted in the light of further information. These initial assessments, or anchors, should not, theoretically, have an influence on our final decision. The evidence suggests, however, that they do. A nice example of this, involving mental arithmetic, is given by Tversky and Kahneman (1974). They gave two groups the task of calculating 8 factorial (i.e. 8 times 7 times 6 times 5, ...1.). One group was instructed to start at the top, i.e. 8 times 7, the other at the bottom, i.e. 1 times 2. Each group was stopped before it could complete the calculation and asked to estimate the answer. The group that started at the top would have a high initial 'anchor' on which to base their assessment, the other group would have a low 'anchor'. Their estimates did, indeed, differ according to their anchor. When carried out with a large number of groups, the mean estimate for the high anchor was 2,250, whilst that for the low anchor was 512. (In fact the correct answer is 40,320.) Our final decision, it would appear, tends to be closer to our initial approximation than is justified. We can make some allowances for the situation, but perhaps not enough.

So far we have been discussing largely cognitive factors that influence our interaction with others. We turn now to a theory which adds some more affective dimensions.

TRANSACTIONAL ANALYSIS (TA)

Transactional analysis is a theory which covers both the structure of personality and the interaction between people. It was developed by the American psychiatrist Eric Berne (1968) but it soon became apparent that it had applications outside the consulting room. Despite its clinical pedigree, however, many psychologists do not regard it as highly as other, more traditional, personality theories. Part of the reason for this may be the terminology that the theory uses which, to some, seems rather 'frivolous'. In our experience a large number of managers do find the theory useful as it relates to understanding organizational behaviour.

First we will deal with the part of the theory that concerns itself with the structure of personality, before moving on to consider the analysis of transactions.

Exercise

Before reading further, read the case study in Appendix 2, draft a reply to each of the memos, and write down your impressions of the personality of Bob Jeffries. Then consider how you felt when reading the memos.

THE STRUCTURE OF PERSONALITY

Berne suggests that the personality consists of three major parts, or 'ego states'; Parent, Adult, and Child. We will start with a brief description of each, together with some considerations of their origins. Before doing so a word of warning is required. The terms Parent, Adult, and Child do not mean the same in TA terminology as they do in everyday speech. Child does not, for example, mean the same as childish.

According to Berne, as human beings we are initially all totally dependent upon our parents, or surrogate parents. Thus, virtually all of our experiences in the first few years of life are determined by our interactions with our parents. These experiences, it is argued, are never forgotten. We develop what he likened to a tape, or video, recording of these early experiences, together with our own learnt responses. Thus, the memory contains all the behaviour of the parents, as observed by the infant. This ranges from experiences of loving, to experiences involving the imposition of rules and demands, and those concerned with the setting of standards. These experiences constitute the 'Parent'.

As well as our memories about the actual experiences, we also remember our reactions to the parental behaviour. Most commonly, this is in terms of the feelings associated with them. These constitute the 'Child'. Such feelings may be those of guilt, joy, rebellion, etc.

Finally, at about the age of ten months, the infant starts to become independent and to explore and test the surrounding world. To the 'taught' Parent and 'felt' Child, is added the information-processing function of the 'Adult'.

This is the basic TA structure of personality and is usually presented diagrammatically as three contiguous circles, as shown in Figure 3.2.

As can be seen, the Parent and Child are subdivided. These subdivisions represent the different ways in which the Parent can control, or the Child may feel.

In the Parent, these subdivisions are those of *Critical Parent, Standard-setting Parent*, and *Nurturing Parent*. In the Child they are the *Free*, (or *Spontaneous*) *Child, Intuitive Child* (referred to by Berne as the 'Little Professor'), and *Adapted Child*. This last category, of Adapted Child, can itself be further subdivided into Compliant Child, and Rebellious Child. Both sorts of Child, as we shall see, are often found within organizations. (The Adult may also be subdivided, but this is not relevant for our purposes.)

The balance between these three 'ego states' will vary from individual to individual. For example, some individuals may have a par-

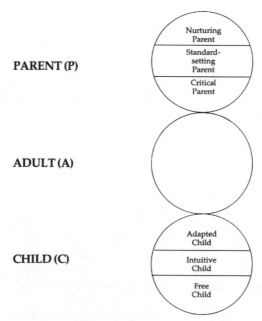

Figure 3.2. Transactional Analysis: structure of personality

ticularly strong Critical Parent. Such an individual will often be seen as authoritarian and inconsiderate of the feelings of others. In our experience, it is likely that many readers will have described Bob Jeffries in words associated with Critical Parent. Other individuals may have a strong Adult, perhaps with very little Child. Such an individual is very logical and rational, but lacks the sense of humour associated with the Free Child. (An interesting, although fictional, example of such a personality is Mr Spock in the Star Trek series.)

What Berne also noticed was that whilst we all have, to a greater or lesser extent, all three ego states, our behaviour at any particular moment is controlled predominantly by only one of them. Thus, a person may behave at different times perhaps as a Critical Parent or a Free Child, but not both at the same time. From this it is perhaps apparent that TA suggests that, although we may have our preferred ego states, we move between all three, often dependent upon what we are responding to at the time.

ANALYSING TRANSACTIONS

We now have the basic information upon which to build our description of Transactional Analysis itself.

The *transaction* is the basic unit of behaviour. It involves a person saying or doing something to another person, and that person responding. For the sake of simplicity, we will concern ourselves largely with verbal transactions, although there are others that are more behavioural, for example shaking a fist.

A transaction originates in one of the ego states. The one from which it originates can be identified by both the content and the way in which it is said. In addition, every transaction is targeted at a particular ego state in the other person. The sender hopes that the receiver will respond from the targeted ego state. This, as we shall see, does not always happen.

Consider the memo from Bob Jeffries (see Appendix 2), which was written from the Critical Parent. Before we consider your memo in reply, let us discuss how you would feel if, in real life, you received such a memo. Critical Parent transactions are targeted at the Adapted Child, and in particular the Compliant Child. In the jargon of TA, the Critical Parent tries to 'hook' the Compliant Child. In our experience, especially with managers, this rarely happens. A more common initial reaction is that of Rebellious Child – 'Who the hell does he think he is?'. (This often happens, we suspect, after a very brief period of 'What have I done wrong?', – Compliant Child.)

What would have happened if you had written the memo back in terms associated with Rebellious Child? The next reply might have been 'Sorry, I realize I was somewhat heavy-handed', but we suspect not. More likely would have been more, and heavier, Critical Parent, resulting in a sequence of transactions known as *uproar*, for obvious reasons.

We more commonly find that the content of the replies are not wholly Rebellious Child, although it is often hinted at in a disguised fashion. (A common veiled Rebellious Child utterance is 'with respect......!'.) More commonly, the response is from the Adult, stating what has been, or is planned to be, done in order to ensure that the same mistake is not repeated in the future.

Parallel and crossed transactions. These alternatives demonstrate a further aspect of TA, the *parallel* versus the *crossed* transaction. These are shown, diagrammatically, in Figure 3.3.

In a *parallel* transaction the initial statement succeeds in hooking the appropriate ego state, and elicits a response from it. In a *crossed* transaction it does not hook the appropriate ego state. In general, a parallel transaction will continue, a crossed transaction will cease. The only way in which a crossed transaction can continue is if one of the individuals moves to the appropriate ego state. Thus, any reply from Jeffries to a memo from your Adult will either have to be in Adult, or contain another attempt to force you to move to Compliant Child. If either refuses to move, memos will soon cease.

Obviously, there are a large number of possible transactions, but we will consider some of the more common patterns. We have, of course, already considered Critical Parent to Adapted Child.

Adapted Child to Nurturing Parent. This is in some ways a mirror-image of the example of Bob Jeffries. Rather than the Parent criticizing the Child, the Child appeals to the Nurturing Parent for help. Taken to the extreme, this may be seen as 'crawling', especially if it is the boss to whom the appeal is made. Used correctly, it can be a highly effective way of resolving some problems. For example, trying to get faulty goods exchanged, is often done from the critical parent. The result is often uproar. Asking for help to resolve your problem is often a more effective approach, as it often hooks the Nurturing Parent.

Critical Parent to Critical Parent. This is a transaction often carried out on training courses, or over a drink. The name often given to this pattern is 'Ain't it awful'; for example:

'This organization never takes any notice of me.'

'I know, my boss never even talks to me.'

Whilst it may be nice to get things off your chest, this does not get things done.

PARALLEL TRANSACTIONS

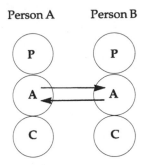

A: 'What time is it?'

B: 'Four o'clock.'

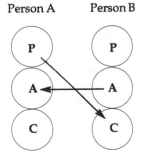

A: 'You look worried. Can I help?'

B. 'Yes please. I don't know how to do this.'

CROSSED TRANSACTIONS

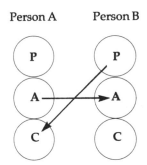

A: 'Where is the Robinson file?'

B: 'How come you never know where anything is?'

A: 'That suggestion is ridiculous!'

B: 'Could you give me the evidence that leads you to that conclusion?'

Figure 3.3. Examples of parallel and crossed transactions

Child to Child. Free Child to Free Child is 'Let's have fun'. This fun may, in its pure form, be harmless. If, however, the Rebellious Child is involved, the motivation is mischievous, rather than fun. For example as in the handwritten memo from Steve Holland: 'Let's get our own back on Jeffries'.

Free Child is often given its head in so-called 'brain-storming' sessions. In such sessions, ideas are produced but neither criticized (Parent), nor evaluated (Adult). Evaluation takes place later.

Adult to Adult. Whilst it may be emotionally beneficial to have a good moan, or to have fun occasionally, it is only when operating from Adult that things get done. Adult to Adult is concerned with information exchange, evaluation, and rational decision-making. Both memos from Bill Owen are written predominantly from the Adult.

IMPROVING TRANSACTIONS

Now that the various transactions have been described, we will now consider how TA can be employed to improve interactions. Recognizing the ego state that is the source of a transaction is the first step in gaining greater control over it. Secondly, you need to be aware of the ego state it is intended to hook, especially if it is the Child, for this is the source of feelings. Finally, decide if you want the transaction to continue. If you do not, then cross the transaction. The other person will either have to follow you (normally to Adult), or give up.

The source of a transaction is indicated in a number of ways. Verbally, both the words used and the tone of voice can indicate the ego state involved, as can the general manner of the person. Non-verbally, gestures and expressions also indicate the ego state involved. Figure 3.4 lists the most common managerial ego states and some of the characteristic words, tones, gestures and attitudes.

Finally there are two points that, whilst not strictly analysis of transactions, may be of some interest. As well as dealing with reality, the Adult also has the job of ensuring that the experiences and feelings of childhood, recorded in Parent and Child respectively, are still appropriate. For example the Parent may still play recordings of 'leave a clean plate' at meal-times. Modern nutritionists, however, question this dictum. Logically there is no longer any nutritional reason why we should have to eat everything placed before us. Nevertheless, the Child may experience inappropriate feelings of guilt. It is the Adult's job to question the rationality, both of the judgement from the Parent and the corresponding feelings of the Child.

Although we have shown the three ego states as being totally separate, sometimes the Adult can become 'contaminated'. When con-

	Critical Parent	Nurturing Parent	Adult	Free Child	Adapted Child Compliant (C) Rebellious (R)
WORDS:	Never Should Ought Do/don't	Let me Don't worry Be careful Well done	Correct Where? Why? What?	Hi Fun Wow Great	Sorry (C) Please (C) Won't (R) No! (R)
VOICE:	Critical Condescending	Sympathetic Encouraging	Confident Inquiring	Excited Free	Apologetic (C) Defiant (R)
EXPRESSION:	Frowning Pointing	Accepting Smiling	Thoughtful Interested	Spontaneous Uninhibited	Helpless (C) Sullen (R)
ATTITUDE:	Judgemental Authoritarian	Understanding Caring	Open Evaluative	Curious Changeable	Agreeing (C) Rebellious (R)

Figure 3.4. Ego state characteristics

taminated by Parent, untested judgements are presented as real. For example, 'all trade union leaders are communists'. The common name for this is prejudice. If, on the other hand, the Child contaminates the Adult, the result is illusion, i.e. wishful thinking presented as reality.

From this discussion, it may have become apparent that transactions need not always be between two people. There can be an internal dialogue; the Parent chiding the Child when things go wrong, patting it on the back when things go well. Again, it is the Adult's job to ensure that both judgement and feeling are still valid in the changing world, and not just the automatic replay of childhood experiences.

EXISTENTIAL POSITIONS

There is one more piece of theory from TA which we have found to be of considerable value to managers. This concentrates on the *existential position* from which people operate. It will be easier to explain the meaning of this phrase once the essential concept has been covered. This concept is whether a person is 'OK' or 'not OK'. Unlike the concepts of Parent, Adult, and Child, the term OK means very much the same in TA as it does in everyday language. If someone is seen as 'OK' then they have value as a person and their views and opinions have to be considered seriously. They are competent, and are generally in control of their life. Someone who is seen as 'Not OK', on the other hand, is perceived as the opposite of this. They do not

I'M OK YOU'RE NOT OK	I'M OK YOU'RE OK
I'M NOT OK YOU'RE NOT OK	I'M NOT OK YOU'RE OK

Figure 3.5. OK corral

appear to be in control, and their views and opinions can be dismissed without consideration. They have little or no value as a human being.

The concept of being 'OK' or 'Not OK' can be applied both to oneself and to others. Thus I can be 'OK' or 'Not OK'; likewise you can be 'OK' or 'Not OK'. Putting these two factors, 'OK-ness' and I/You, together produces four possible combinations, as shown in Figure 3.5. For obvious reasons it is often referred to as the 'OK Corral'.

Let us take each of the positions in turn and consider their implications for our interactions with other people. The diagram was originally devised by Franklin Ernst (1971) for use in psychotherapy. For this reason we will give some clinical as well as managerial examples.

I'm OK, You're Not OK. If I'm OK then I have value as a person and my ideas and views also have value. You, on the other hand, have little or no value. The logical conclusion is that if you don't count, then I am justified in getting rid of you. In its extreme clinical form this is the position of homicidal psychopaths. It is also the position adopted by some extreme religious groups. In managerial terms it is the 'hire-and-fire' culture.

I'm Not OK, You're OK. In many ways this is the reverse of the first box. Everyone else but me appears to be in control, and has value as a person. In this situation, the logical conclusion is to get rid of myself. In extreme clinical cases the ultimate solution is suicide. Indeed, an analysis by Berne of suicide notes revealed that this was a very common position. In organizational terms, the result is often resignation. 'It's my fault again, I'll have to go.' (The memo from James Slater in Appendix 2 is an example of a response from this position.) A milder, and more common, version is to keep a low profile. This is a common feeling during the first weeks or months in a new job.

I'm Not OK, You're Not OK. In this situation no one knows what is going on, and no one is in control. In clinical terms, the outcome is to become insane. 'You may think I'm strange, but you should see my psychologist!' It often expresses itself in a very mild organizational form in the type of office stickers that read 'You don't have to be mad to work here, but it helps'.

I'm OK, You're OK. In this position, both parties have value and are in control. There may be disagreements, but they do not mean that either party disparages the value or ideas of the other. In this situation, the motto is not to 'get rid of' but to 'get on with'. It is the only position from which people can interact effectively.

The theory suggests that people exist in, and operate from, one of these four positions, hence the term 'existential position'. Which position a person is operating from will change, depending on their own preferred existential position and that of the person with whom they are interacting. In everyday life we suspect that most people spend most of their time in 'I'm OK, You're OK'. We also think that most people have a preferred 'fall back' position, which becomes apparent when things go wrong. For most managers, we suspect that the common fall back is 'I'm OK, You're Not OK' – when things go wrong it's someone else's fault (shades of the self-serving attribution bias). The effect of responding from this position is to push the other person to *their* fall back position, which is also likely to be 'I'm OK, You're Not OK'. The result is then likely to be uproar. Judging from their behaviour, we suspect that some drivers operate from 'I'm OK, You're Not OK'. Their behaviour has the effect of pushing other, normally 'I'm OK, You're OK' drivers into the same position. The next most common fall back is probably 'I'm Not OK, You're OK'. This position, however, is very uncomfortable. For this reason we suspect that those who fall back to this position often quickly convert to 'I'm OK, You're Not OK'. (At this point you may have noticed the links between the OK states and the ego states mentioned earlier. 'Not OK' comments always originate in either Rebellious Child or Critical Parent.)

We find that the OK Corral is a very useful aid to managers in their interactions with others. First, it helps them understand when they, or others, are slipping into 'Not OK' positions. Second, it points out that the only way to interact effectively with others is to stay 'OK', both about yourself and those with whom you are interacting. Finally, the position you occupy at any particular time is a voluntary choice. As Eleanor Roosevelt once said, 'No one can make you feel inferior without your consent'. Staying 'OK' may make you feel better and be more effective.

We have now considered the ways in which personality can be described, and how interpersonal communications may be improved. The ability to analyse transactions and construct appropriate responses is an important tool in effective people-management.

INTERPERSONAL INTERACTION AND THE PSYCHOLOGICAL CONTRACT

The different ego states are involved in both the economic and psychological contracts. The economic contract will involve, essentially, the Adult. Needs, other than purely economic needs, will involve other ego states. The matching of the individual's moral and ethical values with those of the organization will involve the Standard-setting Parent. Perhaps most important, however, are the individual's needs for enjoyment, excitement, and emotional support. These are central to the psychological contract, and involve the Child. This is important because, as we have seen, the Free Child is the source of energy, creativity, and motivation. A motivated work-force will have its Child needs satisfied. Finally, the negotiation and ongoing re-negotiation of the psychological contract is likely to be ineffective unless both parties are operating from 'I'm OK, You're OK'.

4

Motivation

An independent consulting firm in the USA recently carried out a survey of employees' attitudes. While most workers were generally satisfied with their pay and benefits, less than half thought that their boss was doing a good job of motivating them. This applied at all levels, from the shop floor to the boardroom. Similar results have been found in the UK.

Exercise

Before looking at various theories of motivation, and their implications for management, we have found that it often helps to think about what it is that motivates ourselves. It is worth spending ten minutes jotting down answers to the following questions:

- Why do I work?

- Why do I work for my present company?

- Why do I work hard (or otherwise)?

Having done this, it is often interesting to answer the questions again (especially the first one) from the point of view of a group of which you are not a member. If you are a manager, try the exercise for blue-collar workers, and vice versa.

What normally results from such an exercise are lists of *needs,* which have some degree of similarity, but which also reveal some individual differences. This is not surprising as it is likely that some reasons for working apply to everybody. Other reasons have particular importance for particular individuals. The list of all our needs is, however, very long. What we require is some form of theoretical structure that will help to organize the large number of needs, or potential motivators, into smaller, more manageable categories. Such a theoretical structure will help us when we consider what it is that motivates particular employees, or groups of employees.

Since the early part of the 20th century theorists have considered what such a structure might be like and it is interesting, therefore, to look at the history of need theories of the motivation to work. Each of the theories has been shown to be lacking as a full explanation of motivation at work, but each has left its influence on subsequent theories.

NEED THEORIES OF WORK

TAYLOR'S SCIENTIFIC MANAGEMENT

The first modern systematic commentator on motivation at work was probably Frederick Taylor (1911). In the first decades of the century he described what he called *scientific management*. Note that we call Taylor a commentator, rather than a theorist. His 'theory' was stated as a set of 'principles', rather than in the form of a comprehensive theory. Taylor's principles advocated strict division of labour based on systematic job analysis, high levels of control, and the use of money as a motivator linked to various objectives. There is no doubt that money is indeed an important motivator, because of its universal ability to be exchanged for other, more practical, motivators. If it did not appear on your list of why you work one might be suspicious. What Taylor overlooked, however, is that people also work for reasons other than money. A survey reported in the early 1980s (Warr, 1982) asked a large sample of British men and women if they would continue to work if it were not financially necessary for them to do so. Nearly 70 per cent of men and 65 per cent of women said they would continue to work. Interestingly, while there was some difference between professional and unskilled manual workers, it was not as large as may have been expected. Nearly 60 per cent of male unskilled manual workers said they would continue working. Harpaz (1989) carried out a cross-cultural study and found very similar figures to those for the UK. Of the six countries studied, Japan had the highest proportion who said they would continue working (93.4 per cent). The UK was lowest at 68.8 per cent, whilst the USA was in the middle at 88.1 per cent. (These results have to be treated with a certain amount of caution. What people say they will do and what they actually do may not be the same.) If they would continue working despite not needing the money, then what other needs must be being met at work?

THE HAWTHORNE STUDIES

The next major revision of need theory came from work done in the USA in the 1920s and '30s at the Hawthorne works of the Western

Electric Company (Roethlisberger and Dickson, 1939). The name most commonly associated with the Hawthorne studies is that of Elton Mayo. Although he used much of the data to support his own theories, Mayo himself was never directly involved (Mayo, 1975).

Initially the researchers were trying to establish the relationship between various physical conditions, such as temperature and lighting, on productivity. What they found was that there was no consistent relationship. Productivity increased both in the experimental group and in a control group. The level of lighting remained constant for the control group, but was varied in the experimental group. At one point, the level of lighting for the latter was equivalent to that of moonlight. Despite this, productivity did not drop. The researchers eventually concluded that psychological, rather than physical, factors were at work.

In order to test this hypothesis they conducted various small group experiments. From the results of these, they concluded that motivation was best explained in terms of 'social relationships'. The productivity had risen in both the control and experimental groups because the members felt that the researchers were taking an interest in them. Indeed, the 'Hawthorne effect' has entered sociological and psychological vocabularies; that is, merely observing people will have an effect upon them.

Although the studies took place over 50 years ago the results are still a matter of discussion and controversy. Most researchers now accept that the studies were poorly constructed and controlled. For this reason the results can be explained by factors other than just social ones. Nevertheless, they have left their mark by drawing attention to psychological needs in motivation.

MASLOW'S HIERARCHY OF NEEDS

The first comprehensive attempt to classify needs was undertaken by Abraham Maslow in the 1940s. Maslow's theory (1971) essentially consists of two parts. The first concerns the classification of needs; the second, how these classifications are related to each other. He suggested that needs can be classified into a hierarchy. This hierarchy is normally presented in the form of a pyramid, as shown in Figure 4.1, with each level consisting of a particular class of needs.

The relationship between the needs is reflected in the pyramid structure. Maslow argues that the lower down the needs lie, the more basic they are. Thus, the most basic needs are those concerned with physical survival. These needs have to be satisfied, at least to some minimum level, before the next level of needs becomes important. Once each level is adequately satisfied, the needs at that level become less important. The only exception to this is the top level, self-actual-

Figure 4.1. Maslow's hierarchy of needs

ization. Self-actualization is the need to become the kind of person you envisage yourself to be. As such, it can never be totally satisfied. According to Maslow, individuals work their way up the hierarchy, but each level of needs remains dependent on the levels below. Thus, if you are motivated at work by the opportunity to 'self-actualize' and suddenly you are made redundant, the whole system collapses, as the need to feed and provide for yourself and dependants becomes the predominant need.

The theory, especially when the redundancy example is used, has considerable appeal to managers. Its message is clear: find out which level each individual is operating at and pitch their rewards accordingly. Unfortunately, the theory is weak in many respects. Some levels of the classification appear not to exist for some individuals, while some rewards appear to fit into more than one classification, e.g. money, which can be used to purchase the essentials of life, but which can also be seen as a status symbol, or an indicator of personal worth. As to the relationship between the different levels, there appear to be considerable individual differences as to what constitutes 'adequate satisfaction' at any particular level.

Empirical research, therefore, has failed to support the theory (see Wahba and Bridwell, 1976), and most psychologists would rate its accuracy, on a scale of 1 to 10, somewhere about 2 or 3 (Locke and Henne, 1986). Despite this, it is still taught on many management courses without its faults being highlighted. This is not to suggest that the theory is without value; the classification of needs is useful as a guide to ensure that all possible types of need are considered. In addition, it is likely that people's needs *are* organized in a hierarchical manner. What has to be recognized is that the nature of this hierarchy will vary from one person to another.

HERZBERG'S TWO-FACTOR THEORY

The next significant theory was that of Frederick Herzberg (1966), which did not look at motivation directly, but at the causes of job satisfaction and dissatisfaction. Herzberg did this using a technique known as *critical incidents* analysis. He asked a group of professional engineers and accountants to describe incidents in their jobs in the recent past that had given them strong feelings either of satisfaction or dissatisfaction. He then asked them to describe the causes in each case. Based on an analysis of their descriptions of what happened and why, Herzberg suggested a 'two factor' theory of job satisfaction/dissatisfaction ('two factor' because the causes of one were distinct from the causes of the other). Herzberg concluded that job satisfaction is the result of what he called *motivators*. These were such things as 'a sense of achievement', 'an opportunity for personal growth', 'the sense of having done a job well' etc. Dissatisfaction, on the other hand, appeared to be caused by *hygiene* factors. These included such things as 'money', 'working conditions', and 'company policy'. According to the theory, these two factors, motivators and hygiene, are qualitatively different and have different effects. If you want to remove dissatisfaction, improve the hygiene factors. Improving them beyond the level at which dissatisfaction disappears will not, however, lead to an increase in satisfaction. The only way satisfaction can be increased further is by giving more of the motivators. The converse also applies. Giving more of the motivators will not by itself remove dissatisfaction.

On initial examination the theory has some merit. Consider the annual pay rise, or an improvement in working conditions. They may have an initial effect on satisfaction, but they are soon taken for granted. Experimental examination of the theory has not been so kind to it. The results can only be replicated using the same sort of people (i.e. professionals), and the same technique (i.e. getting the people themselves to describe the causes of their feelings). If you recall attribution theory (see pages 95–99) you will remember that we have a tendency to blame things 'out there' when things go wrong, but claim 'things in me' when they go right. This would appear to be the explanation for Herzberg's findings. As with Maslow, Herzberg's work is appealing initially, but on further examination turns out to be conceptually flawed. As with Maslow's theory, however, it continues to be taught uncritically.

Herzberg has left his mark, however. His classification of motivators and hygiene factors is disputed, but the distinction may still be seen in the concept of 'intrinsic' versus 'extrinsic' sources of motivation. Intrinsic motivators are those within the job itself (e.g. feelings of accomplishment). External motivators (such as money) are outside the job. As will be seen, the former are more effective, and cheaper!

In addition, Herzberg's concepts of job enlargement and job enrichment are still in use in the area of job and work design. It is to this that we will now turn.

JOB DESIGN

Job design is concerned with the characteristics of jobs and how these affect people's behaviour. Many managers consider that job or work design has little to do with them. This may be so but, in a workplace that is rapidly changing, we think it unlikely. For example, the introduction of word processors in place of typewriters may, on the surface, simply appear to involve swapping an out-of-date typewriter for a more sophisticated one. But the implications often go further, as those who have undertaken such a change will tell you. Even such a simple thing as changing the office in which someone works may have effects on such things as job performance and absenteeism. It may also influence the levels of job satisfaction, anxiety, and depression of those concerned.

Changes in job design have the potential both for degrading and improving jobs. At worst, they can lead to the 'de-skilling' of previously skilled jobs. They have also the potential to enhance and supplement those skills; which impact they have is not solely dependent upon technology. For example, the introduction of word processors has the potential for both de-skilling and enhancement, depending upon *how* it is used. If the operators are now just used to type in the initial material, which is then modified and edited by others using their own terminals, the job will be de-skilled. The operators will become no more than copy-typists. If, on the other hand, the operators are given the opportunity to use their own initiative, the job can be enhanced. For example, operators could be given the job of seeking out the information required to update routine documents, or producing the agendas for regular meetings.

What the effects of job redesign will be, and their magnitude, will depend upon many factors. The practising manager, therefore, needs some form of checklist in order adequately to diagnose and understand this process. This will at least help to ensure that when contemplating changing the way people work, due consideration is given to the major factors. Most importantly, the manager should realize that job design does not apply only to massive changes, such as automated factories, because even apparently minor changes, such as reorganizing office layout, can have an impact on a worker's attitudes and/or behaviour.

In discussing the major implications of job design we will consider aspects of the job itself, the effects of individual differences, and the influence of contextual factors.

THE JOB ITSELF

Job factors may themselves be subdivided into two broad, and overlapping, classes; *quantitative* and *qualitative* factors. Put briefly, quantitative refers to the amount of work involved in the job; while qualitative refers to the perceived quality of that work.

Quantitative changes concern the demands made upon the physical and mental capacities of those involved. When job changes are planned, physical demands are usually taken into consideration because they are most obvious. The extra walking, or the extra muscle power required is something that becomes immediately apparent.

Mental demands are less often considered. In considering these, it is perhaps easiest to draw an analogy between workers and computers. Both, in particular aspects of the job, are information processors. Both can be either over-loaded or under-loaded. The difference is that computers, unlike people, don't get anxious or bored. Continuing the analogy, information processing consists of three broad stages, at each of which demands may be made:

- *Demands on attention*, i.e. recognizing and inputting the information.

- *Demands on memory*, i.e. storing the information.

- *Demands on decision-making*, i.e. processing the information.

The major influences on these factors are, of course, the volume of information and the time-scales involved. Under normal circumstances, these demands are usually well within the processing capacities of the individuals concerned. Problems often arise, however, when demands suddenly increase. To give a tragic example; in July 1988, the American destroyer *Vincennes* shot down an Iranian airliner with nearly 300 people on board. At the time, the destroyer, said to be the most sophisticated anti-aircraft warship afloat, was engaging Iranian warships. According to one of the officers aboard, the highly complex radar systems aboard the ship had to be 'tuned down', because the information being supplied by the computers was too much for the operators to cope with. The consequences of this, it could be argued, are still with us today. It is unlikely that managers will be faced with a job design task with such potentially disastrous consequences, but how can they recognize when overload is occurring?

It is easy to spot overload in computers. They make mistakes or stop working. Humans, on the other hand, usually do not fail catastrophically, rather they go into a gradual decline. The ways in which they cope are by limiting either the input, or the processing. Limitation of input can be accomplished either by stopping it altogether (go on sick leave, or strike) or by reducing it (form queues). Limitation of processing, on the other hand, means that approximations are made which are sometimes correct because of past experience, but which are often wrong in some detail. These wrong decisions, if detected by others and referred back, then join the ever-growing queue. Unfortunately, many workers will use such techniques to cover up the overload, for fear of disclosing what they perceive as their inability to cope. It is easy for hard-pressed managers to ignore such indicators but, if they do, in the long run both the job and the worker will suffer. Managers should be prepared to probe beyond the offered explanations of 'it will be all right soon', 'it's only temporary', and not wait for the inevitable, and possibly disastrous, error.

Qualitative changes are best summarized by the job characteristics model (JCM), which was developed by Hackman and Oldham (1976, 1980), and which is shown in Figure 4.2.

According to Hackman and Oldham, certain central, or 'core', features of the job will influence certain important, or 'critical' psychological states in individuals. These states will themselves then determine people's attitudes and behaviours towards the job. The model suggests, therefore, that the *core dimensions,* on the left, will influence the *critical psychological states,* which in turn will influence the *personal and work outcomes* on the right. The strength of this relationship will, however, be different for different individuals. It will be influenced by the individual differences in *growth need strength, knowledge and skills,* and *satisfaction with contextual factors.* We will return to these shortly.

While the descriptions given in Figure 4.2 for critical psychological states, and personal and work outcomes are easily understood, we

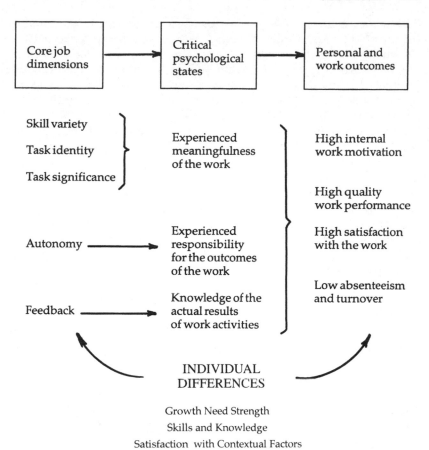

Figure 4.2. Hackman and Oldhams' job characteristics model. (Adapted from: Hackman and Oldham, 1980)

perhaps need to describe the core job dimensions in a little more detail. They comprise:

- *Skill variety* – The extent to which the tasks require different skills.
- *Task identity* – The extent to which the worker can complete a 'whole' piece of work, as opposed to merely a small part of it.
- *Task significance* – The extent to which the work is perceived as influencing the lives of others.
- *Autonomy:* The extent to which the worker has freedom within the job to decide how it should be done.
- *Feedback:* The extent to which there is correct and precise information about how effectively the worker is performing.

The model is in many ways a synthesis of previous theories, and the legacy of Herzberg can be detected. Herzberg differentiated between job enlargement and job enrichment. The former consisted of just giving the worker more of the same – what has been called 'horizontal loading'. Rather than tighten five screws, the worker tightens ten! Enrichment, on the other hand, means including opportunities for intrinsic motivation by expanding the job 'vertically'. In terms of the job characteristics model, the worker thus gains control over a larger piece of work, involving more skills, greater autonomy and a more meaningful task. These will affect the critical psychological states positively and hence improve personal and work outcomes. (We will consider some examples shortly.)

Empirical studies of the model have shown that, while there does appear to be a link between job dimensions and personal and work outcomes, the links of both of these with the critical psychological states may not be as suggested (Wall *et al*, 1978; Wagner, 1994). For the manager, this is a problem that perhaps can be left to the psychologists. The fact that job dimensions affect such things as quality of work and absenteeism is of greater practical importance. However, people's behaviour is influenced by their psychological state, and it would be useful to know what factors of the job have what influence. Broadbent (1985) has argued that job overload will tend to result in increased levels of anxiety; social isolation, on the other hand, will lead to depression; and boring, repetitive work will result in feelings of job dissatisfaction. All of these mental states can, however, be moderated. For example, the provision of social support for those whose work means they are socially isolated can reduce the tendency to depression.

INDIVIDUAL DIFFERENCES

So far it has been tacitly assumed that all people faced with the same job characteristics, in the same contexts, will behave and feel the same way. This is obviously not true. As individuals we differ. The model suggests three main differences that will influence the effect that the job characteristics have upon an individual; these are *growth need strength (GNS), knowledge and skills*, and *satisfaction with contextual factors*.

Growth need strength. People differ in their need for growth in a job. Some require that the job is demanding, whilst others are happy with routine jobs, gaining their needs for autonomy etc., elsewhere. A crude but easy way of defining GNS is by means of Maslow's hierarchy of needs (see page 114). Someone with needs near the top would have a high GNS score, someone near the bottom, a low score. Thus, those with high GNS are characterized as having high needs for autonomy and personal growth from their job. At the other end of the hierarchy are those individuals who view work in purely instrumental terms: 'I'm here for the money and nothing else'. Such individuals may, from a management view, appear to have a rather negative attitude to work. There may be many in this category who derive their major satisfactions from outside activities. These may be leisure-related or may involve public service such as council work. As long as they 'pull their weight' at work, do we have a right to expect everyone to be enthusiastic? If they do not pull their weight, then it is management's job, perhaps using some of the techniques to be described later, to ensure that they do.

The model suggests that the individual's GNS will have an influence on the effects of job characteristics on personal and work outcomes. This is supported by most of the research evidence. People with high GNS tend to respond more positively when their core job dimensions are improved, are likely to be absent less, and are more likely to produce higher quality work (Graen *et al.*, 1986). In addition, there is no evidence to suggest that improving job characteristics has a negative effect on those with low GNS. In general, therefore, improving job characteristics at best produces highly positive responses and, at worst, indifference (Campion and McClelland, 1991).

Knowledge and skills. Any change in a job is likely to require new skills and knowledge. This may especially be the case when a job is being enriched. New skills, both technical and social, may be required. If individuals do not feel that they have the necessary skills and knowledge to cope with the new job demands, the effects are likely to be detrimental. As we shall see in the next chapter, a person's self-perception of their ability to perform well (referred to as *self-efficacy*) can have considerable impact on their later performance. If job enrichment programmes are to succeed, therefore, it is essential that job incumbents receive adequate advance training to enable them to have confidence in their ability to adapt to the new and, it is hoped, motivating job design.

Satisfaction with contextual factors. It may appear obvious, but jobs tend to be done within organizations. It would be strange if aspects of the organization did not have an influence on personal and work outcomes. We have already come across many of the contextual factors that have been shown to have an influence on reactions to job enrichment. Many of them are Herzberg's hygiene factors, such as salary, company policy, etc. Also important, however, are the social aspects of the job and the 'climate' of the organization.

Since the Hawthorne studies, the importance of social contact and support in the workplace have been recognized. Indeed, many companies encourage social, as well as work-related, contact between their staff. Because of its importance, individuals will find ways of increasing their level of social contact if it is low. For example, in one factory studied by the authors, mechanics had collected what they considered to be evidence of sabotage by machine operatives, of whom there were five to a machine. While the machine was being repaired considerable social activity took place between the operatives. When the machines were running, such interaction was not possible because of the noise and locations of the operatives. Another telling example is that of people who occasionally work at home. Anyone who has done this will tell you that, because of the lack of interruptions, you can get a lot of work done. However, it is something that can only be tolerated by most people for a limited period. The lack of social contact is felt after a few days. This factor has yet to be fully taken into account by those organizations which are considering 'electronic offices', which would allow some staff to work at home almost permanently. Given that social contact is, for most people, not only desirable but necessary, how should it affect job design?

The most common way in which job design has been used is in autonomous working groups. In this system, a group is made responsible for a complete particular task. For example, in well reported cases, Volvo and Saab in the 1970s and General Motors in the 1980s established factories based on such working teams. By combining people together in groups, a number of benefits can be obtained. First, because tasks are being combined, there is the possibility for more skill variety, task identity, and task significance. There is also the potential for greater autonomy. All of this is in addition to the satisfaction of social needs. For example, a group may be made responsible for the fabrication of the engine. How they arrange their work is entirely up to them, with the proviso that they maintain a 'buffer' supply of completed engines so that the next group on the production line is not held up.

Another limited example is that of Quality Circles (QCs), where staff working in a particular area are encouraged to meet together during work time to discuss methods of improving product quality and work practices. The results are generally encouraging. In our experience, where QCs fail they do so because of the lack of support from top management.

The introduction of such changes is also dependent upon the 'organizational climate, that is, the array of norms and traditions that have built up about 'how things get done around here'. For example, many job redesigns involve the devolution of greater responsibility to staff, on the assumption that this will be accepted. This may not be the case. For reasons that will be considered in Chapter 6, on leadership and management style, the sudden change from highly controlled work practices to a more participative approach may be met with apathy or, in some cases, even outright rebellion. Large changes in working practice that go against the organizational climate are likely to have one of two effects. First, if the change is persisted with, a period of considerable difficulty will have to be tolerated. Alternatively, and we suspect more commonly, the change is abandoned and the *status quo ante* re-established, but with additional ill-feeling caused by the abortive change.

We are not aware of any research that has studied the relative importance of individual differences and organizational climate, but we believe that the effects of the former are smaller than those of the latter. How people respond to greater autonomy and responsibility is largely dependent upon how they have been treated in the past and the expectations that this engenders. It may be characterized in the often-heard expression, 'I'm not paid to make decisions'. How this may be overcome is left to later chapters.

JOB DIAGNOSIS

There are a number of questionnaires that may be used to analyse jobs along the dimensions of the job characteristics model (e.g. Idaszak and Drasgow, 1987). However, it is possible to use clues about how jobs are currently organized in order to give some indication of the potential for job enrichment. The presence or absence of the following may give some indication (Whitsett, 1975):

- The existence of *quality control departments* and/or inspectors means that some degree of autonomy is removed from the employees. In addition, the amount of feedback is likely to be lower as the feedback is indirect (i.e. via quality control), rather than direct.

- As with quality control departments, *customer relations departments* will dilute the extent of feedback that the employees receive. It is also likely that the employees' perception of the importance of their task to the customer is reduced.

- In response to quality difficulties or other problems, *trouble-shooters* may be used. The employees may see this as a reduction in their autonomy and associated feedback. In addition, skill variety is reduced as some of the more interesting elements of the job are performed by others.

- Trouble-shooters are often used in conjunction with *labour pools*. Whilst these may provide flexibility, they inevitably reduce the sense of ownership of the job, and hence task identity.

- Finally, the structure of the organization may give clues. Too many levels of hierarchy in an organization may indicate excessive control, and hence low levels of autonomy.

If an analysis reveals scope for job enrichment, how can this be achieved? In one organization in which the authors have worked the following steps have been taken:

- The organizational structure has been made 'flatter' by removing some layers of management (fortunately with no compulsory redundancies).

- Autonomous work groups have been established with responsibility for quality, maintenance, etc.

- Employees have been sent on visits to the organization's major customers.

The first two steps have led to an increase in the amount of autonomy, feedback, and skill variety. As for the third step, although a customer relations department still exists, the trips to customers have made the employees more aware of the value of their work and the importance of various aspects of quality. Task significance has thus been increased.

We hope we have demonstrated that the job is capable of satisfying the needs of individuals. However, as we have seen, individuals differ in their needs, and it is to another influential theory of individual needs that we will now turn.

MANAGERIAL NEEDS

David McClelland (1961) is a prolific researcher and writer, and his theories have been the stimulus for hundreds of studies. The popularity of his theory diminished somewhat in the 1970s, but it still remains influential. The theory is concerned with motivation, but from an individual difference perspective. It could easily, therefore, have been included in the chapter on personality. However, since its main concern is with individual differences as they affect motivation, it seemed to fit most comfortably in this chapter.

McClelland's basic assumption is that people learn in early childhood that certain behaviour leads to gratification, and hence they develop a need based on this behaviour. There are, he argues, three basic needs; achievement, affiliation, and power. These are usually referred to by the abbreviations, *n-Ach, n-Aff,* and *n-Power* respectively. Originally, McClelland considered n-Ach to be the most important, but in later work the focus has switched to n-Power.

Need for achievement is, according to McClelland, one of the keys to a country's economic growth. Those who have high n-Ach become active entrepreneurs and businessmen and women, whose joint efforts lead to an increase in economic prosperity.

Such individuals want to take personal responsibility, prefer to take calculated risks, and like immediate feedback on their performance. However, managers high in n-Ach tend to hold fewer meetings than other managers, preferring to work on their own. They also tend to be unresponsive to those around them. The reason is that those high in n-Ach are 'playing the game'. Goals and standards are set internally, single-handed, and they are not dependent on any other person for approval.

McClelland suggests that when people think in n-Ach terms 'things begin to move fast'. Because needs are learnt in childhood, he and his colleagues have examined the n-Ach content in children's and popular literature from many countries, and over many years. This literature should give a good indication of the values that society considers desirable. His results suggested a strong relationship between their n-Ach content and macro-economic performance. For example, in terms of n-Ach content, in 1925 Britain ranked fifth amongst 25 countries. By 1950 it had dropped to 27th out of 39.

McClelland suggests that n-Ach is encouraged by parents who set moderately high achievement goals for their children, but who are warm, encouraging, and non-authoritarian in helping them to achieve these goals. He also claims that n-Ach can be encouraged in adults through appropriate training courses.

Need for affiliation. In the course of his early work, McClelland found that some of the major figures in industry did not, as he had at first expected, score highly on n-Ach. He reasoned that at this level within large organizations goals are achieved by co-ordinating the activities of others rather than by the individual alone. What appears to be the major requirement in these circumstances is the ability to *relate* to other people. Those who have this need are said to be high in n-Aff. Managers with high n-Aff strive for approval, both from their subordinates and their superiors. High n-Affs are sensitive to the needs of others.

Later, however, it was suggested that there are two forms of n-Aff (Boyatzis, 1979), one more managerially effective than the other. The two forms are *affiliative assurance* and *affiliative interest*. Affiliative assurance is a striving for close relationships, because of the security that they bring. Such an individual tends to look for approval, and is anxious about possible rejection. An interest in close relationships because of the support they offer means that energy is concentrated on maintaining relationships. This effort will be at the expense of getting the job done. In addition, the manager high in affiliative as-surance would rather hang on to team members than see them pro-moted. For these reasons, those high in affiliative assurance may not be suited to some managerial jobs.

Affiliative interest, by contrast, is expressed as an interest in the feelings of others, but not at the expense of getting the job done. It is a 'concern' for the legitimate needs and feelings of others. This, it is argued, is the type of n-Aff which will lead to greater organizational effectiveness.

While the combination of n-Ach and n-Aff accounted for the low n-Ach of some major figures in industry and commerce, there were still circumstances that it could not explain. For example, McClelland found that n-Ach and n-Aff did not explain why people became lead-ers, rather than managers.

Need for power. Those with high n-Ach and high n-Aff still had prob-lems of leadership, power, and social influence with which they could not cope. What was needed was something to get people to work together. This he termed the power motive. McClelland (1979) recog-nized that a need for power was often seen as socially undesirable, but why? There appears to be a 'love–hate' reaction to power. This, he suggests, is because power has two faces, one positive, the other nega-tive. Negatively, it is an unsocialized concern for personal dominance at the expense of others. More positively, it shows itself as an interest in persuasion and interpersonal influence.

Once again, this need is learnt during childhood socialization. The original source of power is physical; the older child has power over the others because of his or her greater strength. This exercise of power often leads to positive outcomes, which also lead to positive feelings of accomplishment in the child. As socialization of the child continues, such physical dominance is normally discouraged and the need becomes channelled by *activity inhibition* into more socially ac-ceptable routes of social influence. The extent of this redirection will vary from child to child. Some parents may not inhibit expressions of personal dominance in their children; others may. According to McClelland, the level of such activity inhibition will determine which of the two types of need for power predominates. Those high in ac-tivity inhibition will satisfy their need for power in socially acceptable ways, for example, through interpersonal influencing skills.

Research suggests that people high in n-Power hold more offices, and seek occupations of influence (McClelland, 1979). If they are low in activity inhibition they tend to have more arguments, and may be impulsively aggressive. Interestingly, it is often thought that great leaders dominate their followers. Research by McClelland, who played tape recordings of speeches by leaders such as Churchill and

Kennedy to students, suggests that this is incorrect. Rather than dominate, these leaders increase their followers' feelings of power. They lead by making others feel that they too have power (see Chapter 6).

Although this chapter is concerned with motivation, rather than leadership, the two overlap at some points. N-Ach theory is such a point, and it is perhaps worth briefly mentioning the leadership pattern of need motivation.

Leadership motivation pattern. Research suggests that successful leaders are high in n-Power, low in n-Aff, but high in activity inhibition. They are high, therefore, on interpersonal influence rather than dominance.

In one large American corporation measures of this leadership pattern were taken for a large number of managers. Follow-up studies some eight and sixteen years later found that managers with this pattern advanced more rapidly than the others. The same was also true in a study conducted in the US Navy. These findings, however, only applied to non-technical managers. For those in specialist technical jobs this pattern is not likely to be a predictor of success. Power in these areas seems likely to depend more on knowledge than on interpersonal influence.

So far in this chapter we have largely been concerned with 'what' motivates people. In the theories that follow, we will switch our attention from 'what' motivates, to 'how' they can be motivated that is, the *process* of motivation rather than its content.

EQUITY THEORY

Exercise

Before reading further, please turn to Appendix 3 and try the case study.

Equity theory is concerned with the way in which people judge the fairness, or otherwise, of the way that rewards, including wages, are distributed. As such it is, in fact, only one of many approaches to the issue of distributive justice. The issues of the way that scarce resources are, or ought to be, shared out is a major concern in most societies. On the 'macro' scale, for example, are issues about the way the world's wealth is distributed between different countries. At the more 'micro' level are disagreements about the way a country's wealth is distributed between various sections of society. Our focus will be even more limited, i.e. the way rewards are distributed between individuals, or groups, within organizations. It will be necessary, however, to consider wider issues in describing the theories. Our focus will also be on empirical studies which study the way in which people actually judge fairness. In other words, the emphasis will be upon *how* people judge fairness, not on how they *ought* to judge it. The latter issue is one for moral philosophy or jurisprudence, not organizational psychology.

PRINCIPLES UNDERLYING THE DISTRIBUTION OF REWARDS

People rarely reflect on the principles they use to judge fairness. In fact, they tend to take for granted the assumptions they use when assessing fairness. There are three main categories by which we judge: those based on *contributions*, those based on *equality*, and those based on *needs*.

Contributions. The basic assumption behind the principle of contributions is that people should be rewarded in proportion to their contribution. The more a person contributes to any outcome, the greater the proportion of the rewards they should receive. This principle is probably the most dominant within organizations, and perhaps within Western society as a whole. Like many assumptions it is often accepted so automatically that other possible principles are, indeed, overlooked.

The contribution need not be only in terms of effort. Education, training, experience, and responsibility may also be counted as contributions. There is, in fact, often disagreement as to what counts as a contribution, as will be seen later.

Equality. The equality principle is perhaps the easiest to describe. In short, everybody receives equal shares, independent of their contributions or needs. This form of distribution is generally associated with communist or socialist economies. However, even within Western systems some things are distributed on the basis of equality. In particular, the right to vote in elections; in most democracies each adult citizen has one vote.

Needs. According to the need principle, people should be rewarded according to their personal needs. The size of a worker's family might be considered to be a need. In those countries with state-run health services the availability of treatment is, in theory, based on a person's need.

PRINCIPLES IN PRACTICE

Dornstein (1985) examined the basic distributive orientations of a sample of white-and blue-collar workers. The results, shown in Figure 4.3, suggest that the sample used four different principles when deciding how rewards should be distributed. We have already considered 'contribution' (i.e. education, responsibility and authority, skills, and

Basic orientation	White-collar	Blue-collar
Contribution	32.7	8.1
Need	16.4	40.3
Ascription	9.1	4.8
Disagreeability	41.8	46.8

Figure 4.3. Equity orientation. (Adapted from: Dornstein, 1985)

dedication), and 'needs' (i.e. family size and circumstances). In addition, however, two other principles were added: 'ascription' (i.e. age, seniority in job, and length of service), and 'disagreeability' (i.e. difficult working conditions and inconvenient working hours). These four principles were used by both blue- and white-collar workers. However, the groups differed as to their perceived importance of each of these principles when assessing equity. The groups agreed over the importance of 'disagreeability' and, to a lesser extent, 'ascription'. There was considerable disagreement, however, over the importance of 'contribution' and 'need'. Apparently, there is no one universal norm governing fairness.

The finding that different norms were used by different groups was also supported in a later study (Dornstein, 1989), which used a cross-sectional city sample of 222 Israeli employees.

It would appear that these basic orientations also apply in the UK. Dickinson (1991) used a sample of British business studies undergraduates who were asked to assess wage levels for a number of jobs, including for those unemployed. 'Need' was used by 50 per cent of subjects to justify increases in unemployment benefit or very low wages. All other suggested changes were in terms of 'effort' (53 per cent), 'training' (34 per cent), and 'importance to the community' (29 per cent), all of which can be interpreted as 'contributions'.

The norm of contribution appears, however, to be cultural. Hui *et al.* (1991) used an experimental comparison of reward allocation policies of Hong Kong Chinese and American undergraduate students. They used the 'need' and 'equity' rules to analyse reward distribution for the two cultures. The Chinese used the equality rule more than the Americans, who used equity. The explanation offered by the researchers is that Chinese society is more collectivist than the American, which tends to be highly individualistic.

EXCHANGE AND EQUITY THEORIES

The range of differing principles discussed above can be integrated using two closely related theories; *social exchange* theory and *equity* theory. These theories have applications across a wide range of human interaction, including the distribution of organizational rewards.

Exchange and equity are so closely related that they can be regarded as one theory, with equity being the more general. Both are based upon the apparently universal 'norm of reciprocity'. This norm requires like to be repaid with like. As has been mentioned previously, norms may be seen as both a description about what happens *and* a prescription concerning what should happen. Do people *feel* or *think* that it is right to reciprocate?; probably both.

Social exchange theory works on two very fundamental premises. First, that individuals will tend to engage in those actions that promise to be most profitable in terms of social rewards. On the surface, this would appear to be a very selfish reason for undertaking social interaction and, indeed, it would be, if it were not for the second premise, the norm of reciprocity. This requires that interactions have to be approximately equivalent for both parties over a period of time. If it is not, one of the parties will terminate the relationship.

The theory is, perhaps surprisingly, applicable to a wide range of situations – even marriage and friendship. There is considerable evidence to support the premise that, unless each partner gets roughly equivalent rewards (as defined by the person concerned) from the relationship, then it will end, in spirit if not in law. You may wonder what the rewards could possibly be in some partnerships of your acquaintance but, if they are stable, then they will be there. Another influence determining whether the partnership continues will also be the availability of other partnerships offering greater rewards. The balance is, however, complicated by the time spans over which reciprocity has to be established. Long-standing and close relationships can tolerate considerable periods where one partner is continually giving, while the other is only receiving. (In fact, one way to tell when a relationship is under stress is when the time scale over which the 'balance sheet' is balanced, shortens. In such situations the participants begin to expect almost immediate repayment of favours done, 'I cut the lawn for you, the least you could do for me is. . . '.)

It will probably not have escaped your attention that social exchange is very similar to economic exchange. They differ in some respects, but not in what might be thought to be the obvious way – the presence or absence of money. These differences are, in fact, the extent to which they are specific and formal. Economic exchanges, for example, are usually extremely formal and specific. Costs and benefits can be quantified, and equated one to the other. In addition, they can be openly discussed and indeed may be made legally enforceable through formal procedures. Social exchanges, on the other hand, are far more complex and diffuse, and are generally not enforceable by law. This is not to say, however, that a form of contract does not emerge informally. It is apparent, therefore, that the concept of social exchange can be seen as a major contributor to the concept of the psychological contract.

These two types of exchange are often confused, sometimes deliberately, more often unconsciously. Sales staff, for example, often try to establish social obligations through such techniques as using first names and taking an interest in personal aspects that are unconnected with the sale. This establishes, it is hoped, a feeling that this attention and interest has to be reciprocated, which will, the sales staff hope, make it more difficult for the potential customer to withdraw from the economic part of the exchange. The unconscious confusion of social and economic exchanges often occurs in work situations. As has been pointed out, we go to work for both economic and social reasons; usually the two can be kept separate, but the confusion becomes apparent when difficulties arise. It is often difficult, for example, for managers to discipline those with whom they have a strong personal relationship. The same can sometimes occur when we mix business and pleasure. Doing work on a commercial basis for a friend, or employing a friend, may bring the two into conflict.

Social exchange theory is a useful way of viewing interactions, but it has its limitations. *Equity theory* is an extension of social exchange theory that is made more general by the addition of two extra concepts: *equity ratios* and *investments*.

The main limitation of social exchange theory is the assumption that each party has to gain approximately equal 'absolute' benefits from the exchange. In equity theory, this is modified to state that the benefits of a situation are equitable when the ratio of inputs (e.g. effort) to outputs (e.g. pay) is approximately equal to others in a similar position. To use a rather simple example, someone who works a standard working week does not expect their pay-packet to be the same as a fellow worker who also works overtime. If the ratio of inputs to outputs balances, then all is well. If it does not balance, then the individual will experience tension. Tension is uncomfortable, leading the individual to take steps to reduce it. Again using pay as an example, let us see how tension can be reduced. Consider a situation where a person, or group of people, feels underpaid relative to those with whom they compare themselves. In such a situation there are two obvious, and one not so obvious, ways of restoring the balance. First, and most obvious, is to get a pay rise large enough to restore the balance. Second, if a pay rise is not possible, or is not large enough to restore the balance totally, then an alternative is to reduce the level of effort. The form this reduction will take will depend upon the payment scheme in operation. If the rewards are based upon the number of units produced (i.e. piecework), then it would obviously be counter-productive for the workers to produce fewer. In this case, something will suffer that does not affect wage levels, perhaps quality. If payment is by a time rate (i.e. hourly, weekly, monthly, or an annual salary), then output levels and/or quality may suffer. The same applies when the individual or group, rather than feeling under-rewarded, feels over-rewarded. This, in our experience, is rare! The reason for this can probably be explained by the third method of restoring balance.

We have said that people compare their ratio of inputs to outputs with other individuals or groups. This begs the question, of course, of which particular individual or group is chosen for comparative purposes, and there are many alternatives. You might, for example, compare yourself with others inside the organization or, alternatively, those outside the organization in similar jobs. You may also judge yourself against your own work history: 'I've done well compared with where I started'. This choice of individuals or groups against whom we compare ourselves is important, as it will affect our feelings of equity. If we compare our general life situation with the jet-set (or you may choose your own example here), we may feel somewhat dejected. If, on the other hand, we compare ourselves with most of the population of the Third World, or indeed disadvantaged groups in our own society, different feelings will be evoked about our own position. (Notice we do not say what the particular feelings will be, as these will vary from person to person.) By changing the group to which we refer, that is the *reference group*, we can move ourselves into or out of balance. The third way of restoring balance, therefore, is to change the reference group to one that produces a balance. This may often be overtly used in pay negotiations – 'Ah, but look how well you are doing compared with...'; which the other side often counters by choosing a less favourable example.

Research into which reference groups people choose for comparison suggests that the most important ones are those in the same, or similar, occupations in the 'market' as a whole (Dornstein, 1988). The ability of the organization to pay, and the individual's productive contribution to that organization, appear to play a negligible role in determining the perceived equity of rates of pay. This perhaps explains why workers in loss-making companies make wage claims that appear, to outsiders, not to be justified by the relevant performance indicators. There are, however, some exceptions to individual choice of reference groups. In particular, those who are in general 'satisfied' with the organization tend to compare themselves with others in the organization, rather than with those in the same occupation in other companies.

We have talked a good deal about equity, but if equity is based purely on a comparison between 'effort put in' and 'benefits taken out', there are situations where we all appear to accept apparent inequities. Most shop-floor workers, for example, do not see the difference between what they get paid for a week's work and what a professional person gets paid for a week's work as necessarily inequitable. Why? The answer lies in the second addition to exchange theory, that of *investments*.

'Investments' has a very similar meaning in equity theory to that in economics, in which an investment is something that has a value, and hence a return on that value is expected. Investments in equity theory are not so easy to quantify, however, as they can be anything that people think is an investment (Brown, 1986). Some of these are almost universally accepted; about others there is much disagreement. To return to Figure 4.3 at the beginning of this section, some people may consider 'disagreeability', 'length of service' (ascription), and 'family size' (need), to be investments. Length of service is often considered differently by employers and employees. This may not become apparent until something happens to highlight it. Forced redundancy, for example, often reveals the differing 'weighting' placed on length of service. It is not unusual to find long-serving workers reacting with comments that indicate that they consider their dedication and loyalty to the firm has not been adequately rewarded.

A widely accepted investment is qualifications and skills. The fact that someone has invested time and effort in obtaining them, means that they have investment value. Indeed, to obtain most qualifications, people have to forgo immediate financial rewards for benefits in the future.

Consider, on the other hand, the position of someone who has been 'passed over' for promotion. Such an individual may claim as investments things that those responsible for the decision may not accept. For example, an investment that is often claimed is that of long service – 'I've given my life to this company, and this is how they repay me! Many arguments concerning perceived inequity revolve around agreement as to what counts as an investment, and how great its value is.

Although we may feel intuitively that feelings of inequity will have negative effects, this needs empirical support.

Summers and Hendrix (1991) used a complicated statistical analysis to model the relationship between various 'inputs', (pay equity, pay satisfaction, job satisfaction, organizational commitment, intention to leave) and voluntary turnover. Their model was supported. Five of the input variables (salary level, job performance, pay valence, job level, and hours worked per week) were related to pay equity. The study suggests that pay equity does indeed have an influence on both job satisfaction and organizational commitment and, through these factors, on intention to leave and voluntary turnover.

Other studies have revealed other outcomes of perceived inequity. Cowherd and Levine (1992), for example, examined customer perceptions of product quality for 102 corporate business units. They found that the customer's assessment of the product was related to the degree of pay equity between lower level employees and upper level managers. This suggests that employees' perception of pay equity influences their motivation to produce high quality goods. Harder (1992) examined the effects of over-reward and under-reward on baseball and basketball players. Harder argues that baseball is essentially an individual-orientated sport. For baseball players most of the performance-related effects were found for over-reward. Those who felt over-rewarded performed better. Basketball, on the other hand, is a team sport and here the effects were different. Those players who felt over-rewarded demonstrated high levels of co-operation with their team-mates. Those who felt under-rewarded tended to play for themselves, rather than the team. This was deduced from the observation that those who felt under-rewarded took far more shots at the basket, but scored less. In other words, they were trying to increase their own scores when it would have been more effective to pass to a team member who was in a better position to score.

Greenberg and Ornstein (1983) found that even such things as job titles can have an effect on perceptions of equity. In experiments students were asked to perform proof-reading tasks. Some of the students were given extra job responsibilities, but also a high-status job title to go with it. It was found that the job title was seen as adequate compensation for the extra duties, but only for those students who felt they had earned it.

At this point it is perhaps worth referring to your answers for the case study on pay levels (*Appendix 3*). Comparisons can be made in two ways. First, the differences between different individuals, or groups of individuals. Second, between fair salary levels and actual salary levels. Each of these can be interpreted using the concepts described earlier, especially that of 'investments'. When managers do this exercise the biggest discrepancies between actual and fair levels occur for Devlin and Franks. For Devlin many perceive that they would be paid far more than would be 'fair'. This is reversed for Franks. Once again the question arises 'What counts as an investment?'

At a more general level, there is evidence to suggest that the perception of levels of pay, both by employees and the general public, is inaccurate. Headey (1991) carried out a study in Australia to investigate the relationships between actual incomes, peoples' estimates of incomes, and their assessment of 'fair' incomes, for a range of jobs. He found that the perception of incomes differed considerably from actual incomes. Whilst the perception of the income of primary school teachers was fairly accurate, others showed considerable inaccuracies. The incomes of shop assistants, for example, were over-estimated by 33 per cent. The income of managing directors of large companies, on the other hand, were under-estimated by 74 per cent! The question arises as to how people produced their estimates of salary levels. Headey's data show that there are far smaller differences between estimates of perceived incomes and 'fair' incomes. This suggests that, in the absence of information about income levels, people assume that they are 'fair', and use this as a basis for their estimates. It is interesting that following the disclosure of the salary levels in privatized utilities in the UK there was a public outcry about the inequity of such pay levels. Inequities were suddenly made salient.

Thus far we have been considering the *content* of the exchanges between individuals and organizations. More recently attention has moved away from the content of the exchange to the procedures associated with the exchange. Rather than considering distributive justice, the emphasis of theory and research has shifted to *procedural* justice.

Distributive equity focuses attention on the nature and level of what individuals and organizations exchange. Procedural equity, on the other hand, focuses on the *procedures* that are used to decide how various organizational benefits are distributed.

A particularly nice example of the effects of procedural justice is described by Greenberg (1990). This also has links to the concept of the psychological contract. (It might also serve as a salutary warning to some managers.) Greenberg was asked by the management of an manufacturing organization to look at the effects on the work-force of a particular decision that had been made. The parent company had three manufacturing plants in various parts of the mid-west of the USA. As the result of losing two large contracts the management was faced with temporarily having to reduce its wage bill. Rather than lay workers off, the management decided to impose a temporary cut in pay of 15 per cent in the two plants most affected by the loss of the orders. Rather bravely, the organization allowed Greenberg to write the explanations for the pay-cut that would be given to the workers. In each case the explanations were read out by the company president at a meeting held at the end of the working week. At one plant Greenberg wrote what he refers to as an 'adequate' explanation. A full explanation of the reasons for the pay-cut was given. Graphs and figures were produced to show the effect on company finances of the loss of the contracts. It was also stressed that it was hoped that the pay-cut would only last for 10 weeks. Remorse was expressed and it was pointed out that the 15 per cent cut would affect every member of the work-force, without favouritism. Approximately one hour was spent answering questions.

In the other plant an 'inadequate' explanation was given. The work-force was told that the cut was to be implemented and that it was hoped that it would last for only 10 weeks. Apart from saying that the reason had been the loss of the contracts, no other explanations were given. No statements of remorse were made and the meeting lasted 15 minutes.

Figures for staff turnover and levels of staff theft were collected for the periods 10 weeks before the pay-cut, the 10 weeks during which the pay-cut was operative, and the 10 weeks following the restoration of normal pay levels.

Data on employee theft showed interesting variations across the three plants. In the plant where there had been no pay-cut (and hence no explanation was needed) theft levels remained fairly constant at approximately 3 per cent. In the plant where an 'adequate' explanation had been given the theft rate rose from approximately 3 per cent in the 10 weeks before the pay-cut to approximately 4.8 per cent during the pay-cut. In the 10 weeks following the pay-cut it returned to the 3 per cent level. In the plant where an 'inadequate' explanation had been given the figure for the periods before and after the pay-cut were also 3 per cent. During the period of the pay-cut, on the other hand, it rose to 8 per cent!

The figures for staff turnover showed an even clearer pattern. In the 'adequate' explanation plant the number of people resigning remained constant. In the 10 weeks prior to the pay-cut, one person had resigned. During the pay-cut one person resigned and this figure was the same for the 10 weeks following the pay-cut. In the 'inadequate' explanation plant a different picture emerged. Only one person resigned in the 10 weeks prior to the pay-cut, and only two in the 10 weeks following it. During the period of the pay-cut, however, 12 people (23 per cent of the work-force) resigned.

There are, of course, a number of possible explanations for these effects. It is highly likely, however, that the reasons were associated with the differing explanations given to the work-force. In the plant where no pay-cut was implemented (technically called a 'control group'), levels of theft and resignations remained almost constant.

Greenberg's findings are entirely consistent with equity theory. The reduction in wages is compensated for by increased theft. There are two possible reasons why theft is used to 'restore' equity. For those items that can be sold, the effect is to increase the income of the thief. For those that cannot be sold, the effect is to reduce the assets of the organization. The increased thefts are also interpretable in terms of the psychological contract. The breach of the contract by the organization legitimizes, at least in the eyes of the thieves, the breaches by the work-force.

Greenberg's interpretation is that the increased levels of theft and staff turnover are caused by feelings of inequity concerning pay. This interpretation is supported by the results of questionnaires distributed to the employees during the pay-cut period. Those in the 'adequate' explanation plant reported lower levels of perceived pay inequity than those in the other plant where the pay-cut had taken place. What is also interesting is the difference in levels of theft between the two plants during the pay-cut. Where the 'adequate' explanation was given, the theft level did not rise as much. It would appear that the level of inequity in pay can be offset, to some extent, by the way in which the pay-cut is presented, i.e. procedural equity.

What is implicit in both the Greenberg and other studies is that the reasons given are legitimate. For example, in the Greenberg study it would appear that the employees believed the management's reasons for the temporary cut in pay, i.e. the loss of major contracts. The attribution of the cause is likely, therefore, to be external to the organization, i.e. market conditions. Little research has been carried out into this aspect of equity, but anecdotal evidence would suggest there are limits to the extent to which the management can blame 'external' factors. For example, the staff of many banks in the UK have seen the work-force cut and their conditions reduced over recent years. It would appear that many staff accepted these changes as being the result of 'market forces' (*The Guardian*, 3 June 1995). This may be changing. Customers' complaints have risen, as has the pay of top management. It may be, therefore, that proposed further changes are now seen as 'internally' caused. Rather than being seen as being aimed at improving customer service, or maintaining competitiveness, they are seen as a means of increasing already high profit levels. The resulting strikes may indicate staff perceptions of inequity. Procedural justice may mitigate the effects of distributive injustice, but only if the causes are seen as legitimate.

We have seen that both distributive justice and procedural justice have effects upon employees' attitudes and behaviour. Their effects however, are slightly different. Various studies (e.g. Folger and Knovsky, 1989; Moorman, 1991) have investigated the effects of both distributive justice and procedural justice. The results suggest that whilst distributive justice is associated with individual outcomes, such as satisfaction with pay, procedural justice is associated with organizational outcomes, such as organizational commitment. There is also an interactive effect. Satisfaction tends to be lowest when perceptions of both distributive justice and procedural justice are low. Low distributive justice may, however, not produce dissatisfaction as long as perceptions of procedural justice are high. As we have seen, people will tolerate some unfairness of distribution as long as the procedures that produced it are seen to be fair.

More generally, Tyler and Bies (1990) suggest five norms that contribute towards the perception of fairness:

- adequate consideration of the employees' viewpoint
- lack of personal bias by managers
- consistent application across all employees
- provision of timely feedback following a decision
- provision of an adequate explanation.

What implications does equity theory have for managers? Because feelings of over-reward are relatively uncommon, equity theory is most useful for demotivation situations. In such situations its value is as a diagnostic aid, identifying the ratios and investments concerned. The recent research by Dornstein into reference groups gives some insight into why some groups of workers make wage demands that the organization obviously cannot afford. Rather than comparing themselves with people in different jobs in the same organization, it appears that most of those in Dornstein's study compared themselves with those in similar jobs in other organizations, and with wage rates in the 'market' in general. Wage demands are based, therefore, on general market conditions and what is happening to wages in similar jobs elsewhere, rather than on the organization's profitability.

The other important implication is that procedural justice is important. In other words the *way* in which decisions affecting perceived equity are explained and implemented by management is important. On the evidence of Greenberg it is obvious that negative reactions to undesirable, if necessary, changes can be reduced by providing proper explanations.

MOTIVATION AND THE PSYCHOLOGICAL CONTRACT

The earlier motivation theories that we have discussed in this chapter concerned themselves mainly with the 'needs' that people seek to satisfy at work. The basic needs are, of course, satisfied by the medium of money. Work is exchanged for money, which itself can be exchanged for the necessities of life. Often, little is said in the formal contract about the opportunities available for the satisfaction of higher-order needs. Yet it is in the satisfaction of these higher-order needs that most people find their greatest satisfaction and where motivation is, potentially, at its highest. It is also likely that the opportunity for their satisfaction is an important element in the psychological contract. These may often be overlooked. Social needs, for example, are often neglected in the organization of work. Even small changes in the physical environment or the organization of work may disrupt long-established social networks. Sometimes it may be desirable to disrupt these if, for example, they are interfering with the effectiveness of the organization. More often, however, they are not ineffective, and may even add to the organizational effectiveness. The re-organization of work should always take into account the social effects, as well as the effects on work-flow.

Perhaps the most obvious link between the psychological contract and motivation is evident in equity theory. The study by Greenberg shows clearly how the breach of what is perceived to be the psychological contract can have dramatic effects on worker behaviour. No formal contract *required* the management to give a full and proper explanation of their action in temporarily cutting wages. Yet the failure to do so generated what can be seen as a tit-for-tat response from the work-force. The perceived breach of the psychological contract by management was matched by the work-force. The message to management is clear – breach of the psychological contract is likely to have a cost, just as would breach of a formal contract.

Behavioural Approaches to Motivation

GOAL-SETTING THEORY

Goal-setting theory is at present one of the most influential theories of motivation, yet it is based upon fundamentally simple assumptions.

The name most commonly associated with goal-setting is that of Locke. According to Locke (Locke and Latham, 1984), satisfaction comes from achieving specific goals. The harder these goals are to achieve, the greater the effort and subsequent satisfaction. There is considerable evidence to support these contentions (Locke and Latham, 1991); but first, how does goal-setting work?

It works, according to Locke by

- directing attention
- facilitating a search for appropriate methods
- mobilizing and maintaining effort.

The effect of directing attention towards the task involved is, of course, necessary if the task is to be undertaken. It also has the effect of removing uncertainty about precisely what is expected. Once attention is directed, there has to be a search for appropriate methods of task attainment. When the task is clear and precise it is possible to rule out a large number of alternative strategies and concentrate on those most directly relevant. Finally, goal-setting mobilizes and maintains effort. The fundamental and simple assumption behind the theory is that people will do what they say they will do, and will strive hard to do it!

Goal-setting appears to many managers to be little more than applied common sense, but let us look a little closer. Within the description of why goal-setting works, lies another suggestion about the effectiveness of goal-setting that is borne out by a mass of evidence. That is, the more specifically the goal is stated, the more positive the effects. Goals along the lines of 'do your best' are not effective in directing attention and helping to choose appropriate strategies. The more specific the goal, the better.

There is a wealth of evidence from experimental and 'real-life' studies that supports the basic theory of goal-setting (Locke and Henne, 1986). However, discussion about the theory continues. Recently, this discussion has focused on a specific aspect of the theory; the effects of participation, and goal difficulty.

PARTICIPATION IN GOAL-SETTING

Locke's original distinction between the way goals were set was that of 'assigned' versus 'participative' goal-setting. An assigned goal is one in which there is no discussion with the individual. A participatively set goal, on the other hand, involves the individual in decisions about the goal. Surprisingly, perhaps, initial studies suggest that whether the goal was assigned or set participatively had little effect on performance and goal attainment (Locke and Henne, 1986). Further research has suggested that this is indeed the case, as long as the goal is *accepted* by the individual to whom it applies. This has led to considerable discussion and experimentation about the factors that influence goal acceptance.

One explanation was provided by Locke and his co-workers. For Locke, perhaps the central concept of goal-setting theory is that of 'goal difficulty'. Participation, it is argued, leads to an increase in the level of goal difficulty, thus leading to improved performance. As long as assigned goals are accepted, more difficult goals will also lead to improved performance. Hence there is no difference in the effects of goals that are participatively set, and assigned goals that are accepted. Locke and his colleagues have shown that this does appear to be the case (Latham and Saari, 1982). For similar levels of accepted goals, there was no difference in performance between those that had been assigned and those that had been set participatively.

Other researchers, however, have found that those who have been involved in setting their own goals perform better. According to this view, participation affects performance not through the effect of more difficult goals, but through the *commitment* generated by the participation. As we shall see in a later chapter, it is accepted, almost without question, that participation improves commitment. Many people will have experienced this effect. The opportunity to express their views and to have some control over the goals they are set, seems to have a positive effect on most people's commitment.

Recently this debate appears to have been resolved as the result of a number of joint studies (e.g. Latham *et al.*, 1988). The results of these studies suggest that the major difference between assigned and participatively set goals is the extent to which a reason, or rationale, is provided for the goals being set. It would appear that the critical feature required for goal acceptance is the provision of a *reason*. This reinforces the findings of Greenberg (see pages 135–137) concerning the importance of providing employees with acceptable explanations for managerial actions.

FEEDBACK

So far, nothing has been said about letting people know how close they are to achieving their goal – in other words *feedback*. It has been shown that feedback by itself can lead to higher levels of performance, as does goal-setting by itself. However, the two together are more powerful still. Feedback allows people to plot their own performance. However, it does not have a significant effect on those who are 'on target'; rather it leads to increased effort by those who are falling short.

This, in summary, is goal-setting theory. Its message is simple: set specific, difficult goals that are accepted. In order to gain goal acceptance, the minimum that a manager should do is to provide a clear and understandable rationale for the goals being set. Ideally, however, the goals should be set participatively. (This may not always be possible, a point we will return to in the chapter on leadership.) He should also provide feedback to his people on how they are progressing. As we have said, this sounds simple, but in our experience it is rarely implemented. This contention is supported by the reported experiences of many hundreds of managers attending courses that we have run. With few exceptions, managers at all levels claim that their goals are not clear, and that their boss never tells them how they are doing. And if this feeling is as universal as our experiences suggest, their subordinates would say exactly the same about them!

Many managers will have noticed the similarities between Locke's goal-setting and Peter Drucker's management by objectives (1954). As some commentators have said, MBO is as desirable as 'the flag, motherhood, and apple pie', but the evidence for its long-term effectiveness is largely anecdotal. Many schemes have been implemented, but few have lasted long. The reasons for this are not entirely clear. Our suspicion is that one reason why the schemes fail is because of the lack of specificity in the 'objectives'. Too often objectives are set that, whilst apparently specific, are not actually so. They are too broad, such as 'increase profit margins by X per cent'. The problem with such an objective is that the many ways of achieving it mean that effort is dispersed. In addition, factors that are not under the control of the person involved may influence the goal, hence responsibility is diffused. The result is that the system becomes discredited and gradually falls into disuse. Perhaps the initial emphasis in any goal-setting or MBO system is to set goals that are *specific* – 'develop a scheme to reduce the processing time of routine orders in your department from five days to three days!'.

Goals, as in goal-setting, tend to be expressed in terms of *outcomes*, which are usually expressed as performance levels. But should goals be expressed in this way?

PERFORMANCE OR BEHAVIOUR?

In many of the preceding sections we have talked, rather easily, about 'performance'. Most managers feel that motivation is concerned with obtaining high performance levels from their staff. The term 'performance', however, is not without its difficulties. As we saw in Chapter 1, developing reliable and accurate measures of performance is fraught with problems. For this reason many theorists and practitioners have moved away from measuring performance to measuring behaviour (see Kanfer, 1992). The change may appear to be small, but it has significant implications.

What is measured is behaviour, not the *outcomes* of behaviour. For example, rewarding shop assistants on their level of sales is fraught with problems, not only the problems mentioned above but others also. For example, it is likely that if rewards are based on individual sales levels, assistants will begin to compete with each other. This may have effects that are detrimental to the organization as a whole. For example, assistants will try to avoid performing necessary, but not sales-related activities, such as stock replacement or tidying. The rewarding of behaviour does not have the same inherent problems. A range of behaviours can be rewarded that, taken together, are likely to lead to good sales figures. For example, sales assistants should be close to the merchandise or the point of sale, and customers should be offered assistance if they need it. (For an example of where this approach has been used to improve performance see Komaki *et al.*, 1977.)

This technique, of using behaviour rather than performance as a measure or criterion, has been used in many motivational theories. It also forms a central part of 'organizational behaviour modification'.

ORGANIZATIONAL BEHAVIOUR MODIFICATION

Organizational behaviour modification (referred to as OBMod, for short) developed separately from goal-setting, and has different explanations for behaviour. Nevertheless, in recent years links have developed between the two that make them a powerful combination.

In the chapter on personality we looked at internal, dispositional approaches to understanding behaviour. Organizational behaviour modification, on the other hand, takes a situational, or external, approach. It concentrates on *behaviour* and the events in the environment that encourage or discourage such behaviour, rather than on attitudes or personality.

We have already dealt, in Chapter 2, with the links between personality and behaviour, but what of attitudes? Once again, the assumption underlying the internal, dispositional approach is that attitudes cause behaviour. This assumption, as we have seen, is questionable. There is considerable evidence to show that there is a fairly weak relationship between attitudes and behaviour. Indeed, attitudes often express how we think we would *like* to see ourselves behaving than rather how we *actually* behave. For example, attitude surveys suggest that the general public is against the invasion of privacy by the press. However, newspaper editors have firm evidence that the pictures and stories resulting from such invasions increase sales. Alistair Cooke has reported that over 70 per cent of the American public thought that television coverage of the pre-trial of the American hero O. J. Simpson was undesirable. But over 90 per cent had watched it!

It also appears that the assumption that attitudes cause behaviour is only part of the picture. There is evidence from psychological research to suggest that behaviour can influence the formation and change of attitudes. The attitude/behaviour relationship is interactive. For example, before the wearing of seat-belts was made compulsory, the UK government spent considerable sums of money trying to change the public's attitude to seat-belt wearing. Despite many different publicity campaigns the level of seat-belt usage remained depressingly low. Upon the introduction of legislation making seat-belt wearing compulsory, with financial and other penalties for non-compliance, usage leapt to almost 100 per cent. Although we have no direct evidence, we suspect that this change in behaviour also produced a change in attitude toward seat-belt usage. The same may be true for drinking and driving.

There are a number of possible explanations of why the way we behave should influence our attitudes, but perhaps the most appealing involves the concept of consistency. We like to be consistent and keep our behaviours and attitudes in line with each other. If we behave in a particular way we feel that this must be a representation of our attitudes.

The OBMod approach, therefore, ignores attitudes and personality and concentrates solely upon observable behaviour.

Exercise
Before reading further, you should turn to Appendix 4 and attempt the case study on absenteeism.

The basic postulate of OBMod can be stated very simply — so simply that some may say it is just applied common sense. It is that *behaviour is determined by its consequences*. In other words, people learn to behave in ways that produce rewards, and avoid behaving in ways that produce either no rewards or even punishment. Inevitably, managers will already be using some of the techniques that will be discussed, but without being aware of their theoretical background. By providing a theoretical structure, we will enable managers to make more effective use of the techniques.

OBMod is based on the work of psychologists who studied learning, or to use the technical term, *conditioning*. In particular, the names most commonly associated with the theory are those of Thorndike and, perhaps most commonly, Skinner. Skinner takes the approach that since we cannot observe mental states such as attitudes and personality traits, we should concern ourselves only with observable behaviour. If we extend this to the work situation, what managers should be concerned with is not employees' attitudes, but how they behave (i.e. what they *do*). It is often difficult to get managers to talk only of behaviour. They often, quite understandably, slip into talking about personalities and attitudes. But employees' attitudes should not be the manager's concern, as long as they are behaving correctly. Organizations do not pay people for the attitudes they hold, but for their behaviour. As such, we are perfectly justified in asking someone to behave differently. We are not justified in trying to change their personality or attitudes, even if we could! We cannot change personality; we can change behaviour. As with goal-setting, however, the required behaviour must be described as precisely as possible.

We have said that behaviour is determined by its consequences. How can these be classified? The possible range is shown below:

- we receive something nice
- something nasty is taken away
- something nice is taken away
- something nasty is given

	NICE	NASTY
GIVE	Positive reinforcement	Punishment
TAKE AWAY	Punishment	Negative reinforcement

Figure 5.1. Classification of reinforcement and punishment.
(Adapted from: Kazdin, 1994)

The first two consequences lead to an increase in the behaviour that preceded them. To use the correct technical term, they are *reinforcers*, because they reinforce the behaviour concerned. The first, giving something nice, is called positive reinforcement; the second, negative reinforcement, because something nasty is taken away. The last two are different forms of punishment. They will tend to suppress the behaviour that occurs before them.

All of these may be neatly summarized in a diagram, as shown in Figure 5.1. There is one outcome, however, that will not fit into the diagram, that is if, following the behaviour, it is neither rewarded nor punished. This will lead to the behaviour not being repeated.

Most managers, we find, are fairly happy with positive reinforcement, but negative reinforcement is not as clear. Let us take an example from parenthood. We find it unpleasant when a baby cries. If, by picking the baby up, we stop it crying, we will pick it up the next time it cries. Stopping the cries negatively reinforces our behaviour of picking the baby up, as it stops the nastiness. (Note that, from the baby's point of view, being picked up is nice and hence the crying is positively reinforced. Next time the baby wants to be picked up, it will cry.) Another familiar example is a fire alarm. The loud noise of the alarm is unpleasant and people will try to escape from it. They do so by getting out of the building; leaving the building has been negatively reinforced – the noise stops.

Now that the range of possible consequences has been described, let us consider how effective each one can be at influencing behaviour. This is where, in some respects, common sense and psychology part company. We think you will agree, after considering the arguments, that psychology has the more accurate explanation.

The effectiveness of each of the consequences is largely determined by how frequently it follows, or does not follow, each occurrence of the behaviour. These patterns of how frequently behaviour is rewarded or punished are called *schedules*.

How to maintain behaviour. If we are trying to get someone to learn a new behaviour then it is appropriate to reinforce their successful attempts every time they occur; but what about maintaining behaviour that has already been learnt? Consider a schedule that has already been learnt, where the behaviour is rewarded, let us say, every twenty times it occurs. For example, pulling a lever to obtain a reward. If the mechanism was switched off, how quickly would you realize there was no point in pulling the lever any more? Probably after between 20 and 40 further pulls. Now consider the situation where the reward occurs *on average* every twenty times. The reward could be on the next pull of the lever or many hundreds of pulls later. To determine when this mechanism had been switched off would take a very long time indeed. This is the principle, of course, of one-armed bandit machines. This is also why you keep being trapped by the company 'bore'. You have only to reward them by paying attention once every so often and they will continue to pester you. This is called *variable ratio reinforcement*. Variable ratio reinforcement is far more effective in maintaining behaviour, even undesirable behaviour, than reinforcement that occurs every time (*fixed ratio reinforcement*). The person knows it will pay off at some time, so they keep trying.

(As well as fixed and variable ratios, there can also be fixed and variable times. The effects are similar; fixed time reinforcement is a relatively ineffective way of maintaining behaviour. It remains, of course, the most common way of paying salaries.)

How to stop undesirable behaviour. What options are open to us if we now want to stop undesirable behaviour? The strategies available are those of punishment and non-reward. (Notice here that non-reward is not the same as ignoring. Non-reward means that the person gets no benefit whatsoever as a result of their behaviour.) Which of these strategies, non-reward or punishment, is likely to be more effective in changing behaviour?

All the evidence suggests that non-reward leads to the behaviour being *extinguished*; punishment merely suppresses it. This is not to say that punishment is never effective. Punishment, by itself, can be effective under certain conditions. (When reading further it might be instructive to think of the ways in which society tries to suppress crime.)

Unfortunately for managers (and perhaps for society in general), the ways in which rewards and punishment influence behaviour are not the same. For rewards to be effective in maintaining behaviour they need occur only every so often. (Think of the fruit machine as an example.) Punishment, on the other hand, has to fulfil two criteria if it is to be effective. It must occur *every time* the behaviour occurs, and *as soon as possible* after the behaviour. This may help us understand why hangovers rarely have a long-term influence over drinking habits. The rewards of drinking to excess are immediate, the punishment is some way off. In addition, you may sometimes escape without having a hangover. (Interestingly, one way of treating alcoholics is to use drugs that produce an unpleasant effect immediately after any alcohol is consumed.) The same argument applies to many aspects of preventive medicine, e.g. smoking, diet, etc. The rewards are immediate, the possible negative consequences some way off. It is unlikely that teenagers' smoking habits will be influenced by the prospect of lung disease when they are old.

To summarize: to keep undesirable behaviour going it needs to be reinforced only once every so often (variable ratio reinforcement), to stop it by using punishment requires punishment to be administered every time. It is hardly surprising that prisons are a highly ineffective way of influencing the behaviour of criminals.

As an example of how organizations attempt to use punishment, take the case of trying to deal with persistent lateness by a particular individual. One method commonly used is the memo. A memo pointing out the requirements for strict time-keeping is sent to everyone, including the culprit. This may affect the culprit's behaviour for a short time, but they will then start re-offending. The other effect it will have is on those who are innocent, who may arrive late occasionally but do not abuse the system, and who compensate by working into their lunch break. Often these individuals will rebel, working strictly to the clock.

The other common method is to ignore the problem in its early stages. Each individual late arrival is recorded, but is not commented on. When an unacceptable number have accumulated a 'trigger point' is reached. This is normally a specified number of latenesses over a specified period. What follows is a gradual escalation of punishment. Oral warnings are followed by written warnings. These are then followed by formal dismissal procedures. Under these circumstances, punishment is unlikely to be effective. For it to be so, the individual needs be made aware that each and every incidence will be questioned as soon as it occurs, and that moderate sanctions will be applied. (Very harsh sanctions would probably lead to avoidance through absenteeism.)

It should be apparent that the conditions for using punishment or discipline effectively are very limited. Managers, and other individuals with responsibility for enforcement, are rarely in a position where they can monitor people all the time. The difficulties associated with the effective use of punishment lead us, therefore, to the following conclusion:

Schemes should concentrate on the encouragement of desirable behaviour rather than trying to use discipline to eliminate the undesirable.

So far we have been considering the effects of punishment alone. Most effective, however, is when punishment for the undesirable behaviour is coupled with reinforcement of the desired behaviour. Under such circumstances the punishment does not have to fulfil the requirements just described; even mild and infrequent punishment will be effective. Just raised eyebrows from a boss who uses reinforcement effectively will be enough to discourage unwanted behaviour.

Now that we have dealt with the basic concepts, let us consider some applications. One nice example of the difference between fixed ratio and variable ratio reinforcement is one that will be immediately applicable, if you want to improve the productivity of beaver trappers! One group of beaver trappers in the Canadian forests were given a $1 bonus for every beaver skin. Another similar group were given the chance to roll dice each time they brought in a skin. If they rolled two successive odd numbers they got $4. The cost of each of the schemes was the same. Productivity in the first group rose by 50 per cent, in the latter group by 108 per cent (Saari and Latham, 1982).

Another area in which OBMod has been used is in dealing with absenteeism and lateness. At this point you should turn to your suggestions for solving the problem at Chestnut hospital (Appendix 4). We suspect that you will have adopted a *medical* model (no pun intended) in trying to solve the problem. Such a model sees absenteeism as a symptom of some underlying problem. The assumption is that absenteeism is a symptom of dissatisfaction with some aspect, or aspects, of the job. The solution, therefore, is to improve job satisfaction. This may indeed have some impact, but there is often a limit to what can be done to improve satisfaction. Shift-work still needs to be worked, and many other 'dirty' and undesirable jobs need to be done. In addition, the rewards for staying away from work are powerful, and rarely capable of being influenced by management.

OBMod, on the other hand, looks not at the *influences* that are thought to underlie absenteeism, but rather at the *consequences* to the employee of attendance or non-attendance. It adopts a 'direct action' model. Let us consider some possibilities.

Some schemes have used reinforcement as an alternative. One such example was reported from a factory in Liverpool. The factory was to be closed and the production lines transferred to another part of the country. The workers were under notice of redundancy, but it was essential that production be maintained until the new factory was in production. Unfortunately, the factory was suffering absenteeism levels of 30 per cent and above, due to a 'mystery virus' that appeared to strike mainly on Mondays and Fridays. Because of the law relating to redundancy, pay could not be stopped for these absences. In order to improve attendance, management instituted a weekly prize draw of £500. Participation in the draw was by means of tickets. Each employee received a draw ticket whenever they attended for work on time. Absenteeism dropped to very low levels and the management reported that workers were even turning up on their days off in order to collect tickets. Other schemes have used a cash bonus, paid to every employee who had attended on a number of randomly selected days during a set period – the random choice of days provided the variable ratio.

These further examples demonstrate one of the conditions under which such reinforcement works best; the expenditure of a little additional investment on the part of the individual, together with the potential for a large pay-out – for example football pools and national lotteries. Indeed, the use of prize draws is widely used as a marketing technique.

Some managers object to such schemes on the basis that you are paying people extra to do what they are already being paid to do. This is a perfectly legitimate position to take. If, however, you have tried everything else, what do you do? Your principles may also have a cost – continuing high levels of absenteeism.

It is perhaps worth noting the contrast between schemes that reward attendance, and those that punish absenteeism. Schemes that use punishment usually do so by giving an attendance bonus and then removing it for an absence. (On initial inspection the attendance bonus may sound like a reward, but this was not the way it was perceived, as we shall see.) For example, managers recently tried to improve the attendance of a group of UK civil servants (driving test examiners) by giving a £30 weekly bonus for attendance. The whole sum was forfeited for any non-attendance during the week, no matter what the reason for the absence. The scheme provoked a national one-day strike! It might be worth considering how this, not inconsiderable, sum could have been used to improve attendance by variable ratio reinforcement.

An interesting example of the removal of reinforcers was reported by the Merseyside police. They used to concentrate upon catching those who were stealing car stereo equipment, to little effect. They then switched their strategy to that of identifying those cars whose owners might have purchased stolen stereos. They examined parked cars, looking for incongruities, for example, an old car with a high priced modern stereo, and then contacted the owners for an explanation. As soon as it became known that this was happening, the market for stolen stereos declined sharply.

It is very common, in fact, to find organizations actually rewarding the very behaviour that they say they wish to discourage. Some organizations, for example, give annual budgets to departments. If it is not all spent, it is reclaimed by the centre and next year's budget is cut. As the manager of such a department what do you logically do in these circumstances? – you spend up to your budget limit!

There are also organizations which use positive reinforcement effectively, perhaps without knowing the terminology involved. One of them employs tanker drivers to deliver hazardous liquids and gases to customers. These are delivered through complicated valves and pipes that transfer the chemicals from the tanker to the customer's tanks. Drivers who phone for advice receive a bonus each time they do so. It might be thought that this would encourage drivers to phone for trivial reasons and, indeed, the system may be open to some abuse. Consider however, the situation that may occur where workers are discouraged from asking, usually because they fear some form of punishment, even if only ridicule. Which costs would the company rather bear – some trivial requests for advice, or a tanker exploding in a city street?

The other examples are from two organizations which are probably aware of the theoretical background. Both are large American organizations – Xerox and American Airlines. At Xerox, 'X' certificates, redeemable for $25, were introduced into the personnel department. Every member of the department, not just managers, could give Xs to others. They could be given for any work-related behaviour, for example excellent attendance or co-operation. They could also be given to people in other departments. At American Airlines, passengers are given coupons that they may give to staff whom they feel deserve some recognition. (We are not sure how effectively these schemes might transplant to the culture of the UK.)

A final example concerns the problems associated with routine maintenance procedures (Komaki et al., 1977). All the rewards and punishments are geared to encourage short-cuts. If a part is not checked, it will probably be all right anyway, and the mechanic saves time right now. In addition, there is no reinforcer to encourage them to carry out the checks as specified. If something does eventually go wrong, then what evidence is there to rebut the claim that 'it seemed all right when checked'? The evidence of successive reports by the consumer magazine Which? on the quality of car servicing by garages lends strong support to our analysis.

All of these examples show how behaviour may be influenced by reinforcers, but what different types of reinforcers are there?

REINFORCERS

Reinforcers may be classified in a number of ways. Perhaps the most basic distinction is between primary, secondary, and generalized. *Primary reinforcers* are those that are essential for life, such ₃s food, water, etc. They equate closely to the physiological level of Maslow's hierarchy. For this reason they are common to everyone. Unfortunately they may quickly lose their effectiveness as reinforcers. This process is known as *satiation*. Food, for example, is only a reinforcer if you are hungry. Immediately after a big meal the prospect of food is unlikely to be reinforcing. *Secondary reinforcers* gain their reinforcing strength through association with primary reinforcers. Social reinforcers such as attention and praise originally gained their reinforcing value because other people, e.g. parents, were the source of primary reinforcers. Other reinforcers may gain their power from social reinforcers. Status symbols, for example, are reinforcing because they are approved of by a social group that is important to the individual. Finally, *generalized reinforcers* are so called because of their general effect. The best example is money. This is reinforcing for most people because it can be exchanged for items that they find reinforcing. For this reason generalized reinforcers are particularly powerful. In organizations, however, secondary reinforcers are widely used. We will return to this shortly.

Another important distinction between reinforcers has already been considered briefly in the sections on Herzberg and the Job characteristics model (see Chapter 4). This is the distinction between 'intrinsic' and 'extrinsic' motivators.

INTRINSIC VERSUS EXTRINSIC REINFORCERS

The difference between intrinsic and extrinsic reinforcers lies in whether they originate from the job itself, or from external sources. This distinction is not always clear-cut. As we shall see, some reinforcers may have elements of both.

Perhaps a good example of intrinsic reinforcement is provided by computer games especially, it would appear, for adolescent males. The rewards are so powerful that for some the games become almost addictive. This reinforcement is also an example of what Bandura (1986) would call a 'naturally-occurring' reinforcer. Such reinforcers follow automatically from the behaviour concerned. Many intrinsic reinforcers are naturally-occurring.

Unlike intrinsic reinforcement, extrinsic reinforcement has to be provided 'artificially'. Pay is perhaps the classic example of an extrinsic reinforcer. Behaviour does not automatically produce pay as reinforcement. Administrative schemes have to be developed to ensure that it is delivered.

According to Deci (1975), the distinction between intrinsic and extrinsic reinforcement is not one of merely academic interest. It has considerable practical implications.

Intrinsic reinforcement is, other things being equal, more powerful than extrinsic reinforcement. It is also, from the organization's point of view, the most cost-effective. If individuals get high levels of reinforcement just from doing the job, they are likely to do the job more effectively. As we have seen, jobs can be redesigned so as to enhance such intrinsic reinforcement. It would, however, be naïve to assume that everyone can have a job that is intrinsically reinforcing. For those in this fortunate situation, doing the job is a pleasure in itself.

What happens when extrinsic motivation, such as pay, is 'added' to a task that is already intrinsically reinforcing? According to Deci (1975) the effect of introducing the extrinsic reinforcer is to 'undermine' the strength of the intrinsic reinforcer. If you start paying people for doing things that they presently do because they enjoy doing them, you will reduce the level of intrinsic reinforcement. Individuals, when given such extrinsic reinforcement, seem to switch from being intrinsically motivated, to being extrinsically motivated. This is likely to mean that once you have started extrinsic reinforcement, you will have to continue with it if you want the behaviour to continue. You will not be able to rely on a return to intrinsic motivation producing the same levels of effort.

Whilst initial studies tended to support Deci's theory, later work suggests that the effects of extrinsic reinforcement are not as simple as originally thought. Pay, for example, does not always reduce intrinsic motivation. As a result of these, and other, findings, Deci modified and elaborated his ideas into what is now known as cognitive evaluation theory' (Deci and Ryan, 1980).

Cognitive evaluation theory makes the same basic distinction between intrinsic and extrinsic. It now, however, makes a further distinction between two different types of extrinsic reinforcement. Extrinsic reinforcers may be classified, according to Deci, according to whether they are *controlling* or *informational*. Controlling extrinsic motivation will reduce intrinsic motivation; informational extrinsic reinforcers will not reduce it, and may even enhance it. Information, especially that which is seen as providing evidence of personal competence, appears to enhance intrinsic motivation. On the other hand, people tend to resent being controlled.

Like other aspects of reinforcers, whether they are controlling or informational cannot be determined objectively. Pay, for example, can be seen as either. Pay may be perceived as a method of control – a bribe to behave in a particular way. Alternatively, it may be seen as a source of information, indicating how management evaluates behaviour or performance. Whether it is perceived as controlling, informational, or a mixture of the two, is something that can only be determined *subjectively*. The individual's perception of its nature is what counts. Two individuals may perceive the same pay rise in different ways. This will influence their behaviour. It will obviously be in the organization's interest to ensure that reinforcers are perceived as informational rather than controlling.

The subjective nature of reinforcers is important. Many managers make the assumption that everybody's reinforcers are the same. Indeed, they usually assume that they are the same as their own (another example of the false consensus effect, see page 99). Some reinforcers are, indeed, almost universal. Money is a good example; like most universal reinforcers, it is an example of a generalized reinforcer – it can be exchanged for other things that people want. If, however, the pay-off was a night at the opera, how would you feel? Different people will have different reactions. Some reinforcers are difficult for others to understand. For example, adolescent children often get reinforcement from 'winding up' their parents. The parents find this difficult to understand as they feel that by shouting at their children and sending them to their room, they are punishing them. It may also 'pay off' because, when such arguments occur, real issues can be avoided. (This is 'uproar' in TA terms – page 104.) To take an example that applies to many societies, what are the reinforcers for the hooliganism of a minority of male adolescents? The only method of accurately determining what the reinforcers are is to remove potential reinforcers. When the behaviour stops, you have found the key. We can, however, speculate as to what they might be. It is quite likely that group approval is involved. As we shall see later, social rewards are amongst the strongest reinforcers known. The disapproval of society may, strange as it may seem, also be a potential reinforcer. Appearing in court or in the media may be reinforcing – much like the adolescent and parent situation described earlier. Given that these are some of the potential reinforcers, what can society do about it? As we have seen, punishment is unlikely to be effective. In order for it to work it must occur every time the disruptive behaviour occurs. This is almost certainly impossible. We may be able to remove some of the reinforcers, for example, media coverage. But perhaps the only effective method is to change the hooligans' perception of what is reinforcing for them.

SOCIAL COGNITIVE THEORY

Exercise

Before reading further, please complete the career questionnaire in Appendix 5.

Earlier in this chapter we reminded you of the distinction between internal and external explanations for people's behaviour. Personality theory in general tends to seek an internal explanation for why people behave as they do. OBMod, on the other hand, tends to concentrate on the situation. In its most radical form (e.g. Skinner, 1993), the importance of internal, cognitive and affective (i.e. emotional), factors are discounted altogether. This dichotomy, between either totally internal or totally external explanations is, however, false. Internal and external, as we have seen in the chapter on personality, interact with each other.

In behavioural theory this interactionist approach is best expressed in 'social cognitive theory.' This was developed by Bandura (1986), and grew out of his earlier social learning theory.

Social learning theory sought to explain some elements of behaviour that did not appear explicable in terms of 'radical' behaviourist theory. For example, it is not unusual to observe someone perform a complex sequence of behaviours without there being of any evidence of them having been previously reinforced. Adolescents who are keen to start driving often have a very good idea of what to do in their first driving lesson, despite never having driven before. Radical behaviourist theory would require that these complex behaviours be shaped. Cruder, and then increasingly more accurate approximations to each of the behaviours in the complex sequence of 'driving a car' would need to have been reinforced. Yet the evidence is that learning seems to have taken place, without the behaviour being undertaken and reinforced. This suggests that other processes are taking place.

It would appear that learning can take place cognitively, rather than behaviourally. We do not apparently have to undertake the behaviour in order to learn. Nor do we have to experience reinforcement, or punishment, directly. We can learn indirectly or, to use Bandura's term, *vicariously*. For example, when joining a new company we do not attempt to find out what the norms are about time-keeping, by arriving five minutes later each day until someone in authority objects. Rather, we observe what behaviour in others is rewarded or punished. In other words, we learn vicariously by watching other people. We assume that if we follow their examples we will reap the same rewards, and avoid possible punishment. This process – learning in the absence of any observable behaviour – was originally called modelling. It is now more commonly referred to as *mastery modelling*.

MASTERY MODELLING

The central concept of mastery modelling, as we have seen, is that of vicarious learning. What cognitive processes underlie such learning, and what implications do they have for organizations?

The cognitive mechanisms of mastery modelling are relatively simple. First we have to pay *attention* to the behaviour we wish to model. Second, we set up a *cognitive representation* of the behaviour, a sort of mental plan of action. Then we may *cognitively rehearse* the behaviour. At this point we have to decide whether to try out the behaviour 'for real'. Whether or not it will be tried will depend upon perceptions of the likely consequences. We can mentally rehearse driving a car at very high speed. Most of us do not actually drive at such a speed because we can imagine the possible consequences.

An important distinction needs to be made between modelling and mimicry. Modelling is not just mimicry. The cognitive representation stage of behaviour modelling gives scope for innovation and change. Cognitive representation involves the creation of an abstract model, and this abstract model can be modified so as to allow for experimentation. Such experimentation is essential if people are to adapt the general models to their own particular circumstances. The mental model that the adolescent has of car driving may need to be modified. If they have modelled their behaviour on a driver using a manual gear-change, they may have to adjust when faced with an automatic.

This requirement for adaptation, experimentation, and innovation means that in general it is better to model 'general rules', rather than 'specific skills'. Behaviour that is controlled by an understanding of underlying principles will be capable of greater flexibility. There are, it is true, some situations where there is a single, unchanging, skill that can be taught, but these situations are becoming rarer. For example, the acquisition of typing skills does not need an understanding of the principles of the typewriter. With word processors the situation has changed. Operators will certainly need to understand the operation of a specific word processing package. It is likely, however, that they will need to use other packages. A knowledge of the general principles behind the operation of all packages will obviously be of great assistance when they come to interact with other systems.

Two other important requirements for successful mastery modelling are those of *guided practice* and *early success*. Guided practice allows the development of learning in a non-threatening environment where feedback can be given, and received, in a climate of mutual trust. Early success is essential if the individual is to develop feelings of *self-efficacy*.

SELF-EFFICACY

Self-efficacy is a *set of beliefs* about one's ability 'to organize and execute courses of action required to attain designated types of performances' (Bandura, 1986). It is essentially a process of self-persuasion. (Self-efficacy has a central role to play in the process of self-regulation and self-control. We will return to these in more detail in Chapter 12.)

It is not unusual to find individuals with very similar skill levels producing very different levels of performance. Often this is explicable by reference to their differing levels of self-efficacy. What, therefore, produces self-efficacy, and what are its effects?

The main sources of self-efficacy beliefs are mastery experiences. Success, not surprisingly perhaps, helps the process of persuading ourselves about our own competencies. There are two other main sources of self-efficacy – social persuasion, and physiological states.

We all use, and are subject to, social persuasion. Parents use social persuasion in order to try to induce self-efficacy in their offspring. It is most effective when it originates from someone whose judgement we trust and respect. This may often be the 'expert' on whose behaviour we are trying to model our own.

The state of arousal, or otherwise, of our own body can also be a source of self-efficacy. When aroused we experience certain physiological states, e.g. butterflies in the stomach. These physiological states are the same for many different emotions. The physiological states of fear and excitement, for example, are very similar. What makes the difference is how we interpret these states. If you are about to give a speech to a large gathering and you are experiencing butterflies in the stomach and an increased pulse-rate, your interpretation of the reasons for this is likely to influence your self-efficacy, and hence your performance. There will be a considerable difference between interpreting your increased pulse rate as due to nerves, or to the fact that you have just run up a few flights of stairs in order to be there on time.

Having considered the sources of self-efficacy, what are its main effects? Self-efficacy leads to a general feeling of psychological well-being. This manifests itself in higher levels of motivation and performance. It also helps in resisting the debilitating effects of stress. As we shall see in the chapter on reaction to change, it also defends against the effects of depression in threatening situations.

A concept related to that of self-efficacy is that of locus of control of reinforcement, usually shortened to *locus of control*. This concept has its roots in the work of Rotter (1966). Rotter suggested that people differ in the extent to which they believe they have control over the reinforcers in their lives. In particular, people could be either *internals* or *externals*. The former believe very much that their reinforcers lie largely within their own control; the latter that, no matter what they do, the control of reinforcers lies externally, and is due to such factors as chance or the influence of powerful other people.

Exercise

At this point you should work out your final score for the career questionnaire (Appendix 5) and compare your score with those of other managers, provided at the end of Appendix 5.

The questionnaire was developed by one of the authors in order to measure 'locus of control' in a specific area – career development. A more general questionnaire was developed by Rotter, and a large number of studies have been carried out using it. In general, the findings are that 'internals' are more successful than 'externals'. In one well-known study (Anderson, 1977), a group of small-businessmen in America, whose businesses had been destroyed by a hurricane, were followed over a period of years. Those who were 'internals' recovered from the disaster far better than 'externals'.

If you think back to attribution theory, you will recall the effect that attribution of causality had on our perception of others. In some respects self-efficacy and locus of control are concerned with how we attribute causality for ourselves. It is apparent that our own beliefs about our abilities, together with our expectations about the consequences, have a considerable influence on our performance.

The relationship between self-efficacy and locus of control, and their effect on performance may be best summed up in the following diagram:

$$E \longrightarrow \text{leads to} \longrightarrow P \longrightarrow \text{leads to} \longrightarrow O$$

Efficacy expectation	Outcome expectation
(Self-efficacy)	(Locus of control)

Effort (E) leads to performance (P), which then leads to outcomes (O). An individual's belief that if they exert effort they will succeed, is their self-efficacy. Locus of control, on the other hand, is their belief that they can perform in such a way as to achieve their desired outcomes.

So far we have been considering Social *Learning* Theory. A number of additional concepts have since been added by Bandura to create what is now referred to as Social *Cognitive* Theory. As might be expected, these additions are cognitive in their nature, and are concerned with self-regulation.

As mentioned before, we will deal in more detail with self-regulation in a later chapter. There are, however, two aspects that we will consider here – goal-setting and self-attributions.

GOAL SYSTEMS AND GOAL ORIENTATION

Social cognitive theory, like goal-setting theory, places importance on the setting and attainment of goals. There has, in fact, been mutual influence between the two theories. Bandura has adopted goal-setting, whilst Locke and his co-workers have recognized the importance of self-efficacy. The theories differ, however, in their explanations of the effectiveness of goal-setting. Locke sees the setting of goals, and their achievement, as intrinsically motivating; no 'extra' reward is needed. Bandura, however, believes that 'the motivational effects do not stem from goals themselves, but rather from evaluative responses of people to their own behavior'. Despite this difference, both theories accept the motivational effects of goals.

Like Locke, Bandura considers that goals achieve their effects by guiding effort; they also build beliefs about self-efficacy. Of special importance for Bandura, however, is the nature of the *goal orientation*.

Goal orientation. Bandura draws on the goal orientation theory of Dweck (1992). Dweck distinguishes between *learning* goal orientation, and *performance* goal orientation. (Other writers have used the terms 'task-involved' and 'ego-involved' learning, respectively.)

People who are 'learning' (task) orientated tend to set goals that are determined largely by their own, internal, standards. Their objectives centre on personal improvement and mastery, irrespective of the goals or performance of others around them. 'Performance' (ego) orientated individuals, on the other hand, are more concerned with outperforming others. They assess their performance by reference to the performance of significant others. (This distinction is similar, in some respects, to the concept of self-monitoring which was discussed in Chapter 3.)

The theory and research associated with goal orientation theory has been concerned with the way children learn. It shows that 'learning' orientation leads to greater improvements, and greater persistence in the face of failure. Dweck suggests that an individual's goal orientation is basically dispositional, i.e. like a personality trait. However, it can be influenced by situational factors. If the situation places emphasis on performance relative to others, then 'learning' orientated individuals will tend to move to a 'performance' orientation.

Although the work on goal orientation is concerned with the way children learn, it has obvious implications for organizations. This is especially so for the learning of new skills. There are obviously occasions when it is appropriate to motivate people by the use of competition. Competition is most appropriate with individuals who have high levels of skill and also high self-efficacy. These individuals will tend to set themselves difficult goals which they expect to achieve.

When faced with failure they will probably adopt an attributional style that will protect their self-esteem i.e. attributing their failure to external causes.

In many situations in organizations, however, what is required is for individuals to improve and develop, irrespective of whether others are performing better or worse. The situation should be organized so that a 'learning' goal orientation is encouraged. Performance levels should be judged according to whether the individual is improving, not how they compare with others.

SELF-ATTRIBUTIONS

Whilst self-efficacy is influenced by objective events such as goal attainment, it is essentially *subjective*. It results from a process of *self-persuasion* and is an outcome of our own process of cognitive self-regulation. Cognition is concerned with the way in which an individual processes information. We have seen, in Chapter 2, how information processing can differ from person to person. There are some other cognitive processes that can have important influences on self-efficacy.

We have already looked at the manner in which people attribute causality to events. The way in which causality is attributed can also have significant effects on motivation. In particular, the attribution we place on our own successes or failures will influence our feelings of self-efficacy. We have already discussed the basic distinction made by attribution theory; that between internal (dispositional) and external (situational) attribution. If we attribute our successes to internal factors, and our failures to external factors (the self-serving bias discussed in the chapter on personality) our self-efficacy is likely to be enhanced by success and protected after failure. If, on the other hand, we attribute our failures to internal factors, and our successes to external, we are likely to find our feelings of self-efficacy suffering.

This basic distinction, between internal and external causes is, however, rather too simple. We need to add some more dimensions to increase the power of the theory.

Our performance is likely to be determined by a number of factors. For example, to succeed at almost any task we need the basic aptitude to cope, and we will need to exert effort. In addition, an element of luck may be helpful. Each of these can be used to derive the extra dimensions we need.

Both aptitude and effort are internal, but they differ in terms of their *stability*. Aptitudes, like personality traits, are very stable; there is little that can be done to improve someone's intelligence. Effort, on the other hand, is not. The amount of effort we put into different tasks may vary enormously.

Luck is an interesting case. At first it is likely to be seen as external. However, there are some people who are often referred to as 'lucky' – an internal characteristic. However, the essential feature of luck is that it is, like aptitudes, *uncontrollable*. Effort, on the other hand, is under our own control.

Finally, our attributions for our success, or failure, at a task may also have an influence on our perception of our likely chances of success in other tasks. We may perceive our success or failure as a 'one-off', limited to this specific task. We may, on the other hand, see this as just another example of our global tendency to succeed or fail. The attributions we make, therefore, may be *global* or *specific*.

Figure 5.2 (adapted from Dugan, 1989) sets out the most common explanations for performance, classified according to three of the dimensions of attributions discussed above.

The importance of these attributions is in their influence over our perceptions of our successes or failures. As we shall see, the nature of these attributions will influence how we *feel* about our performance. This, in turn, will influence what actions we are likely to take in future.

	Internal		*External*	
	stable	**unstable**	**stable**	**unstable**
uncontrollable	ability	mood	task difficulty	luck
controllable	typical effort	specific	nature of supervision	dependence on others

Figure 5.2. Common explanations for performance.
(After: Dugan, 1989)

Motivational Effects of Attribution. Weiner (1985) has suggested that attributions can have a motivational effect. This effect is the result of the emotions generated by our attributions for success or failure. According to Weiner, 'the most embracing presumption . . . is that how we think influences how we feel'. Weiner suggests that the creation of these feelings is the result of a two-stage process.

When faced with success or failure our immediate emotions are automatic, and not dependent upon our attributions for the outcome. Thus, success leads automatically to positive emotions, such as happiness. Failure, on the other hand, leads to feelings of sadness. The next stage, unlike the first, is dependent on the attributions made for success or failure. The emotions aroused are dependent, not on specific causes, but on the dimensions of those causes, in particular their locus, stability, and controllability. The emotions aroused then influence the individual's motivation. This is perhaps best explained by taking examples from Figure 5.2.

For most people, attributions associated with success are easiest to explain. These are normally internal attributions such as ability and/or effort. The first 'primitive' emotion of happiness is followed, therefore, by a feeling of *pride*. If others were perceived as having helped, there may also be feelings of gratitude.

Attributions for failure, on the other hand, are rather more complex. If the attributions are external and uncontrollable (task-difficulty or luck) then the feelings produced may be those of *helplessness* (we will return to this shortly). If the attributions are external and controllable (nature of supervision or dependence on others) then the likely response is that of frustration and *anger*. This is usually directed at the perceived cause, for example the supervisor concerned.

Internal attributions for failure are perhaps the most interesting. The most important of these internal attributions are those of effort (both typical and specific) and ability. If the internal attribution is to a cause that is stable but uncontrollable (e.g. ability) the likely feeling is that of *shame*. Because it is stable and uncontrollable it cannot be changed. The motivation, therefore, is to withdraw from the situation so that the feelings of shame are not repeated. Contrast this with internal attributions that are controllable (e.g. effort). If poor performance is seen as due to lack of effort, the likely emotion is that of *guilt*. This is a motivating emotion. If performance is due to lack of effort, it can be corrected. The potential is there for increased motivation. (Note that this only applies when the success or failure has some importance to the individual concerned. For most people this will usually be the case.)

The way that people attribute causality, therefore, can have an important influence on their behaviour. Most people, although subject to the biases discussed previously, do not have a set 'attributional style'. Some people, however, do have such a style. Perhaps the most important of these is learned helplessness.

Learned helplessness. In its original form the concept of learned helplessness did not include attributional concepts (Seligman, 1975). The attributional elements were added later by Abramson *et al.* (1984, 1989).

Learned helplessness can be induced (the original experiments were with dogs) by exposing someone to an unpleasant situation in which they learn that they can do nothing to remove, or escape from, the unpleasantness. In this situation, once the person realizes that nothing they do has any effect, they give up doing anything at all. Unfortunately, this effect does not remain specific to the original situation. It is generalized to other situations. Thus, in situations where a difference could be made, the person still refrains from doing anything. Some theorists have argued that depressive reactions following trauma can be interpreted as learned helplessness. For example, following the loss of a loved one it is not uncommon to find individuals exhibiting behaviour similar to learned helplessness. Nothing will bring the loved one back, therefore why do anything at all? Like learned helplessness, this also seems to generalize to other areas of the person's life.

In adding attributional elements, Abramson has suggested that it is not the objective events themselves that produce learned helplessness, but how they are interpreted. Learned helplessness is characterized by a reversal of the normal self-serving bias. The 'normal' person tends to attribute success to internal, controllable, stable, and global factors. I succeed because of my general ability to cope. Failures, on the other hand, are attributed to external, uncontrollable, unstable factors that are specific to the situation e.g. bad luck. In the depressive, however, this pattern is reversed. If I succeed it is because I happened, this once, to be lucky. If I fail, it's because of my inability, as usual.

Learned helplessness is not a particularly common phenomenon in organizations. When it does occur, however, it is often particularly difficult to deal with. The 'depressive attributional style' does not lend itself to change by reasoned arguments (as anyone who has tried to talk someone out of depression will testify). The treatment of such depressive states is beyond the scope of this book, but a milder form of learned helplessness may sometimes be observed in those who have experienced consistent failure at work. The way of coping with such an individual is to follow the steps, outlined previously, to improve their self-efficacy. This involves setting mastery criteria that are achievable, providing modelling, etc. In addition, verbal persuasion, when coupled with success, may also have a beneficial effect. Försterling (1985) has suggested that such 'attributional retraining' has been consistently successful in increasing persistence and performance.

IMPLEMENTING THE THEORIES

It may have occurred to you that some of the concepts of goal-setting theory, behaviour modification theory, and social learning theory have common elements. Goal-setting, in SLT terms, is the generation of expectancies. Indeed, self-efficacy has been incorporated into goal-setting theory by Locke (Locke *et al.*, 1984), who sees it as an important addition. Reinforcers also appear in all three, although they differ as to the reasons for their beneficial effects.

What, then, are the implications from these two influential theories? To reiterate from goal setting theory, managers should

- set specific goals
- set hard goals
- set goals that the person believes they can achieve
- provide feedback.

To these we can now add that they should also

- ensure that desired behaviours are reinforced
- ensure that undesired behaviours are punished, or not rewarded
- use variable-ratio reinforcement to maintain desired behaviours.

REINFORCERS IN PRACTICE

The problem remains, of course, as to what we, as managers, can use as reinforcers. The most obvious is money.

Performance-related pay. Many organizations have considered, and in many cases, implemented, a system of performance-related pay (PRP). In the light of the guidelines listed above this would appear to be a useful way of motivating employees. The setting of difficult goals, together with positive reinforcement for their achievement, is advocated both by goal theory and OBMod.

It is perhaps worth examining PRP a little more deeply, especially how it is implemented in practice. Rather than relying on the authors' analysis, however, it might be useful for you to carry out an analysis of PRP:

Exercise

Consider the following questions, drawn from some of the theories discussed so far. (This list of questions should not be taken as being exhaustive. You should also develop some questions of your own.)

How easy is it to establish a measure of individual performance that will be considered equitable?

Is the required performance, together with a clear indication of the reinforcement, specified in advance?

What will be the effect on intrinsic motivation of introducing an extrinsic motivator?
What will be the likely effect on goal orientation?

Your answers will probably make you realize that it is not easy to design a system of PRP. For example, few organizations set out, *in advance*, the performance required and the reinforcement that is being offered. Whilst they may be specific about the goal to be achieved, it is rare to find the reinforcement for achieving the goal being specified. This is much more likely to be done *after* the event by comparing the individual's performance with that of others. The amount of performance-related pay is usually determined not by an individual's performance, but by budgetary constraints.

Even if an efficient and fair system of PRP can be devised it is not clear that the results will be totally beneficial. The effects on intrinsic motivation and goal orientation may produce dysfunctional effects. Indeed, these effects have been pointed out by some other than psychologists. The political theorist John Gray is considered by many 'market-orientated' politicians to be their mentor. In his book *Beyond the New Right* (1991) Gray points out the dangers of taking PRP too far. In mature organizations with a climate of commitment, he suggests that the introduction of new contracts with PRP may lead to a change in the commitment of the staff. Their response may be to move from a commitment based on loyalty to one which is instrumental, delivering only that which their contract specifies. He has specifically identified the National Health Service as an example of where this is happening.

Research into the effects of PRP has not been very encouraging for its advocates. The Institute of Manpower Studies (*Performance pay fails to motivate*, reported in Hutton, 1995) carried out a survey of more than 1,000 employees in three organizations with PRP. They found that, in general, PRP tended to lower morale, reduce commitment, and increase staff turnover. In those few circumstances where it was successful its success was dependent on a high level of trust between those being assessed and those undertaking the assessment.

Zenger (1992) has pointed out that, whilst the benefits of PRP are often extolled, the costs are rarely considered. The implementation of PRP means that performance will have to be continually, and formally, monitored. This will entail tangible administrative costs. There are also likely to be intangible costs if the system is not perceived as being fair. Zenger concludes that perhaps PRP should be limited to only certain categories of staff. In particular, those performing exceptionally well, and those performing poorly. The exceptional performers, it is suggested, need PRP in order to prevent them from leaving for better-paid jobs. The poor performers need the incentive to perform better. For the majority, however, the potential costs seem to outweigh the benefits.

There is an additional problem with PRP; most managers have little or no control over the pay levels of those working for them. What reinforcers, therefore, can managers use in their day-to-day interactions with their staff?

Other reinforcers

Exercise

Before reading further, try making a list of what reinforcers you have under your control that you can use. Look back to your list of 'what motivates' for some suggestions. Remember that this has to be a tentative list. As we mentioned before, what is a reward for one individual will not be so for another. Some people enjoy attending courses. The fun of spending time away from home at company expense tends, in our experience, to fade with familiarity. In psychological jargon, they 'satiate'.

Your list of possible reinforcers will obviously be unique to you. Some managers have control over merit awards and promotion. Most, especially in large organizations, have more limited influence. However, there are two that should appear on most managers' lists which are very powerful.

The most powerful reinforcers are *social*. Our own self-image can only be sustained, in the long term, if it is accepted by others. Thus, it is to others that we turn for our rewards. This applies even to those individuals who appear impervious to the praise or disapproval of others. For them, it is probably the case that they obtain their rewards from groups outside the organization. As you will recall from SLT, we can reward or punish ourselves internally, but this will not last forever. The internal rewards need confirmation every so often from real people.

Within the work situation *praise* is used far less effectively than it might be. Variable-ratio reinforcement suggests that praise should not be used on every occasion; indeed, if over-used it will eventually lose some of its value. This being said, the evidence is that it is hardly used at all. Why is this? A survey amongst managers suggested a number of reasons. Some took the view that it was inappropriate – their employees were already being paid well for what they did. For the majority, however, it was the embarrassment of giving praise. It is somehow 'not macho'. Many, however, thought that they already did give praise. Over 80 per cent of managers in one organization claimed to praise their employees for work done well. The researchers then asked those employees about the praise. Only 14 per cent said their manager actually gave praise for good work! Another reason for not giving praise is that we tend to 'manage by exception'. We shout and complain when things go wrong (the exception), but fail to praise when things are going routinely well. Compare the number of times you have complained, for example in shops, to the council, or to other managers, with the number of times you have written complimenting them when they have been particularly helpful.

Praise is a very powerful reinforcer, especially when used on a variable schedule. This schedule should not be indiscriminate or generalized (i.e. the occasional praise for 'work in general'). It should be specific, and it should be clear to the person which part of their behaviour is being praised. Many organizations, Xerox and NCR to name two, are now recognizing that training managers in the appropriate use of praise and recognition has considerable value.

The other reinforcer is less obvious. An American student (Lyons, 1973, quoted in Berthold, 1982), who was working her way through college, made some timings of the average length of time various tasks took in the store where she worked. These timings were averaged across a number of people. Figure 5.3 shows two columns of figures, indicating the length of time taken to do various tasks in two different situations. As you will see, it took 50 per cent longer to complete the tasks in situation B than in situation A. What reinforcers do you think might have been used to obtain the increase in pro-

Task	Timings in minutes	
	A	B
Stock sweet shelves	20	35
Stock cigarette shelves	5	15
Vacuum floor	5	15
Dump rubbish	5	10
Clean store	45	90
Check in orders	30	60
Help pharmacist	50	60
Deliver orders	50	60
Totals	210	345

Figure 5.3. Behaviour under different reinforcement conditions.
(Source: Berthold, 1982)

ductivity indicated by the shorter times? Neither praise, money, nor other tangible inducements were involved.

Many of your suggestions might have produced the desired effect; we cannot be sure. It is unlikely that many of you will have found the actual cause. The only difference was that in column A, a nice job was known to be following a nasty job, while in column B a nasty job was known to follow the nice one. To modify Parkinson's Law, work expands so as to fill the time available for its completion, but only when the work that follows is nastier!

This phenomenon is known as the Premack Principle, after David Premack who first observed it in animals. Put generally, more likeable jobs can be used to reinforce less likeable. Unfortunately, most of us work the other way round. We put off doing those jobs we dislike, finding another job to do in their place. (This is known as 'displacement activity'.) *Work scheduling*, therefore, has considerable potentialities as a reinforcer. It is necessary, however, to determine the nature of a person's hierarchy of job preferences if we are to make use of the Premack Principle. There are two main ways of doing this. First, it is perfectly possible to ask people which tasks they like and which they do not. A second, and perhaps more accurate, method is to observe them. Given a free choice, people will spend most of their time doing those tasks that they enjoy.

Hoyle used the Premack Principle in order to improve the performance of a group of professional engineers (see Makin and Hoyle, 1993). The group were not performing well but this was not due to lack of enthusiasm or dedication. By observing their behaviour he found that they spent too much of their time attending to only those parts of the task that they enjoyed. He then devised a system of goal-setting, with feedback and praise, to encourage them to do the other important tasks that were being neglected. The results were impressive. The section rose, within a year, from being the worst-performing such section in the organization, to being the best.

This use of work scheduling as a technique to improve performance highlights something that has been implicit in what we have been discussing; that these techniques can be used to change our own behaviour as well as that of others. We will return to this in a later chapter.

PRACTICAL EXAMPLES OF OBMod AND GOAL-SETTING

Luthans and Kreitner (1985) have suggested a systematic five-point process for implementing an OBMod programme.

1.   Identify the problem-related performance behaviour.

2.   Measure to identify the current levels of the behaviour.

3.   Functionally analyse the antecedent stimuli which 'cue' the behaviour and the consequences that maintain it.

4.   Intervene by changing the environment to encourage the new behaviour(s) and discourage the old.

5.   Evaluate by systematically monitoring and evaluating the results.

This procedure was used to implement a behaviourally-based approach to safety in a factory manufacturing Cellophane (Makin and Sutherland, 1994). The production process ran on a continuous shift system which operated on a 10-day cycle. The factory had a workforce of approximately 550, and had a continuing and active commitment to safety, including a full-time safety adviser. Various schemes had, over a period of some years, led to an overall 10 per cent year-on-year reduction in accidents. Despite all its efforts, however, the organization had reached a 'base level' of minor accidents, below which it was proving difficult to drop further. New safety campaigns had produced some reduction in accidents, but these were not being maintained.

Identification of behaviours was drawn largely from two sources. First, an analysis was carried out of all accident records for the previous two years. The second source of information was in-depth interviews with a random sample of approximately 15 per cent of the work-force. It is generally accepted that many minor accidents go unreported and it was thought that these interviews would help in discovering such omissions.

From these interviews, together with the data from the accident records, a 'checklist' was constructed for each department, comprising those behaviours most commonly associated with accidents. Examples of these behaviours included 'goggles to be worn when using nail gun', 'cut-resistant gloves to be worn when cutting' and 'long gloves must be used when recovering viscose from acid'. Each of these became a checklist item.

These checklists were then refined by the managers in each of the departments, who were asked for feedback on the appropriateness of each of the items. In addition, the departmental safety committees also aided in this refinement.

A member of each department within the factory was then trained to act as an 'observer', using the checklist. Further refinement of the checklists was undertaken in the light of the experiences of these observers. The observers were asked to undertake, at random times during the shift, at least one survey of their own department using the checklist. Each checklist item was scored as to the number of times 'safe' or 'unsafe' behaviour was observed. The employees were assured that no names would be recorded. In line with the policy of rewarding desirable behaviour, rather than punishing undesirable, it was stressed that no disciplinary action would follow from the results of these observations. The checklists took, on average, about 10 minutes to complete.

Measurement of safe behaviour was obtained by using the checklists for four weeks. This also allowed the observers and the observed to become familiar with the procedure.

Analysis of the benefits gained from unsafe behaviour showed that most were undertaken because they saved time. It was decided that little could be done to change this. The emphasis would, therefore, be on encouraging safe behaviour.

The new behaviour was encouraged by using goal-setting plus the reinforcement of feedback. Display boards were produced for each department, and an enlarged copy of the relevant checklist was displayed publicly in each department. At the end of the four-week period the base-line data were entered on the board in graphical form. (The data were presented in a format which indicated the number of safe behaviours as a percentage of total observed behaviours.) Staff in each department then attended a 'goal-setting' meeting at which the purpose and philosophy of the approach was explained. Once again, particular emphasis was placed on the fact that no individual worker could be identified in the behavioural observations, and that no disciplinary action would follow as a result of the observations. The results of the base-line observations were then presented and each group was asked to agree upon a target that was 'difficult yet achievable' for improvement in safety behaviours. The goal was then entered as a solid line on each of the boards.

Monitoring: Following the goal-setting meetings, the boards were placed in display positions in the respective departments. Observations were continued at the same rate as that during the base-line period and the results were plotted on the boards every Friday.

The results of this approach were impressive, during a typical 16-week period prior to the introduction of the scheme there were 118 accidents. In the first 16 weeks of the scheme the total accident rate was more than halved. Figures some two years after the scheme was introduced showed a total of 49 accidents for a 16-week period. At the same time the number of lost-time accidents had fallen from 22 in the year prior to the scheme, to three.

The impressive results of this study show how effective the techniques can be, Indeed, they are now being applied to quality assurance (see Sutherland et al., 1995), with promising initial results. The study also demonstrates another important factor. Such schemes should not be seen as a 'one off' intervention. For them to succeed in the long term they need to become part of the company's culture – the standard way of doing things. As others have pointed out, the nature of any new programme, whether safety-related or otherwise, will interact with, and have an impact upon, organizational climate and culture (Zohar and Fussfeld 1981; Mawhinney, 1992). This will inevitably produce changes in the way the organization functions, to which we will return later.

Some of the techniques of OBMod may be seen as manipulative. We believe they should be used openly. As we stressed earlier, we are buying and selling behaviour. In doing so, we can be open with the contract – 'This is what I want you to do, how do you want to be rewarded?' The following principles should, however, guide any implementation.

1. Personal relationships: Any scheme should be introduced openly, and people should be free to 'opt out'. Although different rewards may be needed for different people, equity should be maintained. Finally, if the scheme does not succeed, remember that it is the scheme that has failed, not the participants.

2. Technical issues: The factors affecting the effectiveness of reinforcement etc. have been listed above. However, it is worth restating the basics, i.e. that it is behaviour, not outcomes, that is rewarded, and that the emphasis should be on the reward of positive behaviour, not the punishing of bad. It is often useful to establish 'contingency contracts'. These should state the behaviours to be rewarded, which must be directly observable, and detail the benefits for each party. A method for recording the rates of performance and 'reward' should be established. Remember that contingency contracts are like other contracts and should, therefore, be open to negotiation and, if necessary, re-negotiation.

3. Organizational issues: Creating new reward systems can produce 'knock-on' effects. Try, therefore, to use 'naturally-occurring rewards'. Also, assuming that the scheme is successful, it may be necessary to consider the effects of the changed behaviour on other aspects of the work.

Let us end with a fairly light-hearted example. Some time ago *The Guardian* newspaper picked up a report of the use of OBMod in a clinical setting. A wife had developed an aversion such that she could not bear her husband even to touch her, though she still loved him. She was also, it transpired, extremely fond of Polo Mints. The psychologists involved developed a reinforcement schedule which involved the husband using the mints, over a period of time, to reinforce more and more intimate behaviour. Full conjugal relations were finally restored. *The Guardian*, true to form, speculated as to whether the situation could be reversed, in order to get someone who disliked Polos to like them!

THE BEHAVIOURAL APPROACH AND THE PSYCHOLOGICAL CONTRACT

In many respects the behavioural approach fulfils many of the requirements for the psychological contract that we outlined in the Introduction. It requires elements of the contract to be made explicit. In this chapter we have concentrated, implicitly perhaps, on the economic contract, but principles discussed apply just as well to the psychological contract. A clear understanding of how each of the parties expects to be treated by the other is likely to lead to fewer misunderstandings and conflicts.

The nature of the changes in the psychological contract produced by the safety programme described above can be used as an illustration. Even a programme with a limited and specific scope, such as improving safety, can have influences on the psychological contract. The introduction of the new scheme placed a heavy emphasis on shop-floor participation. This change was initially met with some resistance, both from shop-floor workers and middle managers. The former resisted participation because it changed the psychological contract concerning the focus of responsibility. In fact, it made them more responsible for their own actions. Similarly, middle managers saw an area for which they had responsibility being transferred away from them. (We will deal in later chapters with a model of such resistance and how it may be overcome.)

However, once the scheme had been implemented and accepted, both by managers and shop-floor, there was a noticeable change in the psychological contract. Having experienced the successes of participation in one area, the shop-floor workers now expected it in other areas. Managers also seemed to be more likely to respond to these demands. Although we have no quantitative data, our impression was that the 'climate' within the organization improved over the course of the intervention. Shop-floor workers seemed more ready to comment on issues, including those other than safety, and management appeared more willing to listen. More importantly perhaps, they also appeared to be more ready to act on information that had been provided by the work-force in the past. The resurrection of a 'near miss' reporting procedure was such an example. It had been moribund for a long time. Management complained that no near misses were reported. The workers replied that even if they reported such incidents, they were never acted upon. Another tangible piece of evidence for this improved climate was provided by the introduction of a 'hazard spotting' programme. According to managers, the employees attended work in their own time to undertake this exercise! It was the effectiveness of the safety scheme, together with the increased willingness of the work-force to become more involved, that led to the extension of the techniques to quality issues. The main point, from this chapter's point of view, is that almost any change has the potential to change the psychological contract. It is part of the function of leaders to re-negotiate such changes.

Leadership and Management Style

BORN TO LEAD?

When considering leadership, many people begin by recalling those individuals who are, or were, what they thought of as a great leader. Many names may come to mind such as Churchill, Gandhi, or Martin Luther King. (We have chosen dead leaders so as not to be considered guilty of sins of either omission or commission in our choice of contemporary leaders.) All appear to be charismatic, to have something about them that makes them stand out from others, to be 'great men or women'. But does this mean that all good leaders have to be charismatic?

Some would argue that Clement Atlee was an extremely effective post-war British leader, yet Churchill once described him as 'a modest man with much to be modest about'. To redress the balance let us allow Atlee to speak through the words of his own poem.

Few thought he was even a starter,
there were many who thought themselves smarter,
but he ended PM, CH, and OM,*
an Earl and a Knight of the Garter.

If leaders are what we would call 'great men or women', are there any particular traits that can be identified as being associated with effective leadership? We will return to the concept of charisma later in this chapter, but are there any other particular personality traits that can be identified with effective leadership?

Many personality traits have been examined, but few show any relationship to successful leadership. One possible exception is 'intelligence' which is not, however, a personality trait, but an aptitude. According to some early researchers (e.g. Stogdill, 1948) there is some relationship, although it would appear to be a curvilinear, rather than a straight-line relationship. In other words, while leadership ability in-

* Prime Minister, Companion of Honour, Order of Merit.

creases with increasing intelligence, it does so only up to a certain point. Beyond this point higher levels of intelligence lead to decreased leadership ability. Alistair Cooke has, for example, suggested that Jimmy Carter was probably the most intelligent post-war president of the USA. He was not the most effective, according to Cooke, because instead of seeing both sides of a problem, he saw 23 sides!

Some have suggested that great leaders have a need to dominate but, as was seen in the previous chapter, great leaders have their effect by increasing their followers' feelings of power, not by subjugating them. Hunter and Hirsh (1987) used meta-analysis to examine the contribution of traits to leadership. Of those they considered that intelligence explained the highest amount of variance (27 per cent), whilst 'masculinity' explained 11 per cent, and 'conservatism' 4.8 per cent. Many other traits have been examined, but the evidence is mixed, often because the traits measured are themselves woolly and ill-defined (for example, that of 'initiative').

Why are the traits associated with leadership so hard to find? Perhaps, like Shakespeare's great men, 'some leaders are born, some are made, and some have leadership thrust upon them'. In the last category might be placed Rajiv Gandhi. Gandhi was perfectly happy to pursue his career as an airline pilot until the death of his elder brother. At this point he was propelled, by all accounts reluctantly, into the forefront of Indian politics. Once again, the interaction of personality and situational factors is evident. 'Cometh the hour, cometh the man.'

Rather than seek the secrets of leadership through the traits that people possess, researchers shifted their studies to what leaders, and in particular managers, *do*, i.e. what are the behaviours associated with leadership?

BEHAVIOURAL AND CONTINGENCY APPROACHES

Two major studies into behaviour have made their impact upon leadership theory. Both were undertaken at American universities, and both by teams of researchers, rather than by individuals. (For this reason they are usually referred to by the names of the universities, Ohio and Michigan, although the name of Rensis Likert is often linked with the latter.)

The Ohio study took a large number of possible descriptions of the behaviour of leaders. These were then reduced to 130 single descriptions of behaviour, grouped into 12 broad categories (for example, communication), which were put into questionaire format. By administering the questionnaire to a large number of people, they were able to subject their results to 'factor analysis', a statistical technique widely used by personality theorists. The results of this analysis suggested that the behaviours fell into four distinct factors or dimensions. The two most useful dimensions have been given many different, but relatively similar, names over the intervening period. The correct titles are *consideration* and *initiating structure*, but the more common names are 'people-orientation' and 'task-orientation'. These descriptions will be used interchangeably. The two dimensions are mutually independent, hence an individual may be high or low on either or both. Although people may change their behaviour, the theory suggests that individuals have a preferred style with which they feel comfortable.

Someone who is high on the consideration dimension behaves in ways which foster the establishment and maintenance of good inter-personal relations. There is usually rapport between the leader and group members, together with mutual feelings of warmth and trust. Someone high on 'initiating structure', on the other hand, is more concerned with getting the job done than with interpersonal warmth. Such a leader behaves in ways which lead to well-defined communication channels and co-ordination.

To repeat, these two dimensions are independent and hence the combination of these produces a diagram upon which various leadership styles can be plotted. Figure 6.1 shows this diagram, together with some jobs associated with the various preferred styles. Research suggests that those who are high on task-orientation (initiating structure) are perceived as effective, while those high on people-orientation (consideration) are seen as providing a pleasant and satisfying work environment. These dimensions have been used as the basis for many managerial applications, perhaps best known of which is the 'managerial grid', developed by Blake and Mouton (1964).

What effect does each of the dimensions have on morale? Studies by Fleishman (Fleishman and Harris, 1962) suggest that employee turnover and grievance levels go up as task-orientation increases, but go down as person-orientation increases. There appears to be a 'trade-off' between the two, as far as morale is concerned. This trade-off is, however, only one-way. High people-orientation can compensate for high task-orientation, but not vice versa. In real life the requirement to get jobs done means that a high degree of task-orientation is required, often at times of crisis or deadlines. In these circumstances, the possible decrease in morale can be offset by higher levels of people-orientated behaviour. For a leader low in people-orientated behaviour, the situation is not so promising. It might be thought that morale could be increased by reducing task-orientated behaviour. This is not the case. It appears that a moderate

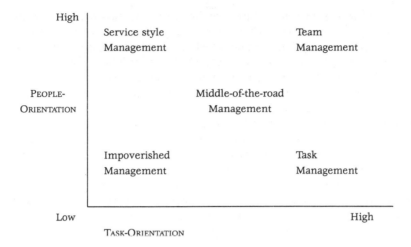

Figure 6.1. The managerial grid.
(Adapted from: Blake and Mouton, 1964)

level of people-orientation is required, irrespective of the degree of task-orientation, if morale is to be maintained.

These two facets of leader behaviour need to be met, but not necessarily by the same person. There are many cases where an effective leadership 'team' may emerge with one individual who is task-orientated and one who is people-orientated. Usually the leader is mainly task-orientated, while the second-in-command smooths the feathers ruffled by their boss.

Since its original statement there have been criticisms of the theory and extensions of the number of dimensions, but the two original dimensions appear to be fairly universal. The main criticism, which, as we shall see, also applies to the Michigan studies, is that it does not take into account the fact that different styles may be needed in different situations.

The Michigan studies differed from those of Ohio in two respects. First, they used only one dimension. At one end were managers who were *production-centred*, at the other those who were *employee-centred*. This assumes that a person cannot be both. Second, instead of looking at 'satisfaction' with various leadership styles, they looked at levels of productivity associated with differing styles. Three main themes emerged. First, that in the more productive groups, the supervisor spent less time doing the same jobs as his subordinates, concentrating instead on co-ordinating and planning activities. Second, that general, i.e. participative, supervision was more effective than close supervision, on the whole. Finally, that employee-centred supervision was more effective than production-centred supervision.

Despite the substantial differences between the two sets of studies, the main themes from the two have had a considerable impact. These themes are those of people- versus task-orientation, together with the emphasis upon general (i.e. participative), supervision. If they are to be effective, managers have to realize that both task and people dimensions have an impact on subordinates' morale. In general, the people-orientated manager is likely to have a more satisfied workforce. They can also afford to increase the level of task-orientation when necessary without a significant loss of morale. Managers also need to recognize that performance will be affected by the closeness, or otherwise, of supervision. General supervision is likely, on the whole, to be more effective than close supervision. Whilst all these factors need to be considered, the problem is that the theories fail to offer specific advice as to which approach should be adopted in specific situations.

FIEDLER'S CONTINGENCY THEORY

As mentioned earlier, one of the main criticisms of the behavioural theories is that they fail to take into account the demands of the situation. Situations change, and with the changes come different leadership demands. To be fair, the later Michigan studies included one situational factor – that of organizational climate. The inclusion of situational factors, however, is a feature of Fiedler's theory.

Fiedler's theory (Fiedler and Chemers, 1984) takes into account the preferred leadership style of an individual as well as various situational factors. According to the theory, the most appropriate style is dependent, or contingent, upon these other factors. For this reason the theory is known as *Fiedler's contingency theory*.

Let us deal first with preferred leadership style. The concept that Fiedler uses to describe leadership style is that of the 'least preferred co-worker' or LPC. Through his early work with psychotherapists, Fiedler detected differences between 'good' and 'bad' therapists. These different groups of therapists appeared to differ in the way that they looked on their patients, as compared with themselves. 'Good' therapists saw the patients as essentially similar to themselves, but with particular problems that were troubling them. 'Bad' therapists, on the other hand, saw themselves and their patients as quite dissimilar. From these observations Fiedler developed not only the concept of LPC, but also a scale by which to measure it, also called LPC. The level of LPC is determined by how favourably, or otherwise, the person describes their least preferred co-worker. Those with high LPC scores describe even their least favourite co-worker in relatively favourable terms.

Those scoring high on the LPC tend to seek self-esteem through interpersonal relations, while those scoring low tend to seek it through task performance. These two orientations appear, on the surface, to be very similar to the two dimensions from the Ohio studies. Fiedler claims, however, that this is not so. Rather he sees them as more of a particular hierarchy of goals, along the lines of Maslow. Different scores on the LPC represent different hierarchies. The nature of these differences is not entirely clear and there has been considerable discussion concerning both the concept and the measurement of LPC. Despite the lack of clarity, many consider that a rough shorthand for high and low LPC are 'relationship' and 'task' motivated, respectively.

The effectiveness of a group, however, is not dependent solely upon the leadership style of its leader, but also upon the extent to which the situation enables the leader to exert influence. According to Fiedler, there are three main factors that have to be considered when assessing the situational characteristics. In decreasing order of importance these are: leader-member relations, task structure, and position power. Each of these can be favourable to a greater or lesser extent. For simplicity's sake, however, the theory considers only two possibilities for each.

Leader-member relations means exactly what it says. Are the relations between the leader and the group members good or poor?

The definition of *task structure* is not so easy, and itself is sub-divided into four factors. 'Decision verifiability' is the degree to which the solution can be verified as being correct – 'How right was the answer we got?' 'Goal clarity' is the degree to which the task goals can be clearly stated, and known by the group members. 'Goal path multiplicity' refers to the number of ways in which the problem can be solved – 'How many ways are there to skin a cat?' Finally, 'solution specificity' refers to the number of solutions that would be considered correct. Combining these four produces a good or poor rating for the task structure.

The final, and least important dimension is *position power*. This has been called 'fate control'. Essentially, it is the capacity of the leader to determine and dispense rewards and punishments to group members.

These are the major elements of the situation, but how do they interact with the leader's preferred style? In essence, as a result of a large number of empirical studies, Fiedler suggests that low LPC (task-motivated) leaders will be most effective when the situation is either very favourable or very unfavourable. High LPC (relationships-orientated) leaders will be most effective when the situation is moderately favourable. This relationship is shown diagrammatically in Figure 6.2, which illustrates leadership style and situation, together with the way they interact. What implications are there for improving group effectiveness?

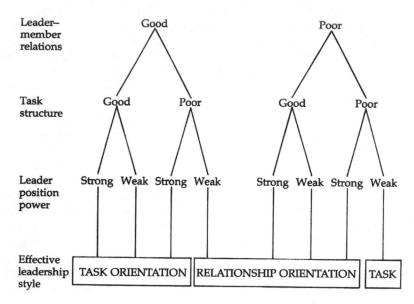

Figure 6.2. Fiedler's model of contingent leadership.
(Source: Bryman, 1986)

To a large extent the situational variables are not susceptible to change. It might be possible to improve leader – member relations, and give the leader more control over rewards, but the other factors are largely determined by the nature of the task. What then of LPC? According to the theory, LPC is very stable and similar to a personality trait. As such it is difficult to change. What Fiedler suggests, therefore, is what he calls 'leader match'. Rather than change the situation, select a leader whose preferred style is most appropriate. This may appear a rather drastic solution. It is, however, what is often done, especially when things are going wrong. In these situations, a task-motivated manager will be moved in, often to replace the relationship-motivated manager for whom the situational factors have now 'gone sour'. Those who have seen the film *Twelve O'Clock High*, which used to be shown quite often on management courses, will recognize the situation.

Fiedler's theory has been the subject of much debate and argument. We have already mentioned the controversy over the nature of the LPC scale, but other researchers have also questioned elements of Fiedler's research methodology. The debate surrounding the methodology is too complicated to be dealt with here, but you should be aware that the theory is far from being universally accepted.

Although Fiedler's theory takes into account what he considers to be the most important situational factors, there are obviously others that he does not consider. Amongst these are two that relate directly to the individual characteristics of the group members. These are incorporated in the model developed by Hersey and Blanchard (1982).

HERSEY AND BLANCHARD: SITUATIONAL LEADERSHIP

Like Transactional Analysis, this model has not found favour in standard textbooks, and there is little research either to support or refute the theory. Nevertheless, we find it a useful way of approaching the major dilemmas of leadership – how participative can I be, versus how authoritarian must I be?

Hersey and Blanchard consider two factors in their theory: leadership style, based very much on the Ohio dimensions, and one situational variable, *maturity*. As the Ohio dimensions of leadership were discussed earlier, we will now turn to the concept of maturity. This will, according to the theory, determine which leadership style is most appropriate.

Maturity is a blanket term which covers two different aspects of behaviour. First, it is applied to the skills required to carry out the task (in fact a more appropriate term might be technical capability). Secondly it is applied to the person's motivational level, or 'psychological' maturity. These, combined together, will decide whether a 'delegating', 'participating', 'selling', or 'telling' style is most appropriate. Descriptions of each of these styles will be given later in this chapter.) The theory is again best summarized diagrammatically, in Figure 6.3. In order to determine the level of maturity, Hersey and Blanchard developed scales by which the manager can rate a subordinate's maturity, and the subordinate rate themselves. The results of these two ratings then form the basis for negotiations between manager and subordinate, so as to identify the appropriate style.

The emphasis in this theory, rather than accepting leadership style as a trait, is to stress leaders' style flexibility. 'Different strokes for different folks' might be a fair way of summarizing it.

As you may have noticed, the general trend in leadership theories has been to increase the number of situational variables that have to be taken into account. Recently, however, the concept of charismatic leadership has undergone a revival.

It has also influenced what has become known as 'new leadership'.

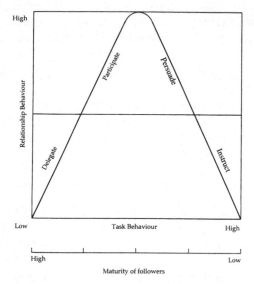

Figure 6.3. A situational leadership model.
(Adapted from: Hersey and Blanchard, 1982)

CHARISMATIC, TRANSFORMATIONAL AND NEW LEADERSHIP

CHARISMATIC LEADERSHIP

The original work on charismatic leadership can be traced to that of Max Weber (1970). Examining the nature of organizations, Weber suggested that they were characterized by the type of authority they used in order to function. He suggested three basic types of authority; rational, traditional, and charismatic.

Rational authority he associated with bureaucracy. In his use of the term 'bureaucracy' he did not anticipate the rather negative associations that the word now has. For Weber a bureaucracy was a particularly rational form of organization. A bureaucracy, in his terms, operated according to logical rational principles. (In TA terms, the Adult would be the predominant mode of operation.)

He associated traditional authority with hierarchical organizations, of which the 'traditional' Church and the Army are perhaps good examples. Authority in these organizations tends to be authoritarian, and based upon the position held by those issuing the orders.

Both rational and traditional authority depend, for most part, not on the characteristics of the particular manager, but on the positions they hold. Charismatic authority, on the other hand, is largely a function of personal characteristics.

The charismatic leader. The central theme of charisma is that it is a personal characteristic. Its essential features are, according to Bryman (1992), the existence of a mission, and the acceptance of this mission by others. The nature of the mission is also important. To be effective, the mission must be seen as the solution to a problem. The problem must be important to those involved, and it must be causing some distress. Indeed, a common characteristic in the emergence of a charismatic leader is that it tends to occur in times of distress.

In some ways charismatic leadership can be seen in terms of a 'social exchange' (see pages 129–132). The important point about this exchange in charismatic leadership is that it involves *emotional*, rather than rational, elements. In TA terms the charismatic leader succeeds in 'hooking' the follower's Child. As the Child is the source of energy and motivation this is potentially a very powerful influence on behaviour.

The emotional nature of the interaction can be seen in those personal characteristics that have been perceived as being central to the charismatic personality. Willner (1984), for example, suggests four aspects of the charismatic leader. They are perceived by their followers as being divine (or at least semi-divine). With this go their possession of extraordinary qualities, an unconditional acceptance of their authority, and emotional commitment. Other personal attributes such as 'hypnotic' eyes and voice, together with high skills of oratory have also been suggested.

Whilst personal characteristics are very important, the situation still seems to be important in the emergence of the charismatic leader. A crisis, for example, seems to assist their emergence. Charisma is also a social creation. Can a leader be called charismatic if they do not have inspired followers? Almost certainly not (although some may claim to see the 'seeds' in those who later become charismatic). This interaction of personal and situational factors makes the identification of the requisite personal characteristics very difficult. Indeed, it makes even a definition of charisma difficult.

If it is impossible to have a charismatic leader without inspired followers, which comes first? Does the leader generate followers, or do the followers create the leader? Almost certainly both. The leader may initially attract the followers. However, the followers, through the creation of myths and legends about the leader, also take part in the social formation of charisma.

Also central to many writers' perception of charisma is the concept of the mission. Peters and Waterman (1982) in their book *In Search of Excellence*, for example, suggested that a strong 'mission statement' was a characteristic of successful organizations. The question arises as to whether the mission causes the charisma, or the charisma creates the mission. As with leader and followers, trying to disentangle the causes and effects of charisma is very difficult. This problem is also evident when trying to explain the disappearance of charisma. Charisma appears to be basically unstable, arising as it does from a 'collective excitement' which may evaporate (Bryman, 1992). Leaders may lose their powers, or the mission may fail to deliver the answers required by the followers. Again, the problem is: which is cause and which effect?

Charisma in organizations. The historical origins of the concept of charisma lie with religious, political, and military leaders. Perhaps the first questions that need to be addressed, therefore, are whether charismatic leadership can emerge in business organizations, and if so, can it persist over any significant period?

By its very nature, charisma usually arises by offering a solution that is a radical break with the established order. This is a problem in many organizations whose 'culture' (see Chapter 8) is not geared to radical, and often potentially risky, solutions. Unlike charismatic political and religious leaders, the staff of the organization are not voluntary followers, but those working for a salary. The major commitment for many will not be the organization or its leader.

Despite these problems, there do appear to be business leaders who may be called charismatic. While some appear to retain their charisma over a long period, others may disappear as quickly as they appeared. Many of the successful organizations discussed in Peters and Waterman's book are no longer so successful, e.g. IBM. A major problem in maintaining a culture based on charisma is that such organizations are likely to grow. (We will return to the nature of such growth in Chapter 8.) This means that charisma will need to become 'routine'. Charisma, by its very nature may not be susceptible to such 'routinization'. This presents a dilemma; if the charismatic leader becomes too closely associated with the creation of routines, their charisma may decline; if, on the other hand, they keep a good distance from the process, there is a danger that the organization will be taken over by the bureaucracy. The massive 'cultural revolution' in China in the 1960s has been interpreted by some analysts as an attempt by Mao Tse Tung to 'rescue' the communist revolution from the hands of bureaucrats.

It has been assumed so far that charismatic leaders are successful leaders. Whether this is so has yet to be proven. Bryman (1992) criticizes many of the studies of the effectiveness of charismatic leaders on methodological grounds. The studies are often of small samples of leaders who have been identified as charismatic *because* they are successful. If, for the sake of argument, we accept that charismatic leaders are desirable, the question remains as to whether they are born or created. Early theorists suggested that charisma was a stable, internal, characteristic. If this is so they can only be selected. If, on the other hand, the techniques of charisma can be learned, then training can help.

Conger and Kanungo (1988) have taken a behavioural and attributional approach to charismatic leadership, trying to determine which behaviours led to the attribution of charisma. They concluded that the most important behaviours were:

- an idealized view of the organization and its goals that conflicts with the *status quo*

- the willingness to take personal risks which increases their trustworthiness

- the use of unconventional methods. (However, they are sensitive to organizational constraints and seek only to implement their vision when the time is right, e.g. triggered by a crisis.)

- if they become 'managers' their charisma tends to fade.

Conger and Kanungo conclude that charisma is not magical. It is true that leaders differ in the extent to which they can transmit their vision. However, the behavioural pattern underlying this is fairly mundane, and can be taught. They suggest that training should concentrate on cultivating five competencies:

- critical evaluation and problem-detection skills

- visioning skills (including creative thinking)

- communication and linguistic skills

- impression-management skills

- Empowering skills (including improving participation, setting high targets, removing bureaucratic constraints).

The impact of charisma on organizations. The most noticeable influence that charisma has had on organizations is in the concept of 'mission statements'. Many organizations now have mission statements. In some respects these may be seen as organizational goals. Like goals, they are meant to improve motivation by increasing effort and improving its direction and persistence. Unlike goals, however, mission statements tend to be general, rather than specific. They also tend to be a compromise between the importance of internal goals, and the maintenance of a certain public image. In the authors' experience this compromise can be seen in the final part of a mission statement. Often one part of the statement will stress the desire of the organization to be profitable, another will stress a commitment to customers. Alternatively, the commitment to customers is replaced by one to 'stake-holders', i.e. shareholders and staff in addition to customers. Whilst such statements are obviously useful in defining an organization's goals, they are perhaps a little too vague, or have elements of mutual contradiction, to influence behaviour directly. At times of financial or other difficulties, it often becomes apparent that some stake-holders are 'more equal than others'. Perhaps it is better that separate departments within the organization develop their own, more specific, mission statements.

Another aspect of charisma that has had an impact on organizations is that of 'empowerment'. Charismatic leaders, contrary to some beliefs, do not achieve their effectiveness by subjugating their followers. In fact the opposite is true. Such leaders make their followers feel more, rather than less, powerful. In doing so they 'empower' their followers. (This is an important concept, to which we will devote a later chapter.) Recently many aspects of charismatic leadership have been absorbed into transformational leadership.

TRANSFORMATIONAL LEADERSHIP

The original definition of transformational leadership was suggested by Burns (1978). Burns was a political scientist who studied political leadership. Observing different political leaders he drew a distinction between transactional and transformational leadership. The former he saw as being characterized by *exchange*, the latter by *change*. These two types also differed in some other ways.

First, they differed in whether the leader sought to satisfy 'lower-order' or 'higher-order' needs. Higher- or lower-order needs can be interpreted in terms of Maslow's hierarchy. Alternatively, they can be perceived as aspects of intrinsic versus extrinsic motivation (see Chapter 5). Secondly, the two styles differed as to whether they concentrated on 'end values' or 'modal values'. Modal values are less abstract than end values. Modal values stress conventional values, such as honesty, that are essential to maintain the normal functioning of organizations and society. End values, on the other hand, are based upon general principles such as justice and equity. (The distinction between these two may be illustrated by if you consider the following problem. A manufacturer is making huge profits from marketing a drug at a very high price. Someone close to you is dying and only the drug will save them. You have no money, and your only way of obtaining the drug is by theft. Do you steal the drug? Honesty would say no! What would be the verdict based on principles of the sanctity of human life?)

According to Burns, transactional leadership is based upon the satisfaction of lower-order needs according to principles of honesty. Transformational leadership, on the other hand, engages the 'full person' of the follower in order to satisfy their higher needs. This results in a relationship of mutual stimulation and elevation.

Thinking of the sort of political leaders that Burns was studying, this distinction can often be seen. The great 'charismatic' leaders of our age, Gandhi, Churchill, Kennedy, Mandela, all appeal(led) to higher-order needs and general concepts of justice. (It is difficult to imagine any of them making the central theme of their election manifestos, 'Vote for me and I will repay you with tax cuts!')

Burns sees transforming and transactional leadership styles as forming a continuum, defined by the relative balance of modal values versus end values. In summary, transformational leadership differs, and transcends, transactional leadership in the following ways:

- The aims of the leader and the followers merge into one.

- Expectations are raised by addressing 'higher-order' needs of followers.

- The 'whole person' of the follower is engaged.

There are obvious similarities with charismatic leadership. Indeed, charisma is sometimes seen as part of transformational leadership. Some even see the terms as being synonymous. Many writers, however, suggest that they are not the same. Bass (1990), for example, sees charisma as part, but only a part, of transformational leadership.

Transformational leadership in organizations. Bass (1990) has taken the original distinction between transformational and transactional leadership and developed it in an organizational context. In doing so he is more specific about the nature and components of transformational leadership. He also suggests that there is not a simple distinction between leaders. Even leaders who are transformational may, when necessary, use transactional techniques.

Bass suggests that transformational leaders raise their followers' propensity to expend extra effort by:

- raising awareness of the importance of certain goals and the means for their achievement

- inducing the followers to transcend their self-interest for that of the organization

- stimulating and satisfying higher-order needs in the followers.

He perceives transformational leaders as having three major characteristics: charisma, consideration, and intellectual stimulation. Charisma is responsible for the arousing of positive feelings, such as group loyalty. Consideration is similar to the use of the term in the Ohio studies. It allows people to become involved through consensual decision-making. Finally, intellectual stimulation involves the perception of problems, and their solutions, in new ways which inspire others.

Transactional leadership, on the other hand, is characterized by management-by-exception. Rather than the positives being highlighted, the emphasis is upon the detection and correction of errors. This usually involves negative feedback and punishment.

In summary, the difference between the two types of leadership can be summed up as follows:

- Transformational leadership: Based on charisma and the communication of a vision, consideration of the individual as a whole, and intellectual stimulation through offering novel solutions.

- Transactional leadership: Where it is bad it is based on management-by-exception; where good, on contingent reward.

(The comments above may appear to conflict with the advice in the previous chapter about contingent rewards. As we shall see in the later chapter on self-management, this is not necessarily so. The use of empowerment and intrinsic rewards is entirely consistent with elements of transformational leadership.)

Just as charismatic leadership became a part of transformational leadership, so transformational leadership has become a part of what is referred to as *new leadership*.

NEW LEADERSHIP

New leadership is a term that developed in the late 1980s. It represents a collective term for an approach that includes elements of transformational leadership and charisma, amongst others.

Trist and Beyer (1990) suggest that the old and new leadership patterns differ as follows:

Old leadership	New leadership
Non-charismatic	Charismatic
Transactional	Transformational
Management	Leaders
Non-visionary	Visionary
Non-magical	Magical

New leadership also differs from the old in where it places its emphasis:

Less emphasis on	More emphasis on
Planning	Vision
Routine	Change
Compliance	Commitment
Contract	Extra effort
Reaction	Proaction

Evidence suggests that people can be trained in the new leadership approach. This involves such things as creativity, and verbal and communication skills.

An important part of the new leadership approach is that of 'empowerment'. Either explicitly or implicitly, all the theories of charismatic, transformational, or new leadership stress the importance of the followers. These followers will need to be able to cope with the new powers they feel they have acquired. They will need to be able to self-manage far more than under traditional leadership styles.

IMPLICATIONS

Selection and training. Bass considers that techniques of transformational leadership can be taught, despite it depending, in large part, upon some personal characteristics. He has developed training programmes for organizations to improve their transformational leadership style. However, he suggests that people should be selected for training on the basis of their intellect, verbal skills, energy, self-confidence, and strong ego-ideals.

In an overview, Bryman (1992) suggests that certain common themes emerge as to which skills should be taught:

- vision (most important)

- communicating the vision

- empowerment.

The question arises, however, as to who should be taught, and when. Zaleznik (1983), for example, suggests that there is a need to identify leaders and managers, and train them differently. Others (e.g. Avolio and Gibbons, 1988) have argued that such training has to be at an early stage in a person's career.

Such selection and training may prove ineffective, however, if the organizational culture and structure is incompatible with new leadership styles. New leadership is hardly likely to survive in a traditional bureaucracy.

Old or new leadership? The distinction between old and new leadership styles has perhaps been over-emphasized. Many writers point out that management and leadership should be considered as different modes. This does not mean, they argue, that management should be denigrated. Both management and leadership are essential to any organization. (The reader of any of the texts quoted, however, is left with the feeling that one is thought to be implicitly 'better' than the other, despite claims to the contrary.)

The central concept of a mission for the organization is important; it provides a general goal for the members. It should not, however, be thought of as an end in itself. The values it embodies need to be stated in far more specific and behavioural terms if it is to have an impact on performance.

Finally, whilst charisma may be an important factor in leadership, there are others. Perhaps only a minority of managers are born with, or can acquire, charisma. All managers can, however, seek to empower their subordinates. Whether or not they will do so will depend upon many factors. In particular, the assumptions they make about subordinates.

ASSUMPTIONS ABOUT OTHER PEOPLE AT WORK

It might be thought that a consideration of our basic assumptions should have come at the beginning of this chapter. We feel, however, that some knowledge of the current theories of leadership is desirable for the appreciation of the power of assumptions. Assumptions are, in effect, our own theories – in this case about why people behave the way they do at work. As such, they have an important influence on our behaviour towards other people. Unfortunately they are rarely, if ever, tested against reality.

Douglas McGregor's (1960) work on the nature of managerial assumptions is now rather old. For us it retains its power to illuminate those assumptions nevertheless. McGregor coined the terms *Theory X* and *Theory Y* to describe what appeared to him to be two fundamentally different sets of assumptions about why people work.

The basic assumption behind Theory X may be stated fairly succinctly – 'people are lazy'. Acceptance of this assumption leads to the inevitable conclusion that the only way to get people to work is by using strict *control*. This control takes two different forms. The obvious way is to use coercion, the threat of punishment if rules are broken or targets not achieved. The problem with threats is that they are only effective if the person being threatened believes that they will be carried out. Modern employment laws, coupled with company-wide agreements, have made this route rather difficult for many managers. For this reason, the alternative method of control is perhaps more common, and perhaps more efficient. It is the carrot approach, what some have called the 'seduction' approach. People have to be seduced by promises into producing the required performance.

Theory Y, on the other hand, is rather more difficult to state as succinctly. It assumes that most people are motivated by those things at the top of Maslow's hierarchy; in other words, people are naturally active, and seek commitment, responsibility, and enjoyment from their work. Most people, given the opportunity, will actively involve themselves in their work, and will have the abilities to contribute in a constructive way toward the solution of problems that may arise.

Which of these assumptions do you think is the more accurate? In our experience many managers say that their own assumptions are closer to Theory Y than Theory X. When, on management training courses, we use a more accurate method of measuring their attitudes, we often find they are more Theory X orientated than they care to admit. In addition, many suggest that while they themselves are like Theory Y, their subordinates are more Theory X.

The vast majority of organizations behave according to the assumptions of Theory X, especially where non-managers are concerned. The emphasis within the organization is on control and the use of money to 'goad' the workers into the correct behaviour. If Theory Y is correct, however, the organization could be more productive by relinquishing control and turning responsibility over to the workers. Why does this not happen?

The reasons there are so few organizations that work from Theory Y are twofold. First, Theory X is, by its very nature, a self-fulfilling prophesy. This is because people develop expectations about how they will be treated. For example, if, as a result of being converted to Theory Y, a manager attempts to implement it, what is likely to happen? The sudden switch from being told what to do, to a situation in which they have to make decisions is likely, in the short term, to lead to a period of considerable confusion and a resulting drop in levels of performance. The effect of this is to convince the manager that his particular workers do not want, and indeed cannot cope with, the new responsibility. The manager's reaction, therefore, is to re-introduce the former controls. Their initial belief in Theory X is strengthened even further – 'I tried it and it failed'. Hence the self-fulfilling prophesy; the initial reaction to the change confirms that Theory X is indeed needed!

DEPENDENCY

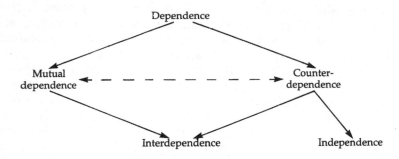

Figure 6.4. Dependency model.
(Source: Cox and Makin, 1994)

To understand why this reaction occurs, we will briefly describe a model with its roots in child and adolescent development (see Cox and Makin, 1994). The central idea of this model (see Figure 6.4) is that of *dependency*. Dependency is just what it says: one individual is dependent on another. In childhood we are dependent upon our parents for everything. At work, under a Theory X regime, we are dependent upon management telling us what to do. This dependency relationship may be accepted for some time, but at a certain stage of childhood, the amount of control exercised by the parent comes to be resented. The child develops the need to control its own life. In the work situation, this dependency is accepted as long as the rewards are big enough and/or the control does not impinge on those areas felt to be personal.

Counter-dependence. When the level of control is felt to be unacceptable, people are driven to what is called counter-dependence, that is, to rebel against authority. There is, however, another way in which counter-dependence can be induced. Perhaps surprisingly, it can be induced by releasing controls too quickly. We often see examples of this at university. Students who have been used to a fairly high level of control, both at home and at school move, in the space of a few weeks, to a situation of almost no controls. Nobody tells them when to come in, or when to work. Lecturers are certainly not going to act *in loco parentis* to those who are legally adults. For all students it is a useful experience but, for some, the release is too abrupt and they go into counter-dependence. Some go 'punk', others join extreme groups, to the dismay of parents. In this example, Theory X is replaced by almost *laissez-faire* management (i.e. very little, or no, control). The reactions are, however, much the same as those that occur at work when Theory X-type practices are suddenly replaced by Theory Y-type practices.

Interdependence. How then can we move from the dependent relationship to a Theory Y-type relationship based upon interdependence? An interdependent relationship is one in which both parties are capable of doing each other's job; however, for reasons of efficiency and convenience, they may specialize. You may remember that we said that there were two reasons why organizations use Theory X. The first is because it is a self-fulfilling prophesy, because of counter-dependence. The second reason is associated with another form of dependence, mutual dependence. The model suggests that there is no direct route from dependence to interdependence. There have to be stages of either counter-dependence or mutual dependence.

Mutual dependence is a situation where both parties mutually agree to regulate their interaction in certain ways. The best example from everyday life is that of marriage: 'I will be responsible for cooking and cleaning, if you accept responsibility for doing the gardening and household maintenance.' Such a relationship is very strong, as long as both parties are present. Unfortunately, when one party is no longer present those activities for which that person was responsible do not get done. We suspect that a lot of managers and their subordinates are in this kind of relationship. The way to find out is to see what happens when you are away on holiday. If in your absence nothing gets done unless someone takes over your position, then the relationship is likely to be that of dependence. If, as is more likely, there is a situation of mutual dependence then what awaits your return will be different. Everyone will have carried on doing their own job, without any need for close supervision. The things that you, and only you, do, will not have been done without outside assistance. In a totally interdependent relationship, it will be as if you had not been away. All the jobs will have been done, without the need for any extra outside help or direction. Your colleagues will simply have worked a little harder in order to cover for your absence.

The route from dependence to mutual dependence is by negotiation: 'You can stay out late as long as you phone and let me know'. At work, in return for accepting more responsibility you will be allowed to do some more of the work that you particularly like. The two routes shown in Figure 6.4, or a mixture of both, are the only ways to move from dependence to interdependence; from X to Y. Each has its advantages and drawbacks. Mutual dependence is cosy. It is more comfortable than interdependence which, contrary to what many may think, can be difficult. It is more difficult because disagreements, rather than being solved by issuing orders, have to be resolved genuinely to the satisfaction of all. This is highly effective, but the process may be painful. The temptation, therefore, is to stay in mutual dependence. The counter-dependence route, on the other hand, is obviously uncomfortable. However, because it is so uncomfortable the transition through it may be quicker. There is, however, another danger associated with counter-dependence. If it proves to be too painful the dependent party may choose complete independence. The adolescent leaves home and is not heard from again; the employee resigns.

You may now think that dependence has its attractions, but it too has its disadvantages. Dependence can be comfortable, especially when the situation is seen as difficult and hard to control. A strong leader, or system of leadership, that promises total support, is often seen as desirable. We can hand all our responsibilities to someone else. We have seen how control that is perceived as too pervasive eventually invites rebellion, or counter-dependence. Even before this, however, there are disadvantages associated with dependence, which culminate in rebellion. Put simply, dependence breeds passivity. This passivity shows itself in a number of different ways. First, as *inactivity*; if all control rests with others there is no point in doing anything until you are told. This, of course, may have undesirable consequences, such as dismissal! Because of this, a more common type of passive behaviour is *over-adaptation*, or extreme compliance. Orders are carried out, but strictly by the book. Finally, a period of *agitation* may follow before pent-up feelings are channelled into counter-dependence. The 'trigger' for the commencement of open hostilities (e.g. a strike), may appear trivial to outsiders, and even to some more remote managers. Benevolent autocrats and over-indulgent parents are often totally confused by the sudden turn of events. It is not the benefits that they provide that are at fault. Rather, it is the fact that they do not allow those in their charge any control or responsibility for their own work or destiny.

The styles we have considered so far might be said to be 'macro' in their approach. We have been concerned with describing leadership and management styles, and discussing when each may be appropriate. What none of the theories suggest is *how* you become participative, or task-centred, or democratic. In order to do this, we have to take a more 'micro' approach and look at the interactions between managers and those for whom they have responsibility. In particular, we will direct our attention toward the interaction between managers and their subordinates, where the purpose is to influence the subordinates' behaviour. All such interactions, we will argue, are in fact mini-appraisals, and we will hence consider them under this broad heading.

STAFF APPRAISAL

In broad terms, staff appraisal involves the collection of information about people and their performance, so that decisions can be made about them. Obviously, the type of information that is collected, and how it is collected, will depend on the type of decision that is being made. Staff appraisal systems are intended to fulfil a number of different, yet related, functions. Randell *et al.* (1984) suggest three major functions:

1) The allocation and distribution of the 'fruits' of the organization's activities, for example pay, power, and status.
2) Improving and developing the present job performance of each individual member of staff.
3) Predicting the level and type of work that an individual is likely to achieve in the future, and how long it will take them to do so.

Although these functions overlap to a certain extent they should, according to Randell and his colleagues, be kept separate, as the techniques, procedures, and information required for each are different. The distribution of rewards should be the subject of a *reward* review, the improvement of performance a *performance* review, and the prediction of future level that of a *potential* review. It is not possible for these different functions to be integrated easily into the same interview. For example, the role of the manager in the reward interview is that of a judge. In a performance review, however, the role required may be closer to that of a counsellor. In addition, the inclusion of any discussion of salary in an interview often colours the whole of the rest of the interview, especially if expectations are not met. Yet it is the below-average performer, who is not getting an increase in salary, who is the very person who needs development.

The responsibility for each of the separate functions also needs to be kept separate. Apart from perhaps small merit rises, salary levels should be determined by the organization as a whole. Small merit rises can have symbolic importance to individuals well beyond their monetary value. On the other hand, overall wage levels, and in particular wage differentials, have the potential to cause problems of equity.

The potential review should also be a central responsibility. The prediction of future potential is a difficult task, even for experts. Whilst the manager may be able to comment on present performance, more sophisticated techniques, such as assessment centres, are required to assess potential (see Chapter 1).

Obviously, managers will have an important role in providing information which may be taken into account in reward and potential reviews, but they should not have overall responsibility for these. Performance reviews, on the other hand, are very much the responsibility of the individual manager. It is clearly the manager's responsibility to develop their subordinates and improve their present performance.

The different types of interview also have different reporting requirements. It is here that the difficult issue arises of how performance is assessed. Many organizations use rating scales, which have the advantage that they can be aggregated and manipulated in various ways. Thus, if it has been decided that the top X per cent of managers will receive a salary increase of Y per cent, this can be calculated from the ratings given by their bosses. Alternatively, if evidence is required for not renewing someone's contract, the relevant poor ratings can be produced. (All of this assumes that ratings are accurate and that those of manager A can be directly compared with those of manager B. This is usually far from being the case.)

If the object of assessment is to improve performance, ratings are *not* required. Lest this appear strange, let us take an example. Many rating forms have a number of dimensions upon which a rating is required. These are often created by others, without any reference to job incumbents. Common amongst them are 'initiative', 'leadership', 'technical competence', and others. These are often marked on a scale from 1 (unacceptable) to 5 (outstanding). You have been given a '3' by your boss. What do you have to do to get a '4'? The rating gives you no guidance whatsoever. What you have to do is discuss specific incidents, covering what did, or did not happen, and how it could be done better in the future. Ratings are for administrative purposes, not for developing the individual's job performance. As we shall see shortly, this clash between administrative needs and developmental needs may be one reason for the inefficiency of many appraisal schemes.

The concept of goal-orientation, discussed in the previous chapter, is also relevant to the use of ratings. If people are to improve they need to concentrate on internal, developmental, goals rather than external, competitive, goals. Ratings may have some developmental uses but they tend, more often than not, to emphasize competitive goals, especially if pay depends on them.

INTRODUCTION OF APPRAISAL SCHEMES

Appraisal schemes are being introduced into many organizations. Even universities are now moving towards formal appraisal of teaching. Many individuals and unions, however, view this introduction with suspicion. In other organizations, schemes that have already been introduced have not lived up to initial expectations. Why is this? It appears that there are often 'gaps' on three key issues; training, objectives, and culture.

The training gap. Schemes are often introduced on the assumption that managers already have the basic skills needed to interview staff. All that is needed, therefore, is an introduction to how the relevant scheme is to be administered. This is a false assumption. If it were true, why would so many managers avoid doing them if at all possible? We do not expect people to learn to drive by watching a video. They have to practise under the guidance of a tutor. The same is true of appraisal interviewing.

The objectives gap. Management often try to 'sell' the idea of appraisal on the basis of staff development. If we accept Theory Y, we must accept that most people want to improve their performance. What most organizations start with, however, is the development of a rating system. Although the employees are not aware of the terminology, what they realize is that rating scales are required for administrative purposes, such as disciplinary procedures. Rating scales are not required for development. Professor Chris Argyris of Harvard Business School (1960) has been studying organizations for several decades, and has come to one unequivocal conclusion; how organizations *say* they work and how they *actually* work are never the same. (In his terms, their 'espoused' theories are never the same as their 'theories in practise'.) In other words, what they say, and what they do, differ. Why organizations say they want to introduce appraisal, and why they actually want appraisal may also be judged in the light of Argyris's comments. This is sometimes reinforced by the fact that the scheme applies to everyone, except the board of directors.

The culture gap. Any appraisal scheme has to fit within the organizational culture involved. To attempt to introduce a developmental scheme within a traditional 'Theory X' structure, would have its dangers. So would the imposition of an administrative scheme on an organization, or department, that was traditionally more 'Theory Y'. This latter case often occurs when such schemes are tried for highly specialist professional staff.

APPRAISAL INTERVIEWS

There is one thing that is true for all but the best appraisal schemes. Managers do not like doing appraisal interviews, will avoid them where possible, and do them only with reluctance. Why?

Appraisal interviews can be stressful. It may be relatively easy to deal with a high flyer, perhaps by channelling his enthusiasm in the right direction. It may also be fairly straightforward, if painful, to deal with those who are performing well below standard. The vast majority of individuals are somewhere in the middle. They do a reasonable job, but are unlikely to rise much higher. Some may be content to stay where they are, others may be unrealistically ambitious. How do you motivate the former, and let down the latter? In addition to being information exchanges, appraisal interviews also have the potential to become very emotional, especially if pay reviews are involved. Social and economic exchanges are often complexly intertwined.

The other main reason why managers are reluctant to carry out appraisals is that they are often seen as a peripheral activity, imposed over their heads, apparently for some administrative purpose. Carrying them out and returning the forms appears to have no influence on subsequent events. Not carrying them out results in various reminders from the personnel department. What then are the functions of appraisals?

Most managers, we suspect, will think of appraisal interviewing as something that is done, formally, once a year. Forms are filled in before, during, or after the interview, and then sent to the personnel department. Little apparently happens except, perhaps, when someone is summoned away to a training course, often at short notice. We would argue that managers are actually doing appraisals all the time, the purpose of which is to influence current and future performance. The only difference is that they are generally informal, and the official forms are absent.

It is not by accident that this section on appraisal occurs at the end of a chapter on leadership and management style, which itself follows chapters on personality and motivation. The appraisal interview, as we have defined it, is where all the elements come together as theory and practice meet.

The first part of a manager's job entails reaching decisions about what happened, why, and how it can be improved upon in the future. In doing so they will attribute *causality* – who, or what, was responsible? Let us take an example where something has gone wrong. Remembering back to the section on attribution theory, bear in mind three phenomena: actor/observer divergence, the self-serving bias, and the fundamental attribution error. The first of these, actor/observer divergence, suggests that your subordinate, as the actor, will attribute causality to the situation, an explanation that also fulfils the self-serving bias. You, however, as an observer, will tend to attribute causality to the subordinate. This may, however, be influenced by their past performance. If the person normally performs well, then the tendency to blame the actor may be reduced. However, the general tendency is still to blame the subordinate. The fundamental attribution error suggests that you will underestimate the influence of the situation.

These biases in attributions are likely to have an important influence upon appraisal. The attributions made by the manager and the subordinate for exactly the same events may differ considerably. In extreme cases they may even lead to *attributional conflict*. If the manager is attributing causes for poor performance to the subordinate, whilst the subordinate is blaming the situation, a problem-solving discussion is unlikely to occur. The manager may even start to be perceived by the subordinate as part of the problem, rather than as part of the solution.

According to Martinko and Gardner (1987) managers should try to reduce the divergence between their perspective and that of the subordinate. This is best achieved by personal interaction and listening to the subordinate's 'accounts'. This is the first function of the appraisal interview: the collection of information. This information collection has to be done before any evaluation takes place. If it is not, the effects may be counter-productive. Bad appraisal interviews, of whatever type, can be worse than none at all. Having gathered all the relevant information about the problem, it has to be decided which style of interaction (ranging from totally authoritarian to totally democratic), is appropriate. The answer to this will depend on many of the factors discussed in the leadership theories. In particular, does the person have the maturity, both in the skills required and the motivation required, to initiate the change themselves? Once again, the only way to answer these questions is to gather information.

How to gather information. Before dealing with specific techniques of information gathering, it is worth making a general point about the nature of the information gathered. We have talked in the last chapter about the importance of concentrating on behaviour. To the benefits of dealing with behaviour that we outlined in the previous chapter can be added another. Discussions concerning behaviour are less threatening than those involving dispositions. To be told by someone that you are a 'cruel' person will probably upset you. To be told, on the other hand, by the same person that 'How you have just behaved makes me feel small in the eyes of others' is not likely to have the same impact. You can do something about the behaviour that caused the other person to feel small. There is very little you can do about a 'cruel' personality. It is both safer, and more effective, therefore, to concentrate on information about behaviour.

The basic building blocks of any information-gathering exercise are questions. One of the quickest ways of increasing effectiveness in any interview is by choosing the correct type of question. First, however, we have to be able to recognize the different types, and be aware of their uses.

Exercise

Questions and their uses. In Figure 6.5 are listed the different types of questions. As an exercise, first familiarize yourself with them, and then analyse some real-life interviews. Any such interviews will do, but we find that the following is often useful in highlighting certain questioning techniques. Compare any 'chat-show' host with more searching interviews. Some of the best of these may be found in cross-examinations of politicians by political correspondents.

Each of the question types listed in Figure 6.5 has its particular uses, but they are, not surprisingly, often found in combination. Some ways of combining the different types of question into sequences are, more effective than others, however. One sequencing of questions that is particularly appropriate for information gathering has been referred to as the funnel technique – so called because the information gathered becomes more and more specific as the sequence proceeds.

Using this technique the discussion about the events in question starts with an open question. This helps the interviewer get an overall view of what happened – for example, 'The production line was stopped this morning; what happened?' Although the open question often elicits a large amount of information covering a wide area, it is often lacking in depth. In order to elicit more detailed information probing questions are used. For example, 'Who did you consult about stopping the production line?' The answer to this question will be more detailed but may still omit specific relevant information. If this is so it may be necessary to follow the probe with a closed question in order to produce answers to specific points. For example, 'Did you get authority from the production manager to stop the line?' Finally, it is often useful to use a summary to check that your information is correct. Appraisal interviews often cover a number of job-related events. It is not unusual, therefore, to find this cycle of open, probing, and closed questions, together with summaries, being repeated as different events are discussed.

The initial use of an open question also has some other advantages. First, it allows the subordinate to put their side of the story. In doing so, it may become apparent how much they feel they were responsible. And they may also indicate the extent to which they have already learnt from the events. It may be that they are already taking the necessary corrective action. Second, the use of an open question indicates that the manager has an open mind and is keen to seek all the information. This avoids defensive behaviour on the part of the subordinate. The immediate reaction to attack, in the form a pre-judgement of 'guilt' on the part of the manager, is defence. Under these conditions the subordinate will not admit to any fault on their

Question/Statement type	Useful for:	Not useful for:
OPEN 'Tell me what happened when....'	Most openings. Exploring and gathering information on a broad basis.	Very talkative interviewee.
CLOSED 'How many widgets did you produce?'	Getting specific, factual answers.	Getting broadly based information.
PROBING 'What precisely happened next?'	Establishing and checking details of events already known, or arising from open question answers.	Exploring emotionally charged areas.
HYPOTHETICAL 'What would you do if...?'	Getting interviewee to think in broader terms, or about a new area.	If situation is outside the interviewee's range.
MULTIPLE A string of questions or statements.	Never useful.	Never useful.
COMPARISON 'Would you prefer a weekly or a monthly meeting?'	Exploration of needs and values.	Where pairs of alternatives are unrealistic.
SUMMARIES 'What we seem to have decided so far is....'	Ensuring agreement about main points raised. Gaining commitment.	If used prematurely.

Figure 6.5. Question types.
(Adapted from: Randell *et al.*, 1984)

part, for fear that the admission will be used to press the attack even further. The tactic becomes one of defending the outer lines, only falling back when absolutely necessary. Such interactions are not likely to be very productive. (In TA terms this is likely to end in 'uproar', as the best form of defence is attack.)

Before moving on to look at ways of influencing behaviour, perhaps we should say something about the question types used by 'chatshow' hosts and political interviewers. Political interviewers use probing questions or, with particularly evasive interviewees, leading questions. For example, 'It is the government's intention to ... isn't it?' A statement is made into a question by adding 'isn't it' at the end. This is the most pointed way of asking for confirmation or disconfirmation. Nevertheless, skilled politicians will often respond with the answer to an entirely different question! It is a technique widely used by barristers when cross-examining hostile witnesses. Chat-show hosts, on the other hand, are normally interviewing people who want to talk. The most appropriate question types are, therefore, open, with the occasional probe. Some successful hosts, however, use closed and multiple questions. Fortunately for them most of their guests are from show business, and treat these as open questions. When 'naïve' guests, especially young children, are interviewed they are likely to treat the closed questions as such, and give one word answers. The embarrassment of the host on these occasions is obvious.

Dealing with emotions. Thus far we have been dealing with the rational and logical process of gathering information. This is part of decision-making skills and, as such, is an obvious part of a manager's role. There is another aspect of the role with which many managers feel uncomfortable. Human beings have emotions and often express them. While managers are trained to deal with information, they are often not trained to deal with emotions.

There is one cardinal rule for dealing with emotions: they do not mix with logically reasoned argument! If your partner, in a highly emotional state, complains that you never wash the dishes, we would not recommend that you show the argument to be logically incorrect because you did wash the dishes last Christmas Day! There are only two ways to deal with emotion. If you have aroused the emotion because of something you did which you now accept as wrong, then an *early* apology will defuse the situation. On many occasions, however, this may not be appropriate. In these circumstances the only solution is to let the emotion run its course. This can be encouraged in two ways. Attentive, but silent, listening, and the occasional use of *reflective* questions. Silence can be difficult to maintain as there is a strong temptation to jump in and correct inaccuracies. Reflective questions do what their name suggests; they use a summary of what the person has just said and reflect it back, without evaluation. For example, 'You feel you've been undervalued by the firm – is that it?' The effect is to allow the emotion to run its course. High levels of emotion are difficult to maintain without support from others, either in the form of agreement or argument. With no evaluation, the emotional level tends to steadily decrease. In doing so, the course of the outburst often follows a spiral. The same ground is gone over again and again, but with the emotional level declining all the time. When it is over, the time is right for logical discussion.

Influencing behaviour. There are many ways of influencing behaviour, but one dimension that should always be borne in mind is that of commitment versus compliance. When people are committed to a course of action they will adopt it as their own and will make efforts to ensure that they succeed, without the necessity of continual monitoring. When they are being compliant they are only undertaking the action because they fear the consequences of non-compliance. In general, people are most committed to their own ideas, and least committed to those that are imposed by others.

Potentially the most successful condition for behaviour change is when no influence at all is required. This is the situation where the person has worked out what they need to change, and has already started the process. All the manager needs to do is check that they agree with the proposed course of action, and monitor it to ensure that it is carried out. But there is a danger, under these circumstances, that managers can actually reduce effectiveness if they are not careful. To be told by someone else what you should be doing, when you have already reached the same conclusion, can be very de-motivating. Once again, the way to avoid this is by the use of open questions.

On the other hand, there are bound to be occasions where commitment is of secondary importance, and where the maturity of staff is such that a directive approach is required. Let us consider the range of options open to a manager to influence behaviour. It includes:

Orders
Requests
Advice/suggestions
Promises
Threats
Explanations
Praise
Criticism
Leading questions

The first three options have certain aspects in common, as they all let the subordinate know what you think they should be doing. They differ in the extent to which reasons are given.

Orders leave the least room for any kind of initiative by the subordinate. In the extreme case, no questions are allowed. Requests may vary somewhat. The difference between an order and a request is that, in theory at least, a request may be turned down. The extent of the latitude to turn down the request will obviously vary. Advice and suggestions offer the greatest latitude for rejection. The message behind an order is 'Because I say so'; and that behind a request is 'Because I would like you to'. The message behind advice and suggestions is 'Because it is in your own best interests to'.

All the other methods of influence work on variations on coercion and seduction. You will recognize promises and threats from the section on OBMod. As discussed there, these may be highly effective, but both require a knowledge of the individual to whom they are to be applied. The major pitfall for managers is that of *projection*. We all have a tendency to project our own needs, aspirations, and values on to others. To assume that what we find rewarding or punishing will also be rewarding or punishing for others is a mistake, as is assuming that their aspirations are the same as ours.

The other pitfall, common both to managers and parents, is to threaten punishments that will not be enforced. The reason may be that you cannot impose them or that you do not want to impose them; the effect is the same, future threats lose their credibility.

Praise and criticism are particular forms of reward and punishment. Both carry information, but the rewards and punishments involved are social rather than tangible.

Leading questions can be used as a method of giving instructions – 'You won't do that again, will you? Phrased as a question, the implications are clear, as is the response expected. The tone will suggest whether it is an order, a request, or advice.

Types of interaction. Now we have the building blocks: question types for gathering information, and the different methods of influencing behaviour. How are these combined in the appraisal to produce the style required?

Wright and Taylor (1994) have identified six main styles of interaction between managers and staff:

Tell
Tell and Sell
Tell and Listen
Ask and Tell
Problem Solving
Ask and Listen

These styles lie along the scale from total control by the manager, to control by the subordinate. As such they differ in the extent to which they allow subordinate initiative. As we have suggested, there is often a relationship between the degree to which a person has control over decisions that affect them, and the extent to which they feel committed to those decisions. Because of this, the different styles will differ in the degree of commitment they are likely to engender in the subordinate. The styles also differ in the degree to which they emphasize information-gathering or giving orders. At one end of the scale is a lot of order-giving but no information-gathering – 'Tell'. At the other end there is a lot of information-gathering, but no ordering – 'Ask and Listen'. Let us now consider each of these types. What influencing

TELL

Uses:	Orders, requests and strong suggestions.
Relies upon:	The manager being right and the subordinate's willingness to accept this.
Advantages:	Saves time and effort.
Disadvantages:	It overlooks the fact that the subordinate may have useful information and may, in addition, create resentment.

TELL AND SELL

Uses:	Orders, requests, advice, suggestions together with explanations, threats and punishments in order to tell the subordinate what to do while also 'selling' the solution to them so that it is accepted.
Relies upon:	The manager being right.
Advantages:	Quick and effective plus, one hopes, some commitment.
Disadvantages:	If the selling doesn't work, possible disaster.

TELL AND LISTEN

Uses:	Orders, requests, advice and suggestions, together with praise and criticism.
Relies upon:	The manager being right together with some participation leading to commitment.
Advantages:	More commitment because the person has been listened to.
Disadvantages:	Possibility of an inconclusive outcome because the effects of 'telling' have been dissipated during the listening phase.

ASK AND TELL

Uses:	Information gathering, followed by orders, suggestions, advice and requests.
Advantages:	As more accurate information has been collected better decisions are likely, together with higher commitment.
Disadvantages:	The decision may still not be accepted, especially if strongly held views have been overruled.

PROBLEM SOLVING

Uses:	Information gathering followed by advice, suggestions, promises, praise and explanations.
Advantages:	Potentially high quality decisions together with high commitment.
Disadvantages:	It is not appropriate when the subordinate has low skill or motivational maturity. Nor when there is little genuine room for manoeuvre.

ASK AND LISTEN

Uses:	Information gathering only.
Advantages:	Only appropriate when views are being sought well in advance of any decision. Its other use is when dealing with emotional problems to which the manager has no solution, in other words being a 'shoulder to cry on'.

Figure 6.6. Types of influence.
(Source: Wright and Taylor, 1986)

techniques do they use? What do they rely on for their effectiveness? What are their advantages and disadvantages?

These are the techniques that any manager can use in his everyday interactions with his subordinates. Managers, who are paid to make decisions and take the responsibility, have a tendency, in our experience, to be at the 'Tell' or Theory X, end of the scale. This is often compounded by the pressures when things go wrong. As a very simple exercise, the next time things go wrong, either at work or at home, before 'telling', just 'ask'. Try a simple open question – 'What happened?' You may be surprised at how much more information you receive, and hence how much better are the decisions you subsequently take.

Asking an open question may also reduce the effects of possible differences in attribution, which can have an influence over the type of interaction. Dugan (1989), for example, found that an 'ability' attribution for failure on the part of a subordinate led to a 'tell and sell' style, with managers reasserting control and adopting an increasingly formal role. Indeed an 'ability' attribution becomes a self-fulfilling prophecy, with managers using punishment in an attempt to improve performance. 'Effort' attribution, on the other hand, led to a 'problem-solving' approach, with shared control. These attributions also have motivational effects, including the possibility of learned helplessness, as discussed in the previous chapter.

Both 'macro' and 'micro' theories of leadership have now been covered. The main point that perhaps needs restating concerns the difference between 'espoused' Theory Y, and Theory X 'in practise' (sic). We believe that managers find Theory X, task-orientated, management-traditional, and hence comfortable. Indeed, as we have seen, it is entirely appropriate in some circumstances. There are, however, situations where more participative management is likely to be more effective. It is in the recognition and adaptation of styles in these situations that we believe that training is required.

As discussed on page 193, the position of interdependence is difficult. It is difficult for a number of reasons. It appears, on the surface, that the manager is relinquishing control. When, in role-playing interviews, managers use 'tell' inappropriately, their excuse is often that allowing the subordinate to make decisions means that they, as managers, have lost control. The role of the manager has traditionally been seen as that of the decision-maker. If the subordinates are allowed to make decisions, there is a feeling that the manager may not be doing their job. Another reason is that interdependence means that each party needs to state their needs openly. This may arouse emotions on both sides. Management has traditionally been seen as a rational, not an emotional, activity. We all realize, however, that it is impossible to separate the two totally, in the work-place as well as elsewhere. As Sir John Harvey-Jones recognizes, you cannot communicate effectively unless you are prepared to show emotion.

These two reasons which, like the low use of praise, are largely cultural in origin, are powerful inhibitors of more interdependent management. There is one very simple step that managers can take. It has been stated before, but bears re-stating because of its importance. Before telling, ask and listen! As managers, your raw data is information. Asking helps to provide that information.

LEADERSHIP AND THE PSYCHOLOGICAL CONTRACT

The nature of the psychological contract will influence, and in turn be influenced by, the interactions between managers and their staff. In particular, the process of staff appraisal can be seen as an opportunity to renegotiate elements of the psychological contract. The existing psychological contract will, however, influence how this negotiation will take place. In an organization where staff have expectations of consultation and participation in decision-making, the use of a 'tell' style of appraisal is likely to be less than effective. In a highly authoritarian organization, on the other hand, a problem-solving approach may trigger counter-dependence. The appraisal interview provides the opportunity to clarify, and possibly renegotiate, both the economic and the psychological contract. The main point, however, is that the process by which this is done needs to be consistent with the current psychological contract.

Group Dynamics at Work

Working with other people in groups is something that is part of every manager's job. Indeed it often appears as if much of the time at work is spent in meetings of one sort or another. These may be just an informal gathering of two or three people to solve a particular problem. In general, the higher people go in their managerial careers, the more time they seem to spend in meetings. The question that has to be asked is, of course, why? Why does so much of what happens in organizations, especially at managerial levels, take place in groups?

The obvious answer is that many organizational goals cannot be achieved by individuals acting independently. Many of them involve tasks which are extremely complicated. There are two ways in which this complexity may show itself. First, the problem may be *technically* complex, requiring the combined skills of professionals, perhaps from a range of disciplines. Second, the problem may be *administratively* complex. This complexity is one requiring liaison and co-ordination. Some problems may, of course, be both technically and administratively complex.

In order to solve these problems, 'formal' groups are established, whose stated functions are to accomplish certain tasks. Such formal groups may be either permanent, such as standing committees, or temporary, such as working parties, depending on whether the tasks involved are recurrent or 'one-offs'.

Organizations, as we know, do not consist solely of formal groups. Friendship and other informal groupings develop. Again, why should this happen? The reason is that such informal groups satisfy 'psychological' needs. According to Schein (1980), these may be classified as follows:

- The satisfaction of the need for affiliation – the simple need to be with other people.

- The establishment and maintenance of self-identity and self-esteem. Who we are, and our relative status is determined by our membership of various groups. This will also influence our perception of our own personal value and hence self-esteem. As we shall see later, personal advancement is usually achieved by attaining membership of a 'higher' group, or by increasing the standing of the present group.

- The testing and establishment of social reality. Groups develop beliefs about the way the organization operates. These may, in some cases, be incorrect. They will, nevertheless, influence the way group members behave. For example, beliefs that increasing output will lead to a reduction in the piece-rate will influence production levels.

- Groups offer a feeling of security and mutual support. By doing so they reduce uncertainty and anxiety.

- The group may act as a problem solver for its members.

Which informal groups will develop will be determined, to a large extent, by the physical layouts required for work. Distance, in particular, has a powerful influence on who will interact with whom. In general, the more frequent the interactions, the more likely informal groups are to form. Because informal groups satisfy important psychological needs, they have a considerable influence upon group members. The norms that groups develop may be either functional or dysfunctional for the organization. Where group norms are in tune with those of the organization, it would do well to capitalize on this. But there is obviously a problem where they are contrary to those of the organization. In such circumstances, the organization will usually try to break up the group, often by removing key members.

The implication so far has been that formal and informal groups are entirely separate. This is not the case. Groupings that started off formally often develop powerful informal relations. As well as being a department, it may be a department of friends. The armed forces deliberately encourage this, as do some Japanese organizations. Once again, social and economic exchanges are intermixed. It is also the case that informal groupings (such as friendships outside work), provide useful channels of communication for the organization. The 'grapevine' is the everyday term for such channels.

Let us consider in more detail what happens when people work together in groups. In identifying what happens we will be in a better position to capitalize on the benefits of working in groups, while avoiding some of the pitfalls we have mentioned above. In particular, we will concentrate on various aspects of decision-making in groups.

GROUP DECISION-MAKING

There are two dimensions that need to be kept in mind when considering the functioning of groups.

Technical quality. When groups have to solve problems and make decisions the only way they can do so is to call on the expertise of those within the group. Each of these individuals will often have their own ideas of what the 'right' decision should be. These initial individual decisions are, however, subject to influence depending upon the inputs of others. The quality of the decision, therefore, will be influenced by two factors. The expertise and knowledge that each participant contributes, and the way the different pieces of knowledge and experience are integrated. The technical quality of the decision is concerned with whether the answer the group arrives at is correct or not. For example, was the money invested in the best way, or did the rearranged production-line work? Technical quality is, of course, essential to the well-being of the organization. This is well recognized, and a large part of our education and training is geared towards making the 'right' decision. Electrical engineers are taught to design distribution systems that are safe and reliable, accountants are taught how to deal with finance, and so on. There is, we would argue, another aspect of group working in which few have been trained. This concerns the organizational quality of the decision.

Organizational quality is not concerned with the technical aspects of the decision. Its concern is with the extent to which those who will implement, and be affected by, the decision are committed to it. This is important because the degree of commitment will influence the speed and effectiveness of implementation with which the decision is implemented. Those who are uncommitted, or even openly hostile, to a decision, are unlikely to apply themselves whole-heartedly when it comes to putting it into action.

On many occasions, therefore, it is necessary to balance the demands for technical quality and organizational quality. It is rare to encounter a problem for which there is one, and only one, correct answer. More often a choice has to be made from a number of options, all of which have some merit. In these circumstances which of these is better – a decision which you think represents the 'best' technical solution, but which is obviously not accepted by someone who will be affected by it; or a decision that is not quite as good technically (at least in your eyes), but to which everybody concerned is wholeheartedly committed? Ideally, of course, what is required is the best decision with total commitment, but life is rarely that simple. As Sir John Harvey-Jones, the former Chairman of ICI, has said: 'There are no perfect solutions, and the best is often the enemy of the good'. The best plan, he suggests, is to 'get a three-quarters right solution and belt on with it'. But what factors influence the organizational quality of the decision?

The most important influence is the way in which the group members work together. What is important for organizational quality is not *what* was decided, but the *process by which* it was decided. And although this process of decision-making mainly influences a decision's organizational quality, it also influences its technical quality, as will be shown. What then, are the main influences on organizational quality?

Participation is perhaps the most important influence. As mentioned earlier, people are generally more committed to those decisions which they feel are, in some way, their own. How is this feeling brought about? There are two main elements in participation: the feeling that your ideas have been properly listened to and assessed, and the feeling that you have contributed to the final decision-making. These may sound like easy targets to achieve, but this is not always the case, as some of your own experiences in groups will probably testify.

To start with, listening is not just the opposite of talking. Too often, the silence that is accorded someone who is speaking is not used for listening to what they are saying, but rather to preparing your own next contribution. This is usually very easy to pick up, especially by whomever has just spoken. If true listening is taking place, then the comments that follow will lead logically from what has just been said by the previous speaker. So often, however, this is not the case. (This is the 'next-in-line effect' referred to in Chapter 3.)

Participation in decision-making is not related just to the extent to which we feel our own ideas have been given a true hearing. We may not succeed in gaining general acceptance of our own views; indeed, we may even come to realize that there are better solutions around. The fact that our ideas are not accepted does not necessarily mean that we cannot be committed. Whether we will be committed or not often depends on our perception of the *fairness* with which the decision is made. Ideally, of course, a consensus is to be desired. This is not always possible and, if a compromise that would attract a consensus is not possible, then other means may be used. A vote is the most common way of making such decisions. At first sight, a vote means that there are winners and losers, and that perhaps the losers may be uncommitted. This need not be the case. As long as the circumstances under which a vote is taken are accepted by all, the 'losers' may accept their position and devote themselves to the consequences of that decision.

Although the benefits of participation have been generally accepted, there has, until recently, been little theoretical explanation for the effects. Recently, explanations have been proposed from two areas that we have considered in earlier chapters. One of these is the concept of procedural justice. People will react more favourably to negative decisions if they feel that the procedures that led to them were fair. The reasons for this may be found in the concept of counter-factual reasoning, which we considered in the section on attribution theory.

When faced with a negative decision, people reflect on the decision-making process that produced it. In doing so they look for an element in the process that, had it been different, might have led to a more positive outcome. The main element is the extent to which they were allowed to participate in the decision-making process. If they did not participate at all it is fairly easy for them to conclude that things would have turned out better had they been involved. On the other hand, if they were actively involved it is more difficult for them to imagine how the decision-making process could have been better. This is likely to lead to a perception that the process was equitable, and hence to greater acceptance.

MONITORING THE PROCESS

Given the importance of the decision-making process to group members' commitment, it is clearly necessary to be able to assess participation within the group. In ascending order of effectiveness, the most common indications of organizational quality are:

- Apathy: no one contributes to the group discussion, not because they are in agreement, but because they are totally disillusioned.

- 'Plops': a suggestion is made, but totally ignored.

- Dominance: one particular individual dominates the meeting. This is often accompanied by apathy from the other members.

- Pairing: this is the simplest form of groups within a group. The psychological support offered by pairing is considerable.

- Voting: this is sometimes the only way to resolve disagreements. There are times, however, when it is appropriate and others when it is inappropriate.

- False consensus: if agreement cannot be reached, one way out of the impasse is to couch the decision in such broad terms that a number of interpretations are possible. A false consensus becomes apparent when the time comes for the decision to be implemented. Each side has a different understanding of what was agreed.

- Consensus: this is the most desirable conclusion. Genuine agreement leads to genuine commitment.

It is also necessary to decide who should be monitoring the decision-making process. Here a problem arises. Work groups are full of technical specialists, whose purpose it is to provide, when required, their professional expertise. As a result of this, they are concentrating not on the process, but on the task. This means that no one may be monitoring how people are feeling about the discussions. Perhaps the person who should be taking an interest is the chairperson, who is often the group leader. Unfortunately, the chairperson is also likely to have his or her eyes firmly on the task instead of the process. For this reason, it is perhaps unfortunate that chairpersons have to be leaders. There is no reason why the most senior member of the group should be the most skilled in interpersonal processes. Someone, perhaps everyone, should be keeping an eye on the process. In extreme cases of disagreement, a neutral chairperson may be appointed, for example, by the arbitration service ACAS in the case of an industrial dispute. They will be regulating the *process* as much as, if not more than, the content of any disagreements. We should not lose sight of the fact such a role is required in any group, albeit informally. It need not, and should not, be the function of the chairperson alone. All group members should bear some responsibility for ensuring the effectiveness of the group.

Some of the indicators of effective and ineffective process were given above. There is one other simple way of finding out. If you feel that a particular individual is less than happy with a particular decision, check it out. Simply ask them how they *feel* about the decision. Notice that you do not ask them what they *think* about it, which would lead you back into the task, rather than towards the process. Questions about feelings will give you information about the organizational quality of the group's decision.

Although all members should take responsibility for the effective functioning of the group, individuals may have preferences for particular roles within the group, and it is to this that we will now turn.

TEAM ROLES

The most comprehensive investigation of team roles is probably that of Belbin (1981). His work is based on studies of groups of managers attending various management courses. A common feature of such courses is group work involving the analysis of case studies, as those who have attended them will testify. Belbin wondered what were the characteristics of groups who did well on case studies. Initially, he tried to 'create' groups who should do well. He did this by using tests to select the most intelligent participants. The top scorers were all then placed in the same group, the so-called 'Apollo' group. In the exercises that followed, these groups, rather than out-performing all others, did disastrously! This led Belbin to investigate and experiment further, using personality tests and a test for preferred team roles, developed by himself. What he found was that successful teams consisted of a *mix* of individuals, each of whom performed a different role. A summary of these roles is shown in Figure 7.1. The names of all but one of the roles match their descriptions fairly well. What characterizes the role of 'plant' is not at all clear from its label. The reason for this is that Belbin discovered that some groups who, on the basis of his research, should have been performing well, were not. The reason, he discovered, was that there was no one in the group who was generating ideas. As soon as he 'planted' such an ideas generator in the group, it started performing – hence the name.

Each person, therefore, has a preferred role or roles and, if the group is to be effective, it needs all these roles to be filled. This might suggest that we need to select people who are going to join groups so as to ensure that they can fill one or more of the roles which the group currently lacks. In an ideal world, this may be so, but most group membership within organizations is predetermined, usually by technical function. How then can a knowledge of Belbin's roles help?

First we must be aware of the role preferences of individuals. You do not have to test people to discover this, just watch how they behave. In doing so, it will become apparent that people differ in the strength of their preferences. Some people will have very strong preferences for just one or two roles. Other people may have their preferences rather less strongly spread across four or five roles. Such individuals, being more flexible, are capable of filling a number of roles. Ideally, people should be given tasks which allow them to operate in their preferred roles. For example, the resource investigator should be allowed to seek out ideas and developments elsewhere which may help the group.

Second, we must realize which roles are missing, and thus contributing to possible inefficiency. For example, Makin *et al.* (1991) investigated why some quality circles continue to meet to solve problems concerned with work, while others cease to meet. They found that all those groups that failed lacked someone whose stated preference was the 'completer' role. Apparently these groups were good at problem and solution generation, but never carried their ideas through.

If an important role is not being filled the obvious solution is to 'import' someone to do it. This, again, is not usually possible, although some boards of directors and senior executives do take this into account when selecting someone to join their ranks. The alternative is to find someone within the group who would be prepared to take on the role, or even adopt the role, if it is not too alien.

ROLE	OBSERVED CONTRIBUTIONS
CHAIRPERSON	1. Clarifying the goals and objectives of the group. 2. Selecting the problems on which decisions have to be made, and establishing their priorities. 3. Helping establish roles, responsibilities and work boundaries within the group. 4. Summing up the feelings and achievements of the group, and articulating group verdicts.
SHAPER	1. Shaping roles, boundaries, responsibilities, tasks and objectives. 2. Finding or seeking to find pattern in group discussion. 3. Pushing the group towards agreement on policy and action and towards making decisions.
PLANT	1. Advancing proposals. 2. Making criticisms that lead up to counter-suggestions. 3. Offering new insights on lines of action already agreed.
MONITOR/ EVALUATOR	1. Analysing problems and situations. 2. Interpreting complex written material and clarifying obscurities. 3. Assessing the judgements and contributions of others.
COMPANY WORKER	1. Transforming talk and ideas into practical steps. 2. Considering what is feasible. 3. Trimming suggestions to make them fit into agreed plans and established systems.
TEAM WORKER	1. Giving personal support and help to others. 2. Building on to or seconding a member's ideas and suggestions. 3. Drawing the reticent into discussion. 4. Taking steps to avert or overcome disruption of the team.
RESOURCE INVESTIGATOR	1. Introducing ideas and developments of external origin. 2. Contacting other individuals or groups of own volition. 3. Engaging in negotiation-type activities.
COMPLETER	1. Emphasizing the need for task completion, meeting targets and schedules and generally promoting a sense of urgency. 2. Looking for and spotting errors, omissions and oversights. 3. Galvanizing others into activity.

Figure 7.1. Belbin's Team Roles.
(Adapted from: Belbin, 1981)

The need to deal with 'people' as well as 'task' processes has now been dealt with at some length, and you may have noticed that only one of the roles (team worker) is explicitly concerned with group relationships. Most of the roles are concerned with 'task' issues, and these will be discussed next.

MONITORING THE TASK

A particularly useful model of what happens when groups are taking decisions has been developed by Thompson and Tuden (1959), who suggest that decisions differ on two dimensions. The way that the decision-making should proceed will depend on where the particular decision lies on these dimensions.

The first dimension they call *preference for outcomes*. Another name for this might be goals, or 'where we want to get to'. The other dimension they refer to as *beliefs about causation*. This is less easy to give an alternative name. Basically, however, it is concerned with our beliefs about what causes what – 'if I do this, the result will be that'. Preferences for outcomes is concerned with where we want to go; beliefs about causation are concerned with how we get there.

On both of these dimensions, Thompson and Tuden suggest that individuals can be either clear or unclear. In fact, we can have varying degrees of 'clarity', but to simplify matters only the two extremes will be considered here. The resulting diagram of four boxes is shown in Figure 7.2.

The top righthand box is, perhaps, the position most people would like to find themselves in, and it means that you are clear about your goals, and also clear about what you need to do to achieve them. In this situation, no decisions really need to be made. Computation is all that is required to make the decision. Contrast this with the box at the bottom left. In this situation you are unclear as to what your goals are and, in addition, you are unclear what the effects of any action you may take would be. In this situation, the model suggests, 'inspiration' is required.

These are the two extremes, however. In most cases, we are fairly clear about at least one dimension. The two boxes that are most relevant, therefore, are the top left and bottom righthand corners. Consider a situation in which you are clear about your goal, but unclear as to what you need to do to achieve it – the situation at the bottom righthand corner. For example, you know where you want to go on holiday, but you don't know how to get there. What you lack in this situation is *knowledge*. And this is the reason that organizations set up R&D and market research departments, and why governments have 'think tanks'. All of these are designed to give expert advice on what

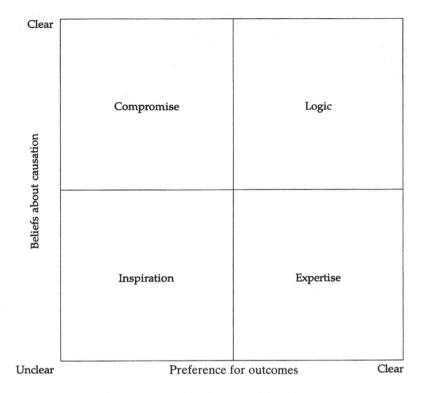

Figure 7.2. Thompson and Tudens' model of decision-making.
(Source: Thompson and Tuden, 1959)

the effects of various strategies will be. What is required are expert, knowledge-based judgements.

Contrast this with the situation at the upper left corner. Here you are aware of how to achieve all the possible goals, but are unclear as to which goal you wish to pursue. This situation is entirely different from the one mentioned above, in that it concerns not knowledge but *personal preferences*. Again consider the example of where to go on holiday. You are trying to decide between two resorts. You are perfectly clear as to how to get to both, but how do you decide between your partner's preference for the beach and yours for sightseeing? No amount of extra knowledge will help you decide. In this situation, the only way to decide is by what Thompson and Tuden call 'compromise'. Their use of the word is slightly wider than normal. There are a number of ways in which a compromise can be reached. First, if an impasse is reached, then the 'compromise' may be to accept the wishes of the majority, often by means of a vote. An alternative, and possibly better, compromise is to find a superordinate goal, in other words, a goal that encompasses all of the alternative goals. Thus, if you can find a holiday resort that has both scenery and beaches, the problem is solved. The last way is to appeal to a higher authority. In organizations this is often senior management who are brought in as arbitrators.

It is important to recognize which of these boxes you are currently in. If techniques of problem resolution are not appropriate, there will be, at the very least, confusion. To give an example from a continuing and controversial public debate, the question of whether, and when, abortion should be allowed raises considerable feelings. In an attempt to decide whether or not it should be allowed, medical experts are often produced by both sides. This is appropriate if the question is 'When is independent life outside the womb viable?' It is not appropriate if the question is 'When does life start?' This latter is a philosophical and theological question. No amount of medical knowledge can provide the answer.

From the explanations given it appears, according to Thompson and Tuden, that all our decision-making takes place in just one box of their model. This is not the case. The object is, in most cases, to move from the bottom lefthand box to the top righthand box, from confusion to certainty. There are two alternative routes by which this may be achieved. One way to do this is to decide first on your goal, then decide how to get there. The other is to look at all the practical alternatives, then decide which goal to adopt. Which of these is likely to be more effective? You may have difficulty answering this. The probable reason is that the most common method is not one or the other, but a combination of the two. The desirability of various goals are assessed, but so are some of the associated practicalities. This is where the implications for chairpersons in particular become apparent.

The chairperson's role should be two-fold. First, to ensure that all members of the group are working on the same dimension. (Identifying which dimension the group is working on is easier than it sounds. Just sit back and listen to the discussion in your next meeting for a few minutes. If one subgroup is working on one dimension and one on the other, there will effectively be two meetings rather than one.) The chairperson should also ensure that there is adequate discussion on the current dimension, before switching to the other. At least tentative ideas should be crystallized before switching to the other dimension. The effects of premature switching are often recognized by those who wish to divert a meeting away from a conclusion that they do not like personally. Realizing which dimension the group is currently working on, they change the discussion to the other dimension. After an inconclusive discussion on that dimension they then initiate a switch back.

To summarize, for a group to work effectively ensure that everyone is working on the same dimension, and that enough time is given to discussion on each to ensure that tentative, interim conclusions are reached.

The problem that Thompson and Tuden do not consider is whether the 'beliefs about causation' are correct or not. How effective, therefore, are groups at problem analysis and decision-making? There are a number of characteristics of groups of which one needs to be aware.

FACTORS IN GROUP DECISION-MAKING

There are both advantages and pitfalls in solving problems in groups. One of the potential advantages is that of increased motivation. If the group is cohesive and all members are committed to a course of action, then the effects are likely to be beneficial. But does a group do any better than the average of the individuals who compose it? Does the technical quality of the decision improve at all?

Obviously, there are some situations where it is not appropriate to use a group to make a decision, as when one individual is clearly recognized as the expert in the field. However, in circumstances in which it is appropriate to use a group to make decisions, the rule appears to be that the group will make a decision that is better than the average of all the members' individual decisions, but not as good as that of the best individual. The problem is, of course, that the 'best' individual solution can only be identified in retrospect.

There are a number of reasons for this. Groups do not appear to be better than individuals at generating ideas. Brainstorming carried out by individuals yields more ideas than when carried out by a group. Where groups gain their advantage is in the pooling and analysis of the ideas. In particular, they are good at detecting errors. This general rule of the greater efficiency of the group is just that, a general rule. There are a number of other factors that influence the effectiveness of the group.

Size and communication will be dealt with under the same heading, as they are, to a large extent, interdependent. The larger the group, the greater the problems of communication. Parkinson's law – 'work expanding so as to fill the time available for its completion' – has already been mentioned. He also commented on the effect of group size on group effectiveness, saying that ineffectiveness increases with size until total ineffectiveness is reached at a group size of 21. Other commentators have suggested that the optimum size is between eight and twelve. In a fairly light-hearted vein, a mathematician has calculated that if Parkinson is correct and that each extra person adds a 'disturbance factor', then the optimum size is, in fact, twelve.

As already suggested, the effects of size result mainly from communication problems, as more and more people wish to contribute to the group discussion. In small groups, therefore, the chairperson's role may be fairly informal. Indeed, a small group of mature adults should be able to control themselves. When groups get larger, however, more formal management may be required. To address all remarks through the Chair in a meeting of six people is perhaps being over-formal. To do so in a meeting of 30 may be a necessity. 'Can we have one meeting please?', is the common cry of chairpersons of large groups.

The channels of communication will influence both the effectiveness of the group, and group members' satisfaction. The main distinction that is made is between centralized and de-centralized groups. Let us consider some examples. For simplicity's sake we will consider a group of four people, but the same points apply both to

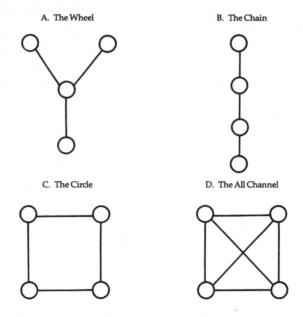

Figure 7.3. Leavitt's patterns of communication.
(Adapted from: Leavitt, 1951)

larger and smaller groups. The different communication patterns are shown in Figure 7.3.

Each dot represents a group member, who is allowed to communicate only along the lines. Thus, in the first case the person at the centre of the wheel can communicate with all of the other members.

They, on the other hand, can only communicate with him or her. If they wish to communicate to other members they can do so only through the same central person. The degree of 'centrality' is highest in the wheel and decreases through the chain and circle. The all-channel, where every member can communicate directly with every other member is totally decentralized.

There are two clear effects of centralization. In general, those in the central positions feel satisfied, while those in peripheral positions feel dissatisfied. The other effect is that those placed in central positions, which give control and power over information-flow, begin to behave directively. In other words, they become 'leaders', irrespective of their personalities.

The degree of centralization also affects the group's efficiency, but this also depends upon the complexity of the task. Once again, for simplicity's sake we will divide the tasks into two categories, simple and complex. In general, when the task is simple, centralized groups like the wheel are faster, and make fewer errors. When the task is complex, the picture is reversed; decentralized groups are faster, and make fewer mistakes. These generalizations are from studies on experimental groups. Unlike managerial problems, all the problems had correct answers. When a range of alternatives are available, rather than one correct solution, additional patterns emerge. These are known as *group polarization* (sometimes called 'risky shift'), and *groupthink.*

Group polarization. The first systematic demonstration of what was then called 'risky shift' was by a postgraduate student in Boston (Stoner, 1961). His dissertation looked at decision-making in groups of business studies students. The problems consisted of a number of case studies. In each of these, there was an element of risk (a stake), plus a possible prize – in other words a choice dilemma. On the basis of the case study, the group had to decide what advice they would give to a person in particular circumstances. For example, what advice would you give to a young electrical engineer? At present she has a good, pensionable, steady, but rather boring job with a large organization. She has been offered a job in a newly established computer firm, with the possibility of a partnership if all goes well. The risks are, of course, also high. The sector is very volatile, with a lot of companies failing each year.

In considering the advice to be given, each individual first makes their own decision. There then follows a group meeting in which everyone reveals their own decision, followed by a group discussion. Each individual then reassesses their own decision in the light of the group discussion. In these circumstances it was found that a high percentage of individuals make a more risky decision following the group discussion, hence the name 'risky shift'. At first, it was thought that the reason for this risky shift could be a reflection of the particular group on whom the experiments were conducted; those in business might be expected to be predisposed towards riskier decisions. This is not the case. The experiments have been repeated across many different groups, in many different countries, with results that are remarkably similar. After a group discussion people take more risky decisions. This is not to say that every individual, or every group shifts to a riskier position. Rather the effect is an average one, across a number of groups and a number of individuals.

Some years after the original work, it was realized that there were a small number of case studies that did not produce a risky shift. In fact, they consistently produced a 'cautious shift'. All the cases that produce such a cautious shift have one characteristic in common. The 'stake' involved is large. To take the earlier example of the electrical engineer, in the case study she is in her early career and the stake is therefore low. What if she were in her late career, and failure of the new company meant that she would stand very little chance of finding future employment?

Although most people's individual decisions err on the side of caution in such cases, a shift does still occur. It is, however, one towards even more caution. It appears that comparing and discussing decisions have the effect of polarizing the initial decision. Risky decisions become more risky, cautious ones more cautious. The final point to be made about polarization is that the amount of shift is not uniform. In general, the more extreme the initial judgement (whether it be risky or cautious), the greater the size of the shift.

Just why does group polarization occur? The first explanation, as mentioned earlier, was in terms of 'special' groups (such as American managers). Another explanation was that people conform to a group norm so that their scores converge towards the group average. Neither of these is correct. Another suggestion was that the group leader was having a large influence. This was disproved when it was found that the risky shift occurred even when the leader was advocating caution.

There appear to be two reasons for the shifts. The rather more obvious one is that of persuasive arguments. Each individual will have made their decision on the basis of risky items outweighing cautious items (or vice versa). The items that each person has taken into consideration will be different. When all these items are shared, there is evidence for an even riskier decision.

The other reason is based in social comparison theory. In general, we all like to see ourselves as 'above average' on desirable qualities. For example, 80 per cent of drivers rate themselves above average. This is of course logically impossible. Consider again the case of the engineer. Most people rate themselves as above average on risk taking. Not so high as to be considered foolhardy, just 'above average'. Accordingly, their decision is based on what they think is above average risk taking. But what is average? At this point they do not know. When they get in the group and share their decisions, however, they find that everyone else has similar levels of risk-taking. This then is the 'average'. When they take their second decision, they now know what 'average' is so they then have to increase their level of risk in order to put themselves where they thought they were in the first place, just 'above average'! Each of these explanations, it appears, has about equal weight. Half the shift can be attributed to persuasive argument, half to social comparison.

Polarization has to be recognized as a potential influence on group decision-making. If a group of normally cautious managers discuss an issue, their final decision is likely to be even more cautious. Likewise, a group of risk-taking managers will make even riskier decisions. However, perhaps a potentially greater danger is that of *groupthink*. The term was coined by Janis (1972) following his study of a number of real-life, and disastrous, decisions within the American presidency. He examined the circumstances surrounding a number of important decisions which turned out to be wrong. In each case warnings about the dangers were ignored. The decisions he investigated included the invasion of North Korea, which brought the Chinese into the Korean war, and the 'Bay of Pigs' fiasco in Cuba. In the latter case, President Kennedy authorized the CIA to help Cuban exiles mount an 'invasion' of Cuba; it got no further than the beach at the Bay of Pigs!

Analysing what happened, Janis suggested that, under certain conditions, commitment to the group began to override the ability to assess situations realistically. This occurs when a number of factors combine: first, the group faces a situation where a very important decision has to be made, often under severe constraints of time; second, the group is already fairly cohesive; third, the group has a tendency to isolate itself from outsiders, finally, the leader has a preferred solution which he or she actively pursues and recommends to the group. Under these circumstances the scope for rational assessment of alternatives may be seriously impaired.

There are a number of symptoms by which groupthink may be detected. These are:

- a feeling of invulnerability

- the rationalizing away of non-preferred solutions

- an appeal to morality

- the stereotyping of opponents in negative terms

- pressure on doubters within the group to conform

- self-censorship

- unanimity

- the appointment of 'mindguards' to censor undesirable information and opinions.

Fortunately for our future survival, Kennedy learnt the lessons from the Bay of Pigs in time for the Cuban missile crisis. His decision-making process was, by then, far more open to external, and dissenting, opinions. Managers need to realize that a group, especially one that is close-knit, may become liable to groupthink. The best defence against this is the introduction of new members with different ideas.

Groupthink, then, is the danger inherent in what might be considered to be a desirable quality of a group – cohesiveness.

Cohesiveness. Other things being equal, cohesive groups will be more effective than less cohesive ones. In general, groups that are together a lot are more cohesive than those with outlying members. Managers will often try to encourage such cohesion as it brings the benefit of high levels of motivation. But the dangers should also be recognized. As well as groupthink, there are potential problems when the group has to deal with other groups. This will be discussed later, when the damaging effects on groups of inappropriate competition and intergroup rivalry are considered.

To sum up, groups have potential benefits. They can, when used properly, increase commitment and motivation, as well as making better quality decisions. They have their dangers, however, notably polarization and groupthink. But when is it appropriate for the group, rather than just one individual, to make decisions?

WHEN SHOULD GROUPS MAKE DECISIONS?

Before going further, consider the following case, which happened to one of the authors some 20 years ago. At the time he was one of five engineers in a particular department of a firm which manufactured heavy current electrical switchgear. One member of the department was required to go to South Wales to oversee the overhaul of some switchgear in a steelworks. Such working away was required every so often. For various reasons, however, none of the five wanted to go. How should the decision be made as to who should go?

One alternative is for the manager to decide who shall go, purely on the information he or she already has. At the other end of the scale, the group itself could be allowed to take the decision. When this situation is used as a case study, the pattern is fairly predictable. In most cases people suggest that the department manager should take the decision, possibly after further consultation with the five engineers. (In fact this was the way the decision was made. The author was the one chosen. He left the firm shortly after.) Some people suggest that the group should be given the opportunity to take the decision, but with the manager reserving 'Tell' (see page 204) as a fall-back. But why should the group not be able to take the decision unaided, even if they decided to draw straws?

There are three major factors we have to consider. Do they have the technical competence to make the decision? Can they cope with the emotional aspects that may go with making a decision? Finally, could they be expected to reach a conclusion? Let us take them one at a time.

1) The decision itself does not require any specific technical expertise.

2) Why assume that mature people are unable to cope with the process of reaching a decision? In other parts of their life they will be doing this all the time.

3) Why should they not be able to come to a decision?

The last one is the reason, after the other two have been discussed, why many managers tend to maintain that *they* have to make the decision. Thinking back to the model of dependency discussed on page 192, you may realize that this is a classic sign of dependency. 'We can't make a decision, you make it for us'. It is an expectation built on experiences of Theory X management. The children of one of the authors exhibit this when trying to decide who should borrow the car. There is a tendency for one, or both, to turn to parents to settle the argument. Why should we? Cannot two adults negotiate an arrangement? If they are made aware that a decision *has* to be reached, then they should be capable of reaching one.

A more sophisticated and prescriptive approach has been suggested by Vroom and his co-workers (Vroom and Yetton, 1973; Vroom and Jago, 1988). They propose a 'decision tree' approach to how problems should be solved. Their theory is often described as a leadership theory, but we prefer to use it in the context of deciding when to use groups to make decisions, as it specifically addresses the issue of *who* should make decisions. According to the model, whichever approach is taken will depend upon three criteria:

- the nature of the task, i.e. technical quality

- whether group commitment is required, i.e. organizational quality

- whether the problem overlaps with the job areas of others.

They suggest that the following questions are answered sequentially by the manager concerned moving along the 'tree'.

i)   Does the problem possess a quality requirement?

ii)   Do I have enough information to make a high-quality decision?

iii)   Is the problem structured, i.e. are all the causal relationships clear?

iv)   Is acceptance of the decision by subordinates important for effective implementation?

v)   If I were to make the decision by myself is it reasonably certain that it would be accepted by my subordinates?

vi)   Do subordinates share the organizational goals to be attained by solving this problem?

vii)   Is conflict among subordinates likely in the preferred solution?

Following the decision tree gives an answer as to which decision-making approach should be adopted, ranging from decision by the manager alone to total group involvement. (The full model may be found in Vroom and Jago, 1988.)

In our experience this model is rather complex for everyday use, but the issues it highlights are extensions of the three criteria listed above. Can the group cope with the technical aspects, the emotional aspects, and the responsibility of coming to a decision? These are answers that require information, not assumptions.

In summary, to produce an effective and committed group the manager must attend to both the task and the process. So far as the task is concerned, all the group members should be working on the same dimension of decision-making at the same time. If half are considering goals whilst the others are considering practicalities the result will be a fragmented meeting.

The manager also needs to guard against possible distortions produced by polarization and groupthink. The effects of both can be minimized by the inclusion of new members with new perspectives. The inclusion of new members with possibly dissenting views carries the potential for disruption. It is here that attention to group processes is particularly important. Discussion should be kept very much in Adult terms (see Chapter 3). In addition, if high commitment is needed it will take time to develop, as it often depends upon the group members feeling that they have been listened to and have had a genuine influence on the final decision. One final word of warning, however. Some managers, realizing the benefits of high commitment, may try to manipulate the group. The group is led to believe that it can reach a decision when, in fact, the decision has already been taken elsewhere. This form of false participation is a very high-risk strategy. If the group at any time realize what is taking place, the effects are likely to be not only counter-productive but disastrous.

As we have seen, the bonds that tie groups together can have their disadvantages. Conflict between groups is another potential disadvantage, and it is this that will now be considered.

INTERGROUP CONFLICT

Any complex organization, whether it be a company or a nation, is faced with the problem of how to establish and maintain effective working relationships between groups which, for whatever reason, have to work together. As we shall see, there are strong pressures, both economic and psychological, within organizations for intergroup conflict to arise.

A number of questions immediately arise when considering such intergroup conflict:

- Is such conflict desirable or not?

- What are the causes and consequences of conflict?

- How can the consequences of conflict be reduced in those situations where it is considered undesirable?

As we shall see, one of the main causes of conflict is competition. However, most managers would agree that some intergroup competition is inevitable and, indeed, desirable. If there was no competition the likelihood is that the organization would become stagnant with few pressures to induce positive change, the result being that its efficiency would suffer. The other extreme, of very high levels of competition and conflict, is also likely to be undesirable. Extreme conflict is likely to lead to counter-productive levels of anxiety and tension in the work-force.

As we have seen, there are advantages to be gained from working in groups. They fulfil some of our own needs and give a sense of identity. In return, they require a degree of conformity to group norms. These norms, together with a feeling of belonging, can have powerful influences on the way people behave. They become heightened when one group is in competition with another. This is, of course, well known to managers. Competitions arranged by management between different departments or branches of an organization are not unusual. Often the effect is to increase effort and improve performance. Such competitions are not, however, without their dangers.

There are circumstances in which they may damage the normal co-operative relationship. For example, in many of the armed services, intercompany football matches and other competitive events are used to heighten feelings of group solidarity. Studies of the US forces in

Vietnam revealed, however, that these feelings of intergroup rivalry then transferred to the battlefield. Even in the face of the enemy, these groups found difficulty co-operating – sometimes with disastrous results.

It is essential, therefore, to be able to determine what level of intergroup competition and conflict is maximally efficient in any particular situation. As will be shown, this decision is one of balancing benefits against costs. It does seem, however, that the pressures that push groups towards conflict are stronger than those pulling them away from it. We will concentrate, therefore, on the pressures that push groups into conflict at levels that are undesirable, and then look at ways in which such levels can be lowered.

CAUSES OF CONFLICT

Turning to the causes and consequences of conflict, we have seen that behaviour may have a number of causes. It may be determined by an individual's 'personality'. It may also be determined by the situation. It is likely to be determined by a combination of both. Arguments continue about the relative influence of each. To what extent, therefore, is conflict between groups caused by the personalities of particular individuals?

There is no doubt that some aspects of a group's interactions will be influenced by the personalities of those involved. However, the effects described below are apparently independent of personality. They happen to everyone. Such phenomena as racial prejudice, chauvinism, and football hooliganism are all within their scope.

One explanation given for why groups compete is that people are competitive. Unfortunately, this is a circular argument – people are competitive because people are competitive. But people do not compete with everybody. If we are to determine the causes of conflict we need to know the conditions which are necessary for it to occur. Tajfel (1972) and his colleagues set out to answer precisely this question by exploring the factors that make one group discriminate against another.

Discrimination. As a European Jew during the Second World War, Tajfel had strong personal reasons for seeking to uncover the source of intergroup discrimination. One obvious reason for discrimination is that one group obtains an objective economic advantage by discriminating against another. Tajfel therefore arranged an experimental situation in which there was no tangible economic advantage to be gained by discrimination. Even in these circumstances discrimination was evident.

What other factors might be causing this continuing discrimination? Although all economic advantages were removed, the group members might assume, wrongly, that they still existed. Yet another reason might be that, although there is no advantage to be gained in this particular instance, a history of hostility exists between the groups. If these potential sources of conflict are also removed, then there should be no further reason for intergroup discrimination. But all the evidence shows that this is not the case! Groups who are currently, or ever have been, in competition, still discriminate against each other. This discrimination goes even further. Let us take another example, again from one of Tajfel's experiments.

You have been asked, in an experiment, to distribute money to individuals. The individuals concerned have been allocated, at random, to one of two groups, but these groups will never meet. Your job is to distribute money to all the individuals in the experiment (£1 being the smallest unit allowed). Each allocation is done in pairs consisting of one individual from group 1 and the other from group 2. The only thing you know about them is which group they belong to. On each allocation you have to distribute a total of £15. You could, for example, give £14 to one individual and £1 to the other. You could also give £8 to one and £7 to the other. How would you allocate the money? Most people say that they would operate `fairly'. Thus, on the first allocation they would give £8 to the individual in group 2. On the next allocation they would reverse the process. In this way they would, at the end, have given the same amount of money to group 1 as to group 2. There is no reason to behave otherwise. You can have no preferences for any of the individuals involved. You do not know who they are, and you never will.

Let us now change the situation very slightly. Exactly the same conditions apply but you have been told that *you* have been allocated to one of the two groups. Again, the groups will never meet and you have nothing to gain by discrimination for or against either group. Again there appears to be no rational reason for behaving other than 'fairly'. This does not happen! Even random allocation to a group with which you will never have interactions leads to discrimination in favour of 'your own' group!

What Tajfel, and Sherif (1966) before him, show is that categorizing an individual as a member of a particular group has effects. The ingroup is then favoured against out-groups. The potential for conflict is present, even where no economic pressures exist – there is tension, even before competition. Think, for example, of public feelings when a fellow national does something particularly praiseworthy or blameworthy. There is no logical reason why Australians should feel pride when an Australian researcher wins a Nobel prize, or the British shame when a group of British football hooligans do something deplorable in a foreign country. We have contributed to neither and therefore share no responsibility.

Another of Tajfel's experiments created a situation in which it was apparent that the two groups could, by co-operating, both increase their incomes. It would still be the case, however, that one group would end up with a higher income than the other. In these circumstances, the groups do not take up this higher profit option. They each appear to be more intent on beating the other, rather than maximizing their income.

If the implications of these findings are not immediately apparent, let us spell them out. When people are allocated to a group they discriminate, at first unconsciously, in favour of that group and against others. This is the case even when they know that they have been randomly allocated to the group, and they will never meet the other members. Think, then, of the potential for discrimination when the group is meeting regularly, and particularly where members can choose the group to which they wish to belong. Why this should happen is not entirely clear. Again, the most likely account is that given by Tajfel, which explains the apparent desire of the groups to beat each other, rather than co-operate to beat the 'system'.

The basic assumption is that we all attempt to increase or maintain our own *positive self-image*. One way of doing this is by belonging to particular groups. These groups can be a source for maintaining or enhancing our self-image. By helping the group improve its standing and prestige, we improve our own self-image. For example, groups of professionals may often resist the erosion of pay differentials. They may do so by objecting to pay rises planned for those groups they consider subordinate to their own. (Remember equity theory and the concept of investments discussed on pages 127–133). The group becomes, therefore, a potential vehicle for defending or improving *our* self-image. Indeed, in large, complex societies our membership of groups (e.g. professions, clubs), is probably the major source of self-image. If the success and prestige of the group increases, so does our own. The way this is achieved is by improving the group's standing compared with other groups – hence discrimination.

Competition. The distinction between groups that co-operate and those that compete is not a strict dichotomy. Every group within an organization will come into at least partial conflict with every other group with which it interacts. Discrimination may be universal, but it will only come to the surface when the groups are pushed into competition by 'economic' factors (in a broad sense of the word).

Economic factors. Each group will have its own goals. The extent to which other groups hinder the achievement of these goals will influence the level of conflict. There are a number of reasons why such hindering occurs. First, groups may be in competition for scarce resources. These resources may be financial, but they may also be non-financial, for example manpower. Specialist employees are often in short supply, and hence may be shared between several groups. There is obvious potential for conflict here.

As well as competition for scarce resources, there may be differences in the actual goals for different groups. For example, the maintenance department of an organization may require a certain level of stock to be maintained, so that spare parts are quickly available. The stock controllers, on the other hand, may have as their goal the reduction of capital tied up in stock. These two goals, both desirable, are potentially incompatible.

Finally, the degree to which groups are objectively dependent upon each other for achieving their goals will have an influence. There are three types of such dependence.

In *pooled* dependence, individual groups merely contribute their own results to a central pool. Independent branches or subsidiary companies are of this nature. None is dependent upon any other for what they do. The potential for conflict here is very low and competition between the branches may be a highly appropriate way of improving performance. Such 'pure' pooled dependence is, however, rare. Branches are often partially dependent upon each other, and may be in competition for scarce resources supplied from the centre.

Sequential dependence is best characterized by production lines. Each stage is dependent upon the one that precedes it, but not the one that follows. Here the potential for conflict is higher, but only with the groups immediately preceding or following yours. Again pure cases are rare.

Perhaps most common is *reciprocal* dependence. Here there is a continual flow between groups, each dependent upon the other. Planning and executing all complex activities involve such dependence. The potential for conflict to occur is here at its highest. Looking at the major groups with which your own group interacts, it is normally fairly easy to determine which of these potentials for conflict are applicable.

These 'economic' factors build on the psychological predisposition for out-group discrimination and push groups into competition.

Psychological consequences. Competition between groups has effects that are perceptual, emotional, and behavioural.

Perceptions involving both the in-group and the out-group are affected, distorting and sharpening distinctions between groups. This does not apply to every characteristic, but only to those characteristics that are considered important for winning the competition, or that have an emotional significance for the group. Whatever the reasons, on those dimensions considered important the in-group enhances its view of itself by denying its weaknesses and exaggerating its strengths, and degrades its views of the out-group. (Notice the potential for groupthink as discussed on page 223). These sharpened distinctions result in stereotypes. As we saw in Chapter 3 these have the potential to distort and exaggerate intergroup differences. In addition, they are very stable and resistant to change.

At the emotional level, almost all of the emotions concerning the other group are negative. The other group is seen as 'hostile' or 'aggressive'. As a result it becomes an enemy – 'them' against 'us'. This emotional reaction also affects perceptions, not only of the abilities of the other group, but also of their motives.

These perceptual and emotional factors inevitably have an effect on behaviour towards the other group. Interactions between the groups become strained. As a result, such interactions decline. When interactions have, of necessity, to take place, group members spend more time attending to their own spokesperson's performance than to what the other group has to say.

WINNERS AND LOSERS

All these effects take place before and during competition. But what are the consequences for the group that wins and for the group that loses? As you might expect, they are different for each group. Edgar Schein (1980) suggests that these consequences can be summarized as follows.

For winners:

- cohesion is retained, and even increases
- there is a release of tension that built up during competition
- there is a switch to person-orientation
- there is a 'fat and happy' feel to the group
- the stereotypes of both in-group and out-group are confirmed.

For losers:

- if the result is ambiguous, then it is denied or distorted
- if the result is unambiguous, then a scapegoat is found, either within or outside the group, e.g. the referee
- there is continued emphasis on task-orientation
- re-grouping for the next stage takes precedence over other activities

- the group becomes tense and 'lean and hungry'

- because the stereotypes have been demolished, there is a high potential for learning.

One other way in which losers deal with their defeat is to reinterpret it. The most common way for this to occur is to claim the 'moral' victory. Although the other group may have won the 'official' contest, the in-group is credited, for example, with being the most virtuous. The effect, both on winners and losers, is to increase rather than decrease intergroup rivalry.

Competition between groups, therefore, brings both advantages and disadvantages. While the competition is under way, there is a high level of group cohesiveness and motivation. What has to be remembered, however, is that these very advantages will adversely affect intergroup relations. If the groups are dependent on each other to any extent, the effect may be to decrease the overall effectiveness of the organization. Given that working in groups is inevitable, how can such intergroup conflict be minimized?

MANAGING CONFLICT

When is competition appropriate? Before looking at how conflict can be resolved, we will first look at when competition is perceived to be appropriate. As we have seen, competition can arise from two sources – economic factors and psychological factors. There is a concept developed from *games theory*, which is particularly useful when considering the economic factors. The concept concerns whether a 'game' (which is defined very broadly in this context) is *zero sum* or *non-zero sum*. A zero sum game is where, at the end of the game, the total of wins equals the total of losses. Hence, they sum to zero. To give an example, any form of gambling for money is a zero sum game. What you lose, others gain, and vice versa. A non-zero sum game is different. As well as there being winners and losers, there is the possibility that both parties can end up winning, or both can end up losing.

In general, and especially within organizations, there are far fewer zero sum games than people imagine. Let us take the example of pay negotiations, or any labour dispute. This surely is a zero sum game: what the employees win in the form of an increase in pay, the organization loses in equivalent profits. But this is not necessarily the case. Most such situations are potentially non-zero sum, that is, both parties can gain or both can lose. Higher pay may be related to, for example, more flexible working arrangements.

Each type of game requires a different approach. If the game is zero sum, then competition is most appropriate. If it is non-zero sum, then both parties have the potential to gain from co-operating. The problem arises, of course, when one side is co-operating but the other is competing. This is dealt with shortly.

While by far the majority of 'games' within an organization are non-zero sum, this is not usually the case between organizations that are operating in the same market. Even here, however, organizations realize that it is, from their point of view, potentially a non-zero sum game. Unfortunately for them, such co-operation (for example price fixing, contact sharing, etc.) is illegal. A true market economy requires competition as a *sine qua non*. (However, many economists argue that the main point made by Adam Smith, the founder theorist of the market economy, was that the *world economy* is a non-zero sum game.) The market can cope with some organizations failing in a competitive environment. But can an organization allow a particular department or branch to fail? Probably not, especially if there is sequential or reciprocal dependence.

Defining a situation as potentially non-zero sum does not, of course, instantly resolve all the problems. There remain the problems of how to establish co-operation, and how to resolve those differences that are bound to occur. One moves here into the psychological rather than the economic considerations.

Trust. We have already said that one difficulty is that of cheating. While one group is dealing in the spirit of co-operation, the other side is dealing competitively. The danger is, of course, that the co-operative group will get 'taken to the cleaners'. This highlights the crucial element in any co-operative venture – trust. Trust takes a long time to establish, but only a single instance of 'betrayal' can destroy it. Trust is intimately linked with the degree of openness between the groups. As trust declines, so does the extent to which each group is prepared to be honest and open with the other. Such openness and honesty carries the risk of cheating. As a result, a downward spiral of decreasing trust and openness sets in.

A good example of a non-zero game where, until recently, there had been little evidence of trust and openness, is the superpower arms race. The problem is how to replace the downward trust/openness spiral with an upward spiral. This is often done on a tentative, step-by-step basis. Then, if the other side does not reciprocate, the losses are limited.

Communication. To say that openness, by itself, is the answer is inaccurate. In the 1960s it was thought that open communications between groups would, by itself, lead to conflict resolution. To translate the old French saying, 'To know all is to forgive all'. It soon became clear that improving communications was not the answer. On occasions, rather than reducing the potential for conflict, it actually increased it. The other group found out *exactly* what you wanted, and found it even more unacceptable than what they *thought* you wanted! Conflicts may sometimes be resolved by better communication, but not always.

Domination. Another method of dealing with conflict is to use power to resolve issues. The group with the greater power imposes its wishes on the other. Dealing with conflict by domination is, we suspect, a common occurrence in organizations. It has the advantage of being quick, but it also has its own problems. Dominance relies upon one group having more power than the other. It is rare, however, for all the power to reside in one of the groups; everyone has some power. For example, it might be thought that the armed forces, together with prisons, represent those situations where power distribution is at its most extreme. Those in authority in both organizations will freely admit, however, that smooth running is dependent, to a large extent, on at least the tacit acceptance of their authority by those who are being controlled. Even the inmates of prisons have some power. If they refuse to accept the authority of the prison officers to control them, the power balance is altered considerably. Examples from some prisoners of war, or prisoners of conscience, who have been tortured are interesting. Some report that, at a particular point in their torture, they decide that they are likely to die. After this, the torturers' power over them disappears. They may kill them, but they can no longer threaten them. (The film *The Hill*, starring Sean Connery, which is set in an army prison, illustrates some of these situations.)

Using power also carries with it the problem of counter-dependence (see Chapter 6). Outright rebellion may not emerge, but the potential for groups to wage 'organizational guerrilla war' may be considerable.

Negotiation. Dealing with conflict by resolution (that is, seeing and understanding the other groups' needs), is not by itself enough. Nor is domination. What is required is negotiation. This negotiation will, of necessity, include elements of both resolution and dominance. To return to resolution, what is required is not 'naïve openness' but 'openness in negotiation'.

To see how negotiations can proceed let us now consider a particular model which incorporates the concept of co-operation, but also adds a second dimension – that of *assertion*. (The model is a general one and hence it can be applied to individual negotiating style, as well as to group interactions.) One of the easiest ways to introduce the concept of assertion is to contrast it with that of aggression. Aggression does not take into account the needs of the party, other than as an opponent. Assertion, on the other hand, is concerned with the legitimate needs of both sides. To be aggressive is to ignore the other's needs and wishes. To be assertive is to recognize that both parties have needs that have to be taken into account if a negotiated settlement is to be achieved.

Combining these two dimensions produces a grid as shown in Figure 7.4. Both dimensions are, of course, continuous, but for simplicity's sake we will consider only high and low extremes on each. This produces four categories, together with a fifth at the point where the four meet.

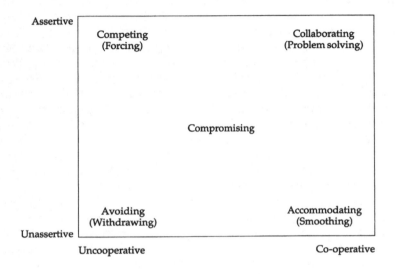

Figure 7.4. Thomas and Kilmans' model of conflict resolution.
(Source: Thomas, 1975)

Avoiding, or withdrawing, is characterized by low levels both of co-operation and assertion. The problems are therefore ignored. This may be the position of both groups, or just one of them. If both are in this position, nothing will be done to resolve the differences. If only one is taking this position, then the other's position is likely to be that of competing, or forcing. The other options are ruled out as, by definition, it takes two to co-operate.

Accommodating is characterized by co-operation, but with little assertion. 'Don't make waves' might be the motto of such a group. If both groups take this line it is likely that some agreement will be reached. This will not, however, be a satisfactory or lasting agreement. In order to achieve it, both sides will have avoided openly stating their real needs. A false consensus is the likely outcome. If only one group adopts this line, the other has two responses. The first is to ignore the co-operation and trade on the other's weakness in failing to present its needs, in other words, to force the issue to a conclusion beneficial to itself. The alternative is perhaps more common. The norms of reciprocity, discussed in Chapter 4, often mean that co-operation is returned. The other group may, therefore, try to go for a problem-solving approach. In doing this, its members may also believe that the others are also asserting their needs. The fact that they are not reveals itself in two ways. The feeling that all is not being disclosed often produces the question 'Are you sure that's OK with you?', or variations on that theme. The other effect may only reveal itself much later, when the false consensus emerges, often producing the comment 'Why didn't you say this when we discussed it?'

Competing, or forcing, allows for only two responses: avoidance, which allows the other group to dominate, or competition. If both groups are assertively uncooperative, the contest will eventually be determined by whichever group can bring most power to bear in that particular situation. (You may have noticed that the squares of conflict resolution model are also interpretable in terms of the OK Corral – see page 108.)

Problem solving. Except in those situations where competition is appropriate, for example in a zero-sum game, it is probably apparent that problem solving is the best form of achieving a negotiated settlement. To be effective such negotiations need to be explicit and open. Openness will encourage trust and hence co-operation. Being precise and explicit will encourage movement on the other dimension, towards greater assertiveness.

This may sound easy to achieve, but it is not. We have already discussed the problems of establishing trust. There are also problems with being more explicit. People within organizations tend to have more contact with each other than they do with outsiders. For this reason it may be thought that they could be more explicit with each other than with outsiders. This may not be the case. Evidence suggests, for example, that such interactions as wage negotiations with trade union officials are likely to be far more explicit about needs than are negotiations within the organization. To understand the reasons for this, we need to return to social exchange theory (see page 129). The contract between the wage negotiators is primarily economic. Each party realizes this, and hence is prepared to express their needs. Within the organization, however, social as well as economic exchanges are involved. Once again, social and economic factors become confused.

TECHNIQUES FOR REDUCING CONFLICT

How then can conflict either be avoided or, if it already exists, be defused? It will be recalled that there are two sources of intergroup conflict, economic and psychological. The economic causes should be avoided by ensuring that win/lose situations are avoided. This may not be as difficult to achieve as it appears. The majority of situations are potentially non-zero sum, despite appearances to the contrary.

So far as the psychological aspects are concerned, there are a number of ways of reducing their impact. A simple way of reducing conflict is to direct attention towards a goal that both groups find acceptable. This is known as a superordinate goal, as it encompasses both of the two subordinate goals. In organizational terms, it may mean substituting conflicting group goals by those that emphasize total organizational effectiveness. The service department and the stores should be given the joint goal of achieving an agreed level of customer service, while keeping stock levels to a minimum. A variation of this is for the groups to identify a common 'enemy', against which they can join forces. The 'war-time spirit' which this engenders leads to the competing groups forgetting their differences, at least for the duration of hostilities.

Other techniques are perhaps more practical. They include ways of breaking down people's stereotypes of other groups. Some techniques involve direct intervention, such as one based on confrontation, in which groups confront each other with their perceptions and feelings. This is obviously a high risk method. The pay-offs are potentially high, but so are the risks. For this reason it is usually done with the help of outside facilitators. Each group is invited to share its perception, both of itself and of the other group. These perceptions are then openly voiced, but without any comments being allowed. The groups then separate to consider the discrepancies and the possible reasons for them. These too are then shared in a joint meeting. This method can produce beneficial results very quickly, but requires expert handling.

A less risky procedure involves the forced interaction of members of the different groups. This may take place at a number of levels. Often, in order to establish credibility, the leaders have to be the first to meet. (It is interesting how President Reagan's 'evil empire' perception of the Soviet Union changed following the Reagan/Gorbachov summit meetings.) Once credibility has been achieved, it can be further developed and maintained by frequent communication and the 'swapping' of group members. It is not surprising that cultural and educational exchanges are common between countries that are trying to improve their relations. After the first inspection visit by three Russian Colonels, a British officer remarked that he had realized, with some surprise, that they were 'normal, nice, blokes'. In fact, within NATO, the armed forces also ensure that officers at all levels spend some time in other units. This is also now becoming more common within organizations, especially when one organization takes over another. In this situation, however, there is a high potential for conflict from boardroom to shop-floor, especially if the take-over was resisted.

To summarize, conflict between groups in organizations is almost inevitable; indeed, some competition is desirable. The inefficiency that it produces is, however, often ignored by organizations. Hard-pressed managers tend to work on short time-scales, and the short-term benefits of competition outweigh the longer-term disadvantages. Managers need to take time to look at the wider perspective and to achieve a realistic balance between the benefits and dangers of inter-group rivalry in their own particular circumstances. If necessary, they should then take steps to eliminate undesirable conflict.

THE PSYCHOLOGICAL CONTRACT IN GROUPS

The psychological contract in groups is concerned with issues of how individuals relate to each other in groups. Do they have to be formal and just get on with the task in hand, or is it all right to be more re-laxed and to have fun? This will influence how hard people work, what commitment they have, and what they expect from the group. There will also be expectations about the amount of participation al-lowed in the decision-making process. If people expect to have more influence than they are actually allowed it may have a detrimental effect on their commitment. To be consulted but then ignored may, in some circumstances, be worse than not being consulted at all. The extent to which participation is allowed will also be related to the perceived role of group members, in particular that of the leader. A climate that discourages disagreements with the leader has the potential to produce such effects as groupthink.

As well as influencing the development of relations within the group, the psychological contract may also contain elements concerning inter-group relations. Expectations will almost certainly exist concerning the levels of co-operation and competition that is expected between groups. There will be informal rules governing when competition is appropriate, and when it is not. Breach of these rules may heighten feelings of mistrust and lead to dysfunctional competition.

It is possible for groups, such as departments or informal working groups, to develop their own psychological contracts. In large organizations, however, the nature of the contract will be strongly influenced by that existing in the organization as a whole. However, as is true in other contexts, if people are to work effectively in a group, they must feel happy with the psychological contract. It is therefore important that these aspects of the group's life are open to review and re-negotiation. Many aspects of team building, particularly techniques such as role negotiation, suggest how this can be done. These are discussed in Chapter 9.

8

Identifying Organizational Problems

Exercise

As an exercise for this section, we would like you to try to answer the following questions about an organization with which you are familiar. This will normally be your present employer, but you can do it for any organization which you know well.

1. If you were asked to give one piece of advice to a new work colleague on how to survive and prosper in the organization, what would it be? (Examples might be 'keep a low profile', 'make yourself visible', etc.)

2. What slogan or motto would best sum up the organization? (For example, 'biggest and best', 'always second' etc.)

3. What animal would you choose to be the organizational mascot? It can be any animal, including birds, fish and reptiles, but should represent the organization as it actually is. You should then choose another animal that would represent the organization as you would ideally like it to be. (Examples that have been given by managers have included dinosaurs, whales, moles etc.)

We will return to your advice, slogan, and animals towards the end of the chapter.

Before attempting to describe and analyse different types of organizations and their problems, we need to define what we mean by an 'organization'. Because organizations are all around us we tend to take them for granted. With the exception of the apparatus of the state and the church, most organizations are of fairly modern origin. It was the changes in production in the Industrial Revolution that led to the creation of the complex industrial and commercial organizations with which we are all familiar. Like elephants, they are easy to recognize but hard to define. Perhaps the easiest way is to list those things that they have in common:

- They consist of individuals, organized into groups and sub-groups.
- These individuals come together to achieve certain goals and objectives. There will usually be varying degrees of clarity and agreement concerning these goals and objectives.
- These individuals perform specific and specialist functions. This means they often have different skills, abilities, and responsibilities.
- Because of the differentiation of people into specialist functions, there is a problem of co-ordinating and controlling the various functions.

One other thing that they have in common is that they persist over time. As we will see, organizations have to adapt and, in adapting, they will change. What will remain constant, however, are the characteristics we have listed above.

The problems that organizations face involve two dimensions; (1) dealing with the external environment, and (2) managing their internal environment. It is with the latter problem, of managing and controlling the internal environment, that we will deal first. Perhaps the classic analysis of how large-scale collective activities should be organized is that of Max Weber (1970). Weber was chiefly concerned with the way that the state apparatus, or civil service, should be run. He was interested in the concept of authority, and the mechanisms by which legitimate authority could exert its control. It was Weber who coined the much-maligned term 'bureaucracy'. Nowadays, this term is synonymous with 'red tape' and inertia but, in Weber's terms, bureaucracy is a way of exerting control effectively and impartially. It is characterized by the following:

- Individuals have specialized tasks, for which they are specifically qualified.
- Tasks are performed within the guidelines of established rules and procedures.
- Each individual can be accountable to only one boss. This boss holds his post on the basis of his technical competence, and exerts power that is delegated from above.
- Relationships, both with 'clients' and co-workers, are based on formally established rules and procedures. Personal likings and preferences are not allowed to influence interactions.

- Employment, as well as being based on technical competence, is protected against arbitrary dismissal.

MECHANISTIC ORGANIZATIONS

Weber's analysis, as mentioned above, concerns the apparatus of the state, perhaps the original organization. Many present-day organizations are based around such concepts of hierarchy, delegated authority, and responsibility. The army and church are prime, and historic, examples. The analogy that is often used of such systems is that they are like machines. Each cog in the machine has a particular function to fulfil, which is highly specialized. As long as all the cogs operate as they should, than the machine performs effectively. Like the machine, such a system is a considerable improvement over individual workers, toiling away in isolation. Just as the machine achieves this improvement by the complex inter-relationship of simple components, so does the organization. The first systematic application of such 'mechanistic' approaches to industrial organizations was by Henri Fayol (1967). His experiences of the organization of French coal mines led him, in the 1920s, to publish his views on the way in which such organizations should be structured.

According to Fayol, to be effective, organizations should be run according to the following principles:

- Tasks should be specialized. This means that there should be 'division of labour'.

- There should be 'unity of direction'. In other words, those with the same sorts of expertise should be grouped together, e.g. all those involved in accounting should be in the same department.

- The manager has broader responsibilities than his/her subordinates, for this reason he/she is given more authority. The higher a manager is in the hierarchy, the more responsibility, and consequently the more authority he or she possesses.

- Authority should be on a 'chain' principle. Each person should answer to one, and only one, boss.

The implications for the command structure and the flow of information are clear: a strict hierarchy, along military lines, with commands being transmitted downwards. The only time the information flow is reversed is when situations are encountered that are not covered by 'standard' procedures. The increasing levels of responsibility and authority, together with the high degree of specialization, leads to a highly centralized and highly formalized system. As you may recall from the section on communication patterns in groups, such a highly centralized system has advantages and disadvantages. On the 'plus' side, it is a system that is highly efficient at dealing with simple and routine tasks, for example, processing and dispatching orders for standard stock items. On the 'negative' side of the balance sheet, however, is the effect on the workers. Such a system is demoralizing and offers little opportunity for gaining job satisfaction. While for some purposes this may not matter, for others the lack of motivation may be important.

ORGANIC ORGANIZATIONS

If an organization is dependent on harnessing the full potential of its workers, then it will have to adopt a structure that enables those individuals to contribute to, as well as take orders from, the system. Rensis Likert (1961) described such an organization as 'organic' rather than 'mechanistic'. The emphasis in such an organization is that communication, information processing, and decision making take place at all levels of the organization. Likert argues that such a system will have the additional advantage that it will be flexible and adaptable. It will be able to respond to the changes, either in the external environment, or in the internal environment as, for example, the organization grows. The organization is seen as a living, growing, developing organism, rather than as a fixed, unchanging, inflexible machine. The growth in communications that an organic structure implies, also produces problems. Likert suggests some ways of dealing with these, which we will consider later.

The proponents of both mechanistic and organic theories suggest that their ideas are correct and desirable. Advocates of either sometimes overlook the fact that both may be effective, but under differing circumstances. We have suggested that mechanistic structures may be appropriate for firms engaged in routine work. An organic structure may be more appropriate for highly complex operations in a rapidly changing environment.

Lawrence and Lorsch (1969) of Harvard Business School, in their study of firms in the plastics industry, went further and suggested that even within the same firm different departments may have different structures. These different structures arise primarily, they suggest, as the result of pressures from different external environments. Where the environment is stable and unlikely to change, such as in basic production processes, then a mechanistic structure is appropriate. Such a differentiation of functions is linked, according to Lawrence and Lorsch, with other characteristics of production departments, in which, for example, there is an emphasis on 'task' rather than 'people', together with relatively short time-horizons. For the R & D department, on the other hand, the environment may be extremely volatile and uncertain, requiring a more organic solution. This is likely to involve a more person-orientated approach, together with relatively long time horizons. The problem is, of course, that all these departments have to work together. As you may recall from the section on inter-group conflict in Chapter 7, differing time-scales and goals may induce conflict. The organic and mechanistic structures are likely to produce such differences. These then, according to Lawrence and Lorsch, require 'integrating' together. The problem remains as to how this integration should be achieved. It could be mechanistically, by the use of formal rules and procedures, or organically by the opening of communication channels. The method chosen will reflect the underlying and predominant philosophy of the organization, and its stage of development.

METAPHORS FOR ORGANIZATION

Organizations are very complex entities and consequently very difficult to understand. We therefore need some way to handle this complexity if we are going to have any hope of analysing and solving organizational problems. One way that we do this is through the use of metaphor. A metaphor is a form of analogy that provides a framework with which we can structure our world so as to make better sense of it. Morgan (1983) describes a metaphor as a 'basic structural form of experience through which human beings engage, organise and understand their world'.

Two of the metaphors that we use have already been mentioned in the previous section – 'organizations as mechanisms' and 'organizations as organisms'. An organization is not a mechanical device, like a piece of machinery, but sometimes it helps to visualize it as though it is. Likewise, it is not an organism like an animal or a plant, but again, it can be helpful to look at it within this framework. What we are doing is using analogies. We are saying that an organization has some of the properties of an organism – it grows, changes through time, gets older and eventually dies. Looking at organization in this way can often give us useful insights. There are, of course, dangers in doing this, since the metaphor will fit only up to a point. Extending the metaphor beyond its useful limits will lead to misunderstanding and ineffectiveness. Pinder and Bourgeois (1982) draw attention to this problem and in fact argue against the use of metaphors at all, on the basis that it is too easy to start treating the metaphor as reality. As they express it 'to the extent that metaphors inter-relate entities that are not identical, we can be misled at some point by pursuing them. The point at which a metaphor stops being of positive heuristic value and starts to become misleading is difficult to detect'.

This difficulty is well illustrated by the work of most of the early writers on organization, who all used a mechanistic metaphor. One negative aspect of this was that it lead to the treatment of human beings within the organization as simply mechanical components, which could be changed and adjusted at will, rather like cogs and levers in a machine. As is now generally realized, this is not an effective way to treat people (although there are still some managers who tend to operate in this way). However, despite these difficulties, metaphors are really the only way we have to cope with the complexity of organizations, but we must bear in mind their limitations.

One particularly important implication of this is that whatever metaphor we are using will determine our approach to, and the type of solution we devise for, the problem we are attempting to solve. Thus, if we use a mechanistic metaphor, we will probably start rearranging the organization's structure – changing who reports to whom and defining what activities each department or section is allowed to do. If we are using an organic metaphor we will think more in terms of *evolving* a solution, consulting with the members of the organization to help them produce their own solutions. A further complication is that much of the time we may not be consciously aware of the metaphor we are using, and hence of how it is structuring our thinking. One example of this is provided by the current British Conservative government, which appears to have only one metaphor for organization, that of 'the market'. This is, almost certainly, an inappropriate metaphor for use with organizations in, for example, the health and education services. These are inappropriately seen as markets because there is not freedom of supply and demand. Using this metaphor can lead to the imposition of ineffective solutions to organizational problems.

One positive aspect of the whole debate on metaphors and their use is that it has made us very much more aware of the process, so that we can be alive to both the positive and negative aspects of any particular metaphor that we are using, and to the fact that we are using it. A metaphor which has been very widely used in recent years is that of 'organizational culture'. This can provide us with extremely useful insights, but like all metaphors, if we extend it too far, and take it too literally, it can be misleading.

ORGANIZATIONAL CULTURE

The 'culture' metaphor is, of course, derived originally from agriculture and the process of growing things, but the concept of organizational culture was arrived at through its analogy with national culture. The notion that different national and/or ethnic groupings have different cultures has been around for some time. The analogy is now extended to the notion that different organizations also have different cultures. Indeed, because organizations exist within national cultures, they can be considered as sub-cultures. One implication of the culture metaphor is that, like organic cultures, organizational cultures also grow and develop.

One way to get a feel of what is meant by organizational culture is to look at some definitions. A relatively early one is provided by Jaques (1951). He defined it as:

'The customary or traditional ways of doing things, which are shared to a greater or lesser extent by all members of the organization and which new members must learn and at least partially accept in order to be accepted into the service of the firm.'

Schein (1984) gives a more complex definition:

'Organizational culture is the pattern of basic assumptions that a given group has invented, discovered or developed in learning to cope with its problems of external adaptation and internal integration, and that have worked well enough to be considered valid, and therefore, to be taught to new members as the correct way to perceive, think and feel in relation to these problems.'

Organizational culture is thus the informal and unwritten rules by which people in an organization know how to behave and react, and are what makes such behaviour in one organization different from that in another. This is well expressed by Wilk (1989),

'There may be no formal rules proscribing certain modes of conduct, yet people in the organization quickly learn to follow unwritten rules to the extent that certain patterns of behaviour become ubiquitous in the organization, and, furthermore, serve to mark it out from other organizations, giving it a distinct identity and a distinct flavour or feel. Once you learn the culture of an organization, you know how to conduct yourself wherever you may venture within it.'

Wilk then gives the following definition:

'We define the culture of an organization as the invariant patterns of organizational behaviour, considered as a whole, that connect, inform, and provide a context for even the most diverse actions of individual managers right across an organization, that help to distinguish behaviour in that organization from behaviour in others, and are not directly encoded in the organization's formal rules.'

It follows, of course, that if the culture is not enshrined in the formal rules of the organization then it cannot be changed by merely changing the rules. Culture change is very difficult and requires time and subtlety of approach (it has even been argued that it is impossible to do deliberately and in a planned way). We will look briefly at culture change in a later section.

Theories of organizational culture. The definitions of organizational culture give some understanding of the concept, but to get more insight we need to look in greater depth. Most theorists in this field see culture as having a number of elements existing at different levels of awareness. Schein (1985) suggests that there are four such levels:

1. *Basic Assumptions.* These are the deepest level and consist of unconscious assumptions about appropriate behaviour and reactions in any given situation. These are the responses we make without consciously thinking about them and are thus taken for granted and unchallenged.

2. *Values.* At the next highest level are 'values' which determine beliefs about how things ought to be and what is important in the organization. Although individuals act most of the time without conscious reference to values, if asked they can usually articulate them.

3. *Norms.* Nearer to the surface of consciousness are 'norms', which guide appropriate behaviour in varying organizational situations.

4. *Artifacts.* These are the externally visible symbols of the organization's culture. They consist of observable behaviours and artifacts such as the rules, procedures and house-style of the organization.

A similar, but perhaps slightly more complex view, is suggested by Hofstede (1991). This is based on national culture, but is equally applicable at the organizational level. It is shown diagrammatically in Figure 8.1. Again there are four layers:

1. *Symbols.* This is the outermost surface layer. It consists of those words, gestures, pictures and objects that carry a particular meaning largely recognized only by those inside the culture, for example, forms of dress, hairstyle, flags and status symbols.

2. *Heroes.* Persons alive or dead, real or imaginary, who possess characteristics which are highly valued within the culture. These can often include the founder of the organization or other individuals who are seen as influential in the organization's history and development.

3. *Rituals.* Collective activities, technically superfluous, but which, within the culture, are considered socially essential and are, therefore, carried out simply for their own sake. These include forms of

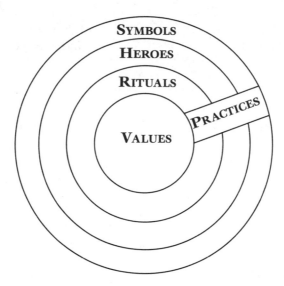

Figure 8.1. The four layers of culture.
(Source: Hofstede, 1991)

greetings (e.g. special handshakes) and social and religious cere-
monies. A good example of a ritual which has high cultural significance in academic organizations is the degree ceremony, which
involves strange forms of dress and arcane rituals, of significance only
to the insider.

The levels of symbols, heroes and rituals are subsumed under the
term *practices* because they are visible to the outsider. Their true significance is, however, fully apparent only to those on the inside.

4. *Values*. These are at the core of the culture and are really what
holds it together. Values are broad tendencies to prefer certain states
of affairs over others and will be held in common by all, or most,
individuals who are part of the culture.

Perhaps a good way to look at culture is as part of what Hofstede calls
an individual's 'mental programming'. He sees three levels of programming, as shown in Figure 8.2. At the most individual level is personality (discussed in Chapter 2). This is, perhaps, partly inherited
but is mainly learned. At a greater level of generality is culture. This
is specific to groups of one form or another, and is entirely learned.
At the greatest level of generality is what he calls 'human nature',
which is common to all humans and, he suggests, is 'in our genes' or,
in other words, is inherited.

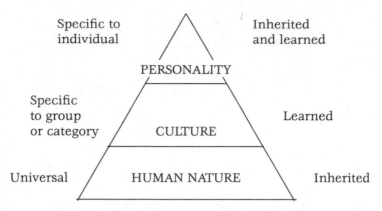

Figure 8.2. Level of mental programming.
(Source: Hofstede, 1991)

Significance of organizational culture. Why is so much emphasis currently placed on the culture of the organization? It is probable that this was originally due to Western interest in, and attempts to explain, the phenomenal success of Japanese organizations in the years since the Second World War. Studies have shown that the assumptions about how people relate to each other (i.e. the culture) are very different in Japanese as compared with Western companies. Much of this difference, of course, derives from differences in the national cultures. It is assumed (probably, quite reasonably) that the differences in performance are attributable to these culture differences.

A further impetus to the study of culture was given by the work of Peters and Waterman (1982), who showed that there were some strong similarities in the cultures of a number of highly successful American companies. These and many other studies all contributed to the belief that culture is a highly significant factor in the success of the firm. The findings of a survey by Gardener (1985) showed, for example, that chief executives see corporate culture as real and an important contributor to success. That culture is not the only important variable is, however, shown by the fact that several of the companies originally studied by Peters and Waterman are no longer so successful.

One important aspect of culture is that it is closely related to the psychological contract existing within the organization. Indeed they are so closely related that it is impossible to say which one causes the other, since the culture determines how people relate, and how they relate determines what sort of contract exists between them.

Origins of organizational culture. As suggested above, at least part of the origin of organizational culture lies in the national culture, so we will start this section by looking at a theory about international differences in culture as they relate to organizations. Based on a worldwide survey within a large and well known multi-national company, carried out within some fifty countries, Hofstede (1984) has suggested that cultures can be differentiated along four major dimensions. It is possible to measure the position of a culture on each of these dimensions in terms of whether it is high or low on that scale, or somewhere in between. The four dimensions are described below.

Power Distance is a measure of the extent of inequality in a society in terms of such things as power, prestige and wealth. It is also a measure of the importance that is attached to these inequalities by those within the culture. In cultures with *high* power distance (i.e. there is a considerable difference in power between those at the top of the hierarchy and those at the bottom), this inequality is formalized in very hierarchical boss–subordinate relationships. Subordinates in such cultures are reluctant to question the decisions of their boss. Low power distance cultures (where there is relatively little difference between the most and least powerful) are characterized by relatively flat hierarchies, where subordinates are prepared to question the decisions of their boss. Many Latin American and some South-East Asian countries (Malaysia and Indonesia for example) tend to have large differences in power distance; most European countries (including the UK) have relatively low differences.

Uncertainty Avoidance is concerned with the extent to which ambiguity and uncertainty are tolerated. Cultures high on this dimension will seek methods of avoiding uncertainty. This is often accomplished by a rather bureaucratic approach to organizations, with formal rules to cope with all eventualities. Those cultures low in uncertainty avoidance can live with uncertainty without the need for formal rules. Latin American countries and some European ones (Greece, Portugal, Belgium) tend to be high in uncertainty avoidance. The UK and Scandinavian countries tend to be low (i.e. they can tolerate uncertainty).

Individualism vs Collectivism refers to the extent to which a loosely-knit or tight social framework is preferred. In 'individualistic cultures' the ties between individuals are loose. Everyone is expected to look after himself or herself and his/her immediate family. In 'collectivist cultures' individuals are integrated into a much wider group, which protects and looks after them, and to which they are responsible. The USA, Australia and Britain have very individualistic cultures. Latin American countries tend to be collectivist.

Masculinity vs Femininity is about the dominant values in the culture. In a masculine culture the predominant values are concerned with assertiveness, dominance, challenge and advancement – all traditionally thought of as male values. In a feminine culture, 'female' values, such as co-operation, caring and security are predominant. Japan, Venezuela, Italy and Mexico tend to have strongly masculine cultures. The Scandinavian countries tend to have feminine cultures. Britain's culture is towards the masculine end of the continuum.

Since each of the above four scales is relatively unrelated to the others, almost any combination of the dimensions is possible. The particular combination which exists has interesting implications for how people interact with each other. To illustrate this we will consider the interaction of just the first two dimensions – power distance and uncertainty avoidance.

- The USA and UK are low on both power distance and uncertainty avoidance. As a result transactions depend on negotiation between (roughly equal) individuals each pursuing their own interest. This type of culture has been called a 'market'. (Perhaps this is why the UK government is so keen on the market metaphor!)

- Some Far Eastern countries are high on power distance but low on uncertainty avoidance. This, Hofstede suggests, is similar to a 'family' type of organization. There are clear leaders who are in control, but the rules governing the relationship between the leaders and the led are not explicitly stated.

- The more 'germanic' European countries are the reverse of the 'family' culture. Low power distance coupled with high uncertainty avoidance means that there are precise rules and regulations to cover most eventualities. Specialist knowledge is respected, not hierarchical power. The boss is obeyed, so long as the boss also obeys the rules. This results in what Hofstede refers to as a 'well-oiled machine'. In organizational terms we prefer to call this a 'rational bureaucracy.'

- The fourth type of culture is one which is high in both power distance and uncertainty avoidance. Hofstede calls this a 'full bureaucracy' and identifies it with 'Latin' cultures. We prefer to refer to them as 'power bureaucracies'. In such cultures organizational allegiance is to individuals rather than to the rules. Bosses are obeyed as long as they deliver the rewards, and subordinates are delegated power on the basis of personal trust. There echoes of a 'family' relationship, but one which is rather power-orientated.

All the above phenomena are at the level of national culture. Hofstede (1991) points out that national and organizational culture are different in nature. The difference is due to the different roles played by each of the manifestations of culture (i.e. values, rituals, heroes and symbols – the last three subsumed under the term 'practices'). Differences in national culture are due mainly to differences in values. Members of different organizations within a nation can be expected to have somewhat similar values. What will determine differences in culture across organizations within a nation, is differences in practices. The differences in the values–practices balance is explained by the difference in the place of socialization for each level. Figure 8.3 shows these different levels. Thus, values are mainly developed within the family and are broadly similar across a nation. Practices are inculcated at the workplace and so tend to be more specific to that situation. Occupational culture is placed midway between national and organizational, signifying that entering an occupation normally means acquiring values as well as practices.

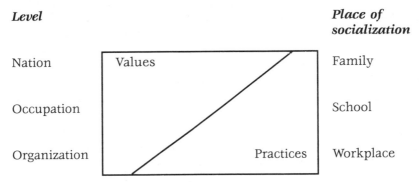

Figure 8.3. Level of culture and place of socialization.
(Source: Hofstede, 1991)

CHANGING ORGANIZATIONAL CULTURE

Since there is evidence that an organization's culture is a key factor in its success, it is important for the organization to have an appropriate culture for its context and type of operation. It is to be expected, therefore, that managers should at times want to change the culture of the organization with the aim of producing better performance. Culture change may, in fact, become desirable for a number of reasons. If the company has grown very rapidly, the culture which was appropriate when it was smaller may no longer suit a larger organization. Takeovers, mergers or other forms of reorganization will also normally require adjustments to the culture, particularly where there are significant differences between the cultures of the organizations concerned. Technological changes in production and changes in the environment, such as increasing competition, will also have cultural implications. It is not, therefore, surprising that 'culture change' has become a growth industry for management consultants.

It has to be said, however, that changing culture, if it can be done at all, is a difficult and long-term process. This is not surprising when it is considered that in most organizations the existing culture is extremely well embedded. It has usually been set by the original founders and in many cases developed and reinforced over long periods of years. Even relatively new organizations will often have absorbed their culture from forerunners or from organizations with which they feel an affinity or which they perceive to be similar. Universities founded in the last half of the twentieth century, for example, have absorbed much of their culture from their medieval forebears. The way we relate to students and the commitment to research and scholarship and many of our practices all derive from this source. It is quite surprising how long some of these practices have survived, even though of doubtful relevance to modern life.

Despite the difficulties, many companies have made quite significant changes in culture; how is this done? Cummings and Huse (1989) provide some practical advice by suggesting a series of stages that must be considered and appropriately managed:

Clear Strategic Vision. It is important to start a culture change with a clear view of the direction and purpose of the proposed change. Why is it necessary to change and where is it hoped to end up? Very often this will be enshrined in a company 'mission statement'. This is a statement of the company's goals and how it intends to achieve them. It is important that this should be a clear and precise statement of operationalizable goals, not just a set of 'motherhood' statements, as is often the case in practice. The importance of the mission statement, from the point of view of culture, is that it will embody the values which the company leadership espouses, and thus provides purpose and direction for the cultural change.

Top Management Commitment. It is important that top management are committed to the change, and are seen to be committed. Culture change can only be managed from the top down. This is because only top management has the power to make changes in the values and deeper structures of the organization.

Symbolic Leadership. Senior managers must behave in ways which are consistent with the new culture. More than this, it is necessary to do so with enthusiasm, so that the new culture is communicated through their actions. Hence the need for real internalized commitment at the top.

Supporting Organizational Changes. It is essential to make changes in the organizational structure, reporting procedures and management styles to bring them into line with the new culture. It is, for example, impossible to move towards a culture embodying participation and empowerment if the organizational systems still require detailed reporting in a strictly hierarchical line system of management. New organizational procedures can also be used to make people aware of the changes that are taking place and encourage the new behaviours which are required.

Change Organizational Membership. Bringing new members into the organization, who already subscribe to the required organizational values and practices is a considerable help to the process of change. By the same token, helping those who do not wish to accept the changes to leave will also speed the process. (An activity which Cummings and Huse rather sinisterly refer to as 'termination of deviants'). One organization we know of has made the change from being a government-funded research organization to become a commercial consultancy. This entailed a change of culture from that resembling a university department to a reasonably aggressive sales-orientated culture. While new mission statements were issued and considerable restructuring took place, one of the main factors in the culture change was a deliberate policy of hiring new personnel with commercial experience and values, coupled with redundancy programmes which enabled those who disliked the new philosophy to leave.

Changing organizational membership, in this context, does not only mean hiring and firing. It is possible to change, by a number of means, the attitudes and beliefs of individuals who remain within the organization. The most obvious of these is through training and development, but other techniques include formal communication programmes, use of role models who display the required new behaviours (often these are provided by new members hired as part of the change programme), counselling programmes and participating with organization members in developing the new culture. Attention to the reinforcement patterns is also important, to ensure that only the required behaviours are being reinforced, and the old patterns which it is wished to change are extinguished. (See the section on behaviour modification in Chapter 5.)

Hofstede has suggested that successful culture change needs the joint action of two parties – a *power holder* and an *expert*. These terms are derived from a German study and are translations of *Machtpromotor* and *Fachpromotor*. In practice the Machtpromotor would normally be the chief executive or a group of senior managers; the Fachpromotor would be an outside expert. The expert's role is to provide a diagnosis of the existing culture. An outside expert is needed for this, as it is virtually impossible for a member of the organization to have a clear and unbiased view of its culture. Based on this diagnosis, the power holder can then make the required culture changes part of the organization's strategy.

By way of summary and in concluding this section it is worth noting Hofstede's view of culture change:

'Although culture is a "soft" characteristic, changing it calls for "hard" measures. Structural changes may mean closing departments, opening other departments, merging or splitting activities, or moving people and/or groups geographically. The general rule is that when people are moved as individuals, they will adopt the culture of their new environment; when people are moved as groups, they will bring their culture along. People in groups have developed, as part of their culture, ways of interacting which are quite stable and difficult to change. Changing them means that all interpersonal relationships have to be renegotiated. However, if new tasks or a new environment force such a renegotiation there is a good chance that undesirable aspects of the old culture will be cleaned up.'

The renegotiation will, of course, include renegotiating the psychological contract. Now that we have looked at what is meant by organizational culture, its significance and how it may be changed, we will move on in the next section to consider a theory of how organizations grow and develop, and what implications this has for the culture of the developing organization.

ORGANIZATIONAL GROWTH

The concepts of 'differentiation' and 'integration', mentioned earlier in the chapter, are also used by Lievegood (1973) in his theory of organizational growth. Organizations do not remain static, rather they grow and develop. The way in which they develop is not, however, random. According to Lievegood, organizations tend to develop through three well-defined phases. These phases he calls *pioneer, differentiation*, and *integration*. Each is characterized by its own style of management, organizational culture, and its own particular way of relating to the customer. In addition, however, each has its own problems peculiar to that phase. As the organization develops, these problems become more acute. It is these emerging problems that are the driving force that push the organization into the next phase of development. We will now describe the phases, together with the problems associated with each.

THE PIONEER PHASE

As its name suggests, this phase is typical of new small entrepreneurial companies. The most common way in which such an organization starts is that an individual, or small group of individuals, identifies an opportunity. They may do this in a number of ways. They may invent a new product, develop a new service, or identify a new, as yet untapped, market. In order to exploit the new opportunity, a company is established, either formally or informally. It may be as small as a 'sole trader'. If any production is required, it is initially 'contracted out'. The firm is too small, at this stage, to invest in or control elaborate production facilities.

The fact that the firm is small, controlled by either one individual or a small group, means that communication channels are short and few in number. This has a number of advantages. Information, for example about changes in the market, or about problems of supply, is quickly transmitted and decisions reached. This enables the organization to respond flexibly and quickly to any such changes.

As the firm grows employees may be added, but the number and length of the communication channels remain small. Most individuals will still report direct to the owner. The structure of the organization and the channels of communication represent the 'hub and wheel' shown in Figure 7.3 in Chapter 7. As a result control tends to be directive and highly centralized. It may even be seen as autocratic. Despite this, motivation is high because the employees can see a direct relationship between their work and the product and goals of the organization. (You may recall the concepts as task identity, task significance, etc. from Chapter 4.)

Organizational culture and style of service. The type of organizational culture and style of service is not directly addressed by Lievegood, but it is in the work of Roger Harrison (1987), who identifies four such types. The overlap between the two theories is not, of course, complete, but we feel that each adds meaning to the other.

The pioneer phase seems to be very much what Harrison calls a power culture, characterized by a power-orientated service style. The power culture is authoritarian and hierarchical, usually dominated by a strong leader or group of leaders. They run the organization on the basis that 'they know best'. This may even extend to the needs of their employees. As long as they are right, they are seen as visionary as far as the needs of the organization are concerned, and as 'benevolent autocrats' by the employees. Within such an organization the way to 'get on' is to develop close relationships with those in power. Status and influence is likely to flow from such relationships. (Here you may like to refer back to your motto and advice to a newcomer to your organization.)

The power orientation tends to be associated with a style of service based upon prestige and status. An example of such a service style is often found in exclusive restaurants or shops. Indeed, restaurants are often a popular business for the entrepreneur. Many are very tightly controlled by the owner, who is often also the chef. This particular type of restaurant often appeals to clients, on the basis of the prestige of the establishment. Advertising is by 'write-ups' in prestigious newspapers and magazines, and there are elaborate mechanisms for keeping out 'undesirable' clientele. Other organizations also give different levels of service based upon certain criteria, such as wealth or status, e.g. first or second class travel. The difference is that the power-orientated service culture, sharply demarcates the top level from the others, and concentrates its service on the former.

Problems of the pioneer phase. The problems associated with each phase are related to a number of themes. These can be to do with service style, communications, and the culture itself. The power/pioneer service style is very much dependent upon the organization's products or service remaining exclusive. Such exclusivity is often ephemeral. In the absence of a large enough clientele, the organization may have to seek other markets. In both cases it is likely to come into competition with other organizations. In the face of this competition it will need specialist advice, either from within the company or from outside consultants. What often happens in such situations is that consultants are engaged to diagnose and provide solutions to the organization's problems. Their solutions often revolve around the creation of specialist functions within the organization e.g. debtor control, marketing, etc.

The growth that leads to the establishment of specialist departments also poses problems of management style and with communication channels. As the number of employees grows, the ability of the founders to maintain communication with each and every employee becomes limited. Methods have to be found by which each employee knows their function, without continual reference to the centre. In addition, the autocratic style that was accepted when the organization was small is no longer appropriate. For example, Walt Disney's company was very much a pioneer organization in its early days. When it had grown to about 1000 employees there was a bitter strike. It is reported that Disney never understood the 'ingratitude' and 'disloyalty' which led to the strike. There is a tendency in such situations to look for 'trouble-makers'. In fact it is the situation that has changed, not the people. The organization has become too large for the original management style and communication systems.

One other important issue that faces organizations with autocratic leaders is that of *succession.* There are many examples of the difficulties of those attempting to take over the founder's role. This is especially the case with father–son succession. The Getty family is a good example, as is the Littlewoods company. In the latter case the founder of the football pools and mail-order empire continued, throughout his life, to exercise highly centralized control over the business empire, in the style of a benevolent autocrat. When his son tried to introduce management practices that he thought were needed to develop the firm, he met so much resistance that he quickly resigned. All these pressures, therefore, push the organization towards the next phase – that of differentiation.

THE DIFFERENTIATION PHASE

The move towards differentiation is an attempt to solve the problems of communication and control, created by the growth of the organization and the associated employment of specialists. It is strongly influenced by the thinking of traditional writers on organizations, such as Fayol. It is perhaps the most common structure within large organizations, and is characterized by specialization and separation on a number of dimensions. For example:

- by function – there are separate departments for production, sales, personnel etc.
- by product – there are separate divisions for each product or product family
- by location – because of the size of the organization there are often different divisions, based on geographic considerations
- by hierarchy – level in the hierarchy becomes important.

With increasing numbers of employees, communication needs to be controlled in some way. One way is to create standardized rules and procedures that will eliminate the need for personal guidance on routine matters. Often there is a specialist department whose sole function is to keep the rule book and systems up to date. This, as we have seen, may have the effect of reducing the levels of employee discretion. This effect may be mitigated by the use of plans and goal-setting, which allow discretion within the established goals of the organization. In general, however, fairly mechanistic systems for managing people are in operation. Jobs are carefully specified and filled by systematic selection procedures. The same is true of disciplinary procedures. The hierarchy is clearly specified and there are formal lines through which people report. The organizational structure is the traditional 'tree', with the chief executive at the top, delegating control through successive levels of management.

Organizational culture and style of service. The differentiated phase is generally characterized by what Harrison refers to as a 'role culture'. Power is not exercised according to personal whim, but by reference to formal systems and procedures. The advice normally given to a new entrant to the organization is 'follow the rules'. The high degree of formalization means that the individual is protected against arbitrary power, as long as they stay within the system.

An extreme example of such a culture is provided by one very large multinational in which one of the authors worked as a consultant. Every individual within the management structure had a reference number, except those at the top of the tree who were described by a letter. Thus, the personnel director was PN. The second in command was PN1. If another individual reported directly to PN, they were PN2. His/her deputy was likewise designated as PN21, and so on. In large departments, such as production (headed by P), there were quite long reference numbers. At the level of first line supervision, numbers such as P21343 were in use. The real significance of the system lay in the strict rule that memos should not be addressed to individuals by name, but by reference number. Typists and secretaries had instructions that, if a memo was addressed by name, they were to replace it with the appropriate code. Not surprisingly, there was a large manual, which had to be updated regularly, containing all the reference numbers. The rationale behind the system was that it was the 'role' that was important – individuals come and go. (In that company, at that time, quite frequently.) It can be imagined how depersonalizing this approach was, and it is only fair to add that the system has since been changed.

The service style of the role culture is the one most commonly found in practice. The central concept around which service revolves is the *transaction*. The customer is also seen as a role, and the system is geared toward making the transactions with that role as efficient as possible. The provision of goods is normally on a large scale with the emphasis on prices, costs, and profit margins. Because of the large scale, the emphasis is upon the typical customer who is 'managed' by the system, much as are the organization's employees. The customer is a statistic, rather than a person. Examples are to be found everywhere. Fast food outlets, airlines, railways, and large stores, for example.

Problems of the differentiation phase. Formal lines of communication in the highly differentiated organization quickly become overloaded. In order to counter this, the organization develops rules and procedures so that trivial information is standardized. As we have seen, this may have the undesirable effect of demoralizing the employees so other methods are developed so that discretion is increased, but within limits specified by the organization. The problem of communication between individuals in different sections or departments is a particular problem. Theoretically, all such communication has to go up the hierarchical 'tree' from its origin, until it reaches a point at which a particular individual has responsibility for both of the departments concerned, and then goes down the tree to the recipient. This is both slow and cumbersome, and adds to the overload on the communication channels.

Because of this difficulty in handling information, the organization becomes slow to adapt to environmental changes. It has been said that the nervous system of the dinosaur was so ineffective that a primitive hunter could cut off its tail and be a mile away before the animal noticed. So it is with some large organizations. One way of adaptation is similar to that adopted by individuals when faced with overload; queues are formed and the system slows down and becomes more prone to errors. (See the section on job design in Chapter 4.)

In an attempt to make the organization more adaptive, there is often a move to create self-contained tasks. This is sometimes called decentralization, and includes concepts such as cost centres, of which the most common forms are by product or by location. Each branch is given the specialists required to operate as a totally independent company. It is responsible for its own costs and profits. This 'pure' form of decentralization is, however, relatively uncommon. Most are hybrids, in which some functions are devolved but others are not. Those departments that are centrally maintained tend to be those where economies of scale are possible, or where the work-load does not justify the employment of local experts. An example of the first might be purchasing, and of the latter, personnel. It is not uncommon to find that organizations in this stage 'cycle' between centralization and decentralization, as they gradually realize that both have their strengths and weaknesses.

Another major problem that the differentiated structure engenders is that it encourages inter-group rivalry and conflict that is likely to be dysfunctional. As we have seen, the lack of communication is an important factor in the generation of such hostility.

People feel undervalued, especially in the early part (i.e. rules and procedures) of the differentiated phase. This applies both to employees and customers. They often have information that could be of value to the organization, but there is no apparent way to get it into the system. For example, in one of our local supermarkets there is on sale a device to stop kettles 'furring up' with lime-scale. It is on sale in one of the 'impulse buying' positions. Unfortunately, the whole of the region has very soft water. So soft, in fact, that it can be used in car batteries in place of distilled water. It is quite likely that the person whose job it was to put these on display is fully aware of this, but the system isn't. Furthermore, the fact that they have been on display for some time suggests that there is no easy way to get the information into the system. The way that organizations attempt to overcome these feelings is by giving the employees more autonomy and making customers feel that they are valued. 'Quality Circles', 'Customer First' and other such schemes are examples of such attempts, and can be seen as ways of starting to change the culture.

In summary, there are two main pressures on the differentiated organization. The channels of communication are based not on actual need, but on *position* within the hierarchy. This means the organization is slow to adapt. Secondly, people in the organization feel, and in fact are, under-utilized. These problems stem from the separation and specialization of functions within the organization. Specialists are required, but need to be integrated rather than separated.

THE INTEGRATION PHASE

It is much harder to define the characteristics of the integration stage of organizational development, mainly because so few integrated organizations exist. Those that do are mainly smaller organizations, such as consultancy firms and advertising agencies. However, within large organizations it is not unusual to find some of the characteristics of integration. Indeed, there may be some sections and departments that are fully integrated. There is a range of methods by which an organization may achieve such integration. The particular method chosen will often be specific to the organization, but there are certain common factors. They are characterized by more adaptable styles of leadership, along the lines of those suggested by Hersey and Blanchard. There is greater emphasis upon teamwork and the performance of the team, rather than on that of individuals. Decision-making becomes more decentralized with the use of more participative techniques. All of these operate from an organic, rather than mechanistic, set of assumptions. The organization is not seen as static, rather growth and change are seen as inevitable and natural.

There are two systems which perhaps typify the integrated organization. These are the concepts of *link-pin* and *matrix*. Link-pin was originally suggested by Rensis Likert (1961). On the surface, it involves only a small change to the way that the organizational chart is drawn (see Figure 8.4). However, it represents a considerable difference in relationships within the organization. The replacement of lines of authority by inter-linking triangles indicates that each group has the responsibility for setting and achieving objectives, at its own level. It is also responsible for signalling to the rest of the system if there are problems in achieving these objectives. This will allow the rest of the system time to adjust to the change in circumstances.

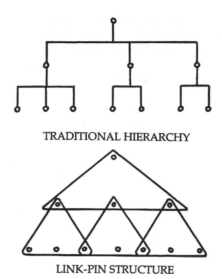

TRADITIONAL HIERARCHY

LINK-PIN STRUCTURE

Figure 8.4. Traditional and link-pin organizational structures.
(Adapted from: Likert, 1961)

The other difference, which gives the system its name, is that many managers are members of two or more groups; they become the 'link-pins'. As such, each manager has the responsibility to ensure that there is compatibility between the groups. This dual membership extends in two directions. Traditionally, links are 'upwards', but they can also be 'sideways'. Thus, a member of one function (e.g. production), may also be a member of the 'personnel' group. If the system works well, this can solve a problem of traditional organizations – communication and compatibility between functions. Traditionally, any requests for information would have to go up the tree and then down again, with the reply following the same path in reverse. The link-pin system allows for quicker and more accurate sideways transfer of information.

In differentiated organizations, such channels are not encouraged. They may develop informally, but if something goes wrong, the 'culprits' are usually instructed to 'follow the correct procedure in future'. The reason for this is that such organizations are built on the premise that authority and responsibility is delegated down the hierarchy. The link-pin system, however, is based upon personal responsibility for setting and achieving objectives, but co-ordinating these with the rest of the organization. As such, it is compatible with *management by objectives*, as long as the objectives are drawn widely enough to allow personal responsibility and discretion, and ideally are set by individuals themselves in consultation with the levels above and below. In passing, it is the authors' belief that the reason for the failure of some MBO schemes is that they are introduced into strong role cultures, which traditionally do not allow such discretion.

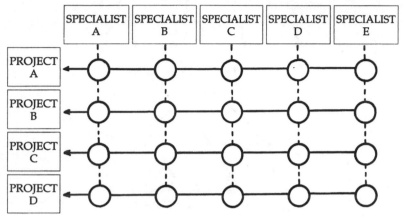

Figure 8.5. The matrix organization.
(Source: Tse, 1985)

Matrix organization, as its name suggests, is built on the fact that many organizations have two dimensions that have to be managed – products and people. This produces a 'matrix' as shown in Figure 8.5. It is perhaps best introduced by way of examples. We will use two, one from our own direct experience and, lest it be thought that it applies only to 'ivory towers', one from the retailing sector.

The Manchester School of Management has a number of 'product lines'. These are the courses that we run. The largest is the under-graduate degree, but there are also various Masters and Doctoral pro-grammes, and 'tailor-made' courses for business and industry. All these products are multidisciplinary. The undergraduate course, for example, covers psychology, accountancy/finance, production, indus-trial relations, and many other specialist subjects. Because of this they require the services of specialist staff from all these areas. The spe-cialist staff are organized into sections (e.g. psychologists, economists, accountants, etc.), each with its own professor at its head. Each of the lecturers will teach on most, if not all, of the product lines (i.e. cours-es). However, sections and the products need to be integrated. There are already section heads in charge of each speciality. What is also re-quired is for each product to have a 'product leader'. In the case of our products these are 'course directors'. They may be from any of the sec-tions and are rarely, if ever, section heads. The 'managers' for each of the dimensions are now established – section leaders and product leaders. All that is required is that each of the circles on the matrix needs to be filled by a particular specialist, e.g. an economist to teach on the Masters degree. The specialist may be any member of that section, including the section head.

The thought that immediately occurs to some people is that the result is that each specialist has at least two 'bosses'. One boss is his section leader, the other is the product leader. While this is true it does not cause problems, because in a true matrix organization the 'bosses' are not controllers but co-ordinators. Since all section heads teach, and none of them are product leaders, they are all both 'bosses' and 'subordinates'. Indeed, the situation often arises where a section head is 'subordinate' to one of his own section members. In industry and commerce, the same principles apply. Individuals working in specialist functions need to be integrated into the production function. As an example of this consider the matrix structure shown in Figure 8.6. This is the matrix structure reportedly used in the engineering department of one of Britain's most successful retailers, Marks and Spencer.

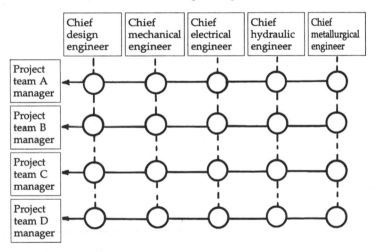

Figure 8.6. The matrix structure of Marks and Spencer's Engineering Department.
(Source: Tse, 1985)

In matrix, as well as in link-pin systems, traditional ideas of authority and responsibility disappear. No one need be permanently 'in charge', but the system can cope with both day-to-day management and emergencies. It would be unwise to claim that such a system has no problems. The matrix structure requires a very high degree of 'inter-dependence' (see Chapter 6). As such it is demanding, but also highly effective. It would also be unwise to claim that there is only one possible type of possible matrix, or that it is appropriate to every situation. Because matrix structures are organic rather than mechanistic, each organization will develop its own variation. In addition, there may be some situations (e.g. production lines) where the tasks are so simple that mechanistic structures are more appropriate.

Culture and service style. There are two cultures and styles that appear to be relevant to integrated organizations. These are *achievement* and *support*. The achievement culture is orientated to making a difference in the world, by achieving a goal or ideal in which it has faith. In this respect its quest is missionary. The members of the organization are also committed to the goal, and are able to use their talents and skills in ways which they find personally rewarding.

The service style derives from the strong internal values and beliefs of the organization. The organization produces what it considers its customers ought to want. The customer becomes the target and 'good' customers accept, without question, the organization's expertise. Such a culture is quite compatible with a power culture. Indeed, many small organizations show elements of both. Again, examples may be found in restaurants. Many are particularly power-orientated, but show achievement-orientation in that they strive for perfection in the food they provide. Often their belief that they are providing such high standards does not allow for contradiction. We know of at least one well-known establishment that throws out customers who have the temerity to ask for any form of extra seasoning. As far as the restaurant is concerned the food is served 'correctly' seasoned. In manufacturing industries, such cultures are often found in smaller 'high tech' organizations (e.g. Apple Computers, or Sir Clive Sinclair's original company).

There are, however, some larger organizations, such as 3M, that appear to be moving towards both matrix structure and achievement, rather than role, culture. Staff are actively encouraged to develop schemes and products to which they are committed. If they can make a good case, they are provided with the resources to develop new products and services. Another way of describing such a culture is that it is 'intrapreneurial'. The members act like entrepreneurs, but within the organization.

The support culture, at least in terms of service, is the opposite of the achievement culture. The achievement culture includes the belief that the customer has, if necessary, to be educated as to what they require. The support culture starts from the premise that the function of the organization is to provide what the customer demands. Again there are restaurants that operate on this philosophy. Whatever the eccentric tastes of the customer may be, the restaurant is there to cater to their needs, and to provide a welcoming and supportive environment. Like the achievement culture, however, the rewards and motivators within the organization are largely intrinsic. In the support culture, these are usually associated with the personal bonds that develop between individuals in the organization, and between the organization and individuals. Employees trust the organization to be responsive to their needs and they, in turn, are responsive to the organization's needs.

In terms of the structure of achievement and support cultures, it may well be that 'matrix' is best suited to achievement and 'link-pin' to support. For reasons we have already stated, this is not a hard and fast rule; each organization will find its own solution.

Problems of the integration phase. The problems associated with the two styles of culture and service are fairly clear. The danger with the achievement culture is that it will produce what no one wants. The classic example is perhaps the Sinclair C5. Alternatively, the organization may produce a better and more advanced device, which is incompatible with previous models. Customers may be happily using these old models, but spare parts become unobtainable. This appears to happen frequently in the computer industry. The danger for the support culture, on the other hand, is that customers become more and more demanding. In addition, the organization may spend a disproportionate, and unprofitable, amount of its resources catering for small minorities.

The organizational problems associated with the integration phase are less easy to describe. Throughout the development, from pioneer, to differentiated, to integrated, solving the problems of one stage produces different problems. It is not yet clear what problems are produced by integration. Possibly just the never-ending one of getting people to work together effectively.

In this section, we have related the stage theory of organizational development to that of culture and service style. This is because we believe that there is a considerable degree of overlap between them. There are, however, some alternatives which complete the picture. Figure 8.7 shows all the possible combinations, together with our views concerning the likely existence of each.

The differentiated organization that has a power culture is an interesting combination. It occurs because, despite the founder's desire to hold on to day-to-day control, the organization becomes so large that this proves impossible. The only alternative is to differentiate, with power very clearly seen as devolved from above.

The pioneer company may also be either achievement- or service-orientated. Whether this occurs, and if so which, will depend upon the beliefs and orientation of the founder. They depend upon the organization remaining small. The problems arise for such an organization when it either grows or is taken over. In growing, it may be that it can 'skip' the differentiated phase and move to full integration. If it is taken over, it is usually by a much larger organization, often one that is differentiated. The subsequent clash of cultures can lead to many problems, and often leads to the departure of many of the original staff.

PHASE

	PIONEER	DIFFERENTIATED	INTEGRATED	
POWER	Classic small entrepreneurial company owned by powerful boss who keeps tight control	Privately owned company too large for owner(s) to control everything; some specialization	Unlikely to occur contrary to the philosophy of integration	
ROLE	Unlikely to occur, small, tightly knit, company does not need role differentiation	Classic large companies	Impossible combination	CULTURE
ACHIEVEMENT	Quite common. Culture defined by pioneer who specifies the mission	Can occur in small pockets within role cultures e.g. research depts.	Classic 'matrix' commitment to jointly defined mission	
SUPPORT	Can occur if pioneer believes in supportive approach	Can occur in small pockets within role cultures e.g. training depts.	Classic 'link pin'	

Figure 8.7. Relationship between an organization's phase of development and its organizational culture

This would be a good place to review your answers to the questions posed at the beginning of this chapter. The purpose is to see what they tell you about the culture and phase of development of your organization. The advice to a new member may be revealing. Does your advice, for instance, suggest that it is necessary to be wary of authority, or to follow the rules? This would suggest a role culture. If the advice is to watch out for political manoeuvring, this could imply a power culture. Similar comments apply to the organization's slogan or motto. Whatever your advice or motto, see how it relates to the four cultures. In the same way what does your animal mascot tell you about your perception of the organization? Animals like dinosaurs or elephants suggest a role culture. More social or co-operative animals (for example bees or wolves) might suggest a support culture, although in the latter case one with predatory overtones.

PROBLEM SOLVING

Exercise
Before reading further you should turn to Appendix 6 and attempt the exercise set out there.

As we have seen, there are a number of problems associated with each phase of an organization's development. In addition to this, each organization will have issues which are specific to itself. These may be concerned with improving co-operation between certain individuals or departments, improving the communication systems, or even changing the basic culture. It is the job of the manager to deal with these problems. This involves 'influencing' within the organization. To do this it is necessary to develop an *influence strategy*, by identifying who needs to be influenced and what is the best way to achieve it.

INFLUENCE STRATEGIES

From an examination of the literature on management, Beck and Cox (1984) suggest that there are four ways of exerting an influence in organizations. These four approaches have considerable pedigrees, being mentioned by writers from as early as Machiavelli up to more contemporary sources. Not all writers mention all four approaches; some mention only one, two, or three. Interestingly, those who mention all four are in a minority. The four influence styles are outlined below. Although the overlap is not perfect, there is a strong relationship between these styles and the four organizational cultures described in the previous section.

The *Political* style relies heavily on informal influence, which is exerted in two characteristic ways. The first of these is the formation of alliances within the organization. These are networks of individuals who have compatible interests, and who hence support each other's causes. This type of network has always been particularly strong in British organizations and, indeed, in society at large. The second method of political influence is by the strategic use of information. By withholding information and releasing it at the right time, and in the right direction, the desired actions can be encouraged. This selective use of information is often accompanied by persuasion and 'selling'.

The individual who uses the political style extensively will tend to see the organization as a 'jungle', where quick thinking and good contacts are essential. As a result they will be careful to maintain a network of contacts and friendships. A useful indicator of a person's preferred style is the way that they approach conflict situations.

Because conflict disrupts the smooth working of informal networks, the political individual will try to keep conflict to a minimum, often by smoothing over problems.

The political style is a very common one, particularly in organizations with power and role cultures. The main reason for this is that it is the only way of challenging control. In the power culture, this control is exerted directly from the centre, while in the role culture it is delegated downwards from the top.

There is often a very strong feeling that politics in organizations is, by definition, a bad thing. This is partly because much political activity is seen as game playing, with the object of advancing personal rather than organizational goals. Also politics can have negative consequences, such as low levels of trust and the wasting of time in manoeuvring for position. However, it is now becoming accepted that some types of political activity can be positive, and because it is often the only effective way of coping with authority, it is widespread within organizations. This being the case, managers need to know about it if they are to be effective.

The various types of political activity, and their consequences, have been neatly classified by Baddely and James (1987). They suggest that there are two independent dimensions to politics. One is 'politically aware' versus 'politically unaware'. To this the present authors would add, politically 'skilled' versus politically 'unskilled'. The other dimension is concerned with whether people are acting with integrity and in the organization's interests, or whether they are playing games and seeking to advance their own interests at the expense of others. The combination of these two dimensions produces four 'types', as shown in Figure 8.8. Each type has its own animal 'mascot'.

Box 1 represents the clever individual who is playing games, but is politically aware and skilled. The mascot of this position is the *fox*. This is the style that has given rise to the traditionally negative view of an organizational politician, and is not recommended. Box 2 is the individual who is playing games, but is politically unaware and unskilled. The mascot here is the *donkey*. This individual is politically inept and blunders around trying to pull off political coups. They are, however, easily out-manoeuvred by more skilful politicians. Box 3 is the individual who is acting with integrity but is politically unaware. The mascot is a *sheep*. This individual is easily taken advantage of (and led to the slaughter) by more politically aware and skilful members of the organization, especially foxes. As a result these individuals are often left wondering 'What happened?', in meetings and other situations where they have been out-manoeuvred. Box 4 is the wise individual, who is politically aware and acting with integrity. The mascot is the *owl*. This is the style of the competent manager who will use the political style only in appropriate situations.

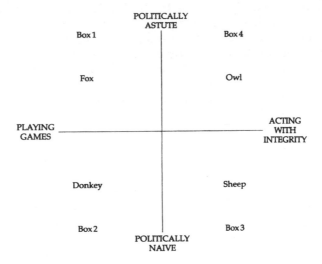

Figure 8.8. Four types of organizational politician.
(Source: Baddely and James, 1987)

The *Formal/Authoritarian* style relies predominantly upon the authority conferred on the individual by the organization, and is therefore usually dependent upon the individual's position within the hierarchy. The way in which the authority is used will be determined by the formal rules of the organization. The individual who uses this influence style predominantly will view the ideal organization as a well-ordered system – 'a place for everything, and everything in its place'. They tend to view the organization in rather 'feudal' terms. Membership means that benefits are accepted but also, as a result, duties are owed. Employees, therefore, owe loyalty to the organization, upon which the formal/authoritarian manager will call. Such an individual, as well as exerting authority, will also respect the authority of those above him or her. In extreme cases the same individual may behave like a tyrant with their subordinates, but meekly follow orders from superiors. The method of resolving conflict is, of course, by reference to higher authority. This higher authority will arbitrate and 'hand down' a decision. This style is well suited to, and hence very common in, differentiated organizations and role cultures.

The *Open* style relies on generating trust and commitment through openness and honesty. The basic assumption underlying this approach is that a consensus can be reached within the organization about what needs to be done. The way that this consensus can be achieved is by dealing openly and honestly with the ideas and feelings involved. It is the style that was widely advocated by social scientists in the 1960s and early 1970s. The individual who predominantly uses this style is probably democratic in orientation, and believes in individual responsibility and joint decision-making. The way in which conflict is resolved is by open discussion, and even by confrontation, between the parties involved. This may prove to be a painful process, as it makes explicit the differences between the people concerned, both regarding the values involved and the actions proposed. These then have to be resolved; like inter-dependence (see Chapter 6), it may be uncomfortable, but effective.

A large number of managers say that this is their preferred style. In our experience it is not so widely used in practice. Once again there is a difference between 'espoused theory' and 'theory in use'. There are, perhaps, good reasons why it is not widely used. Open confrontation with powerful figures is dangerous, especially in power and role cultures. Because of this, it is probably most commonly used between colleagues on the same level or in close working groups. It is a highly appropriate style in achievement and support cultures.

The *Laissez-faire* style is based on the view that if things are going well leave them alone. The *laissez-faire* approach is to set things going, or delegate responsibility, and only intervene if things appear to be going wrong. If used inappropriately, however, the potential for disaster is obvious. For this reason it is perhaps the least popular of the four styles for managers. The manager who uses this style probably values independence and has beliefs about organizations as 'self-organizing systems'. Conflict, in this view, is something that should not exist and hence is to be avoided.

This style is probably most appropriate in achievement cultures, where individuals are highly committed to their tasks. The present authors are members of such a culture, where *laissez-faire* management is highly appropriate. (You may recall that an achievement culture generates products that it believes the customer ought to want. This book is such a product!)

It should be emphasized that all the styles are appropriate in the right context. In pure cultures, one style might predominate, but most organizations are a blend of cultures. It is essential, then, to be aware of the culture within each section or department of the organization, and adjust your influence style accordingly. Flexibility of style is the route to greatest efficiency in influencing organizations. Sometimes the selection of the appropriate style comes by intuition, but more often it requires an analysis of the situation. Useful insights may be obtained by identifying those individuals who seem highly successful in this respect, and comparing their strategies with those who are unsuccessful.

Your choice of strategy in Appendix 6 may give you some indication of your own preferred strategy. Because it is over-simplified it should, of course, be treated with some caution. The four paragraphs are meant to represent the four main styles, in the following order: political; formal; open and *laissez-faire*.

Some guidelines can, however, be given on the selection of an appropriate influence style. This will depend on a number of factors, but particularly on the type of goal, the people involved, and the organizational culture. A summary, which also integrates some concepts from previous chapters, is given in Figure 8.9. From this figure it will be seen that the formal style is likely to work best in a role culture in situations where the goals are clear and relatively short term, and other people's commitment is not necessary. The open style is likely to be most appropriate in support cultures in situations where the goals are complex and long term, and you are working with people who are highly motivated and interdependent. The open style is also important where it is necessary to generate commitment to goals. The political style is probably most effective within a range of situations between the extremes outlined above. As already noted, it is common in power cultures and may be the only way that more junior members in both power and role cultures can cope with authoritarian senior managers. Their *laissez-faire* style is appropriate when dealing with individuals who are highly motivated and committed to their goals and who are able to work independently. This situation will often be found in achievement cultures.

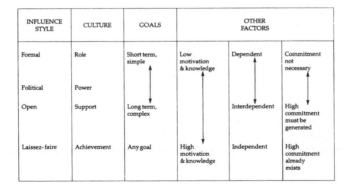

INFLUENCE STYLE	CULTURE	GOALS	OTHER FACTORS		
Formal	Role	Short term, simple ↑	Low motivation & knowledge ↑	Dependent ↑	Commitment not necessary ↑
Political	Power				
Open	Support	Long term, complex ↓		Interdependent ↓	High commitment must be generated ↓
Laissez-faire	Achievement	Any goal ↓	High motivation & knowledge ↓	Independent	High commitment already exists

Figure 8.9. Factors determining a manager's choice of influence style

In our experience there is a danger that managers overuse one favoured approach. Since flexibility is important this means that, by definition, they are at times using that style inappropriately. If this is so, we find that they tend to get a reputation as some kind of organizational 'bastard'. The overuse of the political style becomes a 'scheming bastard', the formal an 'autocratic bastard', the open an 'awkward bastard', and the *laissez-faire* a 'lazy bastard'. An important question for the reader is, what possible reputation do you have?

GOAL CLARITY

In solving problems successfully in organizations it is important to be clear, not only about the influence strategy, but also about the goals you are pursuing. When considering goals or objectives within organizations, there are a number of levels to be considered. A common classification suggests that there are three basic levels, each with three sub-divisions. The three basic levels are those of the personal, team, and organizational. To be effective, clarity is required on all three.

Personal goals are those that satisfy the needs of the individual. There are three levels of such needs. Most obvious are the *task* goals. These are the actual work goals for which the individual is responsible. These may be clear or unclear, self-defined, defined by the supervisor, or jointly defined. In many cases these goals are relatively clear and may even be formally recorded in a job description. Often, however, even where a job description exists, the clarity of these goals may be less than perfect. In such cases, the potential exists for ambiguity about roles.

The individual also needs to be clear about their *development* goals. These are concerned with personal growth and the development of new skills, both professional and personal. These goals are not limited to work; they may include goals that are part of the individual's private life. They are linked to a third group of personal goals that Beck and Cox have referred to as *status* goals. These are concerned with both short-term and long-term career plans. In the short term, issues such as salary and other forms of recognition are involved; in the longer term, career advancement issues are important.

Personal goals are important because they draw attention to, and legitimize, the fact that people work for organizations for personal reward. Because of the emphasis in organizations on task, goals at that level tend to be better defined than at the other two levels.

At this point it would be useful to spend a few minutes defining your own personal goals at task, developmental, and status levels.

Team goals are those of the work group, section, or department. Again, there are task goals and developmental goals, and again the former are usually more clearly defined than the latter. The task goals concern the work objectives that the team is required to achieve, and are similar in nature to those at the personal level. Developmental goals are often concerned with improving team functioning and may, for example, be aimed at improving the way individuals work together. The team may also have status goals. These are often concerned with the team's standing within the organization or in the world as a whole. Goals of this nature are often noticeable in such functions as research, sales and marketing, and advertising.

Again, at this point it may be worth specifying the team goals for your own team, whether it be a section or department.

Organizational goals. Most organizations have very clear statements of their task goals. They are normally enshrined in corporate plans and other policy statements. They define the nature of the business, and set sales and other targets. Developmental goals are concerned with the future of the organization and any programme of changes that might be contemplated. Status goals are often far less clear at this level, but may include such aims as being the 'best' in the field.

Unless you are on the board of directors of your organization, there is probably little influence you can have over goals at this level. This does not mean that it is a pointless exercise to consider them. In fact, for effective goal management it is important to know what they are.

Some would argue that the clarity of goals is one of the most important factors in the success of an organization. The organization needs to be clear as to where it is going, and what type of organization it is. Where such goals exist they are usually heavily value-laden. Warren Bennis (1983), in his study of chief executive officers in US organizations, identifies five essential 'competencies'. The most important of these he defines as follows:

'Vision: The capacity to create and communicate a compelling vision of a desired state of affairs – to impart clarity to this vision and induce commitment to it.'

In the UK, Goldsmith and Clutterbuck (1984), writing of managers as leaders, say that they should 'provide a clear mission, which they believe in passionately themselves and incite others to subscribe to'. Leadership thrives, they suggest, when people have clear objectives. Again in the UK, Cox and Cooper (1988) in their book *High Flyers*, quote one chief executive as saying that an essential skill for the job is 'to be visionary: this is needed to cope with a changing world and to exploit the future'.

In Chapter 5 the importance of setting clear goals for individuals was considered. Such clarity is also required at the organizational level. However, once goals have been specified at each of the levels, it will often be the case that goals at different levels will be in conflict with each other. This will itself require management. Sometimes this will involve compromise or, better, finding a super-ordinate goal. To do this, the techniques discussed in Chapter 7 will need to be used.

THE PSYCHOLOGICAL CONTRACT AND CULTURE

This chapter has examined how the structure and culture of organizations change as they cope with problems, in particular those associated with growth. If managers are to be effective they will need to be aware of the predominant culture of the organization, or part of the organization, that they are trying to influence. The nature of the culture, as we have seen, will determine which style of influencing is likely to be most effective. We have argued that managers tend to have their own preferred style but, because the appropriate style will vary from situation to situation, managers need to develop flexibility. Finally, we suggested that it is essential for managers, when trying to influence events in the organization, to be clear as to their goals, which should be defined at the three levels of individual, team and organization.

All of the above factors are closely related to the psychological contract which exists within an organization. The organization's culture, in particular, defines, or at least provides the framework for, the type of contract that will exist. This is because the bases of culture are norms and values, which will include beliefs about how people should be treated, and how they should relate to each other. Since differences in culture will arise at different stages of development, the psychological contract will change as the organization grows. Failure to realize this and to adapt and re-negotiate the contract as time goes on will lead to dissatisfaction at all levels in the organization, and to industrial relations problems.

Potential differences in the psychological contract in different cultures can be clearly seen by considering the four organizational cultures suggested by Roger Harrison. In a power culture the contract is essentially *alienative*. From the point of view of the manager, the contract is 'I make the decisions, you do as you are told'. The subordinate may be able to make suggestions, but only when the manager allows it. The subordinate's view is 'I am here to do as I am told – I do not have to take responsibility'. The contract is defined and laid down by the power figures at the top of the organization. In fact, a power culture has been defined as one where everyone's reality is defined by the boss. We call this alienative because the lower-level workers do not usually feel like full members of the organization, and may well be totally alienated.

In a role culture the contract is much more a *calculative* one. In this culture the psychological contract comes closer to the formal contract of employment than in any other of the culture types. This is because the culture is based on formal rules which are followed by both manager and subordinate. The basic contract is 'We all follow the rules – I do my job and you do yours'. An important issue in the psychological contract, which will include assumptions about how much work should be done, and in return for what rewards, is 'what do I owe to the organization and what does it owe me?'

The achievement culture and the support culture have some overlap in terms of the contract, as they do in terms of the underlying values. In an achievement culture the contract is a *challenging* one. It is based on an assumption that 'this is a communal enterprise where we challenge each other'. This involves a belief in a common purpose between managers and subordinates in which solutions to problems arise from co-operative interaction.

In a support culture the contract is a *trusting* one. The essence of this contract is that 'this is a communal enterprise where we take care of each other'. The contract is that the individual trusts the organization to respond to his or her needs, and will give to the organization to the best of his or her ability. This is not to say that an achievement culture is not trusting. For it to work there must be a high level of trust. Similarly, a support culture can be challenging and creative. It is a question of where the strongest emphasis lies. The emphasis in the support culture is on mutual loyalty; in an achievement culture it is on personal initiative and self-reliance.

To reiterate, the important issue is that if managers set out to change the organization, they will almost certainly be changing its culture. If the culture changes, so will the psychological contract.

Organizational Change

This chapter is concerned with the way in which organizations change in order to cope with changing conditions. The generic name for the study of such changes is Organizational Development (OD). These changes may be in the external environment, for example markets and competitors, or they may be internal, for example through growth. Internal pressures push the organization into different structures, as discussed in the previous chapter. Whatever the source of the change, they will inevitably have an effect on the people working in the organization. It is with the effects of such changes, and how these can be managed, that we will now be concerned.

Change in organizations is difficult because of two built-in forms of resistance to such change. First, organizations, particularly those in the differentiation phase (discussed in Chapter 8.), are not meant to change. They are specifically designed to be stable. It is expected that they will continue, irrespective of the comings and goings of individual members. Second, the individuals themselves may be unaware of the changes that are taking place in the rest of the organization, and hence the need for themselves to change.

These two factors mean that there is often considerable inertia in the system. If you refer back to the animal mascot you chose for your own organization (in the previous chapter), you may find that resistance, or slowness in reacting to change is a characteristic of the animal. (It may even go as far as the dinosaur which, of course, became extinct.) This issue of resistance to change, and how to overcome it, will be considered later in this chapter. However, before we get into the detail you might like to try the following exercise, which may give you some insight into your own processes of learning and change.

Exercise: Significant learning event

Think of something important that you have learned. Ideally this should have occurred reasonably recently, but so long as you can remember the detail it does not really matter how long ago the learning took place. It is not possible to define what is meant by important; it is something which was important or significant for you. Having thought of something you learnt, now think about how the learning took place – in what context and how it happened. Then read through the following questions and briefly note your answers. We will come back to these later in the chapter.

• Was the learning from a planned event (like a training programme)? If so, was it something you planned for yourself or was it planned by someone else? Alternatively, did it simply arise from something totally unplanned?

• Did it take place at work or outside of work?

• Was the event or situation which gave rise to the learning pleasant or unpleasant?

• Did the learning happen suddenly and all at once, or did it build up over a period of time?

• Did the learning occur while you were alone or was it while you were interacting with others?

• Was the learning related to your job or to life in general?

You might find it interesting to try this with any other significant learning events you can recall, and see if they follow the same pattern.

We will return to this in the section on individual learning, where we will give the results from a large number of people who have responded to these questions and discuss their significance.

INDIVIDUAL CHANGE

Organizational change can take place at three levels – individual, group or team, and organizational. Individual change is really the basis for all change. Unless individuals change in some way, nothing changes. At management levels, management development programmes are the major method by which such change is encouraged. The focus is often on developing the skills the person needs to cope with their present job, but it may also include the development of skills for the future. If any wider programme of organizational change is planned, it will need to include plans for individual change.

How a training programme, or any other individual change programme, is set up will depend on the assumptions that the organizer holds about how people learn. These same assumptions are also fundamental to the strategy taken for any other level of change, so they are worth examining in relation to their implications for the design of change interventions. There are broadly three sets of assumptions about learning, on which social scientists tend to work.

ASSUMPTIONS ABOUT LEARNING

First, there is the *behaviourist* approach, based on the work of Skinner. This was discussed in some detail in Chapter 5, so we do not need to say much about the basic theory here. A change agent working on these assumptions would look for those reinforcements which are producing the current behaviour. Having specified the new behaviour precisely, the object would be to set up a schedule of reinforcement to encourage the necessary change. This sounds somewhat manipulative, and indeed behaviour modification can be done in this way, but it does not have to be. It is quite possible to discuss the change with the participants and help them set up their own specification of new behaviour and schedules of reinforcement, so that control is very much in their own hands. In fact, in our view this is usually the best way to proceed.

Another set of approaches to training is based on *cognitive* assumptions. The behaviourist approach assumes that change is best brought about by considering 'external' factors. The cognitive approach, on the other hand, is based on a belief that behaviour is controlled by 'internal' factors, such as the individual's beliefs, assumptions, and theories about the situation. To change behaviour, therefore, you have to change these internal theories. There are a number of assumptions about how this is done. One view, known as the *structuralist* approach, considers the mind as rather like a computer, and training is a matter of 're-programming' it. This is done by well-designed courses, feeding in appropriate new information. This will work only if the individual is prepared to take on board the new ideas. In recognition of this, another approach is to design training around practical exercises and projects. For this reason, it is known as the *functionalist* approach. It is based on the assumption that people will learn when they realize that they have a practical need for the information offered. This will occur when they are given the opportunity to experiment and learn things for themselves. Training involves a range of activities, from courses designed around case studies and practical exercises, to quite long-term real life projects.

The final set of assumptions which has had considerable influence on change processes, derives from the *humanist* school. One of the most influential members of this group was Maslow (see Chapter 4). Their belief is that, given the right conditions, human beings are naturally committed to growth and development, the potential for which is unlimited. The role of the trainer then becomes that of providing the right conditions. Some insights on how this is done are provided by Rogers (1967). Originally a psychotherapist, his ideas have been widely accepted and used in education and training. In his view, it is impossible to 'teach' anything of value to another person. As he puts it,

'It seems to me that anything that can be taught to another is relatively inconsequential, and has little or no significant influence on behaviour .....I have come to feel that the only learning which significantly influences behaviour is self-discovered, self-appropriated learning.'

This may seem a little extreme, but it does draw attention to the fact that it is impossible to 'teach' someone who does not want to learn. People will only learn (and change), if they want to. The role of the trainer/change agent is to try to bring about conditions where they will want to change.

Thinking along these lines has brought about an approach to training known as *self-development*. In this approach, individuals become responsible for directing their own development. They define their own learning objectives and decide for themselves which is the best way to achieve them, and they evaluate their own progress. The staff of the training department become consultants, helping and supporting people while they do this. Much of the development under this system comes from real life experience, although people may still attend courses, but only when they, themselves, decide that this fulfils the needs they have identified. The use of this approach involves the fundamental belief that people are responsible and will organize their development in a way that is compatible with the needs of the organization, and will be committed to achieving organizational goals. This is, in itself, a humanist assumption.

The values of the humanist movement have had a very strong influence on current practice in training, and on organizational development generally. They are also totally compatible with 'support' and 'achievement' cultures in organizations. Self-development consequently requires a high degree of inter-dependence between the individuals involved. In the more traditional training systems, either cognitivist or behaviourist, there is more likely to be mutual dependence or straight authority/dependence. In general, under these approaches trainees are relatively passive and learn (or fail to learn) what is presented to them, within the framework provided.

In order to make clear the assumptions underlying each of the above approaches, we have tended to concentrate on the differences between them. It is, however, important to note that they are all quite compatible with each other. People learn as the result of reinforcement. They also have internal maps and theories about how the world works, and changing these will change their behaviour. Their internal maps will, in fact, change as a result of changes in reinforcement patterns. There is also overwhelming evidence that learning is, in general, more effective if people are in charge of it themselves. The wise trainer will therefore use all the theories, as appropriate – the contingency approach again!

At this stage you might like to look back at your notes on the key learning event exercise with which we started this chapter, and compare them with the information in Figure 9.1. These are the results of asking the same questions of some sixty adults in professional occupations, who were taking a postgraduate management course, and 500 undergraduate management students. From the table it can be seen that most key learning comes from unplanned events (45 per cent for the professionals and 60 per cent for the undergraduates). Around 30 per cent report that the learning came from events planned by the individual themselves. Only 10–18 per cent came from activities planned by others (e.g. conventional training programmes). It is significant that all those involved in this exercise were, at the time, taking part in full time courses. Not more than 10 per cent of the undergraduates had identified a significant learning related to their course. (It could be less than this, because we do not know that even for that 10 per cent the planned events were related to their *present* course.) This is consistent with Carl Rogers' view of significant learning.

Other implications of this exercise are that significant learning tends to be more related to non-work situations than to work. (For the undergraduates 'work' was defined as anything related to their course.) There is a roughly 50/50 chance that the event will be either pleasant or unpleasant, suggesting that we learn equally well from disasters or good things. Learning tends to be incremental, and is considerably more often accomplished when relating to others. The learning we see as significant is more likely to be related to our life in general than to our job. It is important in interpreting this data to remember that participants were asked for 'significant' events. They may well have learnt all sorts of other things during the same time period which were not as significant and which may have been learnt by other methods. It is to be hoped that the undergraduates were learning something from their course! While providing evidence for the Rogerian view, it does not mean that, as stated above, the other learning methods are not effective in appropriate contexts.

		Professionals %	Undergraduates %
Planned	by self	37	30
	by others	18	10
Unplanned		45	60
At work		40	30
Not at work		60	70
Pleasant		60	50
Unpleasant		40	50
Sudden		27	20
Incremental		73	80
Alone		20	10
With others		80	90
Life-centred		80	80
Job-centred		20	20

Figure 9.1. Classification of significant learning events

TEAM BUILDING

Team building is the second most frequent form of change intervention. Indeed, a review by Porras and Berg in 1978 estimated that 40 per cent of OD interventions involved team building. As already mentioned, teams are an essential part of organizations. They exist wherever several people need to co-operate to complete a task. The emphasis in team building is usually on the manager and his or her immediate group of subordinates. It may also be used at a more casual level, for example with people who work together occasionally, but who are not part of a formal team.

The origins of team building go back to the work of Mayo, who built upon the Hawthorne studies to demonstrate the importance of social relationships at work (See Chapter 4). Other influences are the work of Lewin at the National Training Laboratories (NTL), and the development of the 'T-group' movement. In order to improve a team's effectiveness it is common, in practice, to concentrate on one or more of a number of themes, for example:

- Increasing mutual trust among team members.

- Increasing awareness, both of your own and other people's behaviour.

- Developing inter-personal skills, e.g. listening, giving feedback, bringing others into the discussion, etc.

The decision on which of these themes are to be developed will depend upon a number of factors, but particularly on the theoretical orientation of the consultant working with the team, together with the consultant's diagnosis of weaknesses in the team. Ideally this diagnosis should be made in co-operation with the team members.

STRATEGIES FOR TEAM BUILDING

There are a variety of approaches used in team building. These largely derive from different assumptions about how people learn best (i.e. change), and assumptions about the best sort of environment for effective teamwork.

Sensitivity training is based on the assumptions underlying T-groups and encounter groups. These terms are very broad and hence difficult to define precisely. T-groups (the 'T' simply stands for training) involve a wide range of activities, many of which are very similar to those used in other approaches, such as encounter groups. In general the group consists of some eight to ten people, and the purpose is to learn from their own behaviour and interactions. Emphasis is placed on developing a climate of trust and openness, thus fostering a high level of inter-personal feedback and the acceptance of feelings. The trainer or 'facilitator' is there to help the group achieve these objectives, not as a formal 'expert' teacher; he or she, therefore, operates very non-directively. The focus of the group can be at the level of personal learning and growth, the understanding of group activity, learning at the organizational level, or any combination of the three.

T-groups are very clearly and firmly rooted in the values of the 1960s and early 1970s. These include a strong belief in the value of openness and trust if people are going to work well together. Strong emphasis is placed upon 'authenticity' – being open and expressing inner feelings. Unfortunately, these values are often in conflict with the norms of most organizations. Argyris (1962) has pointed out that the norm in most organizations is to value rationality as effective, and suppress feelings as ineffective. This is based on the belief that as individuals move into expressing feelings they become more emotional. The more emotional a person becomes the less rational they become and hence, it is argued, they become less effective. The natural reaction to this norm is to suppress the expression of feelings, even of perfectly reasonable ones. This becomes so automatic that the person may not even realize that they are being suppressed. Since these emotions are not recognized or expressed, they gradually build up until they burst out, often as anger. The trigger that sets off the outburst may often be a very minor event. Because the person is now so emotional that they are out of control, they may be ineffective, and this can confirm the assumption that feelings and emotions are bad. The individual therefore makes a resolution not to give vent to their feelings in future, and the whole cycle starts again. According to Argyris, the individual needs to recognize the feelings as they develop and deal with them in some way. In classic T-groups, this would be by openly expressing them.

Mainly because of the difference between the values of T-groups and those of most organizations, this approach was never widely accepted and has now fallen into disuse. The clash of values led to poor transfer from the training situation to the 'real world' of the organization. There was even some evidence that people were less effective after such training, although a minority did show positive change. This was probably because open and supportive behaviour were inappropriate in political and formal organizational cultures. Other problems concerned the unpredictable nature of T-groups themselves – because of the open structure, anything could happen (or sometimes not happen). There were also ethical problems. Because T-groups are both powerful and personal, there is a strong case for participation being voluntary. There are, however, strong group and organizational pressures on the individual in such a 'voluntary' situation. In addition, if some members chose not to attend, the effectiveness might of necessity be reduced.

Most OD practitioners in the 1960s and '70s saw T-group values as the way organizations *ought* to be. That is to say, an ideal organization would have a climate of high openness and trust. This is now often, but somewhat disparagingly, referred to as the 'love and trust' model. Most practitioners have now abandoned this approach for the reasons given above, and also because, despite using this approach for some 20 years, nothing has changed in the real world of organizations. They did not become more trusting and open. Most practitioners have therefore abandoned these values and espoused the contingency model of 'horses for courses'. The valuable and valid legacy of sensitivity training in current thinking is to have emphasized that humans are both rational *and* feeling beings.

Role negotiation is, in a way, at the opposite end of the scale to sensitivity training. It was developed by Harrison (1972), in order to take account of the issue of power in organizations.

In preparation for the negotiations implied in the title, each team member considers each of the others and prepares a list of items under each of the following three headings:
It would help me to increase my effectiveness if you would:

• do more of, or do better, the following . . .

- do less of, or stop doing, the following ...

- keep on doing (i.e. maintain unchanged) the following ...

Members then meet in pairs to negotiate the changes that they would like to see, and those they are themselves willing to make. The negotiations are 'genuine' ones, in the form of 'I will agree to do X if you stop doing Y' or, 'I will do A if you will do B'. Negotiations continue until both parties are happy and agreement has been reached. The results are then written down and signed by both parties. It is part of the agreement that if one of the parties does not keep to the bargain, the other can use the sanction of withdrawing their half. The intention is that the negotiations should be done in such a way that there is an incentive to keep to the agreement, so as to gain the benefits promised by the other. Harrison makes the point that it is not legitimate, or necessary, to probe into individual feelings. What is required, however, is honesty. Threats and pressures, on the other hand, may be used, but it should be remembered that their use may lead to defensiveness. The role of the consultant is to help the negotiators to understand and keep to the guidelines, and to help them clarify the requirements for change. It is, of course, important that the consultant does not actually influence the items, but simply helps the individuals clarify their own ideas.

The structured approach is based upon 'cognitivist' assumptions that change is best brought about by providing information and understanding about the processes within groups. The core of this approach is a team-building 'workshop' or training course. This comprises a series of exercises, each designed to focus on some aspect of team working. These exercises are usually of a type known as 'substitute task exercises'. These are tasks that are not related in any way to the normal work of the group, but are designed to highlight some aspect of group process, such as competitiveness, goal clarity, or decision-making. The fact that the task is unrelated to normal work makes it easier for the group to focus on the process, and avoids undue attention being directed on to the particular task being undertaken. It is common to use short questionnaires and other measures to bring out key aspects of team processes. These activities, assisted by interventions from the consultant, help the group and individuals to gain a better understanding of how their present methods of working could be improved.

Packages also provide a virtually 'ready-made' team building programme, which can be taken and 'plugged in' as needed. They are usually fairly highly structured and based on a particular theoretical framework. Often they are aimed more at developing the skills of the team leader than at total team development. A good example is the use of the managerial grid (see Chapter 6). This approach can be used to enable the manager or team leader to clarify his or her current style in terms of 'concern for task' or 'concern for people'. Exercises are then available to enable the individual to develop towards the optimal style, (i.e. high on both concerns). The package can also be used to explore team members' preferences for different styles.

Another widely used package is provided by Adair (1968). This is also mainly directed at the team leader. Adair argues that there are three sets of needs which must be met if the team is to work effectively. These are:

- task needs – practical things to do with getting the work done

- group needs – concerned with group maintenance and keeping a cohesive team

- individual needs – the personal goals which each individual hopes to achieve through membership of the team.

It is important that attention is paid to all three of these; for a fully effective team, all must be fulfilled. It is possible to take the view that ensuring these needs are met is the leader's responsibility, in which case training concentrates on team leadership. Alternatively, if the view is taken that responsibility is shared by all team members the concepts are used as a framework for reviewing how effectively the group is functioning. Exercises are used to highlight the importance of each set of needs, and how well they are being fulfilled.

Interaction process analysis is another approach that enables participants to analyse what type of contribution each person is making to the group, and what the implications are for group effectiveness. It is based on the work of Bales (1951), who designed a rather complex classification of the types of interaction which take place between individuals in groups. The original classification is too complex to master and use quickly, so various simpler versions, such as that shown in Figure 9.2, have been devised.

One way in which this is used is for team members to take it in turns to observe the group, either when it is working normally or in special training sessions, and classify and count the types of contribution made by each team member. Alternatively, the consultant can undertake this task. The results are fed back to the group, who then consider their implications both for individuals and for the group as a whole. It is not uncommon to find that certain individuals' contributions tend to be predominantly of one or two types. They are often surprised to discover this. Sometimes this is true for the group as a whole. There may be, for example, a great deal of *giving* opinions and

In developing appropriate categories of interactions between group members it is almost impossible to give absolute definitions of what should be included in each. Nevertheless, listed below are definitions and examples which should be of assistance for a trainer developing his or her observational and analytical skills.

GIVES SUPPORT
Raises others' esteem   *'Great idea!'*
Gives reward   *'You're looking fine'*
Shows solidarity   *'I'm with you on this one'*
Gives help   *'What was your point, Dave?'*
Builds on suggestions   *'. . . and then we could . . .'*
Agrees   *'Yes, let's do that then'*
Shows acceptance   *'Okay then'*
Understands   *'I see what you're getting at'*
Complies   *'If that's what you want'*
Gives non-verbal signs of encouragement   *'Mm'; nod*

GIVES SUGGESTION
Makes proposals   *'It could be in the by-pass value'*
Suggests direction   *'Let's begin with looking at the*
                                                        sales figures'
Offers autonomy for others   *'What do you think about it, Geoff?'*

GIVES OPINION
Evaluates   *'That's not very helpful'*
Analyses   *'The way I see it, the problem is . . .'*
Expresses feelings   *'I'm annoyed by it'*
Express wishes   *'I hope to get through it all this morning'*
Interprets   *'It seems to me that the situation is . . .'*
Imposes   *'Look, let me tell you'*

GIVES INFORMATION
Informs   *'It's 4.30'*
                                                        'I was amazed'
Repeats   *'What I said was'*
Clarifies   *'I meant the same thing'*
                                                        'That's what I'm saying'
Confirms   *'Yes, that's right'*

ASKS FOR INFORMATION
Seeks facts   *'Where are the figures?'*
Seeks information   *'How did you do that?'*
Asks for repetition   *'What was that?'*

ASKS FOR OPINION
Seeks feelings   *'How do you feel about about that?'*
Seeks wishes   *'What do you want to do?'*
Seeks interpretations   *'How do you see it?'*
Seeks evaluations   *'Do you think that's a good idea?'*

ASKS FOR SUGGESTIONS
Seeks direction and ways of taking action   *'How can we go about this?'*
                                                        'Anybody got any ideas?'

SHOWS DISAGREEMENT
Shows resistance, rejection   *'No, I'm not too sure about that'*
Withholds help   *Silence, non-verbals*
Defends and asserts   *'Not at all!'*
Antagonizes others   *'You really believe that!'*
Attacks others   *'You're wasting my time!"*

Figure 9.2 Examples of categories for interaction process analysis

suggestions, but no *asking*. Sometimes categories such as *gives support* are noticeably lacking. If this is the case, it is necessary for group members to widen the range of contributions they are making.

Team roles. There are a number of theories that suggest that for a group or team to operate effectively there must be a number of specific roles represented. One of the best known is that of Belbin, whose theory was discussed in Chapter 7.

The question arises, of course, as to which of these different approaches to use. This will depend upon a number of factors – namely, the situation, the skills and preferences of the consultant, and the assumptions about how change takes place. One of the important situational determinants will be the organizational culture. In a power culture, role negotiation may be appropriate. In a role culture, a structured approach might work better. The skills and preferences of the consultant should be taken into account when deciding which approach to adopt. There is evidence to suggest that all the techniques we have described can be effective. People tend to do best that which they know best, and are happy with. This also applies to the consultant. The assumptions about change and the way people learn have been discussed above. There are also assumptions about change strategies, which will be discussed later in the chapter.

There is, of course, no harm in taking an eclectic approach, and mixing assumptions and approaches as considered appropriate. This implies that the ideal is for consultants to be flexible in their behaviour and able to use a variety of methods. This is an approach that we have advocated in other contexts. If managers should be flexible in their 'influence styles' so, surely, should consultants.

ORGANIZATIONAL DEVELOPMENT

Organizational development (OD) is concerned with changing the total organization. It has been defined in number of ways. For example, Beckhard (1969) suggests that an OD intervention has five characteristics. It is:

1. planned
2. organization-wide
3. managed from the top, to
4. increase organization effectiveness and health, through
5 planned interventions in the organization's 'processes' using behavioural science knowledge.

The emphasis in OD is, therefore, on the human processes and interactions within the organization. It is not concerned with such aspects as the technology or the production process, although changes in these may be the 'trigger' that makes an OD programme necessary. This link is made clear in another definition of OD, by Bennis (1969):

'OD is a response to change, a complex educational strategy intended to change beliefs, attitudes, values and the structure of organizations so that they can better adapt to new technologies, markets and challenges, and the dizzying rate of change itself.'

Although these two definitions tell us what OD is, they do not describe how it is achieved. This is, however, much more difficult, as there is a bewildering array of approaches and techniques in use. Indeed, Kahn (1974) has suggested that OD 'is a label for a conglomerate of things an increasing number of consultants do, and write about'. Following his lead we will outline some of the typical types of OD activities. French and Bell (1984) have provided a list of what they call the 'major families of OD interventions'. As they point out, no OD programme will contain anywhere near all the possible types of intervention, but the list shows the wide range of possibilities which are available. Any particular programme may concentrate on one, or on a limited range of interventions.

INTERVENTIONS

The list below starts by mentioning briefly those interventions that have already been considered in this book.

Education and training activities. These are designed to improve the skills, knowledge, and abilities of individuals. We discussed these when we considered the topic of 'management development' earlier in this chapter.

Team-building activities. These consist of activities designed to improve the functioning of teams within the organization, and were considered above and in Chapter 7.

Inter-group activities. Organizations need different teams and groups to interact with each other effectively. As we have seen in Chapter 7 this does not always happen. Interventions to improve these inter-group relations were also described in Chapter 7.

Diagnostic activities. Before future goals and strategies for change can be considered, there is a need to know how the organization is at the present time. Methods for undertaking such a diagnosis vary. Traditional methods include organizational surveys and questionnaires. 'Projective' techniques, such as choosing an animal to represent the organization, can also be informative.

Techno-structural or structural activities. These interventions involve changing the structure of the organization. Examples of this were given in the previous chapter, when the 'link-pin' and 'matrix' type of structures were discussed.

Process consultation activities. These are designed to help the client understand the processes that are taking place in the organization, and to develop strategies to improve how people work together. There is a wide range of such activities, which may be aimed at group, inter-group, or organizational level.

Activities based on 'packages'. As with team-building 'ready-made' packages are also available for total organizational development. Perhaps the best known example of this category is, again, that of Blake and Moutons' 'managerial grid'.

Third party peace-making activities. This is another method of resolving conflicts, or at the very least lack of co-operation, between different groups in the organization. The consultant is the third party, whose role is to resolve such conflicts.

Coaching and counselling activities. This involves working with individual members in the organization to help them resolve problems. These problems may be work-related or may be of a personal nature. It has now been largely accepted that employees cannot leave their personal problems totally behind them when they go to work. Problems in personal life inevitably affect work performance. Many organizations are following the lead of companies in the USA and providing counselling services for their employees. These may be either 'in-house' (usually attached to the medical department) or 'out of house' consultants. Such services have generally been shown to be cost-effective, as for example, in the Post Office.

Planning and goal-setting activities. We have already discussed the area of goal management (in Chapter 8). Often OD consultants can be useful in helping to define goals, both at individual, group, and organizational level.

Strategic planning activities. These are designed to help top management define the organization's 'mission', together with the long-term strategies for achieving it.

Behavioural interventions. These are interventions using behaviour modification techniques. As described in Chapter 5, this approach involves defining the required behaviours and setting up appropriate feedback systems to reinforce them. In order to stay within the value-system of most OD practitioners, participants usually define their own behavioural goals and set up their own monitoring and feedback system.

THE PROCESS OF CHANGE

OVERCOMING INERTIA

Whatever type of intervention is being used, change takes energy, since there is always in the system inertia that has to be overcome. Lewin (1947) has suggested that change is a three-stage process, whether it be at an individual, group, or organizational level. These three stages he refers to as unfreezing, change, and re-freezing. He describes them as follows:

Unfreezing: Before any change can take place, the established methods and patterns of behaviour have to be broken down. People may be unaware of these established procedures until their attention is directed to them. Only when they are drawn to attention may their effectiveness be challenged. This demonstration of current ineffectiveness is essential for change to take place. People will only willingly become involved in a change process when they accept the need for change. The early activities of an OD programme are usually designed to bring about this unfreezing.

Change: Once current behaviours are unfrozen it is possible to work on the change process. This can be done using any of the OD interventions described above.

Re-freezing: For people to operate effectively, their behaviour must be reasonably stable. An individual or organization in a state of constant change would achieve nothing. This means that the new behaviour must be allowed to stabilize. Usually people are very good at doing this for themselves. All that is needed is time for re-freezing to occur naturally. Sometimes activities are included towards the end of a change programme that are designed to enable participants to look forward and preview the effects of the planned changes. If these are perceived as beneficial, this preview will aid the change process.

An important point to note is that change does not happen by itself; there must be some source that initiates the change. This source must have sufficient power to be able to influence others in the direction of the desired change. In OD programmes, the source is usually located somewhere in the management hierarchy. There is, in fact, a view that any OD will be successful only if it is initiated by top management. This, it is suggested, is the only group with sufficient power to make the OD programme happen. This is usually referred to as the 'start at the top and work down' approach. In the experience of the present authors, this is not the only possible approach. We have known successful OD projects that have started at the bottom and worked up. It is, of course, true that change is a lot easier with the support of top management and, in some cases, impossible without it. However, power exists at all levels of organizations. An understanding of the different sources of power is, therefore, essential to an understanding of the process of change.

SOURCES OF POWER

A useful classification of the sources of power has been provided by Handy (1985). He has done so by modifying the original classification developed by French and Raven (1959). There are, Handy suggests, essentially five sources of power.

Physical power is derived from the possession of superior physical force. For obvious reasons, it is rarely found in industrial or commercial organizations. It remains, however, the ultimate source of power in society through state control of the police, prisons, and the armed forces. It was also, at one time, widely used in schools, but this has changed. It is still to be found in industrial disputes, often on the picket line. As Handy points out, however, physical power does not have to be used for it to be effective. The fact that it is there, is often enough to endow considerable influence. This influence is expressed through straight-forward *coercion*.

Resource power, as its name suggests, derives from control of resources. These can be physical (e.g. money and materials), or psychological (e.g. the ability to confer status through such things as promotion). These categories are not, of course, mutually exclusive and may overlap. The form of influence derived from resource power is *exchange*. The desired behaviour is produced in exchange for the resources controlled by the power source. It is, in essence, a form of bargaining or negotiation.

Position power is sometimes referred to by the French and Raven title of 'legitimate' power. Position power derives from the position or role occupied by the individual. Managers, by virtue of the position they hold, have the 'right' to control their department. Such rights are often most explicitly expressed in relationships with trade unions as 'management's right to manage'. Position power ultimately relies on being backed up by resource or physical power. The method of influence is primarily through the *rules and procedures* of the organization. To be effective, it relies upon everyone accepting the rules. If these are challenged, then the 'back-up' source of power is called into play.

Expert power derives from the individual having greater knowledge or expertise than others. Having information not available to others is a potential source of considerable power. Influence is wielded by the process of *persuasion*. This can range from the logical presentation of data to support a desired course of action, to the more emotional appeals of advertising and propaganda.

Personal power is derived from sheer force of personality – often referred to as *charisma*. Religious leaders and some political leaders, especially the successful ones, are good exponents of this type of power. High personal power, coupled with high expert power (real or assumed) will give the individual the status of a 'guru'. Influence is by *inspiration*. People do things because they are inspired by a charismatic leader.

Traditionally, that is to say from the 1950s to the 1970s, the prevailing values in OD led to the use of expert power as the influence for change. Many consultants, particularly those of the 'guru' type, also exercised considerable personal power, and some still do. There was a tendency to believe that many of the ills of organizations were the result of using resource or position power. The job of OD, it was argued, was to remove or reduce the use of such forms of power. Physical power was, of course, completely beyond the pale. The ideal, and therefore effective, organization was seen as one where people worked together in an atmosphere of openness and trust, setting goals by consensus, to which there would be a high degree of commitment. This was effectively a blend of the 'support' and 'achievement' cultures discussed in the previous chapter. As we have mentioned before, these 'love and trust' assumptions have had little effect and, towards the end of the century a new spirit of realism is evident. This accepts organizations 'as they are', and plans change within the confines of that reality. This is known, therefore, as the contingency approach.

STRATEGIES FOR CHANGE

While openness and trust remain the ideal of many OD consultants, there is a recognition that most organizations do not operate on these principles. As a result of this acceptance, it follows that change strategies have to be adapted to suit the prevailing circumstances. This has, in reality, always been implicitly accepted. Chin and Benne (1976), for example have defined what they call 'general strategies for effecting change in human systems'. They suggest there are three of these that provide a good framework for defining change strategies, both in organizations and, more widely, in society as a whole.

Empirical–rational strategies: This approach assumes that people are basically rational. Change can be effected, therefore, by showing that it is in the individual's own interest to change. This is sometimes referred to as 'enlightened self-interest'. Change is achieved by the use of data and rational persuasion. The assumptions underlying this strategy lie deep in traditional education, and include a belief in the benefit of research and the general dissemination of knowledge. The source for such a change is primarily expert power.

Normative-re-educative strategies: This group of strategies does not deny the rationality of human beings. It places more emphasis, however, on the belief that behaviour is largely determined by the social and cultural norms of the group or society to which people belong. Individuals have a strong commitment to conforming to, and maintaining, these norms. Successful change is therefore accomplished by changing the norms. This is achieved by a mixture of education and persuasion. Both expert and personal power may be involved in such change strategies.

Power-coercive strategies: These strategies involve the use of physical, resource, or position power to coerce individuals into changing. The use of physical power is widely used by governments when adopting this strategy. At the organizational level, resource or position power is the more usual source. Chin and Benne point out that passive resistance, along the lines used by Gandhi, is also an example of the power-coercive approach. It is effectively a battle of wills between two sources of power.

An interesting example of the use of these strategies is provided by the attempts of the British government to get drivers and front-seat passengers to wear the seat-belts provided in cars. A considerable amount of time and money was spent using empirical-rational strategies. These involved advertising campaigns giving information on safety factors – 'You know it makes sense'. All this had little effect. The government then switched to a power-coercive strategy. Not wearing a seat-belt became an offence, punishable by fines. The result was that seat-belt use leapt over-night to in excess of 90 per cent. The maintenance of this high level of seat-belt wearing, is probably due to normative-re-educative influences. Wearing seat-belts has become the norm. While the threat of fines is still in the background, we suspect that most people would, even without this, continue with the new behaviour. In Lewin's terms, power-coercive strategies were necessary for the unfreezing and change processes. Normative-re-educative strategies produced the re-freezing.

ADAPTATION TO CHANGE

So far we have looked at change strategies from the point of view of someone trying to change others. To complete the picture we need to consider how change takes place within the individual. Kelman (1958) has provided a framework for this. He suggests that there are three mechanisms for change. These can be seen as responses to the attempted influence of others.

Compliance: The individual changes simply because they are unable to resist the pressure being placed upon them. This is a common response to physical, resource, or position power. In some cases if there are rewards, or at least no costs, for the individual the change may become internalized and hence relatively permanent. Often, however, this is not a good way to create change, since the response is, at best, relatively passive. When the pressure is removed the original behaviour is likely to recur. At worst it results in counter-dependence, and individuals may expend considerable energy and ingenuity in finding ways to avoid changing.

Indentification: This is a frequent response to personal power. The person being influenced changes because of their desire to 'be like' the source of power. This may be because of admiration of the individual concerned or because they receive inspiration. Religious conversions are often of this nature, but it can also occur in educational and therapeutic situations. The duration of change by identification may be long, with the change becoming internalized. It may equally be quite short lived, particularly if less admirable aspects of the source of influence suddenly become apparent.

Internalization: This is the most effective form of change, since the individual accepts the change and adopts it as part of their own self-image. Inevitably, this form of change is likely to take longer than the previous two, hence time must be allowed for it to occur. It is likely to be slowed even further if there are strong pressures for change. The individual must be allowed to develop commitment in their own time. However, once this commitment has developed, the change is relatively permanent. The best approach to influence such a change is by expert power.

CHANGE AGENTS

It is a well-accepted principle within organizational development (OD) that it impossible to carry out major changes within the organization without the assistance of an independent consultant. We have, in fact, been making this assumption throughout this chapter. These consultants may be 'internal' or 'external'. In some organizations, usually very large ones, some individuals may be employed full-time to act as change consultants. It is important, however, that they are seen as independent and not associated with any particular power group within the organization. This is often very difficult to do, and hence there are strong arguments for employing people who are genuinely external and independent.

The reason why an independent, external view is needed is very simple. It is usually impossible for the individuals involved to get a clear and unbiased view of their ways of working and interacting. A good analogy is that of the marriage-guidance counsellor. The role of the counsellor is to act as an independent and unbiased observer, who works with both parties to help them understand their situation and plan ways to improve it. The OD consultant fulfils a similar role for the members of an organization, whether they are working at a team-building level, or on wider, organizational change. Unlike marriage-guidance counsellors, they work with large numbers of people rather than just two.

The use of external 'consultants' in organizations is not new, but there are a number of important differences between traditional 'expert' consultants and OD consultants. The term 'change agent' has come to be used as an alternative for the latter, as a way of making these differences explicit. The traditional 'expert' consultant is hired to go into the organization, diagnose what is wrong, and propose an expert solution. They may be experts in accounting, marketing etc., depending upon the problem. The change agent, on the other hand, works with the members of the organization, helping them to identify the problems for themselves and helping them to develop their own solutions. They do not work at the 'task' level like the expert, but at the 'process' level.

The expert consultant is sometimes described as working on the 'medical model' approach because he or she behaves rather like a GP. Symptoms are presented, a preliminary diagnosis is made, then checked by looking for additional confirming symptoms. A cure is then prescribed, which is often actually implemented by the expert. The client organization is relatively passive in this process and takes little responsibility for improving the situation, just as the patient is regarded very much as an object to be repaired. To be fair, this is the traditional view of medicine which is also beginning to change, with greater patient involvement becoming more common.

The change agent works not on a medical, but on a 'therapeutic' model. In this role it is not possible to prescribe a 'cure', because there is no agreed concept of what constitutes 'good health' in interpersonal relationships, just as there is no definition of a 'perfect marriage'. All the change agent can do is to work with the clients to help them towards a solution which they find satisfactory, or at least better than the current situation.

TYPES OF CHANGE AGENT

There are many different theories and classifications of change agents. These tend to be based either on the style or approach of the agent or on the stage in the change process at which they operate or, indeed, a blend of both. Havelock and Havelock (1973), for example, give a four-fold classification:

The catalyst is the individual who sees the need for change and starts to move people towards it. He or she tends to be dissatisfied with existing conditions and starts to upset the *status quo.*

The solution giver has clear ideas on what needs to be done and offers solutions for adoption. The approach is rather like that of the expert consultant mentioned above.

The process helper helps people adapt and cope with the process of change once a course of action has been decided upon. This is the approach which is frequently thought of as the typical OD 'change agent' described above.

The resource linker brings people together who have the necessary skills to deal with a problem and helps the organization make the best use of the resources available.

Although this classification describes four different types of consultant, it is clear that they are all equally valuable and each may make their contribution at different stages of a change process. The catalyst may be the individual who first recognizes the need for change and starts the process going, but the 'solution givers' and 'process helpers' will be needed to effect the actual change, after the need has been recognized. The 'resource linker' also has an obviously useful contribution to make at this stage. In practice, our experience is that most organization development consultants operate in all these styles as appropriate.

A classification which places more emphasis on the timing of the adoption of change is provided by Rogers and Shoemaker (1971). This is a five-fold classification as follows:

Innovators are individuals who are very quick to adapt to change. They will readily try out new ideas, and tend to be risk takers. People who are always quick to buy the latest gadget, or try out the newest technique, may fall into this category.

Early adopters are slightly more cautious than the innovators, but are still quick to pick up on new ideas. They are, perhaps, more evaluative and do not take up ideas simply because they are new. They tend to be more integrated into their society (or organization) than the innovators. They are not seen as quite so extreme.

Early majority. These individuals pick up on innovations once they begin to be accepted. They are relatively quick to adapt, but wait to see how effective new ideas really are before they adopt them. They are quite prepared to change once they are convinced of the value of the change.

Late majority. This group is much more sceptical. They need to be very firmly convinced of its value, before adopting a change. They will watch what happens when others adopt new ideas or procedures, and only after they have seen, over some period of time, that the change is effective will they adopt it.

Laggards. This group are highly suspicious of innovation and are the last to change, or indeed, may never be persuaded to change at all. Their attitude could well be summed up by the phrase 'If it was good enough for my father, it is good enough for me'.

As the name implies most of the population falls into the early and late majority categories. There are relatively smaller numbers of early adopters and laggards, and only a very small percentage of innovators. The relative proportion of each thought to be in the population, based on the normal distribution, is shown in Figure 9.3.

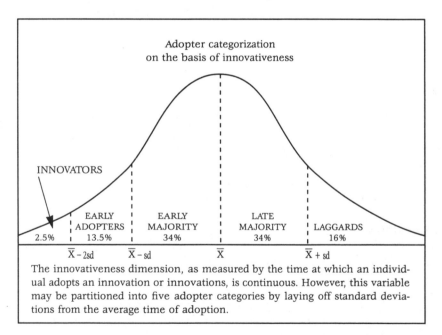

Figure 9.3. Distribution of categories of change agent.
(Source: Rogers and Shoemaker, 1971)

Perhaps the most comprehensive classification of change agents available is that provided by Ottaway (1982). He, in fact, presents this as a taxonomy, an outline of which is given in Figure 9.4. A taxonomy is a specific type of classification with certain clearly defined characteristics, the most important one of which, from our point of view, is that it indicates the hierarchical nature of the relationships between the items being classified. We will return to this point later.

A. Change Generators

1.   Prototypic Change Generators
        – demonstrate the need for change

2.   Demonstrative Change Generators
        i) Barricade demonstrators
        – the 'frontline' of demand for change

        ii) Patron demonstrators
        – support change as benefactors

        iii) Defender demonstrators
        – support change as main beneficiaries

B. Change Implementors

1.   External change implementors
– traditional external consultant 'change agents'

2.   External/internal change implementors
– similar to external change implementors, but are employees of the organization and work entirely within it

3.   Internal change implementors
– implement change in their own group

C. Change Adopters

1.   Prototypic change adopters
– first to adopt the change

2.   Organization maintenance change adopters
– mass of the organization, who accept change when they see that it works

3.   Product (service) users change adopters
– end users of goods or services, who must also accept the change

Figure 9.4. Classification of change agents.
(Source: Ottaway, 1982)

The first stage of Ottaway's taxonomy is based on Lewin's three phases of change, discussed above. This produces the three major classes of change agent:

- *Change Generators* who are concerned with the unfreezing process. Their role is to convert problems and issues into a felt need for change.

- *Change Implementors* whose role is to produce change. Their task is to bring about change after the need has been recognized. It is this group who people usually think of as change agents.

- *Change adopters* who assist the refreezing process. By adopting and practising the change, they establish it as the new norm for the group or organization. They are often unaware of their role in the change process.

There are two main types of change generator. There are what Ottaway calls *prototypic* change generators. These are the people who first start calling attention to the need for change. They are the 'heroes' who are often seen by the public as the primary change agent. They may also be seen as agitators and subversives by management or 'the establishment', because they start, often very vocally, to challenge the *status quo*. In a successful change process they will be followed very closely by *demonstrative* change generators. There are three sub-classes in this group:

- *Barricade demonstrators* who figuratively (and sometimes literally) man the barricades in the streets. These are the people who follow the 'prototypic generators', demanding change. They may organize petitions and demonstrations, or in some other way call attention to what should be done, and put pressure on those who are resisting change. In organizations, trade union representatives, among others, often take the role both of prototypic change generators and barricade demonstrators.

- *Patron demonstrators* who support the change by acting as benefactors. The form of patronage will depend on the individual's resources. Some may give money, openly or anonymously; others may speak or write in support. A director, for instance, may offer support for a particular innovation at board meetings.

- *Defender demonstrators* are often the main beneficiaries of the change. They support change efforts whenever the opportunity arises – at trade union meetings, in the canteen during breaks or at management meetings.

The function of the defender demonstrators is to complete the unfreezing process. At this stage, the second group of change agents can take action. These are the *change implementors*. There are three subgroups of this category:

- *External* change implementors work in the classic mode of change agents described above. They are external to the organization and are invited in to facilitate change. They are usually independent professionals. Because they are not permanent employees of the organization they are able to operate at a fairly high degree of risk. Their function is to help individuals and groups to come to terms with the projected change and to adapt by developing new ways of behaving and working.

- *External/Internal* change implementors are employees of the organization and work wholly within it. They carry out much the same role as the external change agent, but do not have the same degree of independence or risk taking.

- *Internal* change implementors work within their own group or section to implement change. They will probably, but not necessarily, work with other change implementors. A departmental manager who decides that a change in procedure or organization within his group is necessary and sets out to achieve this, is acting as an internal change implementor. He or she may, or may not, call on the help of an external implementor.

The final stages of the change process is brought about by the *change adopters*. This is by far the largest group of change agents. Their part in the process is to normalize the change and thus make it the new reality. There are three sub-groups in this class of change agent:

- *Prototypic* change adopters are the first people in the organization to accept and adopt the change. Their role is crucial and they are the main ally of the implementor. They are not change agents as usually defined within OD, but may see themselves as such. They are the individuals who are keen to accept changes and put them into operation. They are akin to the innovators and early adopters of Rogers and Shoemaker's classification.

- *Organization maintenance* change adopters are the mass of the organization. Their commitment is to maintaining the system and so will change if they see change as important for effective operation. Members of this group do not normally see themselves as change agents, but their adoption of the change is crucial to its success.

- *Product* (or service) *users* change adopters are the ultimate users of the goods or services supplied by the organization. This group is not often considered in the literature on change, but change within the organization will nearly always have some impact on the end users of the organization's products. After all, why else is the change taking place, if it is not, ultimately, to improve the organization's service. Unless this group also accept and adopt the change, it will not have been successfully implemented.

Ottaway states a number of assumptions on which his taxonomy is based. If valid, they have important implications for understanding the change process:

- The change agents are listed in chronological order of their involvement in the change process.

- Everyone is a change agent at some time in their lives.

- Change agent roles become less defined and focused as the change progresses. They also increase in number with this progression, with very few involved at the stage of generation, but many at the adoption stage.

- All three major types of change agent (generators, implementors and adopters) are required in every change process.

- All change agents are equally important.

- A change agent can function in only one of the roles in any one particular change process.

Since we are all, inevitably, involved in change it is important, if we wish to be effective, to understand what our role is and how it fits into the overall process. If a manager wishes to initiate change he or she must take the role of a prototypic change generator and look for likely barricade demonstrators and patrons. If we are on the receiving end of change, should we take the role of prototypic or maintenance adopters, and why? Should we be doing something different? For those involved professionally as change agents, usually as implementors, understanding the process of change is essential. If a desired change is not happening it may be because one stage in the sequence is missing or incomplete. The taxonomy may give some indication of the action which needs to be taken. Perhaps the adopters need more persuasion (or information), or the generators have not built up sufficient pressure for change (i.e. unfrozen the existing patterns of behaviour).

The assumption that an individual cannot operate in more than one role in any particular change process seems, on first consideration, to be valid. An 'adopter' is, by definition not going to be an 'implementor' or a 'generator'. But closer examination does suggest that there is possibly some room for an overlap of roles. Is there, for example any reason why a prototypic generator should not also be an internal implementor? Certainly one type of change agent can influence the activities of others. There would be no point in having consultants (external change implementors) if this were not so. It seems likely that a change agent can influence those who come later in the taxonomy, but not the reverse. This is important in planning change interventions.

RESISTANCE TO CHANGE

Any chapter on OD would not be complete without considering resistance to change, particularly as there are two popular myths concerning it. The first myth is that people universally dislike change, and will attempt to avoid it. While it is certainly true that change programmes occasionally provoke resistance, this is by no means a universal reaction. Indeed, on many occasions people enjoy change and look forward to it. If this were not so, the rapid rate of change in the world, which we have previously noted, would not have taken place. The reality is that the majority of the population of the developed world have happily adapted to enormous changes, both in technology and in their way of life, over the last few decades. It may be, however, that people differ in their readiness to accept change. As outlined above, Rogers and Shoemaker (1971) have suggested that people vary, from being innovators, who accept change quickly and easily, through early adoptors, early and late majority, to laggards at the other end of the scale who are suspicious of change and accept it very reluctantly.

The other myth is that resistance to change is necessarily a 'bad' thing. Sometimes such resistance may be healthy. Both people and organizations need periods of stability to re-freeze and absorb the changes that have already taken place. Also, the existence of resistance may be an indicator that, for some reason, a particular change is not considered desirable. In such cases a closer look is needed at the causes of the resistance.

Where beneficial change is resisted it may be for a number of reasons. Sometimes people believe that the change is likely to be to their disadvantage. On occasions this may indeed be true. It can hardly be a surprise that if a person's job is at risk, they will resist changes. The fear of change is often enhanced by the secretive manner in which change programmes are planned and implemented. This is often done, of course, because management fear that people will find ways of blocking the change, if they are aware of it in advance. Paradoxically, the secrecy itself makes people suspicious and often leads to the very blocking behaviour that the management had hoped to avoid.

Change will always involve some effort, as new ways of doing things have to be learnt. For some people the 'fear of the unknown' will be a major factor, especially if there are high levels of insecurity and dependency. Other sources of resistance may lie in the social system. The existing norms of the group or organization will usually be very powerful. These are necessary, of course, as they provide the rules within which people relate to each other and work together. Change may require that these norms are changed in some way. Problems may also arise if change programmes are instituted in only one part of an organization. This may cause imbalances elsewhere, which are resisted as a means of restoring the balance. Other social type resistances may be due to the change agent threatening vested interests or 'sacred cows'. In OD programmes carried out by outside consultants, there may also be an element of suspicion of outsiders.

O'Connor (1993) has produced a useful classification of the types of resistance to change likely to be encountered in organizations. O'Connor points out that resistance to change can be either overt or covert. That is, it can either be openly stated, or concealed and undefined. Open resistance is usually easier to deal with since it can be discussed and, possibly, fears allayed. Covert resistance may be undetected by those trying to introduce change, and hence not be dealt with. Another dimension refers to the motivation for the resistance. This can be either conscious or unconscious. In the case of unconscious resistance the individual is totally unaware that their actions constitute a resistance to the change. They may even believe that they are adopting it. Conscious resisters will, on the other hand, be well aware that they are setting up a challenge to the change.

These four types of resistance (overt – covert, conscious–unconscious) can be shown on the, by now familiar, two dimensional grid, as in Figure 9.5, giving the four possible positions outlined below:

- *The saboteur.* This style involves covert but conscious resistance. For some reason (perhaps to minimize personal disruption or fear of some potential loss) the individual opposes the change, but does not do so openly. In some cases it may be a matter of hoping that if they ignore it the change may go away.

- *The survivor.* These people often do not seem to realize that any change is taking place, let alone that they are undermining it in any way. Their resistance is covert and unconscious. They simply

soldier on as if nothing is changing, and may well be quite genuinely surprised and hurt when it is suggested that they are not co-
operating with the change.

- *The zombie*. This, at first sight, might seem unlikely – someone who
  is resisting overtly but unconsciously. O'Connor suggests that this
  is an extreme case of the survivor. They agree to the necessary
  changes, but somehow lack the will or ability to carry them out.
  Gradually and openly they revert to their original behaviours.
  When reminded of the need for change they will again make efforts
  but, once more, to no lasting effect. They see themselves as making every effort to co-operate and so do not consider themselves as
  resisting.

- *The protestor*. These individuals are openly and consciously voicing
  their objections to the change. They should certainly be listened to
  because, as indicated above, they may well have valid reasons for
  challenging the change. In general this group is the easiest to deal
  with since they are open in their challenge and will often be using
  rational argument. They are also unlikely to be dependent (see
  Chapter 6). They may be either counter-dependent or interdependent, in which case they will have energy which can be harnessed.
  Dependent individuals, who may take up either the survivor or
  zombie position, have low energy and hence are difficult to motivate. Saboteurs are likely to be counter-dependent and so have high
  energy, which may, with skill, be turned to a positive direction.

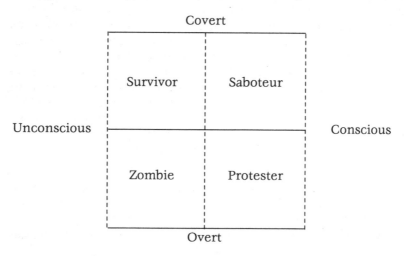

Figure 9.5. Four types of resistance to change.
(Source: O'Connor, 1993)

OVERCOMING RESISTANCE TO CHANGE

O'Connor's classification provides a tool for diagnosing the source and type of resistance which may emerge during change programmes, and thus give some clues on how to deal with it. Unconscious resistance needs to be brought into awareness; this will involve discussion on the effect of the behaviours involved and some exploration of the source of their motivation. The aim is to bring the behaviour into consciousness. Overt conscious resistance requires discussion of the objections being raised, and either allaying these fears and concerns, or adjusting the programme to take account of the issues raised.

There is, however, overwhelming evidence that the best way to reduce resistance to change is to forestall it, by involving in the decision making process those whom it is going to affect. Individuals who have been involved in the diagnosis, planning, and implementation of change are far more likely to feel positively about it. Best of all is if all the necessary information is freely available and the decisions are taken by consensus. There will, however, be occasions when it is not possible to be totally open (e.g. if some of the information is commercially sensitive). The general rule should be that good communication and feedback channels should be established between the source of change and those who are to be affected. Even where there are short-term costs, such as need for re-training, it is necessary to show that there will be long-term benefits, such as better pay or more security. Obviously it will be easier to effect change if there is a general climate of *trust* in the organization, where people feel that their fears will be listened to, and their problems recognized and dealt with in a sympathetic manner. Ideally, the programme itself should be open to change in the light of such feedback.

All of this is, of course, a long-term process, as Marlow (1975) highlights. He suggests that there are four distinct phases in a successful change programme. Although these can be identified and defined separately, in practice they tend to overlap. The four phases are:

Phase 1. Personal acceptance. In this phase the people responsible for introducing the change programme aim to gain the acceptance of the change by all those involved. This may just be certain individuals, a department or function, or the whole organization. This phase can take up to six months.

Phase 2. Expression of resistance to change. This involves bringing into the open underlying fears, hostilities and suspicions regarding the change, so that they can be resolved. It is important that individuals are given every opportunity to express their concerns, and that these are listened to and taken seriously. This phase can also take up to six months.

Phase 3. Identification with the objectives of the change. Underlying fears are now resolved and the objectives of the change begin to be understood and accepted. They should no longer be seen as something being imposed from without. Implementation of the change can now begin. This phase can take up to two years for a major change.

Phase 4. Creating a facility for continuous critical appraisal. The change is now complete, but evaluation and monitoring for adjustments is necessary. In this phase a continuous process for review and planning for improvement should be established. This may take a further year.

Thus, a major change can take up to four years to complete. Perhaps this whole process reflects the implicit 'leitmotif', or recurring theme, of this book. The human resources that the organization has at its disposal are, potentially, its most important asset. Properly managed in such a way that they feel that their contributions are appropriately recognized, the organization and its employees are in a 'non-zero sum game', with benefits for all. What is, of course, implicitly involved in any change programme is a change in the psychological contract. Managers, and others involved in change, need to be aware of these changes, and be prepared to renegotiate them fully and freely if change is to be successfully implemented.

THE PSYCHOLOGICAL CONTRACT IN TRAINING AND ORGANIZATION DEVELOPMENT

The following anecdote is an example of a fairly common occurrence in organizations. One of the authors was about to start a seminar on motivation (of all things!) at the head office of a large and well-known multinational. Just as the seminar was due to start the company training manager noticed that one participant had not arrived. Going to a telephone in the corner of the room he dialled this individual's extension and there followed a short conversation, during which the missing participant was obviously explaining why he was unable to come to the seminar. The conversation was terminated by the training manager saying 'You're supposed to be on this seminar, I want you up here now.' The missing participant arrived a few minutes later, looking not at all happy. The training manager left and we moved into an opening session talking about how people felt about being here. Within a few minutes the reluctant member burst out with 'You heard how I come to be here, what do you think my motivation is like?' This may seem a little extreme, but most trainers have a dozen examples of this type of experience.

It is a clearly established principle that effective learning will only take place when the individual wants to learn, and sees the programme as relevant to his or her needs. It is essential, therefore, for prospective participants to be consulted about both the content of the programme (particularly its relevance to their needs) and the teaching/training methods. Ideally this process starts well before the actual course is due to take place, through discussions with the individual's manager and the training department. Preferably, the individual themselves should initiate the request for training, or it should arise from a joint discussion, perhaps from an appraisal interview. However, it is still very common for people to be drafted on to courses with no prior consultation and no explanation of why they have been sent. The result is that they arrive at the opening session in a state of passive compliance, or openly hostile and angry. Neither is a good basis for an effective learning experience.

Because of this background, and the need for commitment from participants, it is common for training programmes to start with a discussion and negotiation of the 'contract' which is going to exist between the trainer and the course members. We are, of course, talking about the psychological contract. The administrative and legal contracts are usually fairly clear. The psychological contract in this case is about 'How are we going to relate to each other?', 'What expectations do trainees and trainers have of each other?', 'What is the role of each?' Only when these issues have been clarified and agreed can the real process of learning begin.

There are many ways of leading into the contracting process. Sometimes a variant of role negotiation is used (see Chapter 8), where the trainer and the participants independently define their expectations of each other and then negotiate agreed ways of interacting. Another approach is to ask participants (working in groups) to define the 'worst fears' and 'wildest hopes' for the programme. The trainer(s) do the same. This information is then recorded on flip charts and discussed. This process enables fears, often based on previous training experiences, to be brought into the open. They can then be discussed and resolved. Whatever process is used, the aim is to clarify and agree the psychological contract, that is, 'what is to be the relationship between us, and what are we each expected to do?'

Three-cornered contracts. Hay (1992) has pointed out that the implicit contract in training often involves three parties – the trainer(s), the participants and the organization, (represented by whoever is hiring the trainer). All three should be clear and preferably open. However, there can in reality sometimes be collusion between two of the partners at the expense of the third. For instance the trainer and the organization can be in collusion against the participants. One manifestation of this could be when a trainer is reporting back to the organization details of participants' performance, to be used for other purposes. From a training (i.e. learning) point of view this is counter-productive and, in our view, should certainly never be done without the knowledge and agreement of the participants. Alternatively, the trainer and the participants can collude to behave in ways of which the organization would not approve, for example, to plan ways of avoiding legitimate organizational requirements. Participant/trainer collusion occurs where the participants and organization conspire to make life difficult for the trainer. One form of this is where participants and their managers agree that management training is a waste of time, and they might just as well go on the course to have a good time.

Contracting in Organization Development. OD programmes almost always involve some training activity to which all the above comments will apply. However, there are also some additional issues to consider. Any organizational change programme will involve the services of a consultant. This may be someone from within the OD department of the organization or an external consultant. In either case, the procedure is the same. Kolb and Frohman (1970) identify seven stages in such a consulting process:

1. *Scouting.* Identifying the best point of entry, in order to make an effective intervention.

2. *Entry.* Once the entry point is chosen, this next stage involves negotiating a contract as to how the following processes are to be carried out. Some part of this contract will be concerned with procedural and administrative matters, but much of it will be concerned with the psychological aspect, and will be similar to the processes described for training programmes. It is at this stage that expectations will be clarified and agreement reached on the contribution to be made by all parties involved. This process will set the scene for all the subsequent stages.

3. *Diagnosis.* There are two aspects to diagnosis; definition of the problem and identification of the resources available to resolve it. The outcome of this stage may affect the contract, but the details of how it is done are not relevant to the contracting process itself, and so will not be considered here.

4. *Planning.* This follows logically from the diagnosis and involves defining the objectives for change and the generation and evaluation of possible strategies to achieve them. If at this stage it is found that the intervention needs to be wider than originally envisaged, or that additional people need to become involved, it will be necessary to renegotiate the relevant parts of the initial contract.

5. *Action*. The planned intervention is now implemented. Despite careful preparation, it is at this stage that unexpected resistances may occur. If this does happen further planning and re-negotiation of the contract will be necessary.

6. *Evaluation*. This is to determine whether the intervention has achieved the objectives defined at the planning stage. If it has, it should be possible to move to the final stage. If not, it may be necessary to cycle back through the earlier stages. Perhaps the entry point was wrong, the diagnosis incorrect, or a different type of intervention would have been better. This will involve more negotiation and adjustment of the contracts

7. *Termination*. This marks the end of the consultant's contact with the organization, at any rate for this particular intervention. Usually the signal for this to happen will be when the evaluation indicates that the objectives of the change programme have been achieved. How the project is going to terminate should be included as part of the initial contract. Ideally, the objective should be to reach, at the earliest opportunity, a situation where the organization is able to carry on without the assistance of the consultant. In other words, care should be taken that the consultant does not set up a dependent relationship with the client. This does not, of course, preclude the consultant working on other projects within the same organization.

It can be seen from this that any organizational change intervention involves a continuous process of negotiation and re-negotiation of the psychological aspects of the contract, between the consultant and the members of the organization. The skill and care with which this is done will have a very significant effect on the final outcome of the programme.

10

Managing Your Boss

In these final chapters we will make use of many of the theories presented earlier in the book to suggest ways in which you can learn to cope better with certain aspects of behaviour in organizations. So in order to make sense of them you will need to have read the rest of the book. In this chapter we are looking at one of the more important relationships in the organization – that between the individual and his or her boss. We should say at the outset that there are no precise rules, or 'quick fix' solutions for managing your boss. Dealing with other people, and in particular bosses, is very complicated. The large number of variables that influence interactions means that no two cases will be the same. What we can do, however, is highlight the important factors involved, and suggest ways in which they can be used. We will also describe some examples of common 'types' of manager, and consider how they might be influenced.

It is a general rule about all interpersonal interactions that the only person over whose behaviour you can have *direct* influence is yourself. The only way, therefore, in which you can hope to change your boss's behaviour is by changing your own. In deciding what you should be doing, there are three factors that you will need to take into account: your own needs, behaviour, and personality; your boss's needs, behaviour, and personality; and the situation in which the interaction take place. (One particular aspect of the situation is organizational culture, which, as discussed in Chapter 8, will determine the nature of the psychological contract existing between boss and subordinate and which will, in turn, influence the management styles and sanctions which are acceptable.

THE INTERACTION BETWEEN YOU AND YOUR BOSS

As we also suggested in Chapter 8, if you wish to be effective it is essential for you to be clear about what precisely it is that you want to achieve. We suggested that there were three types of personal goals;

task, status, and developmental. These differ both in their nature and their time-scale. Often people are fairly clear about task goals but rather less so about developmental ones. One way of highlighting long-term developmental goals is to pose to yourself the question 'Would I be happy doing my present job for the rest of my working life?' If the answer is *No*, ask 'Is there another job within the organization that I would like?' If the answer to this is also *No*, then start considering other possibilities.

In dealings with your current manager it is likely that there will be disagreement about task and status goals. Problems about 'task goals' are often revolve around lack of clarity about tasks and responsibilities. Problems concerning 'status goals', on the other hand, may often be related to feelings of inequity, arising from perceived under-reward. As we saw in Chapter 4, a common cause of inequity is that the two parties have different perceptions about what are to be taken into account as 'investments'. There are two possible approaches to this situation. The most obvious one is to convince the boss to accept that your efforts do count as 'investments'. However, there is often a difference between what an organization *says* it rewards, and what it *actually* rewards! Once again, 'espoused theory' and 'theory in practice' differ. The other alternative, therefore, is to 'play the game' – identify what it is that the organization really rewards and concentrate on this. The easiest way to do this is to look at those who have recently been successful and, for instance, been promoted.

Your goals will also be influenced by the balance of the needs for achievement, power, and affiliation, identified by McClelland and discussed in Chapter 4. Identifying the balance of these needs may give you some insight into the realism of your goals. Someone who is high in the need for 'affiliative assurance', for example, is unlikely to make a successful 'task-orientated' manager.

As we saw in Chapter 5, behaviour continues only if it is reinforced. In interpersonal interactions there is a continual feedback loop between the behaviour of both parties. Each will influence how the other behaves. The question that you have to answer is, 'Which behaviours of my boss am I encouraging or discouraging?' Another question concerns the compatibility, or otherwise, of your style of working with that of your boss. Are you an 'Adaptor' or an 'Innovator'? Is your behaviour pattern more Type A or Type B?

As we have previously pointed out, the possible number of combinations of needs, behaviours, and personalities is very large. We will therefore describe some of the more common managerial 'types' that we have encountered, and use them as case studies. Before doing so we will consider two possible types of approach, drawing upon theories considered in previous chapters.

The causes of people's behaviour can be considered as either determined by *internal* factors or *external* factors. Transactional Analysis (TA) and McClelland's 'needs' for achievement, power, and affiliation are both explanations based on 'internal' factors. Behaviour modification (BMod) and management 'style' theories, on the other hand, do not concern themselves with internal explanations, but look solely at behaviour and the way that external consequences encourage or discourage the behaviour.

Each of these approaches have their uses but are most powerful when used together. Those based on external consequences are probably safest to use when considering other people's behaviour, as there is no need for interpretations about their personality or motives.

AN INTERNAL EXPLANATION: TA

One of the most useful theories for gaining insight into interpersonal behaviour is that of TA. It is particularly useful when looking at boss/subordinate interactions, as it can take into account the imbalance of power in the situation. In order to understand more fully these interactions we need to introduce one more concept of TA theory – that of stroking. A *stroke* is defined as a unit of recognition, and stroking is concerned with the *feelings* aspect of transactions. Recognition, as we saw earlier, is a powerful need for most people, and in transacting with someone, we of course implicitly recognize their existence. The way in which we do this can vary, and this will have an effect upon the feelings of those involved. First, strokes can vary in their intensity. An example of a mild stroke would be when you nod and say 'Good morning' to a colleague. If you have been away on business for a week, then you would usually get more powerful strokes from your family on your return. Strokes can also be either positive or negative. Positive strokes are intended to make the recipient feel comfortable and good about themselves (e.g. compliments). Negative strokes, on the other hand, are intended to make the recipient feel uncomfortable and bad about themselves (e.g. 'tickings off' and 'put-downs'). Finally, strokes can be either conditional or unconditional. A conditional stroke is, as the name suggests, conditional on you doing something (e.g. praise for a good piece of work). An unconditional stroke is not dependent upon a specific behaviour; it is given merely for 'being there'. (One of the reasons why dogs make such good pets is that they give many such unconditional strokes and, as a result, receive them!) In general, unconditional strokes appear to be more powerful. This is important, as the convention in most organizations is that recognition is conditional. This contrasts with the situation in families, where more unconditional stroking takes place.

The assertion that non-contingent stroking is more powerful than contingent stroking may appear to contradict the advice given in Chapter 5, which explained that rewards should be contingent upon the occurrence of desired behaviour. The apparent contradiction occurs if stroking and rewards are interpreted as being one and the same. This is not the case. The essential feature of unconditional stroking is that it entails the recognition of another individual as a person to be valued because they are a person, not because of what they do. Rewards, on the other hand, should be specifically related to the person's behaviour. For example, to greet another person, and perhaps enquire after their well-being for no other reason than that they are there, is non-contingent stroking. This will make them feel good, but will not have any predictable effect on their behaviour. To praise someone for a specific piece of good work is a contingent reward and also a conditional stroke. It so happens that both work in the same direction and will have a similar effect on the behaviour.

Stroking is closely linked to existential position, which we covered at the end of Chapter 3. The strokes that we give, and hence those that are returned, will depend on our position at the time. These will, in turn, influence the position we then take up. Strokes from the 'I'm OK–You're OK' position will nearly always be positive. Even if we are giving the other person adverse feedback about one of their actions or piece of work, because we feel positively about the *person themselves*, the stroke will still be positive. Receiving such strokes helps to promote or maintain a position of 'I'm OK–You're OK' in ourselves. From other positions, we will tend to give negative strokes, and receiving negative strokes will tend to push us towards our favourite Not OK position (commonly in managers 'I'm OK–You're Not OK'). What often happens is that we get into cycles of stroking, either positive cycles or negative cycles.

It is generally a correct assumption that most people prefer positive strokes. There are some people, however, who actually prefer negative strokes. This occurs, according to the theory, from the stroke patterns established in early life between such people and their parents or other significant adults. These patterns frequently take a form of interaction known as a *game*. A game is an unconscious but predictable set of transactions, which always starts from ulterior transactions and leads to one or both partners receiving negative strokes which, in turn, lead to bad feelings. Berne (1968) describes, analyses and names many such games. Each one follows a set pattern of transactions and has the effect of leaving the individual in his or her favourite bad feeling (known in TA as a *racket*). The significance of the racket is that the individual can go on indulging in negative self-strokes for an extended and indefinite period.

In any large organization you are likely to come across a small number of such individuals. They tend to be unhappy much of the time, and appear 'deliberately' to do things which will generate negative responses from others. They also operate much of the time from one of the 'Not OK' positions. In extreme cases, it will be almost impossible to give positive strokes to these individuals. Those that *are* given will either be ignored or interpreted negatively in some way – 'He's only being nice because he's been told to'. In BMod terms, what is punishment for most people is, for these individuals, a reinforcer.

The inclusion of the concept of stroking makes the analysis of the transactions between you and your boss more complicated, but it is important, as it determines how you feel and, to some extent, your existential position. An ideal relationship would be one in which both you and your boss work from 'I'm OK–You're OK', in which all ego states are freely available and where there is plenty of positive stroking. In our experience this is comparatively rare in British industry. However, once you know about strokes, you can learn to ignore or 'discount' negative strokes which tend to push you towards an ineffective 'Not OK' position. This does not mean that you should ignore any negative feedback concerning your behaviour or performance. This information is, of course, necessary if you are going to adapt future behaviour effectively.

In reviewing the interactions between yourself and your boss it is useful to consider the ego states from which he or she usually operates. It may be that all three are used, but often there is a predominant use either of one or two. Most likely this will be Parent and/or Adult. It is important to consider what effect this has on you – which of your ego states does it 'hook'? As we saw in Chapter 3 heavy Parent will tend to hook your Child, either compliant or rebellious. Once you have analysed the interaction, you may then decide to 'cross' the transaction, perhaps to Adult, again as described in Chapter 3. At first you will almost certainly find it difficult to cross transactions, as it often goes against old and well-established habits. However, with continued practice you will find it becoming easier. Another factor to be aware of is that, when dealing with a Parental boss, he or she usually has a more powerful Parent than you, since they have the backing of the power provided by their position in the organization. This is another good reason for avoiding responding from the 'Not OK' Parent position.

We have been suggesting that Adult–Adult (problem-solving) transactions are preferable to Parental ones, but there are occasions where you may wish to cross one of these transactions. For example, if your boss operates from a predominantly Adult state, then it may be appropriate on occasion to inject some creative Free Child into the transaction.

AN EXTERNAL EXPLANATION: BMOD

Whilst TA is an 'internal' approach, BMod is an 'external' approach. It views behaviour as being largely determined by its consequences. For successful implementation of BMod techniques, attention has to be directed towards specific behaviours. Because of this it is difficult to give examples of applications to 'generic' problems. Where we feel that certain specific behaviours are likely to be common to a particular managerial 'type', we will comment upon them. The theory underlying behaviour modification is discussed in Chapter 5.

SOME MANAGERIAL TYPES

We will now consider some cases, but at this point we should point out that much of what follows is based upon our personal experiences, and those of managers on programmes we have run. There is very little experimental work in this area and therefore generalizations should be treated with caution. In analysing these cases we will take into account the following factors (as discussed at the beginning of this chapter):

Organizational culture: The culture of the organization within which you work will constrain the type of power that the boss can bring to bear. Most readers, we suspect, will be within 'role' cultures. This means that, normally, the forms of power that can be used are those of 'legitimate', 'information' and 'position' power. Occasionally particular managers may have some 'personal' power.

Possible needs: The needs identified by McClelland are useful, in that they indicate what is likely to be reinforcing to a particular manager. What is the balance between your boss's needs for achievement, power and affiliation? As we have said before, you will not be able to change your boss's style but, if you wish to change specific behaviour you will need to establish what reinforcers are keeping the behaviour going. Analysing his or her needs will help to identify the relevant reinforcers.

Personality: The interaction between Type As and Type Bs, and between Adaptors and Innovators was dealt with in Chapter 2. In TA terms you need to identify which particular ego states your boss prefers to use, and respond accordingly. In particular, you need to identify what he or she does that tends to push you into 'Not OK', Parent or Child. Once you have identified this, you can then learn to 'discount' (or ignore) them.

Management style and sanctions: At this point, as well as considering the sanctions that the boss has at his or her disposal, it is worth considering your own sources of power. In Chapter 5 we have seen how important praise and feedback can be as reinforcers. This does not apply only to subordinates; bosses too react to social reinforcers. In terms of power, the main ones that subordinates have at their disposal are those of 'expert power' and 'information power'. Almost everyone has some power through their control of information. They also have a somewhat negative source; almost any employee has the power to disrupt the organization's smooth running by sins of 'omission' as well as 'commission'.

We can now consider the various managerial 'types'.

THE BUREAUCRAT

The bureaucrat is generally pleasant and mild mannered, but is often slow and cautious in making decisions. When faced with a problem or suggestion his or her usual response is to suggest that you check to see if the idea is in accordance with established 'custom and practice'. If the problem, or the suggested solution, is novel his or her response is to send memos to all those who are likely to be affected, asking for their reactions. In addition, a committee or working party might be formed to advise or decide on the issue. If you, as a subordinate, do anything in a way that is not sanctioned by the organizational rules and procedures, then you are likely to receive a reprimanding memo. This memo will be in addition to any possible oral reprimand, and will be concerned with the way you went about the task, rather than about the outcome. Thus, you may actually be praised for what you accomplished, but admonished for breaking the rules to get the task done. These responses can have a de-motivating effect upon subordinates, who tend not to bother taking any initiative. If you want a quite life, you learn how to work to the rules.

Analysis. ORGANIZATIONAL CULTURE: the bureaucrat is mainly found in role cultures.

POSSIBLE NEEDS: Like most managers, the bureaucrat is likely to have a high need for power. The main expression of this is in a need to control others, which can be achieved in a number of ways. According to McClelland, these range from sheer domination to subtle influencing techniques. The particular way in which the bureaucrat exercises control is by strict administration of the rules. In this way, a high degree of certainty and predictability can be achieved. When their needs are blocked by higher authority, they tend to operate new instructions to the letter, waiting for a collapse so that they can say 'I told you so!'.

PERSONALITY: Almost by definition the bureaucrat is likely to be an Adaptor rather than an Innovator, and Type B rather than Type A. For those innovative Type As who have to deal with them, the interactions may be somewhat frustrating. In TA terms, the bureaucrat is highly Parental. However, unlike some other types of manager, the Parent in this case is the internalized 'Organizational Parent'. As with any Parent, the intention is to hook the Child of subordinates. If all is going well, then responses will be from the Compliant Child, but subordinates and others may sometimes rebel. One of the reasons for such a revolt may be that the strict bureaucrat tends to allow his Parent to be in control at all times, even when changed circumstances mean that his Adult should take over to assess and plan for the new situation. Such a bureaucrat would not stop World War III if it meant breaking the rules. Such extremes are, fortunately, rare. Finally, bureaucrats are often low on Free Child, unable or unwilling to 'let themselves go'. They are, however, high on Adapted Child and readily comply with the demands of the system.

MANAGEMENT STYLE AND SANCTIONS: The bureaucrat will tend to be authoritarian, but will stay within the rules, and his or her limits of authority. They will tend to use the powers provided by the organization when dealing with subordinates. These are generally those of *position power*, based on their position within the organization, and *resource power*, based on their control of rewards. When dealing with superiors they will generally be compliant, but if they believe that rules are being broken they may use their control of information as a source of power. This may be used either positively, for example by the 'leaking' of information damaging to the superior, or negatively, by holding back information that would allow the system to take corrective action.

How to Cope. Given that the bureaucrat is usually a Type B Adaptor, any innovations should be presented, if possible, as adaptations of present systems. In addition, do not expect a quick response. In our experience the best approach is to become fully familiar with the rules and regulations of the organization, so that you can present proposals in such a way that they are seen to be consistent with the system. If it is not possible to do this, then avoid pushing your preferred, and possibly innovative, solution. Rather, present the problem, together with your own 'tentative thoughts' on the matter, as a request for help. Under these circumstances bureaucrats often show considerable ingenuity in redrafting your 'thoughts' so that they fit the current systems, or in finding alternative interpretations of the rules.

There will be occasions when you may find yourself being pushed by the bureaucrat's Parent into a 'Not OK' position, either Parent or Child. You should recognize this and stay in 'I'm OK–You're OK' Adult.

Both Child and Parent responses will be counter-productive. The 'Not OK' Parent is particularly dangerous as, in most cases, the boss's Parent carries more 'clout' than yours.

The advice that BMod would offer in coping with such a boss is to examine each specific behaviour of the boss's that you wish to change, and identify the reinforcers that are maintaining it. Then remove the reinforcers and institute a process of change. In looking for the reinforcers, some clues may be gained from considering the balance of needs. The bureaucrat, as we have seen, has a high need for control and order. It is also likely that they have low needs for affiliation. Unfortunately, it is often the case that subordinates have little that they can use as reinforcers with their boss. The exception to this is that they do control their own behaviour. You should analyse specific situations, to see if there are any ways in which your behaviour is actually reinforcing behaviour in your boss that you wish to discourage.

THE AUTOCRAT

Autocrats have very strong views on what ought to be done in any situation. These are derived from his or her own personal convictions concerning what should be done, rather than the rules of the organization. They do not listen very well to their subordinates and issue instructions which are expected to be carried out without question, except on matters where clarification is required. Such a manager is intolerant of those who make mistakes and people who 'do not understand'. He or she will get quite angry in these situations, but in a cold, withdrawn manner. Sometimes such a manager appears inconsistent, since while they are autocratic with their subordinates, they are often helpful to their peers, and even 'fawning' in relations with someone higher up the organization. In the eyes of their subordinates, they can be either 'tyrants' or 'benevolent autocrats', depending upon how the subordinate is treated.

Analysis. CULTURE: The autocrat is probably most common in power or role cultures.

POSSIBLE NEEDS: As with the bureaucrat, the autocrat is high on a need for power but, unlike the bureaucrat, the source of the power is personal conviction, not the rules of the organization. There is research evidence to suggest that those high in need for power are sensitive to power differentials. Their behaviour may vary, however, depending on whether the difference is in their favour or not. This would explain the apparent contradictions between their behaviour to different groups in the organization. If the balance is in their favour, as it is with subordinates, then direct power can be used. Faced with those who have greater power, they gain power by ingratiating themselves. This can be done by doing favours for, or flattering the more powerful individual. There is evidence to show that those managers high in need for power do, in fact, respond positively to such ingratiation from their subordinates. With their peers, the autocratic manager can gain some temporary increase in their power by giving help when asked, especially if the other manager then feels in some way obligated.

PERSONALITY: It is possible that autocrats can be either Type As or Type Bs. Likewise, they may be either Adaptors or Innovators. In TA terms, they are almost certainly highly Parental and low on Child. They are also likely to have a well functioning Adult.

MANAGEMENT STYLE AND SANCTIONS: Like the bureaucrat, the autocrat will use those sanctions that his or her position in the organization provides. These are position power and resource power. If the organization allows they may also use coercive power. The benevolent autocrat is likely to use resource power quite effectively, giving infrequent, unpredictable, but large rewards (variable-ratio reinforcement).

How to cope. As with the bureaucrat, the only way to deal with the autocrat is to stay OK and Adult. Any confrontation should be on the basis of data. Because of their high need for power the technique of ingratiation is often effective, although distasteful to some. Again, because of the high need for power, they are sensitive to power from other sources. If the subordinate has more 'expert' power, and is prepared to 'stand up' to the autocrat, this may be respected. In general, if you have a source of power that is unavailable to the manager (normally 'expert' or 'informational'), then he or she will often cultivate the relationship. This is, however, a high-risk strategy, and should be tried with care. The information or expertise you have may be of only temporary value.

In extreme cases, autocrats are often brought down by a grouping of their subordinates. Realizing that their individual powers are not strong enough to confront the autocrat, political alliances are made between the subordinates, so as to increase their power base. An act by the autocrat that clearly and seriously breaks the organization's rules often then acts as a trigger for concerted action by the subordinates. The autocrat is either removed or their powers strictly defined and limited, often by devolving powers to a committee.

In BMod terms, this type of boss may gain reinforcement from being able to control other people. It is likely, therefore, that he or she will get reinforcement from those situations in which they win a 'fight'. For this reason confrontation should be avoided unless you are certain of victory.

THE WHEELER-DEALER

The wheeler-dealer is often a very senior manager who spends much of his or her time negotiating with other departments over the allocation of resources and such matters as purchasing and sales. He or she clearly enjoys this type of activity and, as a result, spends a lot of time doing it, leaving their own department very much to run itself. They are not always successful in the negotiations, possibly because they are impatient and do not 'suffer fools gladly'. When in the department, they make 'sorties' around the staff, asking how they are getting on, checking on the progress of various projects and generally giving encouragement. Staff are not given much guidance and are often left to 'sink or swim', but initiatives by staff are usually well supported. Non-performers tend to be ignored. There is a general feeling of dynamism in the department, but also a certain amount of chaos. Type A Innovators are likely to find this exciting, but Type B Adaptors are likely to feel uncomfortable in such a climate.

Analysis. CULTURE: The wheeler-dealer is most at home in power, achievement, and support cultures. They are likely to be less happy in a role culture, but may sometimes exist in small pockets of the organization that have their own culture.

PERSONALITY: The wheeler-dealer is almost certainly an Innovator; the rules are made to achieve objectives and, if achieving the objectives means that the rules have to be ignored, so be it. We suspect that most are also Type A, but there is no reason why some should not be Type B. They are likely to be high on need for power and need for achievement. Because they are aware that they need other people in order to achieve their objectives their need for power is more socialized than the autocrat or bureaucrat. Control is achieved by interpersonal influence rather than coercion. In TA terms, he or she is likely to have moderate Parent and an effective Adult. The Child is likely to be very active. In particular, Free Child enthusiasm is very apparent, as is the intuition of the Little Professor.

MANAGEMENT STYLE AND SANCTIONS: The wheeler-dealer's style may range from the consultative, through participative to *laissez-faire.* They often delegate quite considerably but sometimes, especially at times of stress, they may show a flash of authoritarianism. Often they will regret this when things cool down, and smooth the feathers they have ruffled. They often use personal power – people work hard for them because they admire them. Approval is withdrawn from those not performing up to the mark.

How to cope. With this type of manager it is essential to become pro-active. He or she expects their staff to use their own initiative, and only values those who do. It is no use waiting to be told what to do – nothing will happen and you will be written off as ineffective. You should be prepared to make your own decisions about what needs to be done and then get on with them, making sure that the boss is kept informed. The boss should be informed rather than asked, the assumption being that you will go ahead unless there are objections. Keeping the boss informed also means that you keep a high profile with him or her. Problems with this type of boss often centre on getting the more mundane jobs done. The boss does not find these reinforcing and, likewise, does not reinforce those who do them, no matter how well. As a result people learn that doing mundane jobs does not pay off. Often they get thrust on to the most junior member of staff (in terms of seniority or tenure). In this position you need to negotiate with colleagues to ensure that these aspects of the job are shared out evenly. Depending on your colleagues, it may be possible to do this by open agreement or it may be a more political process. Since the boss values enthusiasm and energy (Child), find something to be enthusiastic about, hook their enthusiasm, then point out that mundane jobs are preventing you from devoting your energies to it!

THE *LAISSEZ-FAIRE* MANAGER

This is often the style of a manager who has been promoted because of his or her high level of technical competence. They are not, however, interested in managing. They are very energetic, enthusiastic and creative and give strong verbal support to initiatives. In some respects they are very similar to the wheeler-dealer, but their interests are on the technical aspects of the job rather than managerial. Their interpersonal skills are good and they maintain good relations with their staff. The main problem is similar to that of the wheeler-dealer – the department is largely left to run itself. Because of this, a number of routine jobs are not done well. Again, there are problems about who does these routine jobs, and some team members find this frustrating.

Analysis. CULTURE: Found in almost all cultures, but perhaps most appropriate in an achievement-orientated organization.

POSSIBLE NEEDS: A high need for achievement which is directed towards their profession rather than the organization. They may also be relatively high on need for affiliation, especially on affiliative assurance. This means that they need to be liked by their subordinates. If they have a good working relationship with their team, they are reluctant to lose members, even when it is through promotion of the person concerned.

PERSONALITY: Again like the wheeler-dealer, they are likely to be Innovators. In TA terms, they tend to be low on Parent but with a highly effective Adult, particularly in relation to their professional specialism. They are particularly high on Child, which is reflected in their creativity and their desire to be liked by others.

MANAGEMENT STYLE AND SANCTIONS: The management style is that of *laissez-faire*, with very little use of sanctions. The main sanction is the removal of social contact.

How to cope. Given the similarities between the *laissez-faire* and wheeler-dealer, the method of coping is very similar. There is an additional problem, however, as the wheeler-dealer at least manages the relationships with other departments; the *laissez-faire* manager does not. As a result, the staff will have to manage both internal and external relationships. There will be no problem, however, with the technical output of the department.

Because they have a high need for affiliation, they are susceptible to social reinforcers, especially from the group as a whole. Such social pressures may be used as threats or reinforcement, in order to encourage the manager to undertake those tasks that the group considers to be his or her responsibility.

THE RELUCTANT MANAGER

The reluctant manager has, like the *laissez-faire* manager, been promoted on the grounds of technical competence. The main difference between them is their behaviour towards their subordinates. They generally leave their department to run itself but, unlike the *laissez-faire* manager, they do not encourage their staff in any way. If a technical problem arises then they will offer help, if asked, and this help will be highly effective. The management of the department, both internally and externally, is ignored. In some circumstances, however, the reluctant manager may appear to be bureaucratic. Since he or she is not interested in managing, following the rules of the organization provides the easy way out. When something happens that is not routine, then it is often very difficult to get a decision of any sort.

Analysis. ORGANIZATIONAL CULTURE: Although the reluctant manager may be found in any culture, like the *laissez-faire* manager, they are more likely to be found in achievement cultures.

POSSIBLE NEEDS: They are likely to be high on need for achievement, but low on both need for power and need for affiliation. It is the low level of need for affiliation that is perhaps the most noticeable feature.

PERSONALITY: They are likely to be high innovators but, because they have no interest in management, this shows only in their technical activities. They are likely to be Type B. In TA terms, they are high on Adult, especially concerning their professional expertise. They are particularly low on Child.

MANAGEMENT STYLE AND SANCTIONS: The management style is so *laissez-faire* as to be almost non-existent. Sanctions are rarely used.

How to Cope. The main problem with the reluctant manager is to get them to engage in any interpersonal interactions at all. This, of course, has the advantage that you can get on and do whatever it is you like doing. Indeed, you could almost take over the running of the department yourself, if that is what you want. Because of their dislike of social interaction and management, any request for advice on managerial matters is dealt with in a way which minimizes the time of the interaction. This is in accordance with the Premack principle in BMod, which suggests that we spend longer on those jobs that we like. In these circumstances, it is perhaps best to use your control of information selectively. Present a number of alternatives from which the manager can choose, with your own preferred alternative strongly supported by evidence.

If you are seeking to change any specific behaviour, then you will need to look to see if there is anything in the work situation that he or she finds rewarding. In TA terms, is there anything that hooks their Free Child and gets them excited?

THE OPEN MANAGER

This manager has a very firm belief in the value of participation and getting everyone involved. He or she holds regular meetings to review progress and decide on future actions, as well as *ad hoc* gatherings of sub-groups, or the department as a whole, to deal with issues as they arise. Most people appreciate this, but there is the feeling that on occasions too much time is spent ensuring that all involved are committed when this commitment is not really necessary.

Analysis. CULTURE: Can be found in almost any culture, but is most at home in support or achievement cultures.

POSSIBLE NEEDS: Little need for power, high need for affiliation (supportive rather than assurance), may be high or low on need for achievement.

PERSONALITY: Likely to be middle of the range on Adaptor/Innovator. In TA terms the open manager is flexible and can use all three ego states.

MANAGEMENT STYLE AND SANCTIONS: Highly participative with position and resource power used only if and when required. They may also have some personal power and are admired by their subordinates.

How to cope. There are very few problems in dealing with the open manager, except perhaps in deciding how open you are going to be in return. The danger with being too open, is that the information you divulge may be used to your disadvantage, either at another time, or by other people. A related problem may be that the manager is open in situations that may not be appropriate, for example, in relations with other departments that are behaving politically. The solution to this is to talk openly with the manager about strategies regarding relations with the rest of the organization.

As the open manager engenders commitment, there is also a danger that you will become too involved and take on more work than is good for you. In these circumstances, you will need to learn to say 'no'. Fortunately, because the open manager has all three ego states available this can be done on an Adult–Adult basis.

Appreciation of their openness is probably a reinforcer to these managers. Any lack of enthusiasm from their subordinates will be noticed and questioned.

These, then, are some of the most common managerial 'types' that we have experienced. It is, of course, rarely the case that any particular boss fits one, and only one description. Most bosses are an amalgam of two or three types. If you are to influence your own boss you need to analyse him or her along the lines we have described above.

STRATEGIES FOR MANAGING YOUR BOSS

Having decided what you want to do, you need to have a strategy for its implementation. As outlined in Chapter 8, there are four basic strategies. This applies as much to influencing your boss as it does to influencing the organization as a whole. It is, of course, possible to combine a number of these, or to try one first, and if this proves to be ineffective move to another one of the basic strategies.

THE *LAISSEZ-FAIRE* STRATEGY

We suspect that some reading this chapter will have already experienced the *laissez-faire* reaction. It arises when you come to the conclusion that, having tried other approaches, there is nothing you can do to change your boss or the situation. All you can do is to decide how best to adapt to the situation. This adaptation may simply consist of not allowing the interactions with your boss to push you into a 'Not OK' position, which will mean being careful to work from your Adult. At the other extreme it may mean looking for a new job.

There are no set rules to suggest when this approach is appropriate. Factors that need to be taken into consideration include the degree of rigidity of both your boss and yourself, and the level of effort you think will be required to produce the desired change. There are times when it is quite appropriate to come to the decision that it is not worth trying to change things, because the costs of doing so outweigh the benefits. If you have come to this decision, there are three important aspects to be considered. First, are you sure that you have made a valid judgement about the difficulties and effort involved? Second, have there been any changes in circumstances since you made the decision? An extension of this is to be sensitive to any changes in the future that may alter the relative balance of costs and benefits. Finally, having made the decision, be aware that you will have no further reason to complain about the situation. You have either to accept the situation or leave it.

THE OPEN STRATEGY

This is often the best one to try first, or at least to consider first. Have you tried simply talking openly to your boss about the issue and how you feel? If you choose this approach, make sure that you are working from 'I'm OK–You're OK', and think about appropriate ego states. It is probably best to stick to Adult.

The open style is likely to work best in a support or achievement culture, where the boss also uses an open style (all ego states from 'I'm OK–You're OK'), gives a high level of strokes, and possibly has a high need for affiliation. It will be less effective in a power or role culture, and with bosses who are highly Parental and work from I'm OK–You're Not OK. It could be disastrous in a situation where others are using highly political styles.

THE FORMAL STRATEGY

The formal approach makes use of formal systems within the organization. You should identify any formal appeal procedure that may be relevant. In using the formal system it is essential to stay in Adult (i.e. follow the rules) and, as always, 'I'm OK–You're OK'.

The formal approach will work best in role cultures and with those bosses who tend to be Adult and follow the rules themselves (i.e. bureaucrats). It is unlikely to be effective in support and achievement cultures, which value spontaneity. In political cultures, it is likely to be seen as naïve.

THE POLITICAL STRATEGY

If other approaches do not work, you will have to think of something more subtle. This does not mean, however, that you have to be underhand or negative. The essence of the political strategy is either to develop alliances, or to use information selectively. Only you will be aware of what particular alliances are possible, so we will concentrate on some other techniques of political influence.

One of the best methods is to analyse the boss's behaviour using BMod concepts. What does he or she find reinforcing or punishing? To find out what they consider reinforcing, look at how they spend their time. To find out what they find unpleasant, find those things or situations that they tend to avoid or escape from. These may not be easy to discover, as they occur infrequently. Indeed, they may be discovered only by accident. One of the authors discovered such a punisher in his interactions with a senior administrator. It so happened that the author was, for once, in a highly frustrated and emotional state about a particular issue. When questioned about the issue by the administrator he exploded in what he considered to be righteous indignation. To his surprise he found that the administrator could not cope with this emotional outburst and immediately backed down.

There are some 'political' techniques which are used by salesmen which may also be instructive. All of these play on the other person's desire to display a consistent and socially acceptable image. The 'foot in the door' technique uses acquiescence to a small request as a building block to larger requests. There is research evidence to show that people who have complied with a small request for help on a particular matter will later agree to larger requests about the same matter. A similar technique is what the Americans call the 'low ball' approach. The salesman negotiates a price for an article with the customer but, just before the deal is finalized, he or she suddenly 'finds' that they are prevented from concluding the deal at the original price. The common excuse is that the final price has to be sanctioned by the salesman's boss, whose approval is withheld. Evidence suggests that the customer accepts an increase in the price that they would not have accepted at the start of negotiations. Finally, the 'door in the face' technique plays upon the potential customer's image of themselves as a reasonable person. An original request is submitted that is so extreme that it is immediately turned down – the door is slammed in the face. The refuser realises that this is possibly rude and, hence, is in a position where they seek to establish that they are really a polite person. In this condition, they are more likely to agree to a lower request which itself would have been refused if presented before the outright refusal.

The political approach is often appropriate in power cultures and sometimes in role cultures, where the boss uses positional power very heavily. It may also be the favoured approach where the boss is heavily Parental and controlling, whatever the culture. This is often the case when the boss has a high need for power. It is generally inappropriate in support cultures, and with bosses who are supportive and open.

MANAGING THE PSYCHOLOGICAL CONTRACT

Remember that when attempting to change the relationship between you and your boss you will also inevitably be changing some aspects of the psychological contract between you. It may well be of help in clarifying your feelings about your present situation, and in defining a suitable strategy for change, to think through just what the current contract is, and how you would like it to change. In the process of doing this you may discover some of the 'hidden' reinforcers operating on both yourself and your boss, which will be of use in defining your strategy. As has also been mentioned in previous chapters, some form of role negotiation, to establish a new contract, may also be a very effective way of producing change.

11

Understanding and Coping With Change

Change can be seen as desirable or undesirable, forced or voluntary, major or minor, resisted or welcomed. The one thing that is certain is that it will continue to occur and, what is even more significant because it makes it more difficult to cope with, that the rate of change will continue to increase. Toffler (1970), gives a number of examples of this phenomenon. Perhaps the most dramatic is the rate of change in technological development.

To illustrate this, Toffler suggests that we should consider the last 50,000 years of human history divided into lifetimes of approximately 62 years each. This gives us about 800 such lifetimes. (62 years seems a rather optimistic life span over much of that time, but for purposes of illustration it does not make much difference.) For the first 650 of these lifetimes very little happened in terms of technology. The world was very much the same when someone died as it had been when they were born. It is only in about the last 70 lifetimes that things begin to change. It was at about that point that it became possible to communicate effectively from one generation to the next, through the invention of forms of writing. It is only in the last six lifetimes that printing has been available to the majority. In only the last four lifetimes has it been possible to measure time accurately. The electric motor appeared about two lifetimes ago, and it is only in the final 800th lifetime (and perhaps a little more) that most of the gadgets that we use every day have been developed. In other words, in terms of technological development not only has far more happened during the lifetime of the present generation than had happened in the whole of the rest of human history, but the rate of that development has continued to accelerate exponentially during this period.

This same increasing rate of change is taking place in many fields, for instance population expansion, and the speed and ease of communication. Thus it is in this generation that organizations and individual human beings are having to cope with change on an unprecedented scale.

Many organizations, and the people working within them, have experienced considerable and rapid change in the recent past. Indeed, in many organizations it is still taking place and in yet others it is confidently expected. It is of considerable importance, therefore, to understand how people react to change and how any negative effects may be coped with. This will help us to understand reactions to change, both in ourselves and others. In discussing this we will be introducing some new material, but also drawing on material presented elsewhere in the book.

Perhaps a major distinction is between change that is chosen by the individual, and change over which they have little or no choice. Generally speaking voluntary change is preferred to involuntary change, but this is not always the case. However, there is evidence to suggest that certain aspects of our adaptation to change are the same, irrespective of whether the change is chosen or not.

We will consider aspects of the change process that are common to all change, and probably, to most people. We will also look at the ways in which different individuals pass through the change process. Finally, we will consider how we can move from simply *reacting* to externally imposed changes, to *active* self-management of the change process.

STAGES OF ADAPTATION TO CHANGE

When considering the effects of change on individuals it is useful to start by looking at the effects of relatively large changes. From these 'extreme' changes models can be developed which may then be applied to other, less dramatic, changes.

Perhaps two of the most major negative changes in people's lives are those of unemployment, and the diagnosis of terminal disease, either in oneself or a loved one. Studies of the effects of unemployment (from occupational psychology), and of reactions to terminal disease and loss (from clinical psychology), suggest some common themes, despite the different methodologies (e.g. Fryer and Payne, 1986; Taylor, 1983). These common themes are:

- the regular occurrence of depressive reactions

- the importance of personal control

- the concept of 'stages' of adjustment.

We will start by examining the suggestion that reactions to change may be understood as a process, during which people go through recognizable 'stages'.

There are a number of such 'stage' models, all of which are very similar. Our preference is for that developed by Hopson (Cooper and Makin, 1984), which is based upon Kübler-Ross (1969). Kessler *et al.* (1985) point out that there is little empirical evidence to support stage theories. As they also point out, this may be because the theories are very difficult to test. Our experiences of using the theories with managers, however, leads us to believe that they are useful in understanding and coping with change.

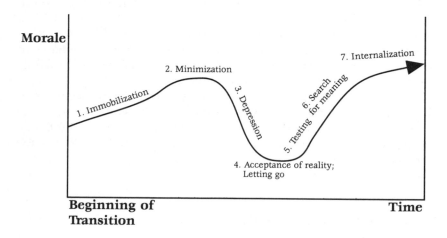

Figure 11.1. Stages of transitions.
(Source: Hopson, 1984)

Hopson's model is general in nature. It seeks to describe a process which is common to all types of change and transition, and to all individuals. It will be noticed that there are no numerical scales attached to either of the dimensions. The horizontal dimension of time, for example, has no specific time periods marked; this is deliberate. As will be seen, although people may go through the same process in adapting to change, they do so at different rates and with different intensities. We will start with a brief description of each of the stages, and then move on to consider individual differences in reactions to change. Finally we will look at three different approaches to understanding the change process, and how to cope with it.

Immobilization. The basic problem of adapting to change is that of maintaining some stability whilst achieving change. If the rate of change is not too fast people do not have great problems in adapting.

Change becomes a process of gradual evolution. Often, however, change is rapid and seems to proceed by revolution rather than evolution. If the change is dramatic and/or fast, the normal processes of adaptation may be overwhelmed for a short time. The initial reaction of many people when faced with such dramatic changes is to 'freeze up', like a rabbit caught in a headlight beam. The freezing is, however, largely cognitive. Behaviourally, the individual in this stage will still continue to function, but may appear to be on 'auto-pilot'. The surrounding stimuli are generally unchanged and so continue to initiate routine behaviours. The individual may often respond by carrying out routine tasks, apparently not having recognized the fact that circumstances have changed. As we shall see, the length and severity of this reaction depends upon such factors as the size of change and the person's perceived ability to cope.

Minimization. The immobilization stage is, by its very nature, a *passive* stage. The minimization stage, on the other hand, is an *active* stage, although at times this may not be apparent. Whilst recognizing that change has occurred, the person minimizes the importance of the change. The change may even be totally denied. These periods of minimization or denial alternate, however, with bursts of recurrent thoughts about the change. This is evidence that the stage is active rather than passive. The individual is actively trying to cope with the change, albeit it in small 'chunks'. The data from experience is being processed and gradually transferred into conscious memory.

Both the immobilization and minimization stages were previously seen as undesirable and dysfunctional. It is now generally accepted that they are necessary stages in the adaptation to change. However, they may become dysfunctional if their length or depth become excessive.

Depression. This stage is the one that is perhaps the most dysfunctional and distressing. Even though it is a 'natural' stage, and as such has value, spending too long in the stage is not desirable either for the individual or those around them. Most people are familiar with the characteristics of depression. The depressed individual lacks motivation, is lethargic, and their mood is generally negative.

Letting Go. Eventually most people become more aware of the reality and permanence of the change. They then begin to accept the new reality. This acceptance also leads to a 'letting go' of the thoughts and feelings associated with life before the change. These thoughts and feelings are the main content of the first three stages of transition, and relinquishing them is a necessary step in the process of adapting to change.

Testing. Although the individual may have let go of the old reality they often do not have a clear idea (or indeed any idea) of where they want to go in the future. There is, therefore, a process of testing out new possibilities. This may either be by actually trying out new behaviours, or by imagining what the new behaviours might be like.

The testing stage is one of increasing energy and motivation. The individual is keen to develop and try out new skills and behaviours. Like many new converts, individuals in this stage are often impatient. This impatience may show itself at times in anger and frustration, especially if things are not advancing as fast as the person would like.

Searching for Meaning. Eventually, following the high levels of activity of the testing stage, the individual finds time in which to reflect on the changes that have taken place, and on their own reactions to that change. Often this search for meaning concentrates on unforeseen but positive outcomes. It is not unusual for individuals to report that they are, in some ways, better people as the result of the experiences.

Internalization. In the internalization stage the new thoughts, feelings, and behaviour become stabilized as part of the normal functioning of the individual.

As mentioned before, the model is general in its nature. The speed with which people move through the stages will vary, as will the intensity of each of the stages. This will depend on many factors, including the magnitude and speed of the change. In addition, there is also the possibility of stagnation and regression. Some individuals may become stagnated in the depression stage. Others, perhaps after a set-back, may regress from the testing stage to the depressive.

Whilst we have concentrated on the effects of change that are perceived as negative, the model, according to Hopson, also has application to positive changes. Even pleasant, self-chosen changes, such as marriage or the arrival of a baby (choose your own example if the previous ones do not apply) produce a process of change as described by the model. Obviously the effects will be different from that of the loss of a loved one, but the general process will be the same.

UNDERSTANDING THE STAGES

Each of the stages in Hopson's model may be interpreted from a number of theoretical positions. We have chosen to use two that we have already covered in some detail, and one additional approach. The behavioural (OBMod) and psychodynamic (TA) approaches have been covered earlier. The *cognitive* approach, we believe, complements these other approaches.

BEHAVIOURAL/ATTRIBUTIONAL APPROACH

The immobilization and minimization stages may be interpreted using a number of behavioural concepts.

As we have seen, a person's perceived 'locus of control' can have a significant influence over their effectiveness. When faced with change there are often considerable uncertainties as to whether control is still possible. In behavioural terms, the individual attempts to regain control over that area threatened by the change. Wortman and Brehm's (1975) 'reactance theory' suggests that any attempt to remove an individual's control over an area of their life will lead to 'reactance'. The individual reacts against the change by actively seeking to regain the 'lost' control. Change in organizations often means changes for managers in the areas over which they have control. Often managers will resist such changes, even though they are offered other responsibilities. Even areas under their control that they may have privately considered peripheral, or even a nuisance, are defended with a vigour that appears to be out of proportion to their importance.

Changes are also likely to have an effect on a person's self-efficacy. The length and severity of the immobilization stage will be determined, to a large extent, by the threat the change is perceived as presenting. Whether the change is perceived as threatening at all will depend upon the individual's assessment of the threat, and their perceived ability to cope. In terms of Bandura's social cognitive theory, this latter assessment is 'self-efficacy'. If the individual feels competent in their ability to cope, the immobilization phase may be very short.

There are obviously threats as the result of change, but why should these produce denial and minimization? In reinforcement terms this reaction is entirely understandable. Threats are unpleasant. Any strategy that removes this unpleasantness will, therefore, be negatively reinforcing. (Remember that negative reinforcement leads to an increase in any behaviour that removes an unpleasant stimulus.) Denial removes the anxiety and hence will be likely to occur again. This removal of anxiety by the process of denial may also explain the bursts of apparent euphoria that often occur in this stage. Activity also has the effect of reducing anxiety (for reasons which we will consider later in this chapter). The activity of resisting any reduction in one's area of control is, therefore, also negatively reinforcing.

As the reality of the change comes to be recognized, attributions will be made. Often these attributions will be external. They will be attributed to those individuals (often the bosses), or situations, that are perceived as having 'caused' the changes. If the changes are seen as unwarranted or unjust the most likely emotional reaction is anger.

The stage of reactive depression has a number of behavioural/attributional interpretations. Perhaps the most influential have been those of Seligman and Abramson. Seligman first offered the 'learned helplessness' explanation to which Abramson added 'depressive attributional style' (see page 162). Another feature of this behavioural syndrome is the persistence of 'fixated behaviour patterns'. These consist of patterns of behaviour that have, in the past, been adaptive but are now inappropriate. Despite the fact that to outside observers the behaviour is now inappropriate, it continues to be exhibited. Managers will be familiar with the situation. Individuals continue to operate old systems, even though new systems have taken over. Often employees will insist on maintaining the old, even whilst operating the new.

This pattern of learned helplessness, depressive attributional style, and fixated behaviour, has considerable similarities to reactive depression. This too is characterized by motivational defects, emotional reactions, and cognitive limitations. (Note that this explanation is only for depression brought on by particular events. There are other types of depression for which a behavioural explanation may be inappropriate.)

In behavioural terms, things that were reinforcers before the onset of the reactive depression appear to lose their force. One possible explanation for this is that the memory of past reinforcement becomes distorted. This is consistent with current theory and research in clinical psychology. This suggests that depression is associated with memory functions, whilst anxiety is associated with the functioning of perception (Mathews, 1993).

During the 'letting go' stage the individual realizes that the old behaviours will not lead to reinforcement. The testing stage, therefore, becomes a search. Either new reinforcers have to be found or new behaviours have to be developed which will lead to a recovery of the original reinforcers.

A behavioural explanation for the 'search for meaning' is somewhat difficult to devise. This perhaps is an object lesson. All the theories discussed in this book have their limitations as well as their strengths. Internalization, however, can be seen as the integration of the new behaviour/reinforcement patterns.

COGNITIVE APPROACH

We have already seen, when discussing person perception, that humans are limited capacity information processors. To overcome this limitation they use heuristics, or information processing 'shortcuts'. These include fitting new information into pre-existing categories. Radical change, however, is likely to disrupt such categorization, and will produce information overload. Denial and minimization may be seen as an attempt to deal with this. Studies of organizational decision-making have shown that threatening situations have a number of effects on managers. These include a reduced motivation to seek out new information and a narrowing of focus in such searches (see Wood and Bandura, 1989).

This explanation may be taken further in accounting for the depressive stage. Another characteristic of depression is the inability to concentrate. It has been argued (Sedek and Kofta, 1990) that this may be the result of 'cognitive exhaustion'. Faced with an unpleasant situation from which they wish to escape, the individual tries repeatedly to develop a plan of action. When all these repeated attempts fail, the person is left 'cognitively exhausted'.

Going beyond this, there are a number of cognitive approaches to the understanding of emotional reactions in general. One has its origins in clinical practice; another has its roots in cognitive psychology and works on the metaphor of human beings as *self-regulating* information-processing systems.

Self-control theory. The cognitive approach to self-regulation is probably the most influential, as it is in other areas of psychology. (This is also sometimes referred to as a 'cybernetic' approach, from the Greek *kubernetes* meaning 'a helmsman'.)

Any form of regulation requires certain functions to be fulfilled. The process to be regulated needs to be monitored, then compared with a standard, and corrective action taken if the standard is not being met. A common, simple, example is a thermostat. The temperature is monitored and if it falls outside the pre-set range heating or cooling systems are turned on or off until the standard is attained.

The classic representation of this approach in psychology is the TOTE model proposed by Miller *et al.* (1960). The letters stand for Test, Operate, Test, Exit. The environment is tested to see if it matches a standard. If it does not then the environment is operated upon to produce change, hopefully in the right direction. The results are then tested. If the standard is still not attained then another operation is carried out. Once the standard is reached the operating cycle is exited, at least for the time being.

To control itself a system must, therefore, be self-monitoring (see Carver and Scheier, 1981). Comparing the current state with the internal standard results in a perceived discrepancy. This discrepancy becomes the source of motivation to act to reduce the discrepancy. For human beings, however, there is one crucial difference. When humans self-monitor (i.e. pay attention to the self), the detection of a discrepancy initiates a process of *self-evaluation*. For reasons that are not clearly understood, such self-focus and self-evaluation produce negative feelings. The converse is not, however, true. Self-focus after a positive outcome does not produce positive feelings. Wood *et al.* (1990) suggest that, because positive outcomes do not require corrective action, there is no reason for self-regulation. (Self-focus can be initiated in a number of ways, by eye contact or even by just looking in a mirror, but perhaps most important from the current perspective is that it is initiated when goal-directed activity is interrupted or disrupted.)

The concepts at the corner-stone of self-control theory are those of *self-focus* which leads to *self-evaluation*. The individual's information-processing focus is not upon the external world, but internally on 'self'. This also has the effect that attributions of causality for the negative events tend also to be on the self. It is a paradox that whilst such self-focus and self-evaluation are essential for self-regulation, if attention is focused on the self for too long it produces negative feelings and emotions. In normal self-regulation the main attention is upon the task to be achieved. Self-focusing only occurs in short bursts, as the results of action are compared with the internal standards. Problems arise, however, when actions to achieve the required standard fail.

Most people, when faced with a situation which it is obvious they can not control, abandon their efforts and hence self-focusing ceases. If the events are, for whatever reason, important to the individual they may continue to go round the TOTE cycle even when others around them realize that this is pointless. This leads to a continuation of self-focusing and negative self-evaluation. It is this, according to cognitive theorists, which initiates and maintains depression.

Whilst abandoning attempts at control is one way to exit the depressive cycle, another way is by changing the internal standards of comparison. In her long-term study of cancer patients, Taylor (1983) found that patients adapted by changing those against whom they judged themselves. Such 'downward social comparison' was achieved by choosing groups for comparison who were worse off than themselves.

Finally, the cycle may also be exited by a total withdrawal from the situation, either behaviourally or psychologically (denial).

In clinical psychology a similar, cognitive, approach is taken by some theorists, most notably by Ellis's 'rational emotive therapy', and Beck's 'cognitive therapy' (see Ellis, 1976; Beck, 1976). The central perspective of Beck's approach to the understanding of emotional reactions is that emotions are not un-focused states, but are rather the result of specific thought processes. An important element of these thoughts is the 'meaning' that people give to events, meanings that are often associated with attribution of causality. According to Beck, however, we are often unaware of the meaning we attach to events. We assume that the event itself has caused the feelings we experience. We remain unaware of the missing link – the meaning we 'unconsciously' attach to the event. Beck calls this a mental 'blank'. To understand the feelings properly we need to 'fill in the blank'. These 'blanks' are the 'internal messages' that are used to monitor and evaluate our own behaviour, and to issue self-instructions. We are all aware of these internal dialogues of self-evaluation and self-instructions. (Although Beck does not take an explicitly self-regulatory perspective, it is implicit in his theory.) In some cases, however, these messages take place automatically, and so rapidly that they are effectively unconscious.

As with the cognitive theorists discussed above, problems arise when the self-monitoring, self-evaluation, and self-instruction systems become, in Beck's phrase, 'over-mobilized'. In such a state they become so mobilized as to become dysfunctional. An example is 'stage fright'. Some managers experience this when required to give presentations. They become over-sensitive to warning signals and negative self-instructions. Such over-sensitivity produces distortions in thinking. According to Beck, these distortions differ between different emotions, but have two characteristics in common; *personalization* and *extreme global judgements*. Personalization takes to its extreme the process of self-focusing. As we have seen, for reasons that are not yet clearly understood, self-focus leads to negative self-evaluation; everything that happens to the individual is perceived as negative. In addition, all these negative events are seen as being self-directed. A good example is paranoia. The paranoid believes that when other people are engaged in conversation they are talking about *them*, and that this talk is invariably negative. For the depressive, if someone else is in a bad mood, they automatically think that it is *their* fault. 'My boss is frowning at me, I must have done something wrong'.

This personalization is reinforced by the tendency to make extreme global judgements. Whilst these are recognized by others as being factually inaccurate, they seem perfectly plausible to the person concerned. Extreme global judgements have two major characteristics, *polarized thinking* and *over-generalization*.

With polarized thinking, events, rather than being perceived in shades of grey, are seen as either black or white; wonderful or terrible. Events will either 'never' happen or will 'always' happen. These are examples of bi-polar thinking – from one extreme. Sometimes the thinking may be uni-polar, anchored at one extreme end. Usually this extreme is the 'bad' end and the person 'catastrophizes'. Everything that happens will, inevitably, be a catastrophe.

Over-generalization is a pattern of thinking that involves a number of distortions. First, the individual 'selectively abstracts' information from events. These are, of course, often the negative aspects of what might otherwise have been a positive outcome. Arbitrary, and usually inaccurate, inferences are then made on the basis of this abstraction. Finally, these inaccurate conclusions are generalized to aspects of experience where they do not legitimately apply. Minor distortions of this nature are, of course, not uncommon. Many of us are ready to interpret the whole of a person's character from, for example, their driving behaviour. It could be argued that some elements of the media also undertake selective abstraction, arbitrary inference, and over-generalization fairly frequently. If taken to extremes, however, these distortions are obviously maladaptive.

The question remains, however, as to why depression, an unpleasant experience, continues. A part of the answer would appear to be that, although depression is, by and large, unpleasant it does provide some benefits. First, it provides a safe and largely unassailable view of the world. This consistency at least allows the individual to predict what is likely to happen. This prediction allows them the perception of control. Even though there may be nothing they can do to change negative events, at least they know what will happen. The second advantage is that it protects the individual against further experiences of the loss that initiates depression. If you take action and produce or acquire something, there is always the chance that this will also be lost. If you do nothing then nothing can be lost.

Except in the most extreme of cases, people eventually cease to self-focus and instead direct their attention outwards. This has two effects; first, it removes the negative self-evaluative focus, and secondly, it focuses attention on the processing of information about the new reality. (An everyday expression, often used when referring to those who are depressed, is that they need 'taking out of themselves'.)

Testing of reality, search for meaning, and internalization may be seen as a process of re-establishing meaningful categories. These will provide the new heuristic short-cuts that will enable the individual to cope in the future.

PSYCHO-DYNAMIC APPROACH

Individuals have habitual ways of perceiving, thinking, feeling, and responding to events. This is evident in both the behavioural and cognitive explanations of reactions to change; similarly with the psycho-dynamic approach (Transactional Analysis). Such habitual ways of thinking and responding tend to operate independently of the current situation. Behaviour that is determined by these habits, therefore, may prove to be dysfunctional.

One of the functions of habitual ways of thinking is that they help create a sense of security. At times of stress, such as periods of rapid change, our sense of security may be threatened. In the face of such a threat individuals will try to defend their habitual view of the world. When the going gets really difficult they may well redouble their efforts to maintain this existing view. There is a range of mechanisms which individuals use to try to maintain their habitual view of the world. These mechanisms account for some of the resistance to change encountered in the Hopson model. This resistance is a characteristic of a number of the stages, in particular the immobilization and minimization stages.

Redefining. One of the mechanisms which people use to maintain a view of the world which is consistent with their script is by the process of *redefining*. Redefinition protects individuals from stimuli which are inconsistent with their frames of reference. It enables them to maintain their established view of themselves, other people, and the world. They achieve this by making a subtle and unconscious shift in the way they view any situation, so that it no longer conflicts with their beliefs. This can most obviously be seen when someone is confronted with a statement they do not wish to accept or deal with. In replying to the statement they shift the ground slightly. On the surface, the reply looks like an answer to the statement, but closer examination reveals that it is not. This is sometimes called a *tangential transaction*, and it occurs because the individual has redefined the original statement. The following exchange provides an example:

Manager to subordinate (who has been absent from his desk for some time): 'I have been looking for you, where were you?'
Subordinate: 'What did you want me for?'

The subordinate has avoided the issue of where he was, by redefining the question to what he is wanted for. With any luck (from the subordinate's point of view), the manager will forget his absence by getting into a discussion about why he wanted him.

Politicians are very adept at this process. When asked, by an interviewer, a question which they do not wish to answer, they will redefine it and answer a slightly different question. If this is subtly done the listener may not even notice. (The authors tend to judge the skill of a politician by the subtlety of their redefining.) This is an activity which is also not unknown among university lecturers! In either case it may also, on occasion, be done consciously and on purpose, in which case it is not a defence mechanism, but a deliberate ploy.

Discounting. Redefining involves *discounting*. This is the unconscious ignoring or minimizing of some aspect of the situation. The person underestimates, in some way, the information which is available, or their own ability to cope. Discounting may well be taking place when you hear someone say, in relation to a forthcoming reorganization, something like 'It won't make any difference to me', or 'I really could never learn to do something like that'. Sometimes, of course, such statements are realistic and rational appraisals of the situation, carried out from the Adult. However, there is always a qualitative difference between a discount and a rational appraisal, which is usually easily recognized, either in oneself or in others. This is because discounting involves *grandiosity*. Grandiosity in TA has a similar meaning to that in self-control theory. It is the purposeful exaggeration or minimization of some characteristic of self, of others, or of the situation. A discounting statement will usually take the form 'You *always* do X', or 'I *never* do Y'.

There are a number of types of discount, which can also take place at a number of levels. These are hierarchical, as illustrated below.

Types of discounting.

- Stimuli: Simply not recognizing or accepting information which is available.

- Problems: Refusing to recognize that there is any problem or need for action or change.

- Options: Not recognizing the range of options which are available in the situation.

Levels of discounting.

- Existence: The existence of new information is simply just not recognized.

- Significance: New information is recognized but its significance is discounted.

- Change possibilities: The situation is seen as new and significant, but there is no possibility of doing anything about it.

- Personal abilities: The situation is seen as new and significant; there are some possibilities for change, but the individual discounts their own ability to take any action.

Figure 11.2 shows all the possible combinations of type and level of discount. The top left-hand box represents the most extreme situation where the existence of new information is discounted. The individual maintains, despite objective evidence to the contrary, that 'nothing

LEVEL	TYPE		
	Stimuli (Information)	Problems	Options
EXISTENCE			
SIGNIFICANCE			
CHANGE POSSIBILITIES			
PERSONAL ABILITIES			

Figure 11.2. The discount matrix

has changed'. The bottom right-hand box represents the situation where the need for change is recognized, as is the availability of options, but the individual discounts their ability to undertake any of them. You might like to try completing the other boxes, while checking whether any of them may represent your own favourite form of discounting. Because of the hierarchical nature of this classification, a discount in any box automatically means that all forms of discount represented by boxes below it or to the right of it, are also brought into play.

Discounting is an important concept in TA, since it is the basic mechanism by which people maintain their existing view of the world and hence resist change. It is important, therefore, to be aware of discounts both in oneself and others. The key is to look for grandiosity. With practice, this is not too difficult to recognize. When discounts are challenged there is a tendency for the individual to move down and discount at the next level. This may itself then require further examination and confrontation.

'Letting go' marks the end of the depressive stage and the beginning of the active and reality-orientated stages. How easy it is for the individual to let go will depend upon the strength and importance of what is being left behind. A useful way of analysing and understanding the nature of these ties is through the concepts of *scripts* and *drivers*.

SCRIPTS AND DRIVERS

In discussing these two concepts we will be making use of ideas already outlined in previous chapters. In particular, the concepts of ego states and existential position (see Chapter 3), and the notion of stroking (see Chapter 10). To these we will add some new ideas.

THE CONCEPT OF 'SCRIPT'

A script in TA has similarities with the use of the term in everyday life. In a play the script determines what the actors will say and do. Similarly, in TA, the script is our own pre-programmed way of perceiving and coping with the world. It is created in early childhood and provides a mechanism by which individuals make sense of their world. This, in turn, influences how they respond to changes. In behavioural terms it represents a pattern of habitual responses.

In TA the script is used to draw a distinction between *autonomous* behaviour and *scripted* behaviour. Scripted behaviour is 'pre-programmed', with its origins in early childhood. In certain situations the script leads to cycles of similar and predictable patterns of behaviour. A common example is the individual whose marriage moves through various difficulties and painful interactions, culminating in divorce. A short while later they re-marry someone with very similar characteristics and personality to their first spouse, and the whole cycle is repeated. Some people go round this cycle several times during their lifetime. In extreme cases it can seem is as if the individual is living their whole life according to a predetermined plan. This plan is referred to as a *life script*. It can be thought of as a series of self-fulfilling prophesies. The individual, unconsciously, organizes their life in order to fulfil these prophesies.

Life script is defined as a 'preconscious life plan'. Anyone who knows the script will be able to predict what will happen and how the scene (or in the extreme, life) is going to end. The process is, of course, unconscious; the individual does not realize that they are following a 'script'. They will be genuinely puzzled and upset that their life keeps following these same old patterns. A common pattern is the individual who, on first entering a new job, appears to be very friendly and easy to work with. Indeed, they are often very conscientious workers. Gradually, however, they begin to 'fall out' first with one person, then another. Finally they leave the job, often by resignation, having upset almost everybody. This pattern then repeats itself in their next job. Not all of our life, of course, is scripted – just how much will vary from individual to individual.

The significance of the script concept is that while we are following script we are not being autonomous. That is, we will be following old patterns of behaviour derived from our childhood which are not totally relevant to our current situation. Transactional Analysis being originally a therapeutic theory, tends to concentrate on the negative, maladaptive side of human behaviour. The purpose of therapy is to move the individual away from such behaviours to effective ones; in this case from script to autonomy. Hence, there is a large body of theory concerning script but very much less on autonomy, although Eric Berne did describe autonomy as consisting of three capacities:

- *Awareness;* being in the here and now. This includes the capacity to respond to current reality without preconceived expectations or value judgements, recognizing feelings and emotions, and not being driven by the past.
- *Spontaneity;* the capacity to choose from a range of options in how we feel think and behave.
- *Intimacy;* the capacity to be open and trusting with others.

(cited in Neath, 1995)

Autonomy means operating freely in the 'here and now' with all ego states available. Fairly obviously, the most effective reaction to change will come from a position of autonomy. Reactions from script will mean that we are bringing outdated and irrelevant ideas and feelings from our childhood into the current situation, which will limit our ability to respond appropriately. To understand how this happens we need to look at the origins and development of the script process.

ORIGINS OF SCRIPT

How an individual's script develops is a complex process and a detailed discussion would be beyond the scope of this book. Briefly, the individual's script arises from the young child's attempt to cope with the pressures of life. The theory suggests that at some point between the ages of four to eight years the child makes a decision on the best strategy for survival. Different authorities suggest that this happens at different times within this range. Perhaps different individuals make it at different times, or possibly, it evolves over a period of time, but within this age range. According to the theory this is always, at the time, a good decision for survival. It is not, of course, a rational and conscious decision, but is an unconscious emotional reaction to *script messages* from parents and other parent-type figures (grandparents, older siblings, teachers).

Script messages can be of two types. Firstly there are *commands,* (more technically called *injunctions*). These are messages about what we should not do or should not be (e.g. 'Don't get close to others', or 'Don't think for yourself'). The second type of script messages are *attributions*. They are concerned with what the child is (e.g. 'You're stupid', or 'You're crazy'). Parents do, of course, also give positive messages, but these do not get incorporated into the script. They are, in fact, known as *permissions* and enable the child to avoid script behaviour. Indeed, a child lucky enough to get only warm positive messages (positive stroking) would not become scripted. The reality for most of us, as parents, is that we give both positive and negative messages, as did our own parents. Most of us, therefore, develop some degree of script.

Script messages can also be expressed in such a way that, on the surface, they seem to be positive (e.g. a parent may say to the child 'Be responsible, take care of your younger brother'), but if this is said in an exasperated tone of voice, just when the child has done something stupid and hurt the younger child, the underlying (and internalized) message may be 'You're irresponsible'. Consciously, the parent may well be motivated by good intentions of instilling socially acceptable attitudes and behaviour, but from the child's point of view it can be seen as a negative 'put down'. The positive message is known as a *counter-injunction* because it is, on the surface, the opposite of the injunction or negative message. Script messages may also be picked up by the process of modelling, where the child adopts 'scripty' behaviour being expressed by the parent. A child may adopt a 'Don't get close' injunction from a parent who always behaves very distantly. The script decision that the child makes in response to these parental messages is how best to adapt and survive in the particular environment. It will set the pattern for future relationships and responses to difficult situations. It will also determine the predominant existential position, preferred types of strokes, and possible games played.

Berne suggested that there are several script patterns that people tend to follow:

- The *never* script. Individuals following this never get or do what they really want, their (internal) Parent forbids it. Their perception, of course, is that events conspire to prevent them, not that they stop themselves. They never get that special holiday or other treat.

- The *always* script. These people show repeating patterns of the same old behaviour – always working too hard or always moving from job to job.

- The *until* script. In this case the individual cannot have a reward, or do something they would like, until they have achieved something else. 'I cannot relax or look after myself *until* everyone else is organized'.

- The *after* script. In this script the individual is set up for trouble after some event or age is reached. 'When your children reach 15, that's when the trouble starts' or 'If I have not made it by the time I'm 35, that's it'.

- The *almost* script. Someone following this script never quite succeeds at what they are doing. For example, the manager who never finishes the job because of all the interruptions.

- The *open-ended* script. This script defines very clearly what a person should do at the earlier stages in life, but stops at a particular point in time. One example of this is the woman who has a very precise script for marriage and family, but nothing for after her children have grown up and left home, and so she is left at a loss. Another case could be the man who is scripted for work-life, but has nothing for retirement. Maybe this is why so many men die soon after retiring. This is not to suggest that having a script is necessarily a bad thing, but if you are living life according to a script, and opportunities for its enactment stop, then you are in trouble.

COUNTERSCRIPT

It was suggested that the script is established in early childhood by an unconscious intuitive decision process. It is reaction to *negative* Parental messages. Some script decisions are also made in later childhood. Because they are made later they are decisions which can be verbalized and brought into consciousness. They consist of a collection of beliefs and principles, often expressed in a form rather like slogans or mottos; 'Stealing is wrong', 'Honesty is the best policy', 'Mothers should stay at home with their children'. These are internalizations of counter-injunctions, and hence are referred to as *counterscripts*. A person's counterscript will also be influenced by his or her cultural background and so will include cultural stereotypes and beliefs about class or ethnic backgrounds. Because much of this system is conscious the individual may believe that, when in counterscript, he or she is acting autonomously, but since it is by definition archaic it cannot totally be a response to the 'here and now'. The counterscript is a reaction to *positive* Parental messages. Normally these messages are socially desirable, and following them can be very effective if done in appropriate contexts. A great deal of the behaviour shown at work, or in other social contexts, is derived from counterscript.

MINISCRIPT

An aspect of script theory which has implications for organizational behaviour and change has been developed by Kahler and Capers (1974). It is known as *miniscript* because it concentrates on 'sequences of behaviour which occur in minutes or even seconds, but result in a reinforcement pattern for life'. They focus on counterscript messages and suggest five basic groupings of such messages. They can be thought of as five very common generalized messages. They are, in fact, so common that most of us can identify with one or, often, more of them. (Kahler even went so far as to suggest that we are in driver behaviour up to 90 per cent of the time, although this seems to us to be rather unlikely.) They coined the term *drivers* as a label for them, because they are to do with the sort of internal pressures we put upon ourselves and which push us to use energy in particular ways. In the definitions which follow, the type of messages which give rise to the driver will be readily apparent.

DRIVERS

Be Perfect. This arises from messages which the child interprets as meaning that in order to be accepted I must 'be perfect'. (I'll be all right as long as I'm perfect.) The individual following this driver strives to do everything perfectly. Everything must be in its place, all jobs finished in the minutest detail, all t's crossed and i's dotted. Such a person is ideal for jobs where minute attention to detail and concern for getting every aspect right is an essential consideration. Computer programming may be an example. The negative side is that the 'be perfect' individual will never feel satisfied. In the real world, no job will ever be completed perfectly. In the extreme they will always feel as though they are failing, because they can never live up to their own expectations.

Hurry Up. People with a hurry up driver are always in a rush. (I'll be all right as long as I hurry.) They scurry from appointment to appointment, or are always terribly busy getting the current job finished, because there are more jobs lined up. The positive side is that they have a lot of energy and often do achieve a lot. However, in their rush things may not be done too well and they may forget things.

Try Hard. With this driver the individual makes great efforts to achieve whatever it is they set out to do. (I'll be all right so long as I keep trying.) They put in a lot of effort, but often don't quite manage to make it – jobs never quite get completed.

Please Me. Often now called *please others* for reasons which will be apparent, this arises when the child determines that, in order to survive and be accepted, they must do as required by the parents or other parent figures. (I'll be all right so long as I do what they want.) The individual with a please me driver spends much of their time 'sussing out' what others want and then setting out to do it. Consequently, they are often very helpful and useful people to have around, particularly in occupations involving service to others. They will strive hard to provide a particular service to the client's satisfaction. The negative side is that they rarely get what they want, because they are so busy pleasing others. They often feel 'put upon' by others.

Be Strong. People operating on this driver spend much of their time being a tower of strength and supporting everyone around them. (I'll be all right as long as I don't show weakness.) They are very good in an emergency and will always be enormously supportive. On the negative side they find it hard to express their feelings. Having feelings they see as a sign of weakness. They may often feel resentful that no one ever does anything for them. Others, of course, never see them as needing anything, because they are always so busy being strong.

A good description of how drivers affect the way people interact in organizations is given by Hay (1992). She relates them to what she calls 'working styles' and then goes on to say:

'Different combinations of working styles will have different effects on relationships. We are likely to have a higher regard for people who share our own orientation. We will also find it easier to understand them, and to empathise with their problems. Even our sentence patterns will match. Hurry Ups will talk rapidly to each other, interrupt each other, and make quick decisions together. Be Perfects will speak carefully, with plenty of long words and specialist jargon, and arrive at considered decisions together. Please People will be very polite to each other, keep checking that the other party is comfortable with the discussion, and aim to find compromises. Try Hards will explore many alternatives, go off at tangents, fail to finish their sentences, and make decisions enthusiastically. Be Strongs will resemble poker players, give little away about how they feel, and make pragmatic, logical decisions.'

As Hay points out, there are both strengths and weaknesses in any particular combination of styles. A team with very compatible styles may find it easy and enjoyable to work together, but may miss out on important characteristics provided by other styles. A team with a mix of styles may complement each other but find it difficult to work together.

As far as the individual is concerned, there are both advantages and disadvantages in working from within miniscript. Many people have maintained very successful careers with behaviour based on one or more drivers. Our research on the careers of successful managers for example (Jennings *et al.*, 1994), suggests (although we cannot prove it) that their behaviour is often very driven. Provided the driver is appropriate for the situation it will lead to very successful performance, simply because there is such strong pressure to follow the particular style of behaviour dictated by the driver. The negative side is that the individual is not operating autonomously and will feel controlled. Although successful, they will often feel that they are not able to do what they really want to. Another important characteristic is that they will find it very hard to cope with change. If the situation changes, they may not be able to change with it. This is because the motivation for their behaviour is rooted in childhood, and hence archaic. As we have previously noted, however, most of the time most people operate from their Adult. In this situation behaviour is determined by a realistic assessment of the current situation, rather than by the pre-programmed script. However, scripted behaviour is not uncommon, especially at times of stress. Unless people can break out of their script and driver behaviour they will not be able to adapt. How they may be able to do this is considered in the next section.

Although there will always be differences in the way individuals respond to change and transition, the Hopson model, we believe, offers an insight into the processes that people go through. There is evidence that organizational changes have much the same effect as other life changes and that, in a similar way, people do recover and start actively to adapt (Crouch and Worth, 1991). But is there anything that can help ease, and perhaps speed, people's progress through the change process?

COPING WITH CHANGE

The usefulness of the Hopson model is that it makes both individuals and organizations aware of the likely consequences of change; just understanding the process has its value.

Individuals realize that their experiences and feelings are not confined to themselves alone. They also become aware that each of the stages that they will experience is valuable and fulfils a necessary function in the adaptation to change. Organizations also need to recognize the elements of the change process and accept the process of change. In addition, they need to accept that different people will progress through the stages at different rates. But whilst acceptance of the change process is useful, what can individuals and organizations do to help ease the passage through the stages?

SELF-KNOWLEDGE

As we have mentioned before, individuals differ in the way they react to change. The length and depth of the various stages differ. It is essential, therefore, to gain some insight into your own progress through the change process, and how this may differ from others'. Perhaps the first question that needs to be answered concerns how you are likely to react to change and how you are likely to cope, specifically:

- Am I an Adaptor or an Innovator?
- Am I a Pioneer, Early Adopter etc.?

Answers to these questions are likely to give some insight into how you are likely to react to change. In addition, however, you need to ask the following question:

- How do I cope with stress, and how could I improve my coping?

Having identified your individual ways of reacting to, and coping with, change, what can the behavioural, cognitive, and TA approaches offer in the way of advice?

BEHAVIOURAL ADVICE

Perhaps the most important advice that the behavioural approach can offer involves 'control' and 'self-efficacy'.

Perceived personal control, as we saw earlier, is one of the common factors that appear throughout the literature on adaptation to change, whether in clinical, educational, or occupational psychology. Indeed, one of the main problems of those suffering from 'post-traumatic stress disorder' is that of control. Those held hostage for a long time, for example, need help to re-establish control over their lives. It is not unusual for long-term hostages to find it impossible to decide what to eat for their first meal of freedom. The 'de-briefing' often includes forcing them to take such apparently simple decisions. Control also has links with perceived self-efficacy. Those who believe they have control over their environment are more likely to have higher levels of self-efficacy.

To recap briefly, the main sources of self-efficacy are

- mastery experiences
- modelling
- social persuasion

Major changes often mean that new skills have to be acquired in order to cope. All the factors that were covered in the discussion of social cognitive theory will need to be taken into consideration. Suitable models will have to be developed. Skill acquisition will have to be arranged such that early failures are avoided and success encouraged. The new rewards that the changes will bring will have to be made clear. If possible, intrinsic rewards should be built into the new working arrangements. These are matters for which the individual and the organization will need to take joint responsibility.

In our experience much change is, perhaps inevitably, driven from the top. However, it is only the initial policy decisions regarding change that need to be made at this level. Decisions about the process and nature of the change do not necessarily need to be made at the highest level. If it is not possible to give individuals actual control over their environment then they should at least be kept fully informed. Being informed allows people to make predictions. This, in itself, gives individuals a form of control.

Organizations should accept the fact that change takes time and that people should be supported and encouraged to help themselves. In particular, the reward system that encourages change should not be devised so as to encourage competition. As we have seen, self-improvement goals are generally more effective than competitive goals where new skills are being acquired. Organizations, by their reward systems, can influence which of these goal orientations people will adopt. As Wood and Bandura (1989) put it:

'To ensure progress in personal development, success should be measured in terms of self-improvement, rather than triumphs over others.'

Rewards should be individually tailored so as to achieve high levels of self-development.

Another influence on perceived self-efficacy and control are the attributions made for successes and failures. We have seen previously how attributions can lead to attributional conflict (Chapter 6), and learned helplessness (Chapter 5). These will have to be handled, often on a one-to-one basis, between managers and their subordinates.

There are other suggestions that the behavioural approach can make towards effective self-management. We will return to these in the next chapter.

COGNITIVE ADVICE

As Campion and Lord (1982) point out, behavioural adjustment tends to be quicker than cognitive. Being active tends to focus attention outwards, rather than inwards. As we have seen, long periods of internal self-focus can have negative effects on the individual. Activity, therefore, reduces both self-focus and anxiety.

Cognitive activities should not, however, be overlooked. A prerequisite for any effective change process is that the individual has an accurate perception of reality and can make assessments based on this knowledge. This is perhaps most difficult to achieve during the depressive stage. As we have seen there is a tendency for distortions of reality to take place, in particular those of 'personalization' and 'extreme global judgements'.

Beck (1976) suggests two methods, 'distancing' and 'decentering', that can be employed to try to reduce the possible distortions.

Distancing involves making a clear distinction between 'I know' and 'I believe'. The former are statements of fact, which may prove to be incorrect. Their uncompromising statement as fact means that they are unlikely to be tested against reality. 'I believe' statements, on the other hand, are hypotheses. These hypotheses are capable of being tested against reality and of being accepted or rejected. The analysis of the situation, therefore, should be phrased as a working hypothesis. This will help to avoid the problems of distortion.

Decentering tries to cope with the problem of personalization. The aim is to create the rational awareness that the individual is not responsible for, or the target of, everything that goes wrong. Observing and talking to other people who are in the same situation is often a good way of de-personalizing. The recognition that others are experiencing the same sort of feelings often removes the belief that everything is self-targeted.

When undergoing periods of change it is worth writing down your experiences, feelings, hopes, and fears. (An even better method is to record them on a tape recorder and then transcribe them.) These thoughts should then be analysed, bearing in mind the concepts we have just discussed.

The techniques of distancing and decentering are largely cognitive. For many reasons, however, perhaps the best method of coping is by becoming *proactive*. Taking action not only achieves results but also breaks the 'depressive cycle'. Attention is focused outwards, on the task, and not inwards encouraging negative self-evaluation. Activity reduces anxiety. (This is probably why anxieties flourish at night, when activity is generally not possible.) The problem, however, is that it is often difficult to make decisions about what activity to undertake, let alone do it. It is said that Carl Jung when treating people who were depressed would ask them 'What would you like to be doing if you weren't depressed?' On receiving a reply he would respond 'Well, go and do it!' A similar technique is that of sticking a pin in a list of activities. Remembering the Premack principle (see Chapter 5), draw up a list of things that you enjoy doing. (This should be done at a time when you do not feel 'down', otherwise you will not feel like doing it.) Then, when you are feeling lethargic, bored, or depressed, with your eyes closed stick a pin in the list. Force yourself, despite your own objections that it is pointless, to do whatever the pin indicates.

PSYCHODYNAMIC ADVICE (TA)

Perhaps the biggest obstacle to change in TA terms is our script. We will become more effective if we can become aware of these script-derived aspects of our behaviour and take steps to break free of them.

Breaking out of script. There are three stages in bringing about change: first there is *awareness*. TA is of value at this stage in that it can create insight and give broader and deeper perceptions of one's own behaviour. Secondly, there is *understanding* of what is experienced. TA offers a model which is diagnostic and relatively easy to understand. Thirdly, there must be *willingness* to change. This is very much an individual matter, but as discussed in Chapter 8, there is considerable evidence that most people are capable of very considerable change, provided they see that the change is in their own interest. Sometimes, however, unwillingness to change may be due to lack of belief in the possibility of change. This may be due to script messages. The Child may be reacting to old Parent messages such as 'Don't ask questions – and don't draw attention to yourself' or 'Don't take risks'. Even the thought of acting against such Parent messages is usually enough to produce anxiety, and even fear, in the Child.'

How then can the individual break out of such script messages? There are two levels at which this can be done. Very deeply embedded script messages may need professional counselling or therapeutic help to uncover and change. This level is beyond the scope of this book, or of any intervention that should take place in organizations. At a more surface level, most of us are following script messages which we can bring into consciousness and make decisions to change. It will require practice and effort. We will not always succeed. When we do, we will occasionally slip back into the old beliefs again, but with perseverance we can break away from the old messages. The secret, of course, is to keep our Adult engaged; become aware of when we are redefining. As a first stage it is easier to learn to recognize redefinitions by others, then become aware of our own. If we are redefining, what is it that we are discounting? Again we can use our Adult to pick up discounts, both in others and ourselves, and then check what evidence we have for our lack of faith.

Another method by which we may identify script messages is to think back to childhood. What messages may our parents have given us, that we are still trying to follow? Are there things that we do, which we recognize as being 'just what our parents did'? It is worth examining these messages to check that they are still relevant to our present lives. Some messages will, of course, still be relevant, particularly those concerned with fundamental aspects of morality. We do not really want to work out our ethical stance from first principles every time we make a choice. However, moral values do change over time and so even these principles are worth questioning from time to time. With time and practice we can become aware of script messages and gradually discard them, and thus take more charge of our own lives and act more autonomously.

CHANGE AND THE PSYCHOLOGICAL CONTRACT

Change of any significance usually involves changes in both the economic and psychological contracts. These will need to be renegotiated, in ways we have discussed in previous chapters. Very rarely, however, is the psychological contract of the *process* of change discussed. Organizations need to recognize the process of change described above and to take it into account when designing change programmes. People need time to adjust to change, and be offered help to do so. One of the greatest sources of stress for individuals, which manifests itself in low morale, is uncertainty. It is difficult, if not impossible, to begin to cope with change if the nature of the change is unknown. Part of the psychological contract, therefore, should be the spelling out of how change, even as drastic as redundancy, is to be handled. Employees' perceptions of equity (see Chapter 4) will be central to this contract.

12

Empowerment and Self-Management

In the last chapter we considered the effects of change. There are many different types of change. However, many of the changes that are currently occurring involve the devolution of decision making, accompanied by the requirement for people to take more responsibility for their behaviour at work. This process is sometimes referred to as *empowerment*. Closely linked with this process is the concept of *self-management*, sometimes referred to as self-leadership. These two trends have been referred to, implicitly if not explicitly, at various points in previous chapters. For example, it was implicit in some of the motivation theories discussed (e.g. the job characteristics model), and explicit in some leadership theories (e.g. the dependency model). It is also implicit in the models of organizational growth, as organizations seek to move from a 'differentiated' structure to one that is more responsive to change.

The roots of this emphasis on self-management are both philosophical and practical. Philosophically, the influence is the belief in the ability of individuals to take more responsibility for their work. Practically, the reasons are three-fold. First, if individuals can take more responsibility then this decreases the requirement for close supervision. Second, increasing the amount of autonomy that individuals have is likely to increase their job satisfaction and organizational citizenship behaviours. Finally, no matter how technically competent a manager is, it is inevitable that the person knowing most about the day-to-day running of any job is the person actually doing it. The approach has been successfully used in many organizational contexts, and under a variety of names. The Rover car group, for example, has devolved considerable power to those working on the car production 'track'. This includes the power to stop the track if necessary, a decision that would have led to automatic dismissal a few years ago.

Such a devolution of power cannot be implemented by managerial diktat. As we have seen, such a step would almost certainly induce counter-dependence. How, therefore, can people be encouraged to self-manage, and what techniques will help them do so?

SELF-MANAGEMENT AND THE INDIVIDUAL

BEHAVIOURAL SELF-MANAGEMENT

The BMod techniques that have been applied to the motivation of others can be used with equal effectiveness in the management of ourselves. Indeed, the five step approach of Luthans and Kreitner (identify the behaviour, measure the frequency, functionally analyse the consequences of the behaviour, implement a modification pro-gramme, and monitor the results) can be applied to ourselves as easily as to others. Indeed, perhaps more so. As we have seen, BMod suggests that we need to be able to monitor behaviour as closely, and as often, as possible. The person to whom we have the ability to do this most effectively is ourselves. In fact, it could be argued that not only the most effective, but the most economical, form of manage-ment is self-management.

To recap, the central proposition of BMod is that 'behaviour is a function of its consequences'. To change behaviour, the reinforcers keeping undesirable behaviour patterns going have, ideally, to be re-moved. Reinforcers then have to be introduced to encourage the de-sired behaviour. In self-management there is another factor that can be used to influence behaviour – the stimuli in the environment that act as a cue to either start or inhibit behaviour. These stimuli may also be involved in influencing the behaviour of others. For example, clock-time is often such a cue, indicating when work (or a tea break) should start and finish. It is, however, generally more important in self-management. These stimuli occur before the behaviour and are hence often referred to as *antecedents*. One of the reasons for referring to them as antecedents is that it produces a nice three letter acronym: ABC (antecedents, behaviour, consequences).

These three components, the antecedents, the behaviour, and the consequences of the behaviour are all capable of being *managed*. If we are to manage our own behaviour effectively we need to consider all three variables.

Managing the antecedents. The antecedents are present in our sur-roundings. The most important concern

- when we undertake behaviour;
- where we undertake behaviour; and,

- the people with whom we undertake it.

Performance can often be improved by changing the time of day when the task is undertaken. Many people are more alert in the morning than in the afternoon. For this reason it may be better to leave more mundane activities to the afternoon. However, more sedentary and boring activities should not, perhaps, be done straight after lunch as there is a danger of falling asleep. You should be aware of your own pattern of alertness and adjust your work accordingly.

Our immediate surroundings often have a powerful influence on our behaviour. For example, some surroundings we associate with relaxation, whilst others are associated with work. It is desirable to keep the two separate. If they are not kept separate there is a danger of the surroundings stimulating the wrong behaviour. At the very least it will cause confusion as we try to decide which behaviour is appropriate. For example, we normally associate bed with sleeping. Frequent bouts of insomnia, in which you lie awake in bed, will confuse this association. Bed will become associated with lying awake, often worrying. For this reason it is better to get up and return to bed when you feel ready to sleep. Likewise, you should try to keep the surroundings in which you relax different from those in which you work. If you want to relax at work, move to another chair, or another part of the workplace.

As we have seen elsewhere, other people are an important element in influencing our behaviour. They are the source of some of the most powerful reinforcers. In addition, social cognitive theory demonstrates their importance as 'models' for behaviour. We can influence our own behaviour by choosing the company we keep. This will, of course, also vary with time. At work we may choose those who act as a work-related model. Outside work, other factors will influence our choice.

Managing the behaviour. In managing the behaviour there are two major points that should be borne in mind.

- First, it is essential to have clear indications as to when the desired behaviour has been achieved. 'Mastery criteria' for success should be established and should be as precise and unambiguous as possible.

- Second, most complex skilled behaviours cannot be learnt in one step. Progressive small steps, which meet specific mastery criteria are required. Progression to the next stage should not take place until these criteria are fulfilled.

A particularly nice example of the use of mastery criteria is given in a light-hearted experiment conducted by researchers at Bowling Green State University (Simek and O'Brien, 1981). This experiment also demonstrates the advantage of having reinforcers as close to the behaviour as possible. The experiment involved teaching two groups of novices to play golf. The 'traditional' method of teaching golf starts with the drive from the tee. The experimenters argued that the main reinforcement was not driving the ball, but seeing it go into the hole. Therefore, they developed a coaching scheme based upon starting with putting and working back to driving. For each part of the coaching sessions specific behaviours were developed, together with specific mastery criteria. Examples of these are shown in Figure 12.1.

Step	Shot	Mastery Criterion
1	10 inch putt	4 putts consecutively holed
2	16 inch putt	4 putts consecutively holed
3	2 foot putt	4 putts consecutively holed
5	4 foot putt	2 holed, 2 out of 4 within 6 inches
9	20 foot putt	4 consecutively within 18 inches
13	65 foot chip	4 out of 6 within 6 feet
17	75 yard shot	4 out of 6 within 30 feet
19	125 yard shot	4 out of 6 within 45 feet
23	Driving	

Figure 12.1. Steps in a behavioural approach to learning golf.
(Adapted from: Simek and O'Brien, 1981)

As can be seen, the behaviours are specific and proceed in small, but progressive, steps from putting to driving. Two experimental groups were used; one received eight lessons of traditional coaching, the other group eight lessons using the behavioural approach. All the participants were novices and were allocated at random to one or other of the two groups. The final test of the effectiveness was to play the two groups against each other. The 'behavioural' group beat the 'traditional' group by an average of 17 strokes over 18 holes!

Managing the consequences

Exercise

Before reading further you may wish to try the following exercise.

- Working alone, identify your main job activities.

- Rank the items on the list in their order of 'preference' i.e. from 'liked' to 'disliked' (high to low probability).

- Get one of your colleagues to do the same for their job and then exchange your lists (but *not* the rank order of preferences).

- Rank the other person's items according to your preferences.

- Compare your rankings with the other person's, and discuss any differences.

We have discussed the concept of reinforcement in an earlier chapter (see Chapter 5). Reinforcement is what keeps behaviour going. Therefore, when trying to change any behaviour, including our own, we need to operate on two fronts. Desirable behaviour should be reinforced, and those reinforcers that are maintaining the undesirable behaviour need to be identified and removed. For example, cups of coffee taken with others, as well as being thirst quenching, often have social reinforcers that lead to prolonged breaks. Taking coffee in one's own office does not.

Reinforcers vary from person to person. In order to self-manage effectively you need to develop your own list of reinforcers.

The exercise above is a method of identifying the naturally-occurring reinforcers in your job. It is based on the Premack Principle (see page 168). Preferred aspects of your job can be used as reinforcers for doing the less-liked parts. You should also try to identify other things that you can use as reinforcers. The easiest way is by making a list. Another way of discovering what we find reinforcing is by self-observation. Given a free hand, we will tend to spend more time on those activities we enjoy. Self-recording our own behaviour may lead us to discover reinforcers of which we were unaware.

As we have seen, the attainment of self-set goals can act as a reinforcer. Improvements in our performance are, however, often incremental rather than dramatic. In order that we can keep track of small, but steady, improvements a prominent record of successful progress to date should be kept. (This is a technique often used in weight reduction programmes.) A nice example of such self-monitoring and self-management, albeit by a group rather than one individual, came as a result of teaching these techniques to managers. (We are grateful to Bob Ballard of Courtaulds for the use of this example.) A group of managers decided to try to improve the efficiency of their meetings. Following the procedure described earlier for improving safety (see page 169), they developed a checklist of desirable behaviours (see Figure 12.2). Self-observations were then recorded in a similar way to that for the safety checklists. Although quantitative data are not available to the authors, the plot of percentage of desirable behaviours showed a strong upward trend.

1.   Meetings to start no more than two minutes late

2.   No one to arrive after the meeting starts (count number late)

3.   No one to leave meeting without explanation (count number)

4.   No deviation from planned routine (count number of times)

5.   Action points passed over without clarification (count number)

6.   Action points agreed but not recorded (count number)

7.   Action points not progressed by next meeting (count number)

Figure 12.2. Behaviour checklist for meetings

Social reinforcement, as we have seen, is a very powerful source of reinforcement for most people. For this reason it is often useful to involve someone actively in your self-management programme. As we mentioned above, self-reporting at weight reduction classes often leads to weight loss. Evidence suggests, however, that whether the weight loss is maintained depends on the support of others, in particular the person's spouse or partner.

The timing of reinforcement is also important. Final goals, such as an increase in annual sales, are often far in the future. In order not to become disheartened, small, but immediate, 'interim reinforcers' should be used to maintain the behaviour leading to the desired goal. Reward yourself after you have made a certain number of customer calls.

Finally, and on a related note, it should be remembered that the following is common to all attempts to change behaviour:

An immediate consequence is stronger than a delayed consequence, whether it is reinforcement or punishment.

In other words, immediate reinforcers (even small ones) are stronger than delayed consequences, whether they are strong punishment or even a stronger reinforcement. In the same way immedi-

ate punishment is stronger than delayed reinforcers e.g. looking fool-
ish when practising a new skill (immediate punishment) is stronger
than the delayed reinforcement of successful skill acquisition.

Anything that can be done to ensure that reinforcement is as immediate as possible will assist the desired change. It is interesting to
note that the speed with which drugs have their effect is related to the
speed with which they produce their pleasant effects. Nicotine takes
about two seconds to reach the brain after inhalation. (This is perhaps
why 'crack' cocaine is so addictive. Its effects are almost instanta-
neous.)

So far we have looked at how the antecedents and consequences
can be changed in order to produce desired changes in your own behaviour. In doing so we have drawn on the 'basic' BMod described in
Chapter 5. Let us now consider the extensions made by social cognitive theory and see how these may be harnessed in order to improve
our own performance.

COGNITIVE SELF-MANAGEMENT

Social cognitive theory, whilst recognizing the importance of reinforcement, also places emphasis on thought process and beliefs,
especially those concerning the 'self'. These beliefs, especially self-efficacy, have an important influence on goal-setting. The setting of
goals and the development of plans for their achievement play an important part in self-management. Such self-management techniques
can be used to achieve goals that we have been set by others. In many
cases, however, self-management involves not only the management
of the behaviour required to achieve the goal, but also deciding what
these goals shall be.

Self-management requires therefore:

• choosing what goals and standards to apply

• preparing a plan of action

• taking action

• evaluating the results of the action.

Choosing goals and standards. We have already discussed the two
main influences on the goals that people will self-set. Self-efficacy,
our belief in our ability to achieve our goals, will obviously have an
influence on the goals we set ourselves, in the same way that it influences other people's goal setting. This will be influenced by the factors we discussed earlier. For example, it is likely to be heavily

influenced by our past performances and, in particular, by our attributions for our past success or failure.

Another influence will be the discrepancy between our current performance and our new goals. The size of the perceived discrepancy between these two will have effects on our motivation. As we have seen, people will tend to set standards that they feel they have a realistic opportunity of achieving. Whilst a moderately sized discrepancy will be motivating, too large a discrepancy will be de-motivating. This will obviously influence, and also be influenced by, self-efficacy.

This self-creation of discrepancies highlights another essential difference between regulating systems and self-regulating systems. Most simple regulating systems, such as a thermostatically controlled heating system, are designed to *reduce* any discrepancy between the current state and the set standard. A self-regulating system, on the other hand, sets its own standards. This means that it can also change those standards. In doing so it can deliberately introduce discrepancies. For example, even though they have achieved a standard, people will often then set themselves an even higher standard and try to attain that. We need only watch people playing computer games to see an example of this.

Planning. Planning, like choosing, is essentially *cognitive*. As a consequence, planning and choosing are closely linked, and influence each other. For example, our assessments of the probable success or failure of our plans will influence the goals we set. The planning and choosing stages can be seen as a form of cognitive simulation. Possible behaviours and their likely outcomes and consequences are tried out mentally, before being tried 'for real'. In fact the whole of the cycle described above is tried out mentally and modified as the result of this simulation.

We have discussed elsewhere (page 156) the way in which behaviours are modelled. As part of this modelling Bandura (1986) suggests that a cognitive representation of the behaviour is formed. This then forms the basis for mental rehearsal of the behaviour.

There is another aspect of this mental rehearsal that has, until recently, received less attention. This is the mental simulation of the outcomes and consequences of the imagined behaviour. These also form part of the representation, often referred to as *mental imagery*.

Mental imagery. The use of mental imagery techniques has recently moved into fashion in organizational psychology (e.g. Neck and Manz, 1992). Such techniques have long been advocated by 'popular' authors such as Norman Vincent Peale in books with titles such as *The Power of Positive Thinking* (1990). Until recently, however, such techniques tended to be 'looked down on' by many professional psychologists.

One reason for this was the lack of any theoretical basis for the techniques. Developments in cognitive psychology and in clinical psychology have, however, provided theoretical and empirical support. In practical terms the techniques of mental imagery have had most application in clinical psychology. More recently they have been applied, apparently with considerable success, in sports psychology (see Neck and Manz, 1992).

Mental imagery entails the mental creation or recreation of the whole, or part, of an event. This occurs in the absence of the sensory stimulation normally associated with the event in real life. We have already discussed the role of mental imagery in the planning of the behaviour. Possible alternatives can be imagined and strategies tentatively worked out to cope with them. This applies not only to behavioural strategies, but also to emotional strategies. This is especially useful where the emotions associated with the behaviour are stressful. For example, speaking in public is considered by many to be stressful. For those who have done it many times, however, the repeated experience leads to a gradual reduction in stress levels. The repeated mental imagining of the behaviour acts in some ways like having the experience itself. Although not as vivid as the actual experience, the mental imaging allows emotions to be anticipated, and coping strategies developed. (This technique is sometimes used in the treatment of phobias. People suffering from an irrational fear of, for example, spiders are taught relaxation exercises. They then have to maintain the relaxed state whilst imagining that there is a spider nearby.)

There is another function fulfilled by mental imagery that is less obvious. Surprisingly perhaps, the outcome of an imagined event will influence the individual's level of confidence in their ability to perform successfully. If the event is imagined as having a positive outcome the level of confidence will be higher than if a negative outcome is imagined. Why should this be so, when it is happening only in the imagination?

In an earlier chapter we looked at some of the effects of human beings as limited capacity information-processors. As we saw, in order to cope with this limited capacity people use certain 'short-cuts' when processing information. These normally work well but may in certain circumstances lead to 'biases' in our judgements. One of these affects the way we estimate of the likelihood of an event occurring.

As a general rule, the more frequently we have experienced a particular event, the easier it is to recall. The information-processing 'short-cut' that we use when estimating the probability of it happening again is based on this reasonable assumption. This is known as the *availability heuristic*. We judge the probability of an event occurring in the future by the ease with which we can recall it having happened in the past (Tversky and Kahneman, 1974). This method of estimating probabilities usually works quite well. It is, however, subject to other influences which produce the 'bias'. In short, anything that increases the ease with which we can recall an event will lead to an increase in our estimates of probability of it happening again. For example, one of the factors that can influence probability estimates is extensive media coverage of events. Programmes that report and recreate crimes are likely to increase people's estimates of the probability of crime occurring. An interesting example of this was reported on BBC Radio. The report investigated the growing number of parents in the UK who will not let their children travel to school alone. The reason given by parents was the fear of attacks on their children, in particular fatal attacks. The programme pointed out, however, that the murder rate of children was, in fact, higher in the 1960s than in the 1990s. The number of children murdered by strangers in the UK has remained, according to the programme, relatively stable since the Second World War, averaging 5 per year. Many people are also surprised to find that the overall murder rate in the UK is almost the same in the 1990s as it was in the 1930s. This figure is also half of what it was in Victorian times! Yet many people think we live in a more murderous society. Similarly, the UK is a safer place, in terms of violent crime, than Canada, Australia, and New Zealand. Within the UK the group *least* at risk is women over the age of 64. Interestingly, however, people's *perceptions* of the risk of being a victim of violent crime is highest in the UK, and also highest in women over 64. These over-estimations may be interpreted as media coverage increasing the ease with which these events can be recalled and hence our estimates of their occurrence. (This is also, perhaps why lotteries seek to publicize big wins. It increases our estimate of the chances of winning, and hence we are more likely to buy a ticket.)

Ease of recall can also be influenced by imagination. Imagining an event has much the same effect as recalling it. Indeed, the more often an event it is imagined the more probable it is to be judged as likely to occur. For example, people who have a fear of flying often find themselves imagining plane crashes with increasing regularity as the time for their flight approaches. (Any parent who has lain awake waiting for a teenage child to return home in the early hours will have experienced a similar effect.)

We can now see how mental imagery of successfully achieving a performance goal can increase the possibility of it occurring. By repeated mental imagery of success the person's probability of success is increased. This, in itself, increases self-confidence and feelings of self-efficacy. This leads to an increased likelihood of success, which itself has a positive effect on self-efficacy. In fact a 'virtuous' (rather than a 'vicious') circle is created.

Mental imagery is one method of cognitive self-regulation. An associated technique is that of positive 'self-talk'.

Self-talk. The most powerful method by which we regulate, or are regulated by, others is through the medium of language. It is the same for self-regulation. Much of our behaviour is influenced by 'internal communications' (Beck, 1976).

The way in which self-talk influences performance is slightly different from the way in which mental imagery has its effect. Both mental imagery and self-talk influence performance by influencing 'thought patterns' (Neck and Manz, 1992). Whilst mental imagery has a *direct* influence on thought patterns, the effect of self-talk is *indirect*. To be precise, self-talk, according to Neck and Manz, has its effect by influencing our 'emotional state', which then influences thought patterns. These then influence performance.

The mechanisms by which self-talk has effect are not as well understood as those of mental imagery. However, it is possible to speculate as to how it achieves its effects. One way is likely to be by self-attribution. As we have seen previously, attributions for success or failure have an emotional effect. This emotional effect will then have an effect on our thought patterns. These thoughts are likely to be what is referred to as 'mood congruent'. In other words, there is a tendency for thoughts to influenced by, and similar to, the prevailing mood. When we are depressed thoughts tend to be generally negative. Another likely mechanism by which self-talk influences behaviour is via its influence upon perceived self-efficacy. As Bandura (1982) points out, self-efficacy is a process of 'self-persuasion'. Such self-persuasion often takes the form of an internal dialogue. (In TA this would be interpreted as internal transactions between the various ego states.)

However self-talk achieves its effects, there is evidence to suggest that positive self-talk can have an important and beneficial effect on performance. In clinical settings both Ellis and Beck advocate its use in treating emotional disorders. As with mental imagery, it is perhaps in sports psychology that the technique is most widely used (see Neck and Manz, 1992).

The methods of self-talk vary slightly, but those suggested by Bandura (1986) are common to many, including Beck (1976).

Positive 'self-talk' involves the following steps:

1. Monitor thoughts. As with the five step approach to behavioural change (see Chapter 5), the first step is to identify the thoughts concerned, and how often they occur.

2. Pin-point negative talk. Some self-talk will be positive, some

negative. The negatives need to be identified and their contents analysed. In TA terms the content will need to be subjected to analysis by the Adult. Are the thoughts rational or, as is more likely, is discounting occurring?

3. Stop negative thoughts. Following behavioural principles, behaviour to be discouraged should be punished as soon as it occurs. There are a number of techniques for doing this but one of the most effective is probably 'thought stopping'. As soon as the negative thought is detected, you should say out loud (or under your breath if out loud would be embarrassing) 'STOP!' This has the effect of interrupting the thoughts. At first you may find yourself doing this fairly frequently and loudly. After a time, however, you will find the thoughts occurring less frequently, and you may not even have to verbalize the 'stop'. (This technique is also useful for suppressing recurrent thoughts that may prevent you getting a good night's sleep.)

4. Accentuate the positive. Not only must the negative be consistently punished, but the positive thoughts should be reinforced. You may try to use tangible reinforcers, as discussed in the section on behavioural self-management. It is more likely, however, that your reward will be self-administered praise. (The internal Adult stroking the internal Child.)

Some examples of self-talk, given by Quick and Quick (1984), are shown in Figure 12.3.

Positive self-talk is, in itself, only a tool. You must undertake behaviour if improvements are to be achieved. As we have noted before, behavioural change is quicker than cognitive change. In addition, changing behaviour often leads to a change in attitudes.

Situation	Typical Mental Monologue	Constructive Self-talk Alternative
Difficulty with a superior at work	'I hate that person' 'He makes me feel stupid' 'We'll never get along'	'I don't feel comfortable with him' 'I let myself get on edge when he's around' 'It will take some effort to get along with him'
Driving to work on a day which you know will be full of appointments and potentially stressful meetings	'Oh boy, what a day this will be!' 'It's going to be hell' 'I'll never get it all done' 'It'll be exhausting'	'This looks like a busy day' 'The day should be very productive' 'I'll get a lot accomplished today' 'I'll earn a good night's rest today'

Figure 12.3. Constructive self-talk.
(Source: Quick and Quick, 1984)

Having either taken action, or imagined it, the next stage is to evaluate the outcome.

Evaluation. Evaluation involves the comparison of the current state with the self-set standard. The process of evaluation keeps our behaviour in line with those standards. Alternatively, it may lead us to revise those standards.

The emotional and motivational effects of evaluation are probably best understood in terms of attribution theory (see page 95). That discussion was, at least implicitly, about standards or goals that had been set by others. There is an additional factor to be taken into account with self-set standards and goals. In talking about standards we have assumed that they are set in a social vacuum, i.e. without reference to other people's standards. This is obviously not the case. The standards of others will naturally have some influence on our own, as will our goal orientation (see Chapter 5).

Consideration of the evaluation stage brings us full circle back to the choice, or standard-setting stage. If the standard has not been reached, further decisions have to be taken. Further effort may be invested, or standards changed or reassessed. Self-efficacy may be enhanced or diminished. Alternatively, it may be decided that it is pointless investing further effort into what may be perceived as a hopeless task. Many of these factors will be influenced by the support that the organization provides to encourage effective self-management.

SELF-MANAGEMENT AND THE ORGANIZATION

Many of the steps that the organization can take to help people become more empowered and self-managing are covered in other sections of the book. However, there is one further technique that will help one move from managerial control to self-control. This technique has been developed so as to minimize the possibility of anxiety and counter-dependence.

TRANSITIONAL CONTINGENCY CONTRACTING

Contingency contracting (Homme and Tosti, 1971) is a technique for negotiating a contract for change, and bringing it about. It is done openly, normally between supervisor and subordinate. The basic process is that the behaviour required, and the reinforcement being offered, are clearly specified. There are a number of rules that guide the way the contract is specified:

1. It must be clear, fair, and based on reinforcement, *not* punishment.

2. The initial contract should require immediate reinforcement for the achievement of small steps (shaping).

3. The criteria for achievement should be clearly specified. The criteria should include both quantity and quality specifications, and should require independent accomplishment, *not* obedience to authority.

The procedure requires that control, both of the tasks to be performed and the reinforcers received, is gradually transferred from the manager to the subordinate. For this reason the whole process is known as *transitional* contingency contracting. Homme and Tosti present a logical structure by which this may be achieved. They suggest that there are five different *levels* and three different *forms* of contracting. These are shown in Figure 12.4.

On the left-hand side of the figure (level 1) the manager has control over both the task being done and the reinforcement being offered. The decisions are the manager's alone. At the right-hand side (level 5), control of both task and reinforcer has been transferred to the sub-

Level

Form	1	2	3	4	5
1	R–M T–M	R–MS T–M	R–MS T–MS	R–S T–MS	R–S T–S
2		R–M T–MS	R–S T–M	R–MS T–S	
3			R–M T–S		

R   = control of the reinforcer
T   = control of the task

M   = control by manager
S   = control by subordinate
MS = joint control by both manager and subordinate

Figure 12.4. Transitional contingency contracting.
(Adapted from: Berthold, 1982)

ordinate. The decisions now lie with the subordinate alone. In between these levels are the transitional levels and forms by which control is gradually transferred. These involve situations in which there is a mix of decision-making. Sometimes the manager decides what the task or reinforcer should be. Sometimes the subordinate decides, and sometimes the decision is a joint one. These levels (2, 3, and 4) are more complicated, and require a little explanation. This is perhaps best achieved by using a 'points' system.

Control by the manager (M), either of task (T) or reinforcer (R) counts as 3 points. Control by the subordinate (S), either of task (T) or reinforcer (R) counts as 1 point. Joint control (MS) involves the manager and the subordinate deciding *together* what task shall be done and what reinforcement will follow. This joint control counts as 2 points. Using this system it is clear that level 1 scores 6 points (both task and reinforcer are under the manager's control; 3 points each). Level 5, on the other hand scores 2 (both task and reinforcer are under the subordinate's control; 1 point each). It is now easy to calculate the degree of control at each level. In level 3, for example, the total points are 4. There are three different ways in which the total of 4 points can be achieved. Form 1 achieves this by $2 + 2$, form 2 by $1 + 3$, and form 3 by $3 + 1$.

This may seem to be an elaborate process, but there is evidence that it is necessary to go through all the stages if the transfer of control is to take place smoothly. Berthold (1982), for example, reports a case where production requirements prompted a manager to move quickly through the sequence, omitting some stages. This created 'total confusion' and 'a growing sense of resentment among workers'. This is counter-dependence, created by too rapid a release of control.

Transitional contingency contracting is one way of moving from dependence to interdependence, via mutual dependence. It is a gradual process, negotiated at each stage. The subordinate ends up in control both of the task and the reinforcement, and is capable of working totally independently. In appropriate systems this might be a possibility. However, in most organizational settings it will be necessary to co-ordinate tasks and negotiate how new tasks are to be handled. In most situations, therefore, the aim of transitional contingency contracting will be to produce an outcome somewhere between mutual dependence and inter-dependence, ideally closer to the latter.

The aim of transitional contingency contracting is to overcome dependence in such a way as to avoid the worst of counter-dependence. The approach adopted by TA has a concept similar to that of dependence, known as symbiosis.

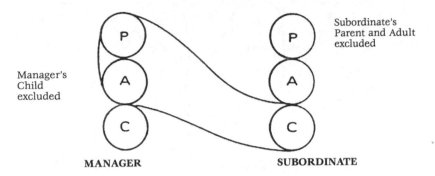

Figure 12.5. Symbiosis

SYMBIOSIS

In hierarchical, authority-based, organizations most managers operate primarily from Parent and Adult, and the subordinate from Adapted Child, with the Adult and Parent excluded. Miyajima and Cox (1987) found evidence that this is, in fact, the relationship preferred by British managers. In TA this relationship is known as *symbiosis* (Schiff 1975) and is shown diagrammatically in Figure 12.5. What the diagram illustrates is that the subordinate has needs which he or she believes can only be met by the manager. When the manager and subordinate are operating in this way they are, in effect, acting as one person, rather than as two interrelated, autonomous individuals. It is also very common in organizations for 'symbiotic chains' to exist (as in Figure 12.6). Each level of management operates from Parent and

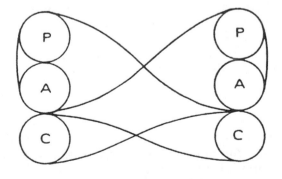

Figure 12.6. Mutual symbiosis

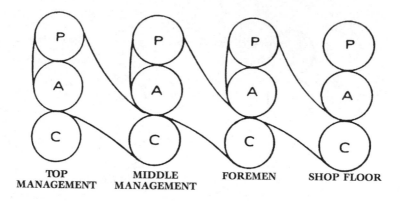

Figure 12.7. Symbiotic chains

Adult to the Child of their subordinates, but in turn relating to their superiors from Adapted Child. Mutual symbiosis (as in Figure 12.7) can also occur, and is the equivalent of mutual dependence.

The effect of a symbiotic relationship is that the dependent partner believes he can only get strokes (recognition) by pleasing the other. The stroke supply is seen as limited, and conditional upon compliance. A further characteristic of this situation is that individual growth is limited, and effective adaptation to change is difficult. This is because one partner (the subordinate) believes that they cannot judge, think or decide effectively for themselves. The other partner (the manager), feels that they are not allowed to care for their own needs, but must always care for, or control, the other. Both partners are likely to experience frustration, feelings of inadequacy and depression. (Some marriages and partnerships may be symbiotic.) This can be acute at the lower end of a symbiotic chain where the individual has no subordinates, and therefore spends their whole working life in the dependent position. At this stage the frustration is likely to escalate into a general feeling that 'There is nothing I can do', and productivity is replaced by *passivity*.

PASSIVITY

Passivity is the probable result of a symbiotic relationship, and there are four possible types of passive behaviour:

- Simply doing nothing. Often this stems from the general feeling that there is nothing that can be done. In more extreme cases this can be accompanied by feelings of resentment and depression. In this case Child energy is being used to inhibit responses or, in other words, in passive resistance. (There are obvious links with the concept of learned helplessness.)

- Over-adaptation. This is extreme compliance. The person carries out whatever is asked of them, often appearing very anxious to please. However, the activity is characterized by lack of involvement and creativity, as energy is being used in compliance. The person may become very anxious if their efforts to please appear not to be recognized.

- Agitation. This is the use of energy in purposeless non-productive activities, for example, excessive and irrelevant talking, pacing about, and lighting cigarettes.

- Incapacitation or violence. This is the last stand against change and the possible breaking of symbiosis. The person simply becomes ill (gets ulcers, asthma, headaches) or loses their temper. Either way the dominant partner is effectively kept in control either by having to look after the other, or calm them down. The dependent partner can happily stay in dependence.

This situation in organizations has been very well described by Wallgren (1975);

'In organizations where the symbiotic relationship exists, the total organization is ineffective. In an effort to expand the direct span of control the top management makes and enforces rules in such a way as to reduce the ability of the individual member to accomplish in a stroke producing manner. In an effort to maintain a more favourable stroke balance members adopt passive behaviour patterns. They do the minimum possible amount of work, i.e. they do nothing. They compliantly do only what they are ordered to do, i.e. they over adapt. They file grievances over meaningless issues, i.e. they agitate to avoid the real issues. They engage in power plays, which may include violent acts of organizational sabotage. The organizational impact of passivity is decreased effectiveness and increased frustration for all personnel.'

Reducing passivity and dependence. Passivity involves discounting. The symbiosis is maintained because both partners discount their own abilities for independent action. The way to break out is to confront the discount, by presenting Adult data. What this will often do is to move the individual down the discount matrix, to discounting at a lower level. In terms of behaviour this moves the individual down the sequence of passive behaviours. If the 'do nothing' stage is challenged, the individual moves to over-adaptation, to show that they really want to be co-operative; when this is challenged they become agitated. At the final stage, if they become ill this 'proves' that they really do need to be looked after.

One of the authors once experienced this exact sequence when running a training programme. It was with middle managers from a very authoritarian but benevolent organization. The first day of the programme was characterized by a high degree of compliance. Participants were politely doing as they were asked, but with no enthusiasm. No one was learning anything. When the trainers drew attention to this behaviour, the group moved straight into over-adaptation. The next session happened to be a practical exercise and the participants went busily about everything they had to do, with a great appearance of wishing to be helpful. They came back at the end, sat down and looked expectantly at the trainers, waiting to be told what to do next. Still no learning. When this was confronted they went into agitation – 'We're doing our best, what else do you want us to do?' When the trainers said 'We want you to take responsibility for learning', they began to get angry. This was followed by a fairly confrontational discussion of what the programme was about, which lead to some role negotiation (see Chapter 9). The trainers built in a little more structure and the participants agreed to take more control. People began to learn things. What this sequence did was, at least partially, to break out of the symbiosis which the managers were transferring from the organization to the trainers. Discussion of this issue provided some insight for the participants, who were, it is hoped, able to transfer some of this learning back to the organization.

We have so far talked about reducing the possibility of counter-dependence and symbiosis in the subordinates. However, the effect on the managers should not be overlooked. Ideally, the process should not 'jump' levels. The contracting should be between the subordinate and their immediate boss. This leads to the transfer 'cascading' down the organization.

This fact was brought home to two of the authors when they were implementing a behaviourally-based safety scheme in a large factory. The scheme (described in Chapter 5) required that the shop-floor workers become responsible for deciding on 'safe behaviours' and monitoring their own performance. The decision to employ the authors as consultants and to implement the scheme had, of course, been taken at board level. A senior manager was given the job of assisting the authors and, eventually, taking over the on-going scheme. The presence of this manager had considerable advantages. It demonstrated, for example, that senior management were committed to the scheme and thought it important. Senior management were, therefore, devolving power directly to the shop floor. Some way into the scheme the authors noticed signs of anxiety and resistance among middle managers. On investigation they realized that the middle managers felt threatened by their perceived loss of control. They felt 'bypassed' and isolated. Increasing the control of one individual, or group of individuals, may often be seen as reducing the control of others.

This demonstrates two important lessons. First, any change in an organization will have effects other than those for which it is directly intended. Some of these may be foreseen, others may not. Second, even experienced professionals sometimes make mistakes! Later, within the same organization, the authors were involved in the introduction of a behaviourally-based approach to quality. Every attempt was made to ensure that the middle managers were actively involved in the introduction of the scheme. Care should be taken, when empowering some, that others do not feel that they are losing power. Everybody should feel empowered. It should, if at all possible, be a 'non-zero sum game' (see page 233).

EMPOWERMENT, SELF-MANAGEMENT, AND THE PSYCHOLOGICAL CONTRACT

Empowerment and self-management, almost by definition, involve a major change in the psychological contract. From the individual's perspective there is greater opportunity for autonomy, and the possibility of greater control over one's work. With this comes the opportunity to fulfil higher-order needs, but also additional responsibility. For the organization the potential for a more motivated and committed work-force is balanced against the possible costs of errors due to decisions being taken at lower levels. These dangers can, however, be minimized using the techniques we have discussed. A well-planned and openly re-negotiated move to greater self-management is essentially, however, a non-zero sum game. Both parties stand to gain from the new psychological contract.

APPENDIX 1: TYPE A QUESTIONNAIRE (*ADAPTED FROM: BORTNER, 1969*)

Please circle the number which you feel most closely represents your own behaviour.

a) Never late   5 4 3 2 1 0 1 2 3 4 5   Casual about appointments, easygoing

b) Not competitive   5 4 3 2 1 0 1 2 3 4 5   Very competitive

c) Anticipates what others are going to say (nods, interrupts, finishes for them)   5 4 3 2 1 0 1 2 3 4 5   Good listener

d) Always rushed   5 4 3 2 1 0 1 2 3 4 5   Never feels rushed (even under pressure)

e) Can wait patiently   5 4 3 2 1 0 1 2 3 4 5   Impatient whilst waiting

f) Goes all out   5 4 3 2 1 0 1 2 3 4 5   Casual

g) Takes things one at a time   5 4 3 2 1 0 1 2 3 4 5   Tries to do many things at once, thinks about what he or she is about to do next

h) Emphatic in speech (may pound desk)   5 4 3 2 1 0 1 2 3 4 5   Slow, deliberate talker

i) Wants good job recognized by others   5 4 3 2 1 0 1 2 3 4 5   Cares about satisfying himself/herself no matter what others may think

j) Fast (eating, walking, etc.)   5 4 3 2 1 0 1 2 3 4 5   Slow doing things

k) Easygoing   5 4 3 2 1 0 1 2 3 4 5   Hard driving

l) Hides feelings   5 4 3 2 1 0 1 2 3 4 5   Expresses feelings

m) Many outside interests   5 4 3 2 1 0 1 2 3 4 5   Few outside interests

n) Satisfied with job   5 4 3 2 1 0 1 2 3 4 5   Ambitions

SCORING

Each item scores on an 11 point scale, but some of the scales are reversed i.e. sometimes 1 is the '5' at the the left hand side and sometimes the '5' at the right. The '0' always score six.
The following scales score from 1 on the left to 11 on the right:

b, e, g, k, m, n

The following scales score from 11 on the left to 1 on the right.

a, c, d, f, h, i, j, l

Your score is the sum total of all the scales.
For an interpretation of your score see the text (page 76).

APPENDIX 2: *CASE STUDY – 'TAKE A MEMO'*

You are John Andrews, the manager of a department in a large civil engineering firm. The function of one of the sections of your department is to examine contracts, in fine detail, to ensure that the firm receives every payment to which it is entitled, and that payments to sub-contractors are justified. Mistakes can be extremely costly.

Answering to you are 16 clerks, some of whom have been trained by the company, others who have been recruited from other, similar, companies. There is a range of experience in the group, and a small number receive extra salary in recognition of their greater experience. These individuals do not, however, have any formal seniority and are at the same level as the others. Although much of the work follows a pattern, non-standard situations do occur. The rules state that any queries or problems that are encountered have to be referred upwards to you. Your department has, on rare occasions, to send someone to assist on contracts elsewhere in the country. These temporary postings are not liked by your staff. At present you are just about coping with your present numbers of staff.

Recently a serious mistake occurred on one of the contracts, resulting in the company being unable to recover £150,000 for work it had done. On investigation you find that a less experienced clerk, James Slater, had come across a problem and, rather than approach you, sought advice from one of the more experienced clerks. As it turned out, the advice was incorrect. You interviewed the clerk responsible for the job, who admitted going outside the official channel, even though he was fully aware of the rules. He also admitted that he had every opportunity to come and seek your advice. The only explanation he can offer is that he 'didn't want to bother you'.

On arriving at your desk this morning, you find some memos await-
ing you from the following people.

Bob Jeffries: Contracts Director (Your boss's boss)
Bill Owen: Contracts Manager (Your boss)
Steve Holland: One of the managers of a department with which
                 you have to liaise and work
Mary Gibson: Manager of the Personnel Department.
James Slater: The clerk who made the error.

MEMORANDUM A

To: J Andrews
From: Mr B Jeffries – Contracts Director

It has come to my attention that, because of a mistake by your department, the company stands to lose at least £150,000 on the
Lakeside contract. I hold you personally responsible.

I will not tolerate this kind of inefficiency and slackness in managers who are under my control. I demand an immediate explanation
and to know what you are going to do about it.

MEMORANDUM B

To: All Departmental Managers
From: Mr B Jeffries – Contracts Director

It has been brought to my notice that timekeeping in my part of the
company is bad.

All departmental managers will send a memo concerning this matter to every member of staff under their control.

MEMORANDUM C

To: Mr Andrews
From: J Slater

As a result of the error concerning the Lakeside contract I feel that I
have no option but to offer my resignation.

Although I accept that I broke the rules concerning this matter, I
followed the course of action that has become common practice in the
department and believed, at the time, that I was behaving correctly.

MEMORANDUM D

To: John Andrews
From: Bill Owen

I've just had a meeting concerning the payments on the Lakeside contracts which you told me about yesterday. I now consider this to be 'water under the bridge' but perhaps you could you let me have your suggestions as to what we can do in order to ensure it doesn't happen again.

MEMORANDUM E

To: John Andrews
From: Steve Holland

John.

Can you possibly help me, I'm really in a jam. One of my clerks is leaving on Friday and his replacement will not arrive for three weeks. Any chance that you can help me out by lending me one of yours until then. I'm really stuck and would appreciate it.

Cheers!
Steve

Handwritten note, stapled and marked 'confidential', from Steve Holland.

John

Have you seen the memo over timekeeping from that sod Jeffries! Typical of him! What about meeting for a pint after work today and figuring out how we can get our own back? I'm really fed up with his attitude towards us.

Steve

MEMORANDUM G

To: John Andrews
From: Bill Owen

The Contracts Director has informed me that three of your clerks are required on the contract in the Shetland Islands for a period of four weeks, starting next Monday.

I appreciate that this will put your department under pressure for this period, and that it will not be popular with those sent, but there are very good reasons why their presence is essential.

MEMORANDUM H

To: John Andrews
From: Mary Gibson – Personnel

I've heard that three of your clerks are required in the Shetlands from next week. Not a very popular posting by all accounts.

Is there anything that I can do to help in the way of making their lives a little more comfortable while they're up there?

APPENDIX 3: *CASE STUDY: PAY REVIEW*

Please read each of the case studies below. In each case decide:

a) what annual salary you estimate the job would command in the 'open market'
b) what annual salary you would consider to be 'fair'.

Adams: Age 45, a Chartered Civil Engineer married with one child. Has to spend long periods away from home on various construction sites. Is considered very competent and has been with the organization since leaving university.

Brown: Age 39, with a first degree in languages and a Master's degree in Business Administration (MBA). For the last five years has been a director of a large merchant bank with responsibility for corporate mergers and take-overs. Married with two young children, plus two other children from a previous marriage which ended in divorce. Works long hours, but the department is the most profitable in a highly profitable organization.

Carter: Age 48. An unskilled manual worker on a rubber products production line, working in dirty, smelly, and noisy conditions. A good worker who has been with the firm over fifteen years. Married with five children, including one with Down's syndrome.

Devlin: Age 45, the second son of an earl, educated at Eton and Oxford. Non-executive director of a clearing bank for the last ten years. Married with three children. Attends one board meeting a month. Is also on the board of a number of public companies, including 'the family firm'.

Edwards: Age 32, a Chartered Accountant. Head of credit control for a large company, responsible for a staff of 30, reporting through three supervisors. Since appointed to the job two years ago the company's cash flow has improved dramatically. Often works late. Unmarried, lives with elderly mother who is partially disabled.

Franks: Age 48, a fireman with 20 years' experience, but no formal qualifications. Held in high regard by fellow workers and management. Works shifts. Married with two 'grown up' children.

APPENDIX 4: *CASE STUDY: ABSENTEEISM*

(Adapted by D.S. Taylor from Stephens, T.A., and Burroughs, W.A. 1978) An Application of Operant Conditioning to Absenteeism in a Hospital Setting. *Journal of Applied Psychology, 63,* 518–521. Copyright by the American Psychological Society. Adapted by permission.)

Chestnut Private Hospital is having a problem with absenteeism among its nurses, porters, and administrative staff.

As with many organizations, the hospital has a sick-pay scheme that means the employees receive full pay for absences of up to six months. Self-certification is required for absences of up to three days, beyond which a doctor's certificate is required. The present problem is with a large number of short-term absences of between one and three days.

The present approach to excessive absences has involved the use of various sanctions. These have included a series of formal warnings which lead, eventually, to termination of employment. Secondary sanctions have included threats relating to opportunities for promotion and pay increases. Only 15 per cent of the staff involved belong to a trade union.

Although the daily cost of the absenteeism has not been calculated, it has been estimated that it is substantial, especially where agency nurses have to be employed to cover for absent staff.

The pay rates are well above those in the National Health Service and there is no problem with staff turnover. Because of the high pay levels the quality of staff is excellent. There is no problem with either productivity or the quality of the work. The problem seems to be solely related to short-term absenteeism.

As a consultant you have been asked to give advice as to a cost-effective solution. What do you suggest?

APPENDIX 5: *CAREER QUESTIONNAIRE*

a) I believe that the individual has little control over his career path. _____

b) I will not push for promotion until I feel the time is right. _____

c) I feel that most people exaggerate the influence they feel they have over their career path. _____

d) I sometimes feel that my career is out of my control. _____

e) In this organization it tends to be who you know rather than what you do that leads to promotion. _____

f) I feel the support of powerful people is more important than job performance in determining promotion in this organization. _____

g) It is important to be 'well-in' with the powers that be in order to get promotion. _____

h) I feel that I can improve my chances of promotion only by concentrating on those aspects of the job which my superiors will notice. _____

i) I think I needed a great deal of luck to get to my present position. _____

j) It doesn't matter how hard you work, if luck is against you, you will not succeed in a career. _____

k) There is a lot of truth in the saying that you have to be in right place at the right time in order to get promotion. _____

l) I think that you have got to have a lot of luck if you are going to get very far in your career. _____

Answer each question using the following key:

1: Strongly disagree   2: Moderately disagree
3: Slightly disagree   4: Neither agree nor disagree
5: Slightly agree   6: Moderately agree
7: Strongly agree

SCORING

Put your score for each question in the spaces provided, and carry out the calculations shown.

$$(8 \ - \frac{}{(a)}) + (8 \ - \frac{}{(b)}) + (8 \ - \frac{}{(c)}) + (8 \ - \frac{}{(d)}) \qquad = \underline{\qquad} \ (\mathbf{I})$$

$$\frac{}{(e)} + \frac{}{(f)} + \frac{}{(g)} + \frac{}{(h)} \qquad = \underline{\qquad} \ (\mathbf{P})$$

$$\frac{}{(i)} + \frac{}{(j)} + \frac{}{(k)} + \frac{}{(l)} \qquad = \underline{\qquad} \ (\mathbf{C})$$

The **I** scale measures the strength of your belief that control over your career is under your own control.

The **P** scale measures the strength of your belief that control over your career is under the control of powerful other people.

The **C** scale measures the strength of your belief that your career is controlled by luck or chance factors.

You might like to compare your score on each of the scales with those of a sample of British managers. The first figure for each scale is the average score. The second figures show the range within which approximately two-thirds of the managers' scores lay.

Internal	19	15–23
Powerful Others	16	11–21
Chance	14	10–18

APPENDIX 6: *CASE STUDY: CHANGE STRATEGIES*

You have an excellent idea for an improvement to existing procedures which will result in considerable cost savings. However, implementation of the idea will require changes in the operating procedures of several departments, and the way they interact. From past experience you expect that several heads of department will resist these changes, offering a variety of reasons as to why they will not work.

As Chief Executive which of the following approaches would you be most likely to take?

1. Discreetly sound out the reactions of each head of department,

partly to test the strengths and weaknesses of your idea, but also to establish their reactions, so that you can enlist the aid of the more enthusiastic managers to help you convert the others.

2. Send a memo to all heads of department outlining the plan and stating your intention to implement it. Follow this up with meetings with individual mangers to brief them on the necessary changes and set a timetable for change.

3. Call a meeting of all heads of department, outline your idea, and then explain that the purpose of the meeting is to consider all the implications, both positive and negative, and then make a decision about implementation. You are happy to abide by the outcome of this meeting.

4. Sound out the reactions of the heads of department. If they are strongly negative accept that the time is not right and leave the change until a more suitable occasion, on the basis that it is better to get it done properly at a later date, when conditions are more favourable, than go for a half-hearted attempt now. If they turn out to be enthusiastic, you would, of course, go ahead now.

If, after selecting one of the above, you wish to suggest some other alternative, you should make a note of it.

REFERENCES

Abramson, L.Y., Seligman, M.E., and Teasdale, J.D. (1978). Learned helplessness in humans: Critique and reformulation. *Journal of Abnormal Psychology, 87*, 49–74.

Abramson, L.Y., Metalsky, G.I., and Alloy, L.B. (1989). Hopelessness Depression: A Theory-based Subtype of Depression. *Psychological Review, 96*, 358–372.

Adair, J. (1968). *Training for Leadership.* London: Mcdonald.

Agho, A.O., Price, J.L., and Mueller, C.W. (1992). Discriminant Validity of Measures of Job Satisfaction, Positive Affectivity and Negative Affectivity. *Journal of Occupational and Organizational Psychology, 65*, 185–196.

Anderson, C.R. (1977). Locus of control, coping behaviours, and performance in a stress setting: A longitudinal study. *Journal of Applied Psychology, 62*, 446–451.

Argyris, C. (1960). *Understanding Organizational Behavior.* Homewood, Ill.: Dorsey.

Argyris, C, (1962). *Interpersonal Competence and Organizational Effectiveness.* Homewood, Ill: Dorsey.

Arvey, R.D., Carter, G.W., and Buerkley, D.K. (1991). Job Satisfaction: Dispositional and Situational Influences. In Cooper, C.L., and Robertson, I.T. (Eds) *International Review of Industrial and Organizational Psychology.* Chichester: Wiley.

Asch, S.E. (1946). Forming Impressions of Personality. *Journal of Abnormal and Social Psychology, 41*, 258–290.

Asher, J.J. and Sciarrino, J.A. (1974). Realistic Work Sample Tests: A review. *Personnel Psychology, 27*, 519–533.

Avolio, B.J., and Gibbons, T.C. (1988). Developing Transformational Leaders: A Life Span Approach. In Conger, J.A., and Kanungo, R.N. (Eds). *Charismatic Leadership: The Elusive Factor in Organizational Effectiveness.* San Francisco: Jossey-Bass.

Baddely, S. and James, K. (1987). Owl, fox, donkey and sheep: Political skills for managers. *Management Education and Development, 18*, 3–19.

Bales, R.F. (1950). *Interaction Process Analysis.* Cambridge, Mass: Addison-Wesley.

Bales, R.F. (1951). *Interaction Process Analysis: A method for the study of small groups.* Reading, Mass: Addison-Wesley.

Bandura, A. (1977). *Social Learning Theory.* Englewood Cliffs, NJ: Prentice-Hall.

Bandura, A. (1982). Self-efficacy mechanism in human agency. *American Psychologist, 37*, 122–147.

Bandura, A. (1986). *Social Foundations of Thought and Action: A Social Cognitive Theory.* Englewood Cliffs, NJ: Prentice-Hall.

Barrick, M.R., and Mount, M.K. (1991). The Big Five Personality Dimensions and Job Performance: A Meta-analysis. *Personnel Psychology, 44*, 1–26.

Barrick, M.R., and Mount, M.K. (1993). Autonomy as a Moderator of the Relationships between the Big Five Personality Dimensions and Job Performance. *Journal of Applied Psychology, 78,* 111–118.

Bartram, D, (1992). The Personality of UK Managers: 16PF Norms for Short-Listed Applicants. *Journal of Occupational and Organizational Psychology, 65,* 159–172.

Bass, B.M. (1990). From Transactional to Transformational Leadership: Learning to Share a Vision. *Organizational Dynamics, 18,* 19–31.

Beck, A.T. (1976). *Cognitive Therapy and the Emotional Disorders.* Harmondsworth: Penguin.

Beck, J. and Cox, C.J. (1984) Developing organizational skills. In C.J. Cox and J. Beck (Eds) *Management Development: Advances in practice and theory.* Chichester: Wiley.

Becker, H.S. (1960). Notes on the Concept of Commitment. *Journal of Sociology, 66,* 32–42.

Becker, H.S. (1963). Personal Change in Adult Life. *Sociometry, 27,* 32–40.

Beckhard, R. (1969). *Organizational Development: Strategies and models.* Reading, Mass: Addison-Wesley.

Belbin, R.M. (1981). *Management Teams, Why They Succeed or Fail.* London: Heinemann.

Bennis, W.G. (1969). *Organizational Development: Its nature, origins and prospects.* Reading, Mass: Addison-Wesley.

Bennis, W.G. (1983). The artform of leadership. In S. Scrivastra and associates (Eds) *The Executive Mind.* San Francisco: Jossey Bass.

Berne, E, (1968). *Games People Play.* Harmondsworth: Penguin.

Berne, E. (1972). *What Do You Say After You Say Hello?* London: Corgi.

Berry, A.J. (1994). Spanning Traditional Boundaries: Organization and Control of Embedded Operations. *Leadership and Organizational Development Journal, 15 (7),* 4–10.

Berthold, H.C. Jnr (1982). Transitional contingency contracting and the Premack principle in business. In R. O'Brien, A. Dickinson and M. Rosow (Eds) *Industrial Behavior Modification: A Management handbook.* New York: Pergamon.

Bettman J.R., and Weitz, B.A. (1983). Attributions in the Boardroom: Causal Reasoning in Corporate Annual Reports. *Administrative Science Quarterly, 28,* 165–183.

Blake, R.R., and Mouton, J.S. (1964). *The Managerial Grid.* Houston: Gulf Publishing.

Blau, P., and Schoenherr, R.A. (1971). *The Structure of Organizations.* New York: Basic.

Blinkhorn, S., and Johnson, C. (1990). The Insignificance of Personality Testing. *Nature, 348,* 671–672.

Bortner, R.W. (1969). A short rating scale as a potential measure of pattern A behaviour. *Journal of Chronic Diseases, 22,* 87–91.

Boyatzis, R.E. (1979). The Need for Close Relationships and the Manager's Job. In Kolb, D.A., Rubin, I.M., and McIntyre, J.M. *Organizational Psychology.* (3rd Ed.) Englewood Cliffs, NJ: Prentice-Hall.

Bradburn, N.M. (1969). *The Structure of Psychological Well-being.* Chicago: Aldine.

Bradbury, T.N., and Fincham F.D. (1990). Attributions in marriage: Review and critique. *Psychological Bulletin, 107,* 3–33.

Bradford, L.P., Gibb, J.R. and Benne, V.D. (1964). *T-Group Theory and Laboratory Method*. New York: Wiley.

Broadbent, D.E. (1985). The clinical impact of job design. *British Journal of Clinical Psychology, 24*, 33–44.

Brown, R. (1986). *Social Psychology: The second edition*. New York: Free Press.

Bryman, A. (1986). *Leadership in Organisations*. London: Routledge.

Bryman, A. (1992). *Charisma & Leadership in Organizations*. London: Sage.

Burns, J.M. (1978). *Leadership*. New York: Harper and Row.

Campion, M.A., and Lord, R.G. (1982). A Control Systems Conceptualization of the Goal-Setting and Changing Process. *Organizational Behavior and Human Performance, 30*, 265–287.

Campion, M.A. and McClelland, C.L. (1991). Interdisciplinary examination of the costs and benefits of enlarged jobs: A job design quasi-experiment. *Journal of Applied Psychology, 76*, 186–198.

Carver, C.S., and Scheier, M.F. (1981). *Attention and Self-Regulation: A Control Theory Approach to Human Behavior*. New York: Springer-Verlag.

Cattell, R.B. (1965). *The Scientific Analysis of Personality*. Harmondsworth: Penguin.

Cattell, R.B. (1995). The Fallacy of Five Factors in the Personality Sphere. *The Psychologist, 8*, 207–208.

Cattell, R.B., Eber, H.W. and Tasnoka, M.M. (1970). *Handbook for the Sixteen Personality Factor Questionnaire (16PF)*. Champaign, Ill: Institute for Personality and Ability Testing.

Chin, R. and Benne, K.D. (1976). General strategies for effecting changes in human systems. In W.G. Bennis, K.D. Benne, R. Chin and K.E. Carey (Eds) *The Planning of Change*. (3rd ed.) New York: Holt, Rinehart and Winston.

Collins, J.M., and Schmidt, F.L. (1993). Personality, Integrity, and White Collar Crime: A Construct Validity Study. *Personnel Psychology, 46*, 295–311.

Conger, J.A., and Kanungo, R.N. (1988). The Empowering Process: Integrating Theory and Practice. *Academy of Management Review, 13*, 471–482.

Cooper, C.L. and Makin, P.J. (1984). *Psychology for Managers*. Macmillan and The British Psychological Society. Out of print, available from libraries.

Cotgrove, S. (1967). *The Science of Society*. London: Allen and Unwin.

Cowherd, D.M., and Levine, D.I. (1992). Product Quality and Pay Equity Between Lower-level Employees and Top Management: An Investigation of Distributive Justice Theory. *Administrative Science Quarterly, 37*, 302–320.

Cox, C.J., and Cooper, C.L. (1988). *High Flyers*. Oxford: Basil Blackwell.

Cox, C.J. and Makin, P.J. (1994). Overcoming Dependence with Contingency Contracting. *Leadership and Organization Development Journal, 15* (5), 21–26.

Crouch, A., and Worth, A. (1991). Managerial Responses to Mergers and Other Job Changes. *Journal of Managerial Psychology, 6*, 3–8.

Cummings T.G. and Huse E.F. (1989). *Organization Development and Change*. (4th edn) Saint Paul, Minn: West Publishing.

Davies, H. (1994). Making it Happen: Supporting Lifelong Career Development. In *Promoting Lifelong Career Development, Anniversary Lectures*. Cambridge: Careers Research and Advisory Centre.

Davis, C., Elliott, S., Dionne, M., and Mitchell, I. (1991). The Relationship of Personality Factors and Physical Activity to Body Satisfaction in Men. *Personality and Individual Differences, 12*, 689–694.

Davis-Blake, A., and Pfeffer, J. (1989). Just a Mirage: The Search for

Dispositional Effects in Organizational Research. *Academy of Management Review, 14,* 385–400.

Deary, I.J., and Matthews, G. (1993). Personality Traits are Alive and Well. *The Psychologist, 6,* 299–311.

Deary I.J., MacLullich, A.M.J., and Mardon, J. (1991). Reporting of Minor Physical Symptoms and Family Incidence of Hypertension and Heart Disease–Relationships with Personality and Type A Behaviour. *Personality and Individual Differences, 12,* 747–751.

Deci, E.L. (1975). *Intrinsic Motivation.* New York: Plenum Press.

Deci, E.L., and Ryan, R.M. (1980). The Empirical Exploration of Intrinsic Motivational Processes. In Berkowitz, L. (Ed.). *Advances in Experimental Social Psychology. Vol 13.* New York: Academic Press.

Deiner, E., and Emmons, R.A. (1985). The Independence of Positive and Negative Affect. *Journal of Personality and Social Psychology, 47,* 1105–1117.

Dickinson, J. (1991). Values and judgements of wage differentials. *British Journal of Social Psychology, 30,* 267–270.

Dornstein, M. (1985). Perceptions regarding standards for evaluating pay equity and their determinants. *Journal of Occupational Psychology, 58,* 321–330.

Dornstein, M. (1988). Wage reference groups and their determinants: A study of blue-collar and white-collar employees in Israel. *Journal of Occupational Psychology, 61,* 221–235.

Dornstein, M. (1989). The fairness judgements of received pay and their determinants. *Journal of Occupational Psychology, 62,* 287–299.

Downs, S., Farr, R.M., and Colbeck, L. (1978). Self-Appraisal: A Convergence of Selection and Guidance. *Journal of Occupational Psychology, 51,* 171–183.

Driver, M. (1982). Career Concepts: A New Approach to Career Research. In Katz, R. (Ed.). *Career Issues in Human Resource Management.* Englewood Cliffs, NJ: Prentice-Hall.

Drucker, P. (1954). *The Practice of Management.* New York: Harper.

Dugan K.W. (1989). Ability and effort attributions: Do they affect how managers communicate performance feedback information? *Academy of Management Journal, 32,* 87–114.

Dulewicz, V., and Fletcher, C. (1982). The Relationship Between Previous Experience, Intelligence and Background Characteristics of Participants and their Performance in an Assessment Centre. *Journal of Occupational Psychology, 55,* 197–207.

Dweck, C.S. (1992). Motivational processes affecting learning. In DeLoache, J.S. (Ed.). *Current readings in child development.* Boston: Allyn and Bacon.

Ellis, A. (1976). *Humanistic Psychotherapy: The Rational-Emotive Approach.* New York: Julian Press

Eriksen, E.H. (1973). *Childhood and Society.* Harmondsworth: Penguin.

Ernst, F. (1971). The OK Corral: The grid for 'get on with'. *Transactional Analysis Journal, 1,* 4.

Eysenck, H.J. (1975). *The Equality of Man.* London: Fontana.

Eysenck, H.J. and Eysenck, S.B.G. (1977). *Psychoticism as a Dimension of Personality.* London: Hodder and Stoughton.

Eysenck, H.J. and Eysenck, M.W. (1985). *Personality and Individual Differences: A Natural Science Approach.* New York: Plenum.

Eysenck, H.J., and Nias, D.K.B. (1982). *Astrology: Science or Superstition?* London, Temple Smith.

Fayol, H. (1967). *General and Industrial Management.* London: Pitman.

Fiedler, F.E. and Chemers, M.M. (1984). *Improving Leadership Effectiveness: The leader match concept.* New York: Wiley.

Fiske, S. T. (1993). Social Cognition and Perception. *Annual Review of Psychology, 44,* 155–194.

Flanagan, J.C. (1954). The Critical Incident Technique. *Psychological Bulletin, 52,* 327–358.

Fleishman, E.A. and Harris, E.F. (1962). Patterns of leadership behaiour related to employee grievances and turnover. *Personnel Psychology, 15,* 43–56.

Fletcher, C. (1991). Candidates' Reactions to Assessment Centres and their Outcomes: A Longitudinal Study. *Journal of Occupational Psychology, 64,* 117–127.

Folger, R., and Konovsky, M.A. (1989). Effects of procedural and distributive justice on reactions to pay raise decisions. *Academy of Management Journal, 32,* 115–130.

Försterling, F. (1985). Attributional retraining: A review. *Psychological Bulletin, 98,* 495–512.

French, J.R.P. and Raven, B. (1959). The bases of social power. In D. Cartwright (Ed.) *Studies in Social Power.* Ann Arbor: Institute for Social Research, University of Michigan.

French, W.L. and Bell, C.H. (1984). *Organizational Development.* (3rd edn.) Englewood Cliffs: Prentice-Hall.

Freud, S. (1974). *New Introductory Lectures on Psychoanalysis.* Harmondsworth: Penguin.

Friedman, M.D. and Rosenman, R.H. (1974). *Type A Behaviour and Your Heart.* New York: Knopf.

Fryer, D. and Payne, R. (1986). Being Unemployed: A Review of the Literature on the Psychological Experience of Unemployment. In Cooper and Robertson (Eds). *International Review of Industrial and Organizational Psychology.* Chichester: Wiley.

Gardener M. (1985). Creating a Corporate Culture for the Eighties. *Business Horizons, Jan/Feb,* 59–63.

Gauquelin, M. (1978). *Cosmic Influences on Human Behavior.* (2nd edn.) New York: ASI.

Gibson, J.L., Ivancevich, J.M. and Donnelly, J.H. Jnr. (1985). *Organizations: Behavior, structure, process.* (5th edn.) Pano, Tex: Business Publications.

Goffman, I. (1961). *Asylums.* Harmondsworth: Penguin.

Goldsmith, W. and Clutterbuck, D. (1984). *The Winning Streak.* London: Weidenfeld and Nicholson.

Graen, G.B., Scandura, T.A., and Graen, M.R. (1986). A Field Experimental Test of the Moderating Effect of Growth–Need Strength on Productivity. *Journal of Applied Psychology, 71,* 484–491.

Gray, J (1991). *Beyond the New Right: Markets, Government and the Common Environment.* London: Routledge.

Greenberg, J. (1990). Employee Theft as a Reaction to Under-payment Inequity: The Hidden Cost of Pay Cuts. *Journal of Applied Psychology, 75,* 561–568.

Greenberg, J., and Ornstein, S. (1983). High status job title compensation for underpayment: A test of equity theory. *Journal of Applied Psychology, 68,* 285–297

Hackman, J.R, and Oldham, G.R. (1976). Motivation through the design of work: Test of a theory. *Organizational Behavior and Human Performance, 16,* 250–279.

Hackman, J.R, and Oldham, G.R. (1980). *Work Redesign.* Reading, Mass: Addison-Wesley.

Hall, D.T. (1976). *Careers in Organizations.* Santa Monica: Goodyear.

Handy, C.B. (1985). *Understanding Organisations.* Harmondsworth: Penguin.

Handy, C.B. (1994a). *The Empty Raincoat.* London: Hutchinson.

Handy C.B. (1994b). Making Sense of the Future. In *Promoting Lifelong Career Development, Anniversary Lectures.* Cambridge: Careers Research and Advisory Centre.

Harder, J.W. (1992). Play for Pay: Effects of Inequity in a Pay-for-Performance Context. *Administrative Science Quarterly, 37,* 321–335.

Harpaz, I. (1989). Non-Financial Employment Commitment: A Cross-National Comparison. *Journal of Occupational Psychology, 62,* 147–150.

Harrison, R. (1972). When power conflicts trigger team spirit. *European Business, Spring,* 27–65.

Harrison, R. (1987). *Organization Culture and Quality of Service.* London: Association for Management Education and Development.

Havelock, R.G. and Havelock, M.C. (1973). *Training for Change Agents.* University of Michigan: Institute for Social Research.

Hay, J. (1992). *Transactional Analysis for Trainers.* London: McGraw-Hill.

Headey, B. (1991). Distributive Justice and Occupational Incomes: Perception of Justice Determine Perceptions of Fact. *British Journal of Sociology, 42,* 581–596.

Heider, F. (1958). *The Psychology of Interpersonal Relations.* New York: Wiley.

Hersey, P. and Blanchard, K.H. (1982). *Management of Organizational Behavior: Utilizing human resources.* Englewood Cliffs: Prentice-Hall.

Herzberg, F. (1966). *Work and the Nature of Man.* Cleveland: World Publishing.

Hewstone, M. (1989). *Causal Attribution.* Oxford: Basil Blackwell.

Hofstede, G. (1984). *Culture's Consequences.* Beverly Hills: Sage.

Hofstede, G. (1991). *Cultures and Organizations: Software of the Mind.* London: McGraw-Hill.

Homme, L. and Tosti, C. (1971). *Behavior Technology: Motivation and Contingency Management.* San Rafael: Individual Learning Systems.

Hopson, B. (1984). Transition: Understanding and Managing Personal Change. In Cooper, C.L., and Makin, P.J. *Psychology for Managers.* London: Macmillan and The British Psychological Society. Out of print, available from libraries.

Hough, L.M. (1984). Development and Evaluation of the 'Accomplishment Record' Method of Selecting and Promoting Professionals. *Journal of Applied Psychology, 69,* 135–146.

Hough, L.M., Keyes, M.A., and Dunnette, M.D. (1983). An Evaluation of Three 'Alternative' Selection Procedures. *Personnel Psychology, 36,* 261–276.

Hui, C.H., Triandis, H.C., and Lee, C. (1991). Cultural differences in reward allocation: Is collectivism the explanation? *British Journal of Social Psychology, 30,* 145–157.

Hunter, J.E., and Hirsch, H.R. (1987). Applications of Meta-analysis. In Cooper, C.L., and Robertson, I.T. (Eds). *International Review of Industrial and Organizational Psychology.* Chichester: Wiley.

Hunter, J.E., and Schmidt, F.L. (1982). Fitting People to Jobs: The Impact of Personnel Selection on Rational Productivity. In Dunnette, M.D., and Fleishman, E. (Eds). *Human Performance and Productivity.* Hillsdale, NJ: Lawrence Erlbaum.

Hutton, W. (1995). *The State We're In*. London: Cape.

Idaszak, J.R., and Drasgow, F.A. (1987). Revision of the Job Diagnostic Survey: Elimination of a Measurement Artifact. *Journal of Applied Psychology, 72*, 69–74.

Janis, I.L. (1972). *Victims of Groupthink*. Boston: Houghton Mifflin.

Jaques E. (1951). *The Changing Culture of a Factory*. London: Tavistock.

Jennings R., Cox C., and Cooper C. (1994). *Business Elites: The psychology of entrepreneurs and intrapreneurs*. London: Routledge.

Jung, C.G. (1923). *Psychological Types*. London: Kegan Paul.

Kahler, T. and Capers, H. (1974). The Miniscript. *Transactional Analysis Journal, 14 (1)*.

Kahn, R. (1974). Organizational Development: Some problems and proposals. *Journal of Applied Behavioral Science, 10*, 4.

Kalma, A. (1991). Hierarchisation and dominance assessment at first glance. *European Journal of Social Psychology, 21*, 165–181.

Kanfer, R. (1992). Work Motivation: New Directions in Theory and Research. In Cooper, C.L., and Robertson, I.T. (Eds). *International Review of Industrial and Organizational Psychology*. Chichester: Wiley.

Katz, D., and Kahn, R.I. (1966). *The Social Psychology of Organizations*. New York: Wiley.

Kazdin, A.E. (1994). *Behavior Modification in Applied Settings*. Homewood, Ill.: Dorsey.

Kelman, H.C. (1958) Compliance, internalization and identification: Three processes of attitude change. *Journal of Conflict Resolution, 2*, 51–60.

Kessler, R.C., Price, R.H., and Wortman, C.B. (1985). Social Factors in Pathology. *Annual Review of Psychology, 36*, 531–572.

Kirton, M.J. (1984). Adaptors and Innovators: Why new initiatives get blocked. *Long Range Planning, 17*, 137–143.

Kolb, D. and Frohman, A. (1970). An Organization Development Approach to Consulting. *Sloan Management Review, 12*, 51–65.

Komaki, J., Waddel, W.M., and Pearce, M.G. (1977). The Applied Behavior Analysis Approach and Individual Employees: Improving Performance in Two Small Businesses. *Organizational Behavior and Human Performance, 19*, 337–352.

Kübler-Ross, E. (1969). *On Death and Dying*. New York: Macmillan.

Latham, G.P., Erez, M., and Locke, E.A. (1988). Resolving Scientific Disputes by the Joint Design of Crucial Experiments by the Antagonists: Application to the Erez-Latham Dispute Regarding Participation in Goal Setting. *Journal of Applied Psychology, 73*, 753–772.

Latham, G.P., and Saari, L.M. (1982). The Importance of Union Acceptance for Productivity Improvement Through Goal Setting. *Personnel Psychology, 35*, 781–787.

Latham, G.P., Saari, L.M., Pursell, E.D., and Campion, M.A. (1980). The Situational Interview. *Journal of Applied Psychology, 65*, 422–427.

Lawrence, P.R. and Lorsch, J.W. (1969). *Developing Organizations: Diagnosis and action*. Reading, Mass: Addison-Wesley.

Leavitt, H.J. (1951). Some effects of certain communication patterns on group performance. *Journal of Abnormal and Social Psychology, 13*, 151–156.

Lefrancois, G. (1983). *Psychology*. Belmont, Calif; Wadsworth.

Levinson, D.J., Darrow, C.N., Klein, E.B., Levinson, M.H. and McKee, B. (1978). *Seasons of a Man's Life*. New York: Knopf.

Lewin, K. (1947). Group decisions and social change. In T. Newcomb and E. Hartley (Eds) *Readings in Social Psychology*. New York: Holt, Rinehart and Winston.

Lievegoed, B.C.J. (1973). *The Developing Organization*. London: Methuen.

Likert, R. (1961). *New Patterns of Management*. New York: McGraw-Hill.

Locke, E.A. (1976).The Nature and Causes of Job Satisfaction. In Dunnette, M. (Ed.). *Handbook of Industrial and Organizational Psychology*. Chicago; Rand-McNally.

Locke, E.A., and Henne, D. (1986). Work Motivation Theories. In Cooper, C.L., and Robertson, I.T. (Eds) *International Review of Industrial and Organizational Psychology*. Chichester; Wiley.

Locke, E.A. and Latham, G.P. (1984). *Goal Setting: A motivational technique that works*. Englewood Cliffs: Prentice-Hall.

Locke, E.A., and Latham, G.P. (1991). *A Theory of Task Setting and Goal Performance*. New York: Prentice-Hall.

Locke, E.A., Frederick, E., Lee, C. and Bobko, P. (1984). Effect of self-efficacy, goals, and task strategies on task performance. *Journal of Applied Psychology, 69*, 241–251.

Luthans, F., and Kreitner, R. (1985). *Organizational Behavior Modification and Beyond*. Glenview, Ill: Scott Foresman.

MacCrae, R.R., and Costa, P.T. (1986). Personality, Coping, and Coping Effectiveness in an Adult Sample. *Journal of Personality, 54*, 385–405.

MacCrae, R.R., and Costa, P.T. (1991). Adding Lieve und Arbeit: The Full Five Factor Model and Well-being. *Bulletin of Personality and Social Psychology, 17*, 227–232.

Magerison, C. and Lewis, R. (1980). Management Educators and their Clients. In Beck, J., and Cox, C.J. (Eds) *Advances in Management Education*. Chichester: Wiley.

Makin, P.J. (1989). Selection of Professional Groups. In Herriot, P. (Ed.). *Handbook of Assessment in Organizations*. Chichester, Wiley.

Makin, P.J., and Hoyle, D.J. (1993). Using the Premack Principle to Improve the Performance of Professional Engineers. *Leadership and Organization Development Journal, 14 (1)*, 16–21.

Makin, P.J., and Robertson, I.T. (1983). Self Assessment, Realistic Job Previews, and Occupational Decisions. *Personnel Review, 12 (3)*, 21–25.

Makin, P.J., and Sutherland, V.J. (1994). Reducing Accidents Using a Behavioural Approach. *Leadership and Organization Development Journal, 15 (5)*, 5–10.

Makin, P.J., Eveleigh, C.W.J., and Dale, B.G. (1991). The Influence of Member Role Preferences and Leader Characteristics on the Effectiveness of Quality Circles. *International Journal of Human Resource Management, 2 (2)*, 193–204.

Marlow, H. (1975), *Managing Change: A Strategy for Our Time*. London: Institute of Personnel Management (now the Institute of Personnel and Development).

Martinko, M.J., and Gardner, W.L. (1987). The leader/member attribution process. *Academy of Management Review, 12*, 235–249.

Maslow, A.H. (1971). *The Farther Reaches of Human Nature*. New York: Viking.

Mathews, A. (1993). Biases in Processing Emotional Information. *The Psychologist, 6*, 493–499.

Mawhinney, T.C. (1992). Total Quality Management and Organizational

Behavior Management: An Integration for Continual Improvement. *Journal of Applied Behavior Analysis*, 25, 525–543.

Mayo, E. (1975). *The Social Problems of an Industrial Civilization.* London: Routledge & Kegan Paul.

McClelland, D.C. (1961). *The Achieving Society.* Princeton: Van Nostrand.

McClelland, D.C. (1979). The Two Faces of Power. In Kolb, D.A., Rubin, I.M., and McIntyre, J.M. *Organizational Psychology.* (3rd edn).Englewood Cliffs, NJ: Prentice-Hall.

McGee, G., and Ford, R. (1987). Two (or more?) Dimensions of Organizational Commitment: Reexamination of the Continuance and Affective Scales. *Journal of Applied Psychology*, 72, 642–648.

McGregor, D. (1960). *The Human Side of Enterprise.* New York: McGraw-Hill.

Meyer, G.J., and Shack, J.R. (1989). Structural Convergence of Mood and Personality: Evidence for Old and New Directions. *Journal of Personality and Social Psychology*, 57, 691–706.

Meyer, J.P., Allen, N.J., and Smith, C.A. (1993). Commitment to Organizations and Occupations: Extension and Test of a Three-Component Conceptualization. *Journal of Applied Psychology*, 78, 538–551.

Meyer, J.P., Paunonen, S.V., Gellatly, I.R, Goffin, R.D., and Jackson, D.N. (1989). Organizational Commitment and Job Performance: It's the Nature of the Commitment that Counts. *Journal of Applied Psychology*, 74, 152–156.

Miller, G.A., Gallanter, E., and Pribram, K.H. (1960). *Plans and the Structure of Behavior.* New York: Holt, Rinehart and Winston.

Mischel, W. (1968). *Personality Assessment.* New York: Wiley.

Mischel, W. (1986). *Introduction to Personality.* New York: Holt, Rinehart and Winston.

Mitchell, T.R., and Larson, J.R. (1987). *People in Organizations* (3rd edn.) New York: McGraw-Hill.

Miyajima R., and Cox C. (1987). A Transactional Analysis of Manager–Subordinate Relationships in both British and Japanese Cultures. *Occasional Paper No. 8701.* Manchester: UMIST.

Moorman, R.H. (1991). Relationship between organizational justice and organizational citizenship behaviors: Do fairness perceptions influence employee citizenship? *Journal of Applied Psychology*, 76, 845–855.

Morgan, G. (1983). More on Metaphor: Why We Cannot Control Tropes in Administrative Science. *Administrative Science Quarterly*, 28, 605–622.

Moskowitz, G.B. (1993). Individual differences in social categorization: The influence of personal need for structure on spontaneous trait inferences. *Journal of Personality and Social Psychology*, 65, 132–142.

Mowday, R.T., Porter, L.M., and Steers, R.M. (1982). *Employee–Organization Linkages: The Psychology of Commitment, Absenteeism, and Turnover.* New York: Academic Press.

Myers, I.B., and McCaulley, M.H. (1985). *Manual: A Guide to the Development and use of the Myers-Briggs Type Indicator.* Paulo Alto, Calif: Consulting Psychologists Press.

Neath, M. (1995). Evaluating Transactional Analysis as a Change Strategy for Organizations. *Leadership and Organizational Development Journal*, 16 (1), 13–16.

Neck, C.P., and Manz, C.C. (1992). Thought Self-Leadership: The Influence of Self-Talk and Mental Imagery on Performance. *Journal of Organizational Behavior*, 13, 681–699.

Nias, D.K.B. (1982). Astrology: Fact or Fiction? In Davey, D.M., and Harris, M. *Judging People.* London: McGraw-Hill.

O'Brien, R., Dickinson, A. and Rosow, M. (Eds) (1982). *Industrial Behavior Modification: A management handbook.* New York: Pergamon.

O'Connor, C.A. (1993). *The Handbook of Organizational Change.* Maidenhead: McGraw-Hill.

O'Reilly, C.A. (1991). Organizational Behavior: Where We've Been, Where We're Going. *Annual Review of Psychology, 42,* 427–458.

Ones, D.S., Viswesvaran, C., and Schmidt, F. (1993). Comprehensive Meta-analysis of Integrity Test Validities: Findings and Implications for Personnel Selection and Theories of Job Performance. *Journal of Applied Psychology, 78,* 679–703.

Organ, D.W., and Konovsky, M. (1989). Cognitive Versus Affective Determinants of Organizational Citizenship Behavior. *Journal of Applied Psychology, 74,* 157–164.

Osipow, S.H. (1973). *Theories of Career Development.* New York: Appleton-Century-Crofts.

Ottaway, R.N. (1982). Defining the Change Agent. In Evans, B., Powell, J. and Talbot, R. (Eds), *Changing Design.* Chichester: Wiley.

Peale, N.V. (1990). *The Power of Positive Thinking.* New York: Simon and Schuster.

Pervin, L.A. (1989). Persons, Situations, Interactions: A History of a Controversy and a Discussion of Theoretical Models. *Academy of Management Review, 14,* 350–360.

Peters, T.J. and Waterman, R.H. (1982). *In Search of Excellence.* New York: Harper and Row.

Piaget, J. (1952). *Origins of Intelligence in Children.* New York: International Universities Press.

Pinder, C.C. and Bourgeois, V.W. (1982). Controlling Tropes in Administrative Science. *Administrative Science Quarterly, 27,* 641–652.

Porras, J.I. and Berg, P.O. (1978). The impact of organizational development. *Academy of Management Review, 3,* 249–266.

Pratkanis, A.R., Breckler, S.J., and Greenwald, A.G. (Eds) (1989). *Attitude Structure and Function.* Hillsdale, NJ: Erlbaum.

Pyszczynski, T. and Greenberg, J. (1987). Self-Regulatory Perseveration and the Depressive Self–Focusing Style: A Self-Awareness Theory of Reactive Depression. *Psychological Bulletin, 102,* 122–138.

Quick, J.C., and Quick, J.D. (1984). *Organizational Stress and Preventative Management.* New York: McGraw-Hill.

Randell, G.A. (1973). Performance appraisal, purposes, practices and conflicts. *Journal of Occupational Psychology, 47,* 221–224.

Randell, G.A., Packard, P. and Slater, J. (1984). *Staff Appraisal,* 3rd edn: London: Institute of Personnel Management (now the Institute of Personnel and Development). Out of print, available from libraries.

Reilly, R.R., and Chao, G.T. (1982). Validity and Fairness of Some Alternative Selection Procedures. *Personnel Psychology, 35,* 1–62.

Robertson, I.T. (1994). Personnel Selection Research: Where are we now? *The Psychologist, 7,* 17–21.

Robertson, I.T., and Downs, S. (1989). Work Sample Tests of Trainability: A Meta-analysis. *Journal of Applied Psychology, 74,* 402–410.

Robertson, I.T., and Kandola, R.S. (1982). Work Sample Tests: Validity,

Adverse Impact and Applicant Reaction. *Journal of Occupational Psychology*, 55, 171–183.

Robertson, I.T. and Makin, P.J. (1986). Management Selection in Britain: A Survey and Critique. *Journal of Occupational Psychology*, 59, 45–57.

Robertson, I.T., Gratton, L., and Sharpley, D. (1987). The Psychometric Properties and Design of Assessment Centres: Dimensions into Exercises Won't Go. *Journal of Occupational Psychology*, 60, 187–195.

Robertson, I.T., Iles, P.A., Gratton, L., and Sharpley, D. (1991). The Psychological Impact of Personnel Selection Methods on Candidates. *Human Relations*, 44, 963–982.

Robinson, D.D. (1981). Content-oriented Personnel Selection in a Small Business Setting. *Personnel Psychology*, 34, 77–87.

Robinson, S.L., and Rousseau, D.M. (1994). Violating the Psychological Contract: Not the Exception but the Norm. *Journal of Organizational Behavior*, 15, 245–259.

Roethlisberger, F.J., and Dickson, W.J. (1939). *Management and the Worker.* Boston, Mass: Harvard University Press.

Rogers, C.R. (1967). *On Becoming a Person.* London: Constable.

Rogers, E., and Shoemaker, F. (1971). *Communication and Innovation.* New York: Free Press.

Rotter, J.B. (1966). Generalized expectancies for internal versus external control of reinforcement. *Psychological Monographs*, 80, Whole No. 609.

Rousseau, D.M. (1990). New Hire Perceptions of Their Own and Their Employer's Obligations: A Study of Psychological Contracts. *Journal of Organizational Behavior*, 11, 389–400.

Saari, L.M. and Latham, G.P. (1982). Employee Reactions to Continuous and Variable Ratio Reinforcement Schedules Involving a Monetary Incentive. *Journal of Applied Psychology*, 67, 506–508.

Schein, E.H. (1977). Increasing Organizational Effectiveness Through Better Human Resource Planning and Development. *Sloan Management Review*, 19, 1–20.

Schein, E.H. (1978). *Career Dynamics: matching individual and organizational needs.* Reading, Mass: Addison-Wesley.

Schein, E.H. (1980). *Organizational Psychology.* Englewood Cliffs: Prentice-Hall.

Schein, E.H. (1982). Individuals and Career. *Technical Report No. 19.* Office of Naval Research.

Schein, E. (1984). Coming to a New Awareness of Organizational Culture. *Sloan Management Review*, 25, 3–16.

Schein, E. (1985). *Organizational Culture and Leadership.* San Francisco: Jossey-Bass.

Schiff, J.G. (1975). *Cathexis Reader, Transactional Analysis Treatment of Psychosis.* New York: Harper and Row.

Schmidt, F.L., and Hunter, J.E. (1977). Development of a General Solution to the Problem of Validity Generalization. *Journal of Applied Psychology*, 62, 529–540.

Schneider, R.J., and Hough, L.M. (1995). Personality and Industrial/Organizational Psychology. In Cooper, C.L., and Robertson, I.T. (Eds) *International Review of Industrial and Organizational Psychology.* Chichester: Wiley.

Sedek, G., and Kofta, M. (1990). When Cognitive Exertion Does not Yield

Cognitive Gain: Toward an Informational Explanation of Learned Helplessness. *Journal of Personality and Social Psychology, 58,* 729–743.

Seligman, M.E.P. (1975). *Helplessness: On Depression, Development, and Death.* San Francisco: Freedman.

Shakleton, V.J., and Newell, S. (1991). A Comparative Survey of Methods Used in Top British and French Companies. *Journal of Occupational Psychology, 64,* 23–36.

Sherif, M. (1966). *Group Conflict and Cooperation: Their social psychology.* London: Routledge & Kegan Paul.

Simek, T.C., and O'Brien, E.M. (1981). Total Golf: A Behavioral Approach to Lowering Your Score and Getting More out of Your Game. Huntington, NY: Mod Associates. Quoted in Martin, G., and Pear, J. (1988). *Behavior Modification: What it is and How to do It.* (3rd edn.) Englewood Cliffs, NJ: Prentice-Hall.

Simon, H.A. (1990). Invariants of human behavior. *Annual Review of Psychology, 41,* 1–19.

Skinner, B.F. (1993). *About Behaviorism.* Harmondsworth: Penguin.

Smith, J.M., and Robertson, I.T. (1993). *The Theory and Practice of Systematic Personnel Selection.* (2nd edn.) Basingstoke: Macmillan.

Smith, P.C., Kendall, L.M., and Hulin, C.L. (1969). *The Measurement of Satisfaction in Work and Retirement.* Chicago; Rand-McNally.

Somers, M.J. (1993). A Test of the Relationship Between Affective and Continuance Commitment using Non-Recursive Models. *Journal of Occupational and Organizational Psychology. 66,* 185–192.

Spector, P.E. and O'Connell, B.J. (1994). The Contribution of Personality Traits, Negative Affectivity, Locus of Control and Type A to the Subsequent Reports of Job Stressors and Job Strains. *Journal of Occupational and Organizational Psychology, 67,* 1–11.

Staw, B.M., and Ross, J. (1985). Stability in the Midst of Change: A Dispositional Approach to Job Attitudes. *Journal of Applied Psychology, 70,* 469–480.

Steiner, C. (1974). *Scripts People Live: Transactional Analysis of Life Scripts.* New York: Grove Press.

Stephens, T.A. and Burroughs, W.A. (1978). An application of operant conditioning to absenteeism in a hospital setting. *Journal of Applied Psychology, 63,* 518–521.

Stewart, I. (1989). *Transactional Analysis Counselling in Action.* London: Sage.

Stogdill, R.M. (1948). Personal Factors Associated with Leadership. *Journal of Psychology, 25,* 35–71.

Stoner, J.A.F. (1961). *A Comparison of Individual and Group Decisions Including Risk.* Unpublished Master's thesis, School of Management, Massachusetts Institute of Technology.

Summers, T.P., and Hendrix, W.H. (1991). Modelling the role of pay equity perceptions: A field study. *Journal of Occupational Psychology, 64,* 145–157.

Super, D.E. (1957). *The Psychology of Careers.* New York: Harper and Row.

Sutherland, V.J., Makin, P.J., Bright, K., and Cox, C.J. (1995). Quality Behaviour for Quality Organizations. *Leadership and Organizational Development Journal, 16 (6),* 10–15.

Synder, M. (1974). Self-Monitoring of Expressive Behavior. *Journal of Personality and Social Psychology, 30,* 526–537.

Tajfel, H. (Ed) (1972). *Differentiation Between Social Groups: Studies in the social psychology of intergroup relations*. London: Academic Press.

Taylor, S.E. (1983). Adjustment to Threatening Events: A Theory of Cognitive Adaptation. *American Psychologist, 38,* 1161–1173.

Taylor, F.W. (1911). *Scientific Management*. New York: Harper.

Tett, R.P., Jackson, D.N., and Rothstein, M. (1991). Personality Measures as Predictors of Job Performance: A Meta-analytic Review. *Personnel Psychology, 44,* 703–742.

Thomas, K. (1975). Conflict and conflict management. In M. Dunnette (Ed.) *Handbook of Industrial and Organizational Psychology*. Chicago: Rand McNally.

Thompson, T.E, and Tuden, A. (1959). *Comparative Studies in Administration*. Pittsburgh: University of Pittsburgh Press.

Toffler, A. (1970). *Future Shock*. London: Pan Books.

Trice, H.M., and Beyer, J.M. (1990). Cultural Leadership in Organizations. Quoted in Bryman (1992). *Charisma and Leadership in Organizations*. London: Sage.

Tse, K.K. (1985). *Marks and Spencer: An anatomy of Britain's most efficiently managed company*. Oxford: Pergamon.

Tsui, A.S., Porter, L.W., Pearce, J.L., and Tripoli, A.M. (1993). Reconceptualizing the Employee–Organization Relationship: An Inducement-Contribution Approach. Unpublished manuscript, University of California. Quoted in Shore, L.M., and Tetrick, L.E. (1994). The Psychological Contract as an Explanatory Framework in the Employment Relationship. In Cooper, C.L., and Rousseau, D.M. (Eds) *Trends in Organizational Behavior, 1.*

Tversky, A. and Kahneman, D. (1974). Judgement under Uncertainty. *Science, 85,* 112–1131.

Tyler, T.R., and Bies, R.J. (1990). Beyond Formal Procedures: The Inter-personal Context of Procedural Justice. In Carroll, J. (Ed.) *Applied Social Psychology in Organizational Settings*. Hillsdale: Erlbaum.

Vroom, V.II. and Yetton, P.W. (1973). *Leadership and Decision Making*. Pittsburgh: University of Pittsburgh Press.

Vroom, V.H., and Jago, A.G. (1988). *The New Leadership: Managing Participation in Organizations*. Englewood Cliffs, NJ: Prentice-Hall.

Wagner, J.A. (1994). Participation's effects on performance and satisfaction: A reconsideration of research evidence. *Academy of Management Review, 19,* 312–330.

Wahba, M.A., and Bridwell, L.B. (1976). Maslow Reconsidered: A Review of Research on the Need Hierarchy Theory. *Organizational Behavior and Human Performance, 15,* 212–240.

Wall, T.D., Clegg, C.W., and Jackson, P.R. (1978). An Evaluation of the Job Characteristics Model. *Journal of Occupational Psychology, 51,* 183–196.

Wallgren, K.R. (1975). The Managerial Corral. *Transactional Analysis Journal, 5,* 373–375.

Warr, P. (1982). A national study of non-financial employment commitment. *Journal of Occupational Psychology, 55,* 297–312.

Weber, M. (1970). Bureaucracy. In O. Grusky and G.A. Miller (Eds) *The Sociology of Organizations*. London: Free Press.

Weiner, B. (1985). An Attributional Theory of Achievement Motivation and Emotion. *Psychological Review, 92,* 548–573.

Westoby, J.P. (1994). The Development of a Job Personality Instrument.

Unpublished MSc dissertation, University of Manchester Institute of Science and Technology.

Whitsett, D.A. (1975). How are your Enriched Jobs? *Harvard Business Review,* January–February, 74–80.

Wilk, J. (1989). Culture and Epistemology: Media of Corporate Stability and Strategic Change. *International Journal of Systems Research and Information Science, 3,* 143–167.

Willner, A.R. (1984). *The Spellbinders: Charismatic Political Leadership.* New Haven: Yale University Press.

Wistow, D.J., Wakefield, J.A., and Goldsmith, W.M. (1990). The Relationship Between Personality, Health Symptoms, and Disease. *Personality and Individual Differences. 11,* 717–724.

Wood, J.V., Saltzberg, J.A., Neale, J.M., Stone, A.A., and Rachmiel, T.B. (1990). Self-Focused Attention, Coping Responses, and Distressed Mood in Everyday Life. *Journal of Personality and Social Psychology, 58,* 1027–1036.

Wood, R., and Bandura, A. (1989). Social Cognitive Theory of Organizational Management. *Academy of Management Review. 14,* 361–384.

Wortman, C.B., and Brehm, J.W. (1975). Response to Uncontrollable Outcomes: An Integration of Reactance Theory and the Learned Helplessness Model. In Berkowitz, L. (Ed.) *Advances in Experimental Social Psychology.* New York: Academic Press.

Wright, P.L. and Taylor, D.S. (1994). *Improving Leadership Performance* (2nd edn.). Englewood Cliffs: Prentice-Hall.

Zaleznik, A. (1983). The Leadership Gap. *The Washington Quarterly, 6,* 32–33. Cited in Bryman (1992).

Zenger, T.R. (1992). Why do Employers Only Reward Extreme Performance? Examining the Relationships among Performance, Pay, and Turnover. *Administrative Science Quarterly, 37,* 198–219.

Zohar, D., and Fussfeld, N. (1981). A Systems Approach to Organizational Behavior Modification: Theoretical Considerations and Empirical Evidence. *International Review of Applied Psychology. 30,* 491–505.

Zucker, L.G. (1983). Organizations as Institutions. In Bacharach, S. (Ed.) *Research in the Sociology of Organizations (Vol 2).* Greenwich, CT: JAI Press.

SUGGESTED READING

GENERAL

Cooper, C.L., and Robertson, I.T. (Eds) *International Review of Industrial and Organizational Psychology.* Chichester: Wiley.

This is published yearly and contains review articles on various topics in Industrial and Organizational Psychology. Many of the articles review material covered in this book.

THE PSYCHOLOGICAL CONTRACT

Cooper, C.L., and Rousseau, D.M.(1994). *Trends in Organizational Behavior, Volume 1.* Chapters 7 and 8. Chichester: Wiley.

SELECTION, PLACEMENT, AND CAREERS

Smith, J.M., and Robertson, I.T. (1993). *The Theory and Practice of Systematic Personnel Selection,* 2nd edn. Basingstoke: Macmillan.

White, B., Cox, C.J., and Cooper, C.L. (1992). *Women's Career Development: A Study of High Flyers*. Oxford: Blackwell. •

PERSONALITY AND INDIVIDUAL DIFFERENCES
Pervin, L.A. (1980). *Personality: Theory, Assessment and Research*, 3rd edn. New York: Wiley.
Cooper, C.L., Cooper, R.D., and Eaker, L. (1988). *Living with Stress*. Harmondsworth: Penguin.
Cooper, C.L. (1996). *Handbook of Stress, Medicine and Health*. Boca Raton, FL: CRC Press.

INTER-PERSONAL PERCEPTION AND INTERACTION
Forgas, J.P. (1985). *Interpersonal Behaviour: The Psychology of Social Interaction*. Oxford: Pergamon Press.
Hewstone, M. (1989). *Causal Attribution: From Cognitive Processes to Collective Beliefs*. Oxford: Blackwell.
Stewart, I and Joines, V.S. (1987). *TA Today: A New Introduction to Transactional Analysis*. Nottingham: Lifespace.
Harris, T.A. (1969). *I'm OK–You're OK*. London: Pan.

MOTIVATION
Steers, R., and Porter, L.W. (1991). *Motivation and Work Behaviour*, 5th edn. London: McGraw-Hill.
Robertson, I.T., Smith, M., and Cooper, D. (1992). *Motivation: Strategy, Theory and Practice*. London: Institute of Personnel and Development

BEHAVIOURAL APPROACHES TO MOTIVATION
Martin, G.L., and Pears, J. (1991). *Behavior Modification: What It Is and How to Do It*, 4th edn. Englewood Cliffs, NJ: Prentice-Hall.
Cox, C.J. and Makin, P.J. (Eds) (1994). Behavioural Approaches to Organizational Change. Special edition of *Leadership and Organization Development Journal*, 15 (5).
Kazdin, A.E. (1994). *Behavior Modification in Applied Settings*. Pacific Grove, CA: Brooks-Cole.
Luthans, F., and Kreitner, R. (1985). *Organizational Behavior Modification and Beyond*. Glenview, Ill.: Scott Foresman.
O'Brien, R., Dickinson, A., and Rosow, M. (Eds) (1992). *Industrial Behavior Modification: A Management Handbook*. New York: Pergamon.

LEADERSHIP AND MANAGEMENT STYLE
Bryman, A. (1992). *Charisma and Leadership in Organizations*. London: Sage.
Bryman, A. (1986). *Leadership in Organisations*. London: Routledge.
Randell, G.A., Packard, P. and Slater, J. (1984). *Staff Appraisal*, 3rd edn. London: Institute of Personnel Management (now the Institute of Personnel and Development).
Wright, P.L. and Taylor, D.S. (1994). *Improving Leadership Performance*, 2nd edn. Englewood Cliffs: Prentice-Hall.
Jennings R., Cox C., and Cooper C. (1994). *Business Elites: The psychology of entrepreneurs and intrapreneurs*. London: Routledge.
Fletcher, C. (1993). *Appraisal: Routes to Improved Performance*. London: Institute of Personnel and Development.

Wright, P.L. (1995). *Managerial Leadership*. London: Routledge.

GROUP DYNAMICS AT WORK
Schein, E. (1988). *Organizational Psychology*. Englewood Cliffs, NJ: Prentice-Hall.
Payne, R., and Cooper, C.L. (1981). *Groups at Work*. Chichester: Wiley.

IDENTIFYING ORGANIZATIONAL PROBLEMS
Hofstede, G. (1991). *Cultures and Organizations*. Maidenhead: McGraw-Hill.
Williams, A., Dobson, P. and Walters, M. (1989). *Changing Culture*. London: Institute of Personnel Management (now the Institute of Personnel and Development).
Harrison, R. (1987). *Organization Culture and Quality of Service*. London: Association for Management Education and Development.
Beck, J. and Cox, C.J. (1984). Developing organizational skills. In C.J. Cox and J. Beck (Eds) *Management Development: Advances in practice and theory*. Chichester: Wiley.

ORGANIZATIONAL CHANGE
Argyris, C. (1992). *On Organizational Learning*. Cambridge, Mass: Blackwell
Carnall, C.A. (1990). *Managing Change in Organizations*. Hemel Hempstead: Prentice-Hall.
McCalman, J. and Paton, R.A. (1992). *Change Management*. London: Paul Chapman Publishing.
O'Connor, C.A. (1993). *The Handbook for Organizational Change*. Maidenhead: McGraw-Hill.
Hay, J. (1992). *Transactional Analysis for Trainers*. London: McGraw-Hill.
French, W., and Bell, C. (1994). *Organizational Development: Behavioural Science Interventions for Organization Improvement*. Englewood Cliffs, NJ: Prentice-Hall.

UNDERSTANDING AND COPING WITH CHANGE
Fisher, S., and Cooper, C.L. (1990). *On the Move: The Psychology of Change and Transition*. Chichester: Wiley.
Clan M. (1980). *Lives People Live*. Chichester: Wiley.
Beck, A.T. (1976). *Cognitive Therapy and the Emotional Disorders*. Harmondsworth: Penguin.
Cartwright, S. and Cooper, C.L. (1996). *Managing Mergers, Acquisitions and Strategic Alliances*. Oxford: Butterworth Heinemann.

EMPOWERMENT AND SELF-MANAGEMENT
Hay, J. (1992). *Transactional Analysis for Trainers*. London: McGraw-Hill.
Kazdin, A.E. (1994). *Behavior Modification in Applied Settings*. Homewood, Ill.: Dorsey.
Martin, G.L., and Pears, J. (1991). *Behavior Modification: What It Is and How To Do It*, 4th edn. Englewood Cliffs, NJ: Prentice-Hall.
Sims, H.P., and Lorenzi, P. (1992). *The New Leadership Paradigm: Social Learning and Cognition in Organizations*. London: Sage.

INDEX Compiled by Sue Ramsey